ENCYCLOPEDIA OF COMPUTER SCIENCE AND TECHNOLOGY

VOLUME 19

INTERNATIONAL EDITORIAL ADVISORY BOARD

ENCYCLOPEDIA OF COMPUTER SCIENCE AND TECHNOLOGY

EXECUTIVE EDITORS

Allen Kent   *James G. Williams*

UNIVERSITY OF PITTSBURGH
PITTSBURGH, PENNSYLVANIA

ADMINISTRATIVE EDITOR

Rosalind Kent

PITTSBURGH, PENNSYLVANIA

SUPPLEMENT 4

CRC Press
Taylor & Francis Group
Boca Raton London New York

CRC Press is an imprint of the
Taylor & Francis Group, an **informa** business

CRC Press
Taylor & Francis Group
6000 Broken Sound Parkway NW, Suite 300
Boca Raton, FL 33487-2742

First issued in paperback 2019

© 1988 by Taylor & Francis Group, LLC
CRC Press is an imprint of Taylor & Francis Group, an Informa business

No claim to original U.S. Government works

ISBN-13: 978-0-8247-2269-2 (hbk)
ISBN-13: 978-0-367-40335-5 (pbk)

LIBRARY OF CONGRESS CATALOG CARD NUMBER: 74-29436
ISBN: 0-8247-2269-8

**Visit the Taylor & Francis Web site at
http://www.taylorandfrancis.com**

**and the CRC Press Web site at
http://www.crcpress.com**

CONTENTS OF VOLUME 19

CONTRIBUTORS TO VOLUME 19

GREGORY M. BEDNAR, Ph.D.,   Senior Technical Staff Member, International Business Machines Corporation, Charlotte, North Carolina: *Optical Character Recognition*

ELOISE COUPEY,   Access Technology, Inc., South Natick, Massachusetts: *Access Technology, Inc.*

DINEH M. DAVIS, Ph.D.,   Assistant Professor and Coordinator, Interdisciplinary Studies Program, Bentley College, Waltham, Massachusetts: *Computer-Aided Composition*

YOGENDRA P. DUBEY, Ph.D.,   Associate Professor, Department of Library and Information Science, Banaras Hindu University, Varanasi, India: *Decision Support Systems: Development and Trends*

NICHOLAS V. FINDLER, Ph.D.,   Research Professor of Computer Science and Director of the Artificial Intelligence Laboratory, Computer Science Department, Arizona State University, Tempe, Arizona: *Air Traffic Control, A Prototype of a Man-Machine Environment for the Study of*

ERNEST H. FORMAN, D.Sc.,   Professor and Director of Information Systems, The George Washington University School of Government and Business Administration, Washington, D.C.: *The Analytic Hierarchy and the Personal Computer*

IVAN T. FRISCH, Ph.D.,   Director, Center for Advanced Technology in Telecommunications, Brooklyn, New York: *Local Area Networks*

KAZUHIRO FUCHI, Ph.D.,   Director, Research Center, Institute for New Generation Computer Technology (ICOT), Tokyo, Japan: *Fifth Generation Computers Systems Project*

AUDREY N. GROSCH,   Professor and Assistant to the University Librarian for Information Systems, University of Minnesota, Minneapolis, Minnesota: *Microcomputer, Selection of a*

INTEL CORPORATE COMMUNICATIONS,   Intel Corporation, Santa Clara, California: *Intel Corporation*

MAHIEDDINE LADJADJ, Ph.D.,   School of Engineering, Rensselaer Polytechnic Institute, Troy, New York: *Automatic Test Generation–The Subscripted D-Algorithm*

JOHN F. McDONALD,   Professor, Electrical Computer and Systems Engineering, Rensselaer Polytechnic Institute, Troy, New York: *Automatic Test Generation–The Subscripted D-Alogorithm*

YU N. MARCHUK,   All-Union Center for Translation of Scientific & Technical Literature and Documentation, Moscow, U.S.S.R.: *Machine Translation in the U.S.S.R.*

MARY ANN SELLY,   Director, Decision Support Software, Inc., McLean, Virginia: *The Analytic Hierarchy Process and the Personal Computer*

HENRY C. SMITH,   Senior Scientist, Lockheed Aeronautical Systems Company, Marietta, Georgia: *Database Design*

J. M. SHEARER,   Department of Mathematical Sciences, University of St. Andrews, St. Andrews, Scotland, United Kingdom: *Symbol Manipulation Packages*

DANIEL STEIGER,   Marine Systems Branch, Naval Research Laboratory, Washington, D.C.: *Oceanographic Data Systems*

M. A. WOLFE,   Department of Mathematical Sciences, University of St. Andrews, St. Andrews, Scotland, United Kingdom: *Symbol Manipulation Packages*

ENCYCLOPEDIA OF COMPUTER SCIENCE AND TECHNOLOGY

VOLUME 19

ACCESS TECHNOLOGY, INC.

Access Technology, Inc., is the developer of 20/20, an integrated spread-sheet modeling package for microcomputers, minis, and mainframes.

A spreadsheet is, quite simply, a natural extension of a decision maker's paper, pencil, and calculator, only much, much quicker and far more accurate.

Spreadsheet are used by sales managers, bookkeepers, marketing directors, inventory control specialists, corporate planners, and manufacturing supervisors. And a spreadsheet's applications are just as varied as its users—planning, budgeting, scheduling, project management, finanical reports, and cash flow analysis are just a few.

Integrated spreadsheets are better, more sophisticated versions of this crucial planning tool. Like 20/20, most integrated programs start with an advanced spreadsheet and then add powerful business planning and analysis tools. This integration of features lets more and more professionals of all levels incorporate spreadsheet modeling into their daily planning.

Access' most recent spreadsheet product is 20/20, an advanced spread-sheet combining graphics, data base management, and project modeling. The 20/20 package's powerful links to other software programs have encouraged many leading computer and software companies to incorporate 20/20 into their office automation systems. Typical of such strategic arrangements are the Quotron Q1000 workstation, Information Builders' FOCCALC, the Onyx Office, and NCA's MAXCIM.

The prevalent corporate need to standardize the company planning performed on multiuser computers is successfully addressed by 20/20. The package was designed to allow personal computer and mainframe users to work together on corporate applications. Entire models—data, text, and formulas—can be moved between a wide variety of micros, minis, and main-frames, regardless of operating system. This enables users to plan in a shared environment, not in isolation.

The 20/20 package is typically used in business situations that require a large spreadsheet, utilizing data stored on other application packages and central data bases, combined with graphics, goal seeking, and project modeling. Spreadsheets may be created to a size of 1,000 rows by 1,000 columns, and a context-sensitive, on-line help file is readily available with a single keystroke.

In addition, command files, which automate routine or complex tasks, enable the creation of work-sheet templates, as well as instruction for their use within one file. It is possible to automate extremely complex tasks by using 20/20's branching capability, so that one command file will invoke another. Command files are created with either the spreadsheet file or a text editor.

The 20/20 package's complete documentation contains thorough tutorial and reference sections. "Learning 20/20" introduces novice users to spread-sheet modeling and quickly gets them up to speed on 20/20. More experienced users will find succinct explanations of 20/20's advanced features.

Training is available from Access Technology, either on-site or in-house. In addition, Access markets a 2-hour training videotape, which provides consistent on-site training at the user's convenience. The video is divided into three sections: (*a*) using a 20/20 model, with instructions for entering values and printing models; (*b*) building a 20/20 model, including entering and editing data, labels, and formulas; and (*c*) advanced topics, with information about graphics, data base query capabilities, and command files.

Access Technology was founded in 1979 by Allen Kluchman, the company's president. Kluchman was the first director of advertising at Digital Equipment Corporation. In 1969 he became the first director of marketing at Data General, where he was instrumental in launching the NOVA minicomputer.

Access Technology is a privately owned corporation, with its company headquarters located beside the Charles River in South Natick, Massachusetts. European operations are managed from London, England.

BIBLIOGRAPHY

"Access Technology's 20/20," *Attage*, 39 (August 1985).

"Access Technology, Inc.'s 20/20: Is it 1-2-3 for Unix?" *Computerworld* (January 14, 1985).

Avant, Harry, "20/20: The 1-2-3 of Unix-Land?" *UNIX/World*, 58–65 (June 1985).

"Beyond '1-2-3' and 'Framework'," *PC Week* (April 23, 1985).

Boulanger, Noel J., "20/20 Vision," *Digital Rev.* (December 1984).

"Financial Planning Software," *PC Week* (February 19, 1985).

"Searle Sees 20/20, By Access, as Its Software Solution," *PC Week* (March 26, 1985).

Shannon, Terry C., "Spreadsheets," *DEC Professional Magazine*, (July 7, 1985).

"20/20: An Integrated Spreadsheet for DG Users," *Data Base Monthly* (June 1985).

"20/20 Multi-User Spreadsheet," *ICP Bus. Software Rev.* (European ed.), 32 (August 1985).

ELOISE COUPEY

AIR TRAFFIC CONTROL, A PROTOTYPE OF A MAN-MACHINE ENVIRONMENT FOR THE STUDY OF

INTRODUCTION

A novel prototype of a man—machine environment (MME) has been designed and implemented. It incorporates a number of new tools useful for training and routine operations in air traffic control (ATC). Before we describe the six large-scale programming systems embedded in the MME, it is necessary to discuss some approaches to the question of normative and descriptive theories of decision making and planning. We also examine decision support systems that increase the effectiveness and efficiency of human judgmental processes by extending their range, capabilities, and speed.

DECISION-MAKING AND PLANNING PROCESSES

Decision making, in general, represents a time—sequence of choices that constitutes the basis of action. Viewed in this way, decision making may be considered a response mechanism operating in a task environment and guided by a problem-solving strategy. The consequences of a decision may be understood in advance completely, partially, or not at all, and in a determi-nistic or probabilistic manner.

The goals of decision making may be positive (to attain certain objec-tives) or negative (to avoid certain events). These goals may be of the short-range or long-range type. In the latter case particularly, a *planning process* precedes the actual decision making, which contrasts and, in some sense, tries out alternative methods of attack in a coarse-grained way. Planning applies a (crude) model to a task, consisting of the current and the desired situation, to compute a sequence of (major) action steps for achieving the goal, that is, to reach the desired situation.

In general, plans are continually refined and incrementally modified. A part of the plan may take care of the *resource allocation* among three activities: gathering more information if necessary, refining and modifying the plan if necessary, and making progress in carrying out the plan. The modification of the plan makes economic sense as long as the cost involved with it is less than the expected increase in the utility of the modified plan. This simple and plausible statement implies that there are many indi-spensable pieces of information available for the human or computer analyst performing the operation, such as

- Measures on the cost and complexity of planning
- Reliability values of alternate plans
- Utilities of individual goal achievement
- Probabilities of achieving goals as the consequence of an ordered sequence of actions
- Trade-off among alternate subgoals, and so forth

However, this type of information is rarely available, and if it is, its reliability is rather low. The difficulty is aggravated by changing environments and goals and the lack of heuristic guidance in combating *combinatorially explosive search domains*.

Returning to the problem of decision making, we can distinguish between *situations of conflict*, in which different decision-making strategies compete to accomplish some mutually exclusive goals, and situations in which no antagonistic confrontation occurs and decisions are made, say, *vis-à-vis nature*. If the goal is not a scalar numerical or a single symbolic entity but a multidimensional objective, its (vector) components need not be orthogonal (e.g., one component may be the minimum deviation from the prescribed flight path of all aircraft, and another, the adherence to the published timetable of flights). In fact, there may be various constraints with and partial conflict between such components.

In real-life situations, the conditions for "rational" decision-making do not prevail. Namely, a "rational" decision maker [1] is assumed to be fully aware of (a) the set of alternatives open to choice, (b) the relationships between the outcomes (pay-offs) and his choice, (c) the preference ordering among outcomes. He can therefore make a choice, the consequence of which is at least as good as that of any other choice—in other words, he is capable of making consistently optimum decisions.

Simon [2] has replaced the above, idealized and abstract actor with the "satisficing man". This individual's environment is complicated, vague, and uncertain. Instead of optimizing, he is content if his current level of aspiration is met ("satisficed"). This model considers incomplete and inconsistent information, conflicts, limited information processing ability, limited perceptions, and desires. He is, however, able to learn and to modify both the structure and contents of his goals. Such "bounded rationality" is realistic at the level of both individual and organizational decision making [3].

BASIS OF THEORETICAL STUDIES

Students of decision making and planning include researchers in artificial intelligence, management science, operations research, statistics, psychology, economics, human engineering, and some "fringe" areas of other disciplines. The motivation comes from one or several of the following aims: to understand, explain, predict, and improve human judgmental processes and to enhance and replace them, partially or fully, with computer systems.

In science, one usually distinguished between *descriptive* and *normative theories*. The former tells us what and possibly why an entity, an individual, or an organization does something under certain conditions. Sociology and cognitive psychology are examples of the disciplines that provide descriptive theories of aspects of human behavior. In contrast, normative theories tell us what to do in order to accomplish certain goals. Linear programming and other optimization techniques yield normative theories of tasks that are well defined and mathematically formularizable tasks.

Social judgment theory, information integration theory, and attribution theory emphasize the descriptive aspects. On the other hand, the normative aspects of decision making are referenced by mathematical decision theory, behavioral decision theory, and psychological decision theory.

Considerable efforts have also been spent by researchers in artificial intelligence to understand and to automate the *planning process*—at least in relatively small and well-defined universes [4—9]. Without going into the details of the work in this area, it can be safely said that much research needs to be done before computer-based planning systems can be made responsible for large-scale, real-life activities.

In view of the difficulties pointed out in the first section, an interactive man—machine system, combining the strengths of both computers and humans, may provide the right tool for the complex tasks of planning and decision making. This idea is discussed in the next section.

DECISION SUPPORT SYSTEMS

Computer-based decision support systems (DSS) assist decision making and planning in semi—structured tasks; they support, rather than replace, human judgment; and they improve both the effectiveness and efficiency of human decision making by extending its range, capability, and speed. There is a growing body of literature [10, 11] describing case studies and general principles of building DSS. These systems are flexible, robust, user—friendly, inexpensive, and based on some high-level interaction between man and the computer. Graphics display systems, possibly enhanced with color capabilities, augment human perception and make it easier for the user to assess a situation and its critical factors.

Some or all of the following characteristics of a task environment make a DSS useful:

1. The database is too large for a human to access or to make conceptual use of.
2. To arrive at a solution requires significant processing of the available information.
3. There is time pressure to carry out the computations (the environment changes) and/or to obtain the solution (action is needed *on time*).
4. Delicate judgment is needed as to which variables are relevant and what their current values are.

A NOVEL MAN—MACHINE ENVIRONMENT (MME)

We describe a MME that can provide the necessary tools for both training human decision makers and planners, and enabling them to perform these tasks on a regular basis in an effective and efficient manner.

Figure 1 shows the proposed schema. Events from the "Real World" update the representation of the affected objects in the computer. The updating can be directed in three ways:

1. With a user-defined frequency (time-driven updating)
2. Whenever one of a set of conditions is satisfied, that is, a set of user-specified events takes place (event-driven updating)
3. On user command, regardless of the time elapsed since the last update or conditions currently satisfied (user-driven updating)

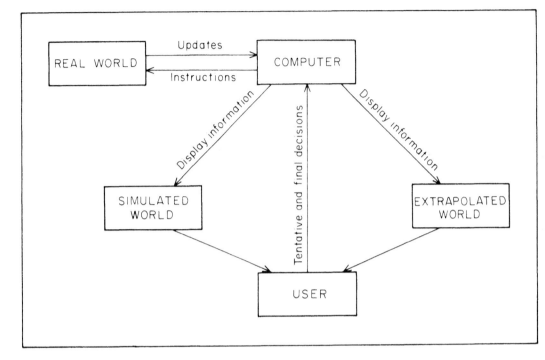

FIGURE 1.   A schematic diagram of the interactive environment.

The relevant features of the real world appear on one display denoted as "Simulated World" (the *current world*).   The user makes tentative decisions on this basis, say, at time t_0 and transmits them to the computer.   He then specifies a time point for extrapolating in the future, t_f, and the computer computes the consequences of his decisions at periodic time increments (the size of which is also specified by the user) up to the final time point, t_f.   If any of these calculations results in a "conflict situation," as defined by the user, the calculation is interrupted, and the conflict and the corresponding time are displayed on the second screen denoted as "Extrapolated World."   If no conflict occurs between the time points in question, t_0 and t_f, the relevant features of the world, showing the consequences of the tentative decisions at t_f, are displayed on the second screen.

If the user is satisfied with the resulting world, he finalizes his tentative decisions by informing the computer accordingly.   Otherwise, he makes a different set of tentative decisions and goes through the above cycle as many times as necessary, time permitting.

Finally, we note that the image of the Extrapolated World is computed according to a computer-resident model that can, of course, be incomplete and erroneous to a certain extent.   The following learning process should increase the predictive precision of this model.   The image of the Extrapolated World is stored, and when real time "catches up" with t_f, the Simulated World is compared with the stored image.   The user is warned if there is more than a tolerable difference between the two.   Such discrepancy may indicate that either the Real World has been affected by unexpected and significant factors during the period of extrapolation (about which nothing can be done) or the world model in the computer is less than staisfactory. In some areas of application, a self-correcting *learning process* may improve an appropriately constructed model.

SIMULATED AIR TRAFFIC CONTROL ENVIRONMENT

The task of ATC is highly labor sensitive and requires considerable intelligence to perceive the essential aspects of situations and to make satisfactory decisions under time-stressed conditions. To increase the productivity of ATC, significant research efforts are being made within the Federal Aviation Administration and at other centers (MITRE Corp. [12], The RAND Corporation [13], University of Texas [14], University of Illinois [15], etc.) on how to delegate more tasks to computers.

Our work, at a considerable smaller level [16–18], attempts to contribute to the theoretical understanding of the ATC processes as well as to provide practical aid in educating human controllers and in the ultimate automation of the whole task.

The following aspects of the ATC environment make it especially suitable for our studies:

- The task is complex enought to be challenging
- One can identify problem areas of different sizes that could be attacked successively
- One can define plausible metrics along several dimensions to measure the performance of a proposed system
- Until a subsystem is fully developed and tested, it can operate in a realistic simulated world
- A successful system for automatic ATC would share with systems working in other environments the important capabilities of planning, problem solving, and decision making under uncertainty and risk, in dynamically changing domains while satisfying a hierarchy of constraints.

Interest in automating the ATC task has increased over the past few years. The need for radical modernization of the current mode of operation is due partly to the economics of this expert labor-intensive task and partly to the potentially disastrous consequences of human errors. The basic problems can be formulated as follows.

When an aircraft flies from one airport to another under instrument flight rules (as military and commercial planes do), it passes through the jurisdiction of a series of ATC centers. These centers track each flight within their sector on radar and try to keep it on its appointed path, according to a desired time schedule. The control actions must also satisfy a number of constraints. Some are constant, such as the government-prescribed rules for minimum horizontal and vertical separation, and the physical limitations of aircraft capabilities. Others arise from the situation, such as unfavorable weather conditions and emergency landing priorities. In addition to safe and timely take-offs, flights and landings, fuel economy and noise pollution over inhabited areas must also be considered.

The above microcosm is well structured in terms of state changes over space and time. The commands and pilot actions are drawn from a small standardized set. The measures of aircraft performance are simple, such as flight time, fuel consumed, and number and degree of constraint violations. The competence of the system can be measured along the dimensions of the number and the duration of validity of commands and (assuming perfect adherence to the commands) all measures of aircraft performance.

Sources of uncertainty are due to imperfect adherence to commands, fuzziness in location of aircraft on radar images, suboptimal commands issued, unexpected environmental events/weather, incoming aircraft, and so forth.

SOME ISSUES OF IMPLEMENTATION

We have implemented a fairly general-purpose MME that encompasses the ideas described above. Several important design decisions had to be made. We explain them in the terms of our first area of application, simulated air traffic control (SATC).

In setting up the environment, we define a set of *objects* inhabiting it. *Conditions* affecting the objects can be constant over time (e.g., the location of a mountain range) or subject to change (e.g., current weather). Objects can also affect each other (e.g., two planes with intersecting flight paths). An object passes through different *phases* in its interaction with the environment. A phase can be considered as a distinct stage in the life-time of the object—the period of its sojourn in the environment. During a phase, the object may perform certain *functions* toward achieving a subgoal. The achievement of the subgoal places the object in another phase. (For example, the six major phases a plane passes through are take-off, climb, cruise, descent, approach, and landing.) The overall goal is, of course, the safe and timely flight between origin and destination.

Associated with each object is a set of *attributes* that define the constant and varying properties of the object, including the phase it is in. The number and type of attributes are determined by the domain of application. The user defines the functions that may alter the values of the attributes every time a user-specified *incremental parameter* (usually time) value elapses. There is a trade-off consideration here. If the incremental parameter is small, more computing is done, but there is less chance that a conflict "sneaks through" unnoticed in between two attribute updatings.

It is important to point out that the attributes of the objects in the Simulated World change independently of those in the Extrapolated World and vice versa. This separation of *scopes* is a basic necessity when the causal relation between decisions and consequences is sought.

A fairly large knowledge base needs to be prepared for a given domain of application. (The term knowledge base is used as opposed to database in view of the artificial intelligence techniques that make use of the information stored.) For the SATC environment, for example, the knowledge base includes

- The physical characteristics of one or several airports (length and location of airstrips; height and location of potential obstrutions, such as mountains and towers; direction of radio beacons, etc.).

- The physical characteristics of all planes participating (symbolic notation for manufacturer/model, landing speed, approach angle, approach speed, descent angle, descent speed, maximum and average cruising speed, climb angle, take-off speed, turning radius, fuel capacity, fuel consumption in different phases, etc).
- Dictionary and syntax needed in the communication between pilots and the air traffic controller.
- Interpreter for the above communication, and links between controller instructions and functions making attribute value changes accordingly.

IMPLEMENTATION OF THE SIMULATED AIR TRAFFIC CONTROL ENVIRONMENT

Hardware

As a first attempt, we decided to drive the displays of the Simulated World and the Extrapolated World from two different computer accounts that could communicate with each other through common files. This approach was slow, inefficient, and error prone. We then asked the Engineering Development Shop at Arizona State University to design and build a device switch that could direct, under software control, graphics signals from a serial I/O port to either of the display units. The criteria of the design were (a) simple maintainability, (b) cost-effective and easily obtainable parts, (c) adherence to interface standards for multipurpose applications, and (d) flexibility in switching characteristics and baud rates.

The idea is that on receipt of a special character (at a selectable baud rate), the device in question intercepts the output stream from the host computer, toggles the output switch, and transmits the stream to the other display.

Software

Figure 2 shows the SATC environment with the left-hand side display unit illustrating the Simulated World and the right-hand side unit the Extrapolated World. Figure 3 shows the simulated radar scopes in more detail. These are patterned after the scopes in use at the Federal Aviation Administration's TRACON center in Phoenix, Arizona.

The display presents a map that is approximately 100 miles in radius and contains a "control sector" — an area for which a group of controllers is responsible. The map is centered over the location of the radar dish generating the display, and circular grid lines are shown 5 miles apart. The locations of the airways, radio beacons, mountain peaks, and other relevant landmarks are also indicated in a standard symbolic format.

In real life, ATC displays produce only the blips on the screen, whereas a transponder system can superimpose additional information on the map about planes in the region as needed. This information providing the airplane's identification, ground speed, altitude, and other data is presented in a block connected with a line to the exact location of the plane on the screen. Our display simulates this process.

We have kept the simulated environment as realistic as possible but, to enhance the system, we have made three changes, as compared to real-

FIGURE 2. Two graphics display units for the air traffic controller—the Simulated World is shown on the left-hand side and the Extrapolated World on the right-hand side (Colors omitted).

life radar scopes. First, we have made use of the color capability of the display units to make the identification of various groups of symbols easier. Second, the user is given the ability to center the display over any part of the map and to zoom it in and out as necessary to obtain a more detailed view of potential problem areas. Finally, the addition of a system clock, a text window for presenting the status of the system and the airplanes, and a menu display was desirable in our implementation.

The menu system allows the user to select or change any of the simulation parameters that are not associated with the behavior of the airplanes. Menu selections are made using a stylus and a digitizing tablet next to the display. Via the menu system, one can vary the time parameters of the simulation, initialize an extrapolation, change the color of a group of symbols, or alter the center and scale of the map as described above.

A second display mode is provided wherein the vertical profile of a plane's motion can be viewed. In this mode, the display is centered on a target aircraft, and the viewing plane is rotated so that the target is always moving perpendicular to the controller's line of sight. Although current ATC radar scopes do not have this capability, this mode was provided to enhance the man—machine interface in certain situations.

The internal structure of the program handles each plane as an independent object, complete with its own performance and behavior characteristics. Airplane objects carry information about their flight plan, commands

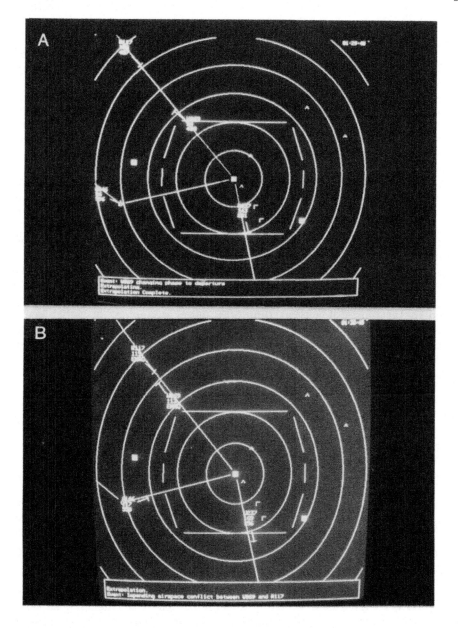

FIGURE 3. The simulated radar scopes showing in detail the necessary features of the Simulated World and the Extrapolated World, respectively. (Colors omitted.)

previously issued to them by the controllers, a full description of their current status, and a pointer to a generic block or "frame" of information containing the performance characteristics of a class of airplanes (e.g., DC-9, Boeing 747, etc.) Thus, any environment can be described in terms of the properties of all airplanes in that environment.

The data structures used allow for easy manipulation of the *system time*. To update the environment to a new time, a set of operations needs to be performed on each airplane representation. Extrapolation is accomplished by taking the current state of the environment and updating it repeatedly by the time increment parameter until the specified time is reached and the display is triggered (assuming no conflict occurs; otherwise, the extrapolation process is interrupted, warning sound and light signals are given, and the conflict at that time point is displayed). Also, the environments can be saved periodically to allow the controller the benefit of an "instant replay."

A novel addition to our simulation is a versatile *reminder system*. The controller is able to describe a variety of anticipated situations using the menu system. When the program senses that a predefined situation is about to occur, it alerts the controller with a tone and a message describing the triggering condition. This subsystem may save a controller valuable time by providing retrieval cues for previously generated plans.

Finally, although the controller can modify simulation parameters via the menu system, commands and requests are sent to the simulated airplanes through an Interstate Electronics voice recognition system. The system is limited to 100 words at a time; thus, the basic vocabulary is rather small. However, we have solved the problem of efficient uploading and downloading blocks of words and completed a reasonably sophisticated open-ended parser for controller utterances. The user can now communicate with the system in a small subset of English and ATC jargon, utilizing several blocks of 100 words.

PARTICIPATING PROGRAMMING SYSTEMS

We are engaged in several interrelated long-term projects concerning the ATC task. Each of them aims at contributing to a different problem area of ATC but all make use of the MME. These are described briefly in the following text.

The Quasi-Optimizer System [17, 21]

Let us consider an environment in which one or several decision-making strategies attempts to achieve some goal. (One can assume, for the sake of generality, that a *goal vector* is specified whose components need not be independent in real-life confrontations; e.g., in ATC, the number of aircraft kept on their appointed flight paths and the weighted average deviation from the desired time schedule are obviously interrelated goal components.)

Each of the strategies evaluates the environment by measuring certain variables (numerical or symbolic) available to it, which the strategy considers relevant. Such variables may be the real or assumed distance between aircraft, the perceived state of the landing strips, availability of air corridor space, criticality of local weather patterns and fuel reserves, and so forth. An important component of a strategy is aimed at interpreting these measurements and incorporating them in the process of making decisions that can lead to goal achievement.

The environment as perceived by the strategy is unclear because some information may be unavailable, missing (risky or uncertain, according to whether or not the relevant a priori probability distributions are known, respectively), or obscured by noise. If the decisions based on such incomplete and/or inconsistent information are incorrect, resources will be wasted and goal achievement will be farther removed.

Let us now consider how the Quasi-Optimizer (QO) System can generate a new strategy [19–21]. It must construct a model (a *descriptive theory*) of every participating strategy through observation and measurements. It must then assign to each component of the model, some measure of quality, that is, an outcome-dependent *allocation of credit* must be made.

The strategy obtainable from the best ocmponents of the model strategies is a *normative theory*, which is potentially the best of all available ones, on the basis of the information accessible by us.

The QO System performs these tasks by automatically generating computer models of the strategies observed, and from these, it constructs a QO strategy that is a normative theory in the statistical sense.

We note that the QO System may also provide a solution to the fundamental problem of expert systems, namely how to acquire the large amount of knowledge required from human experts and how to store it appropriately.

One application of the QO System in the MME discussed is to have ATC trainees demonstrate their control strategy in the SATC environment. The QO System codifies this strategy and makes sure that it is complete, unambiguous, and consistent. The consequences of the decisions are evaluated according to the objective measures listed previously, and quality measures are calculated. Information about the strength and shortcomings of the strategy is then fed back to the trainee for his benefit.

Alternatively, ATC experts would specify their control strategies to be modeled again by the QO System. A normative theory can then be generated from the best components of these expert strategies—obviating the expensive and error-prone systems programming effort. As a by-product of the above, the metastrategy noted previously would indicate in which region of the whole problem space a given strategy is most proficient—leading to an optimum way of dividing the total task into performing components.

The QO System has been completed and electronically connected to the MME. Our experiments, so far only with novice controllers, indicate that the objectives have been accomplished.

The Advice Taker/Inquirer System

The objective of the Advice Taker/Inquirer (AT/I) System is to establish a MME environment in which a human advisor can teach strategies on–line, though *principles* and high-level *examples* [22]. The principles and examples normally consist of situations and recommended actions. (Principles describe rather general situations defined in a flexible manner, whereas examples are specific and illustrate appropriate behavior in a general situation by analogy with a particular one. Actions can either adhere to some general guidelines or follow a set of sharply defined prescriptions.) Whenever the system finds the advice given to be vague, incomplete, or inconsistent with previously imparted knowledge, it makes inquiries and asks for clarification. The advisor can define and redefine the components of a principle at any time. He can also override temporarily the strategy taught so far by issuing an *order*.

The system does not start out with a blank memory. It knows the rules governing the environment, the basic variables, and the range of their values within the situation space. The advisor can at any time,

1. Define variables, functions, general and specific actions, confrontation-related adjectives, nouns, and verbs—in terms of constants, confrontation parameters, current values, overall and moving averages of statistical variables, basic confrontation actions, and Boolean and relational operators.
2. Defines principles of a strategy that connect a situation (specified as a Boolean combination of ranges of statistical variables—again current values, overall or moving averages) to some general or specific action.
3. Give high-level examples by connecting sharply specified situations to direct confrontation actions.
4. Make inquiries about definitions, principles, and values of statistical variables stored so far.
5. Issue an order that temporarily overrides the strategy acquired so far.

In turn, the system can

1. Ask for clarification whenever new definitions are vague or conflict with stored ones, or the strategy is incomplete in not covering the whole confrontation space.
2. Return exemplary actions in user-specified confrontation situations, in accordance with the strategy acquired.
3. Display definitions, principles, confrontation parameters, values of variables, and so forth.

In general, it is more efficient and less error—prone to teach a strategy to a system by telling *how* to do things than by providing detailed algorithms of *what* to do in every relevant situation. Very high-level communication with computers, a most important goal of computer science, would have to incorporate the ideas described here.

We list four possible applications for the AT/I system, still under development, in a SATC environment:

1. *The Controller.* An experienced air traffic controller advises the AT/I in the SATC environment. The AT/I then acts as a controller in it.
2. *The Assistant.* An experienced air traffic controller advises the AT/I in a subset of his activities that are most suitable for automation. The AT/I then acts in it, handling some of the air controller's tasks, thus allowing the controller to concentrate on other tasks.
3. *The Trainer/Advisor.* An AT/I is advised by an expert ATC trainer. The AT/I then monitors the decisions of a trainee in the simulated environment, and critiques and advises the trainee.
4. *The Trainer/Simulator.* The AT/I is advised by an ATC trainee. The AT/I then controls a simulation according to its synthesis of the trainee's strategy. The trainee can then try hypothesized

decisions and view a simulation of the resulting future situation. This accounts for the expected future decisions of the trainee as well as the calculated effects of the simulation.

The Generalized Production Rules System

In decision making, we distinguish between *open variables,* which can be observed at any desired time, and *hidden variables,* whose values can be identified only intermittently or periodically. At other times, when necessary, the values of hidden variables have to be estimated. The Generalized Production Rules System (GPRS) has been designed to do this estimation [23, 24].

GPRS establishes a knowledge base that consists of an ordered set of generalized production rules connecting certain mathematical properties of open variable behavior (the predictor part) and certain known values of hidden variables (the predicted part). Each rule has a rigorously defined credibility level. As more information becomes available, both the number of rules and the credibility level of the rules change. Rules that are "similar enough" are automatically merged, and their credibility level increases.

The GPRS can provide either point or functional estimates of hidden variables values. Furthermore, it can take care of situations in which the data collection is performed at several locations and the knowledge bases themselves are distributed over space.

The GPRS is an independent program that can be plugged into any expert system in need of numerical estimates of hidden variables. We use it in conjunction with the QO and AT/I systems to identify situational variables, decisions, and reasons underlying decisions when they are not directly observable.

The Distributed Planning System

In a Distributed Planning System (DPS), multiple processors cooperate to achieve a common set of objectives [25]. We can visualize such a task to arise within ATC. Assume each plane has a computer that communicates with other airborne machines and with a central processor that has overriding authority. We are concerned with two major issues: (a) what architectural principles should guide us in interconnecting the processors and (b) what planning techiques and control structures each processor should adopt.

Each processor has to go through the sequence, sensing → planning → evaluation → execution. The planning mechanism (as well as the rest of the program for the above quadruple) is duplicated for each aircraft but with different databases (plane characteristics, priority hierarchy, destination, model of the surrounding world, etc.)

We have designed several distinct architectures, each with different modes of operation. We are investigating the reliability and cost-effectiveness of these, both theoretically and experimentally. We are studying the trade-off along the dimension of conflict resolution between completely rule-based operation, at one end of the spectrum of planning activity, and completely negotiation-based operation, at the other end.

Summing up, the characteristic features of planning by spatially and possibly functionally distinct processors are as follows:

- Widely dispersed data gathering/sensing
- Limited and, at times, nosiy communication channels
- Time-stressed demands on decision making
- Natural clustering of activities, both spatially and functionally

The objectives are as follows:

- Error-free and on-time routing
- Reduction of uncertainties that potentially lead to unresolvable conflicts
- Assurance of horizontal and vertical separation
- Conservation of resources (fuel, manpower)

Our studies are not only expected to contribute to the automation of ATC but also to shed light on the manner in which humans organize their knowledge and coordinate their actions. In a broader context, we hope to develop a *unified framework* for plan generation by distributed processors, which can then be easily *customized for different domains of application*. This system is now completed.

The Causal Modeling System

The Causal Modeling System (CMS) is a tool for investigating the cause-and-effect relationships in a well-defined task environment over a specified time interval [26]. The system first constructs a causal model from several information sources under the interactive guidance of the user. The constructed model may be thought of as a directed graph in which the nodes are events (states or changes in states of systems that are significant to the user) and the arcs are causal relations (relationships between events that have temporal and probabilistic properties). Once the model is constructed, the user is able to query the CMS, using the causal graph as a database.

The CMS could be a valuable tool in the realm of air accident (and near-accident) investigation. An investigator would be able to give the system all of the known facts about an accident, weighted hypotheses about what happened, and simulation models of the aircraft and any other dynamic entities involved. In addition, the investigator may choose to bring in libraries of information about general causal relations (e.g., natural laws) or statistical causal relations from previous accidents. Once the causal graph has been constructed, the investigator could ask the system questions, such as:

- What were the principal causes of the accident?
- What event or events could have prevented the accident?
- What is the most probable chain of events from event A to event B?

There are two ways in which the CMS could make use of the MME. In the first, the MME extrapolator's model of the Real World would be displayed on the Extrapolated World screen, whereas the recorded Real World events

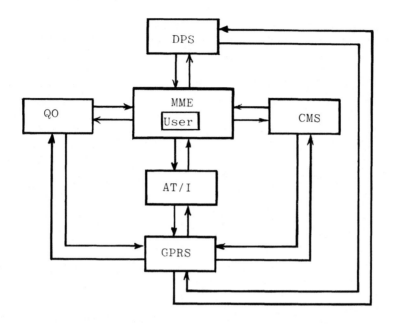

FIGURE 4. The connection between the participating systems and the MME. (QO) Quasi-Optimizer System; (DPS) Distributed Planning System, (MME) man-machine environment; (AT/I) Advice Taker/Inquirer System; (GPRS) General Production Rule System; (CMS) Causal Modeling System.

would be displayed on the simulated world screen, with no time lag between the two. By viewing what actually happened on one screen while viewing what *should* have happened on the other (via the "normal" model in the extrapolator), a user should be able to pinpoint important events and hypothesize about causal relations in the real world domain. The second way the CMS could make use of the MME is to display the state of the real world on one screen at some time point and simultaneously, display the state at a later time point on the second screen (note that the extrapolator model would not be needed here because all of the real-world information within the time interval of interest would be recorded). Using this configuration, a user should be well-equipped to hypothesize about events in the domain, because he can potentially see causes and effects displayed at the same time. The above approaches using the CMS are being implemented.

Figure 4 shows the connection between the systems described above.

EVALUATION OF THE MAN—MACHINE ENVIRONMENT

To evaluate the MME concept, a series of experiments were designed and performed. The objective of the experiments was to compare the proficiency and efficiency of human planning and decision making in a complex, real-time problem domain, with and without the aid of an interactive extrapolation facility.

   The experiments utilized the ATC implementation of the MME, providing a human subject with the (somewhat simplified) task of an en-route air traffic controller. The subject was first presented with a routing task in which only the real-time information was presented to him. The subject was then given a statistically equivalent task (the problems were randomly generated), but an extrapolation facility was available, which enabled him to look at "snapshots" of future situations. The performance of the subject in each case was evaluated according to the number of airspace conflicts (near collisions) that occurred during the session and the efficiency with which aircraft were routed through the subject's control sector. (Note that the configuration of the air corridors and the large number of participating aircraft were introduced deliberately to generate many conflicts for the benefit of the experiments.)

Experimental Setup

As stated above, the ATC implementation of the MME was used for the experiments, with the subject's task being restricted to the en-route phase. In half of the experiments, the extrapolator was simply disabled to obtain a control group of task sessions.

   At the beginning of each session, a number of straight-line airways across the control sector were randomly generated. As the session progressed, a number of aircraft were generated with randomly chosen take-off times, airways, altitudes, and airspeeds. The subject could issue directives to individual aircraft, telling the aircraft to change either its heading or altitude or resume its requested flight plan. Additionally, in the experiments in which the extrapolator was used, the subject could request an extrapolation to some specified time point, the results of which would be displayed on the second terminal as soon as the processing was complete. The session automatically terminated as soon as the last plane left the subject's control sector.

   The following parameters were used in all of the experiments:

- Number of airways: 3
- Number of aircraft: 26
- Requested speed range: 350–550 mph
- Requested altitude range: 19,000–22,000 feet
- Time increment for the simulated world: 5 seconds
- Time increment for the extrapolated world: 10 seconds
- Conflict criteria: within 5 miles horizontal and 1000 feet vertical separation

   At the end of every session, the following statistics were calculated and recorded:

- Number of conflicts: Incremented for every aircraft in a conflict situation (as defined above) at the end of every internal increment of time.
- Average off distance: The difference in miles between each aircraft's requested straight-line route and the sum of the distance it actually traveled throught the sector and the distance from the point it left the sector to its destination.

- Average climb distance: The total distance in feet each aircraft was told to climb during its flight through the sector, plus the difference between its requested altitude and its altitude upon leaving the sector (when positive).

Results

Twenty experiments, lasting approximately 45 minutes each, were performed—10 with the extrapolator and 10 without. The results of the tests were as follows:

10 sessions without extrapolation
    Average conflicts/session: 48.2
    Average off distance/plane: 0.01424 miles
    Average climb distance/plane: 654.6 feet
10 sessions with extrapolation
    Average conflicts/session: 22.20 (54% fewer)
    Average off distance/plane: 0.00797 miles (44% less)
    Average climb distance/plane: 545.0 feet (17% less)

Conclusions

The experimental results clearly indicate that for this particular task, the subjects' performances with the extrapolator were significantly better than their performances without it. Part of the difference in performance can be attributed to the fact that the MME was implemented on a time-sharing system, making the simulated world run a little faster (in real-time) when the extrapolator was disabled, thus making the task slightly more difficult. However, the difference in speed was small enough (especially with several users on the system) that the results should still represent an accurate evaluation of the usefulness of the MME.

Although the use of the extrapolator improved the subjects' performances, we found that the facility could be abused as well. For example,

- After gaining some experience in the use of the extrapolator, it is easy to become complacent when no conflicts show up on the extrapolation, when in reality, conflicts may occur within the time interval between the simulated world and the extrapolated world.
- If extrapolations are continually requested for short time intervals, the majority of one's attention is moved from the simulated world to the extrapolated world—again resulting in the possible oversight of conflicts in the immediate future.
- In "crisis" situations in which many decisions must be made in a short period of time (e.g., several conflicts are imminent), the extrapolator can be more of a hindrance than a help. When faced with such a confusing situation, a seemingly "safe" thing to do is to run an extrapolation into the near future. However, this action usually just results in wasting valuable time, during which directives should have been issued and the situation resolved.

These observations indicate that although the extrapolation facility can be a useful tool in real-time planning and decision making, it should be relied on only as an auxiliary source of information—the decision maker should always focus his attention on the unfolding of events in the simulated world.

ACKNOWLEDGMENTS

The work reported above was carried out by a team of dedicated and talented students in the Artificial Intelligence Lab. I am indebted (in a random order) to Ron Lo, Bob Cromp, Neal Mazur, Tim Bickmore, Mike Belofsky, Cher Lo, George Sicherman, Steve Feuerstein, John Brown, Han You, João Martins, Ernesto Morgado, and Skip Lewis. I also thank Bob Morrison of Arizona State University's Engineering Development Shop for designing and constructing the device switch used with the twin display units.

REFERENCES

1. A. Simon, "A Behavioral Model of Rational Choice." in *Organizational Decision Making* (M. Alexis and C. Z. Wilson (eds.), Prentice-Hall, Englewood Cliffs, NJ, 1967, pp. 174—184.

2. H. A. Simon, *Models of Man*, Wiley, New York, 1957.

3. W. J. Gore and J. W. Dyson (eds.), *The Making of Decisions*, Free Press of Glencoe, New York, 1964.

4. E. D. Sacerdoti, *A Structure for Planning and Behavior*, Elsevier/ North-Holland, Amsterdam, 1977.

5. R. C. Schank and R. P. Abelson, *Scripts, Plans, Goals, and Understanding*, Lawrence Erlbaum Press, Hillside, NJ, 1977.

6. D. McDermott, "Planning and Acting," *Cognitive Sc.* 2, 79—109 (1978.

7. K. Konolige and N. J. Nilsson, "Multiple-Agent Planning Systems," in *Proceedings of the First Annual AAAI National Conference*, 1980, pp. 138—142, The American Association for Artificial Intelligence, Stanford, CA.

8. M. Stefik, "Planning with Constraints (MOLGEN: Part 1)," *Artif. Intell.*, 111—139 (1981).

9. M. Stefik, "Planning and Meta-Planning (MOLGEN: Part 2),"*Artif. Intell.*, 141—169 (1981).

10. P. G. W. Keen and M. S. S. Morton, *Decision Support Systems*, Addison-Wesley, Reading, MA, 1978.

11. R. H. Bonczek, C. W. Holsapple, and A. W. Whinston, *Foundations of Decision Support Systems*, Academic Press, New York, 1981.

12. G. F. Swetnam, Jr., "A Preliminary Characterization of the AERA Man-Machine Interface for ATC Computer Replacement," in *MITRE Working Paper*, WP-81W00135, 1981, MITRE Corp., Washington, D.C.

13. R. Steeb, S. Cammarata, F. Hayes-Roth, P. W. Thorndyke, and R. B. Wesson, "Distributed Intelligence for Air Fleet Control," in *RAND Corporation* Report R-2728-ARPA, Rand Corp., Santa Monica, CA.

14. R. B. Wesson, "Planning in the World of Air Traffic Controller," in *Proceedings of the IJCAI-77* (International Joint Conference on Artificial Intelligence), Cambridge, MA, 1977, pp. 473—479.

15. R. T. Chien, "Artificial Intelligence and the Human Error Prevention Study in ATC Systems," *Final Report* to the Department of Transportation and Federal Aviation Administration, Washington, D. C., 1982.

16. N. V. Findler, "Some Artificial Intelligence Contributions to Air Traffic Control," in *Proceedings of the Fourth Jerusalem Conference on Information Technology*, 1984, pp. 470–475, Institute of Electronics and Electrical Engineering, Computer Society Press, Silver Springs, MD.

17. N. V. Findler, "The Role of Strategies in Air Traffic Control" in *Proceedings of the Eighteenth Hawaii International Conference on System Sciences*, Vol. 1, 1985, pp. 522–529.

18. N. V. Findler, T. W. Bickmore, and R. F. Cromp, "A General-Purpose Man-Machine Environment with Special Reference to Air Traffic Control," *Int. J. Man-Machine Stud.*, 23, 587–603 (1985).

19. N. V. Findler and J. van Leeuwen, "The Complexity of Decision Trees, the Quasi-Optimizer, and the Power of Heuristic Rules," *Inf. Control*, 40, 1–19 (1979).

20. N. V. Findler and J. P. Martins, "On Automating Computer Model Construction—The Second Step Toward a Quasi-Optimizer System," *J. Inf. and Optimization Sci. 2*, 119–136 (1981).

21. N. V. Findler, "An Overview of the Quasi-Optimizer System," *Large Scale Syst. Theory Appl.*, 5, 123–130 (1983).

22. N. V. Findler, G. L. Sicherman, and S. Feuerstein, "Teaching Strategies to an Advice Taker/Inquirer System," in *Proceedings of the European IFIP79* (International Federation of Information Processing) *Conference*, London, England, 1979, pp. 457–465.

23. N. V. Findler, J. E. Brown, R. Lo, H. Y. You, "A Module to Estimate Numerical Values of Hidden Variables for Expert Systems," *Int. J. Man-Machine Syst.*, 18, 323–335 (1983).

24. N. V. Findler, and R. Lo, "A Note on the Functional Estimation of Values of Hidden Variables—An extended Module for Expert Systems," *Int. J. Man-Machine Syst.*, 18, 555–565 (1983).

25. N. V. Findler and R. Lo, "An Examination of Distributed Planning in the World of Air Traffic Control," in *Distributed and Parallel Processing*, 3, 411–431 (1986).

26. N. V. Findler and T. W. Bickmore, "A Casual Modelling System," 1986 (submitted for publication).

NICHOLAS V. FINDLER

THE ANALYTIC HIERARCHY PROCESS
AND THE PERSONAL COMPUTER

This article will discuss how the analytical hierarchy process (AHP), when implemented on a microcomputer, produces a man-machine synergy that enables people to make better decisions about complex problems.

INTRODUCTION—MULTICRITERIA DECISION PROBLEMS

What constitutes a complex problem, making a decision difficult? The measure of complexity must be related to the human thought process. The first ingredient of complexity occurs when we are required to choose from a number of alternatives; the greater the number of alternatives, the greater the complexity.

Complex decisions require us to make judgments. In order to make judgments, standards on which judgments can be based are required; the dictionary calls these criteria. Without criteria we would have no basis for judging. The second ingredient of complexity occurs when there are several, often competing, criteria.

We will consider a problem to be complex if it possesses the following two characteristics: (*a*) numerous (at least two) feasible alternatives and (*b*) numerous (at least two) criteria or objectives.

The "complex" problems that we will discuss, that is, those having several alternatives and several criteria, have come to be called multicriteria decision problems. The complexity stems not so much from the size of the problem itself but from the fact that multicriteria are often at odds with one another.

According to Cook and Hammond [1], "Reaching a decision will ordinarily involve making trade-offs between the factors affecting the decision, and this is a difficult and poorly understood aspect of decision making. Research conducted over the past quarter century has demonstrated conclusively that people have a poor understanding of how they make such trade-offs."

Jones [2] cites experimental evidence that shows that ". . . people do find it difficult to make consistent judgments when more than one attribute is involved." He also states that there is ". . . a strong argument for providing some structured means of helping them 'think through' their choices."

IDENTIFICATION OF ALTERNATIVES, CONSTRAINTS, AND CRITERIA

When confronted with a problem, we consider alternatives and then choose the one (or combination) that best meets our goal. In order to make the "best" decision, we must first identify alternatives, eliminate those that are not feasible, and then choose according to our criteria.

Identification of Alternatives

Identifying alternatives to a problem is often more of an art than a science. A popular technique often used by a group of people is called brainstorming. The objective of brainstorming is to determine all possible alternatives to a problem, regardless of feasibility or merit.

Identification of Criteria

In order to judge the feasibility and merits of the alternatives to a problem, we must judge how well each of the alternatives satisfies our requirements. Criteria are the standards on which we can make such judgments. Brainstorming can also be used to identify criteria, as well as alternatives.

Kepner and Tregoe [3] have proposed that we consider two classes of criteria: "musts" and "wants." Distinguishing between must and want criteria, although not essential, is often easy to do and simplifies the subsequent analysis. In theory, there is not always a clear distinction between a must and a want. We often say we *must* have something when, in fact, we mean we *want* something very badly. In practice, however, it is often an easy matter to make the distinction between musts and wants.

If it is obvious that an alternative identified during brainstorming is not a viable alternative, by stating why it is not viable, one has identified a must criteria, or constraint. For example, in selecting a mode of transportation to be used on the highways, most adults might have a safety requirement that the vehicle possess more than two wheels, eliminating motorcycles and mopeds.

Must Criteria (Constraints)

Each must criteria is a constraint that, if not met by an alternative, will eliminate that alternative from further consideration. In other words, in order for an alternative to be considered feasible, it must satisfy each and every constraint.

If brainstorming is used to generate alternatives, many, if not most, of the alternatives would not really make much sense. For example, in selecting a vehicle for transportation to and from work, a golf cart might be eliminated because there is no route between home and work on which it would be legal to drive a golf cart. That is, we can identify a constraint that requires that a route exist between home and work that accommodates the vehicle and another constraint that it be legal to operate the vehicle on that route. Any vehicle that does not satisfy either constraint is considered to be infeasible and is eliminated from further consideration.

A question to ask when brainstorming for must criteria is, What is the absolute minimum that an alternative must possess with respect to a certain characteristic?

Wants

Those criteria that do not specify absolute minimums are wants. In practice, most criteria are wants. A question to ask when identifying criteria classified as wants is, What characteristic might influence me to choose this alternative as opposed to that?

After identifying alternatives and criteria, categorizing the criteria into musts and wants, and then eliminating those alternatives that do not satisfy all of the must criteria, the problem is narrowed to consideration of the remaining alternatives with respect to the want criteria.

The problem of how to best satisfy wants is endemic to every facet of human endeavor and has, until recently, eluded a reasonable solution. The AHP provides a reasonable solution.

COMPLEXITY AND ORGANIZATION

Complex problems require organization. The greater the number of criteria, the greater the complexity is. The greater the number of alternatives, the greater the complexity is. There is, however, a limit to the ability of the mind to relate and discriminate among and to accurately choose from a large number of alternatives, even if there were only one criterion.

According to James Martin [4], if a person "has to choose from a range of 20 alternatives, he will give inaccurate answers because the range exceeds the bandwidth of his channel for perception. In many cases, seven alternatives are the approximate limit of his channel capacity." Martin's conclusion is based on the results of numerous psychological experiments, including the well-known study "The Magical Number Seven, Plus or Minus Two: Some Limits on Our Capacity for Information Processing," by G. A. Miller [5].

Martin observed that "Seven is a low number when we are concerned with complex problem solving." But he also observed that "Fortunately, there are several ways of increasing our effective channel capacity. The first is to enable the subject to make relative rather than absolute judgments. The second is to organize tasks so that the subject makes several judgments in succession" [4].

Another dimension of problem complexity is related to what Martin refers to as the capacity of the human short-term memory—the number of items that the brain can store for immediate processing and which will lose its contents very quickly if not reinforced. Psychologists have also measured the capacity of the human short-term memory and have concluded that the short-term memory can hold about seven separate items (this varies by plus or minus two for normal subjects in different situations.)

Fortunately, we can accommodate conflicting criteria, as well as compensate for our limited mental channel capacities and short-term memories by organizing a problem into a meaningful structure. What form should this organization take?

HIERARCHICAL ORGANIZATION

Our minds structure complex reality into its constituent parts and these, in turn, into their parts, and so on. This hierarchical organization is a natural thought process. Saaty [6] has pointed out that our tendency to think that hierarchies were invented by corporations and governments is false. Hierarchies are basic to the human way of breaking reality into clusters and subclusters. Whyte [7] expressed this thought as follows:

The immense scope of hierarchical classification is clear. It is the most powerful method of classification used by the human brain-mind in ordering experience, observations, entities, and information.... The use of hierarchical ordering must be as old as human thought, conscious and unconscious...

Herbert Simon, nobel laureate, observed the following:

Large organizations are almost universally hierarchical in structure. That is to say, they are divided into units, which are subdivided into smaller units, which are, in turn, subdivided and so on.... Hierarchical subdivision is not a characteristic that is peculiar to human organizations. It is common to virtually all complex systems of which we have knowledge. . . . The near universality of hierarchy in the composition of complex systems suggests that there is something fundamental in this structural principle that goes beyond the peculiarities of human organization.... An organization will tend to assume hierarchical form whenever the task environment is complex relative to the problem-solving and communicating powers of the organization members and their tools. Hierarchy is the adaptive form for finite intelligence to assume in the face of complexity [8].

Saaty describes how theory reflects what appears to be an innate method of operation of the human mind:

When presented with a multitude of elements, controllable or not, which comprise a complex situation, (the mind) aggregates them into groups, according to whether they share certain properties. Our model of this brain function allows a repitition of this process, in that we consider these groups, or rather their identifying common properties, as the elements of a new level in the system. These elements may, in turn, be grouped according to another set of properties, generating the elements of yet another "higher," level, until we reach a single "top" element, which can often be identified as the goal of our decision-making process [6].

THE AHP

The AHP enables decision makers to visually structure a complex problem in the form of a hierarchy. Each factor and alternative can be identified and evaluated with respect to other related factors. Although there are many variations of a hierarchy, a typical one contains a goal, below which are criteria, below which are levels of subcriteria and, finally, alternatives. Figure 1 illustrates the first three levels of an AHP hierarchy (Fig. 1 will be explained in the case study presented later in this text).

The ability to structure a complex problem and then focus attention on specific components amplifies one's decision-making capabilities. The capacity for making judgments is expanded beyond the limits imposed by, what psychologists call, the limited channel capacity and short-term memory of the human mind.

Once a hierarchy is established, expert judgments are solicited from the decision maker relative to each facet of the decision problem. The method-

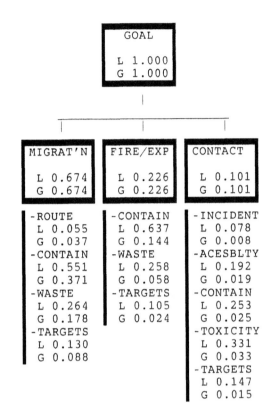

GOAL   --- Evaluate potential hazards to environment
ACESBLTY   --- Accessibility of hazardous substances
CONTACT   --- Direct contact mode
CONTAIN   --- Containment category
FIRE/EXP   --- Fire and explosion hazard mode
INCIDENT   --- Observed incident
MIGRAT'N   --- Migration hazard mode
ROUTE   --- Route characteristics category
TARGETS   --- Targets category
TOXICITY   --- Toxicity/persistence
WASTE   --- Waste characteristics category

L   --- LOCAL PRIORITY: PRIORITY RELATIVE TO PARENT
G   --- GLOBAL PRIORITY: PRIORITY RELATIVE TO GOAL

FIGURE 1 Evaluate potential hazards to environment—GOAL.

ology goes beyond conventional decision analysis techniques by not requiring
numerical guesses. Subjective judgments on aspects of a problem for which
no scale of measurement exists are easily accommodated.

The expert(s) providing the judgments can do so entirely in a verbal
mode; no numerical guesses are required. For example, they can enter

judgments about the importance of criterion A versus B, where criterion A is strongly more important than criterion B. Alternatively, the experts can provide judgments in a numerical mode in the form of a ratio scale, where criterion A is four times more important than criterion B.

The judgments are used in deriving relative priorities for the decision criteria and alternatives. This is accomplished by calculating what mathematicians call eigenvalues and eigenvectors of matrices that represent the pair-wise comparisons of criteria and alternatives. This methodology has been shown to provide remarkably accurate results.

The methodology also develops a measure of inconsistency. This measure is useful in identifying possible errors in judgments, as well as actual inconsistencies in the judgments themselves. The decision maker can request suggestions for improving consistency. It is important to note that the methodology does *not* preclude inconsistencies in judgments. On the contrary, many decisions must be made recognizing inconsistencies that exist in the real world.

After the decision maker conveys his expert judgments relative to the many facets of the decision being contemplated, the results are synthesized into overall priorities. In addition to developing the overall priorities, each of the components that contributes to these overall priorities is presented so that the decision maker can assess the results, implementing them if they seem appropriate or refining the model to reflect additional insights that have been acquired.

Absolute vs. Relative Judgments—Pair-Wise Comparisons

There are two basic kinds of judgments: absolute and relative. In making an absolute judgment, we compare one "thing" against a recollection from our long-term memory. In making a relative judgment, we make a pair-wise comparison of two things, one to the other. Humans can make much better relative judgments than absolute judgments because they have the ability to discriminate between the members of a pair by judging the intensity or preference for one over the other with respect to some criterion.

Pair-wise comparisons are as natural for humans as binary counting is for computers. The AHP uses pair-wise comparisons, as have many other judgment schemes in the past. What makes AHP so different and effective is that (a) judgments can be made verbally (because numerical guesses are not required, subjective judgments can be accommodated), and (b) the mathematical analysis performed on the judgments produces results that are amazingly accurate and robust and that include a measure of the consistency of the judgments.

People are generally wary, if not distrustful, when numbers are introduced into the traditional process of decision making. In some situations, however, appropriately chosen numbers can represent variations in feelings more faithfully than words or rhetoric can.

Two diametrically opposite schools of thought about numbers are (a) that numbers precisely represent quantitative characteristics and (b) that numbers cannot represent qualitative characteristics.

Each of these ideas is too extreme. Numbers neither represent quantitative characteristics to humans in a manner as precise as we think, nor are numbers completely out of place when we deal with qualitative or subjective characteristics. Numbers are sometimes artifacts that give us the illusion of greater precision than we may be capable of feeling.

The use of numbers can be extended in some reasonable, easily under-standable way to reflect our feelings on various social, economic, and political matters.

Scales of Measurement

We cannot measure without a scale, but traditional scales such as time and money limit the nature of ideas we can deal with. Thus, we need "new" scales.

Should we be afraid to develop new scales? To answer this question, let us consider the history of some of our well-accepted scales.

We should not think of our existing scales as being sacrosanct. In fact, existing scales were developed in an attempt to "quantify" what was, at the time, qualitative or subjective. Scales that are precise today, based upon international standards, were once imprecise and intended to repre-sent and communicate qualitative or subjective characteristics.

Consider the brightness and color of light. Are these qualities quanti-tative or subjective? For most of our day-to-day purposes, the answer is subjective. Yet we do have precise scales and devices to measure both the brightness (e.g., footcandles) and color (e.g., hertz) of light.

How about time? Many of us now use digital watches that are accurate to within a few seconds a month. But, for most of our purposes, such as judging the amount of time remaining in our lunch "hour," we probably get more useful information by looking at the minute hand of an analog clock than the digits on a digital clock.

To most of us, temperature is more subjective than time. We don't usually wear thermometers and often say things like "Sure feels hot today"! Yet we do have precise scales and devices to measure temperature, as well. One of these devices, the mercury thermometer, was invented by Gabriel Farenheit in the 18th century. This scale was based on what was, at the time, subjective. Normal body temperature was arbitrarily assigned a value of 100 degrees (100°F) (later found to be 98.6°F), and the temperature of the coldest thing Farenheit could produce in his laboratory, a mixture of salt and ice, was assigned a value of 0°F.

Even when we have precise quantitative measurements, we must pro-vide some subjective interpretations when making decisions. For example, 20°F is not twice as warm as 10°F. And even if we were to use the "ab-solute" scale, the relationship between the amount of heat in the atmosphere and a human's comfort is not linear. We try to model our subjective feel-ings by defining other "models," such as wind-chill factors and tempera-ture—humidity indices.

What can executive decision makers do to "feel" for the right decision? What scales can they use to measure corporate image and employee morale? Almost every decision is strongly influenced by subjective criteria and judgments (including politics).

Just as scales were developed in the past, new scales will be developed in the future. As such scales are developed, our notions of what is objec-tive and what is subjective will change again. There *is no reason* for us to be afraid to develop or use new scales.

Natural Ratio Scale

A "natural" scale used by the AHP consists of forming the ratio of two things. For example, when comparing the weights of two objects, they may be equal or, perhaps, one may be twice as heavy as the other. The scale is natural in the sense that we do not have to measure against some standard, such as a pound or a kilogram. In comparing the brightness of two lights, we may judge that one is three times as bright as the other, without resorting to measurements against a standard such as footcandles.

The scale is universal in that it can be used to compare anything with respect to a characteristic of interest. It can even be used to compare apples and oranges! With respect to weight, an apple and an orange are about equal. With respect to size, an apple and an orange are about equal. With respect to brightness, an orange is brighter than an apple. How much brighter? Twice as bright? Three times as bright? Can we make such a judgment without a light meter? Of course! Will such judgments be *accurate*? In the sense of accurately reflecting your subjective feeling, the answer is yes, by definition. What about in the sense of agreeing with measurements made with a light meter?

Modes of Comparison

Saaty [9] has demonstrated the feasibility of expressing the relative importance of one element over another with respect to a given criterion either verbally or numberically. Table 1 illustrates both modes.

On the numerical scale, 1.0 implies that the elements are equally important, 2.0, that one element is twice as important as the other, and 9.0, that one element is nine times as important as the other. Experience has confirmed that a scale of nine units is reasonable and reflects the degree to which we can discriminate the intensity of relationships among elements.

When making comparisons in a social, psychological, or political context, it is usually more appropriate to make verbal comparisons. When comparing economic or other measurable factors, numerical comparisons *may* be more appropriate (however, not always, because we have a tendency to overlook the nonlinearities in our utility when we use such numbers directly.)

Almost every decision involves one or more criteria for which no quantifiable scale exists. In fact, the higher the level of decision making within an organization, the more important these nonquantifiable criteria become and the greater the benefit of AHP. The natural ratio scale and the verbal comparisons can be meaningfully applied to criteria that are typically thought of as being nonquantifiable and subjective.

Redundant Judgments

When making judgments in the form of pair-wise comparisons, the relative importance of n factors can be arrived at by making only $(n - 1)$ judgments. For example, if we were comparing the relative importance of three factors, A, B, and C, and we judged that A is three times more important than B and that A is six times more important than C, we could surmise that B is three times as important as C. However, each of our two judgments might contain some error. The common statistical approach to minimizing errors is to take additional observations. The AHP does something similar by asking the decision maker(s) to make judgments about all possible pairs of $n*(n - 1)/2$ of factors, instead of the minimum $(n - 1)$ judgments.

Thus, in the above example, when asked to judge the relative importance of B and C, we might say that B is two times more important than

TABLE 1   Verbal and Numerical Judgment

Numerical Scale	Verbal Scale	Explanation
1.0	Equal importance of both elements	Two elements contribute equally to the property
3.0	Moderate importance of one element over another	Experience and judgment favor one element over another
5.0	Strong importance of one element over another	An element is strongly favored
7.0	Very strong importance of one element over another	An element is very strongly dominant
9.0	Extreme importance of one element over another	An element is favored by at least an order of magnitude of difference
2.0, 4.0, 6.0, 8.0	Intermediate values between two adjacent judgments	Used for compromise between two judgments
Increments of 0.1	Intermediate values in increments of 0.1 (Example: 6.3 is a permissible entry)	Used for even finer gradations of judgments

C. This judgment, redundant in the sense that we could have calculated that B was three times more important than C from the first two judgments, may be more accurate than either of the first two judgments. Thus, by using judgments about all possible pairs, the effects of errors in judgments can be minimized by "averaging." In addition, a measure of inconsistency can be derived from the set of pair-wise comparisons.

Calculating Priorities

The mathematical calculation of priorities derived from pair-wise comparisons with the AHP does indeed reduce the effects of errors in judgments. Although the details are somewhat involved, the results are impressively accurate.

The details involve the calculation of eigenvalues and eigenvectors of reciprocal matrices formed from the decision makers' judgments (see Saaty [9]). The process is easily understood by engineers and mathematicians, although the many calculations for a complex problem are usually laborious. Fortunately, the process can be implemented on a personal computer so that a decision maker is not the least concerned with the theory or the complexity of the calculations.

Can we use the process to compare subjective qualities, such as taste? Certainly! I may prefer apples twice as much as oranges, and you may prefer oranges twice as much as apples. Of course, there is no "correct" judgment. Each of us is the "expert" when making such judgments, and judgments of this type are implicit in almost every high-level decision-making process. Fortunately, the AHP now enables us to measure intangible, subjective qualities.

Consistency

A very interesting and important aspect of the AHP approach to deriving priorities is that a measure of inconsistency follows from the calculations performed on the pair-wise judgments. This measure, called a consistency index by Saaty [9], is zero when all judgments are perfectly consistent with one another and becomes larger, as the inconsistency becomes greater. In order to interpret the meaning of a large index, Saaty simulated a very large number of random pair-wise comparisons for different size matrices, calculating the consistency indices and arriving at an average consistency index for random judgments. He then defined the consistency ratio as the ratio of the consistency index for a particular set of judgments to the average consistency index for random comparisons for a matrix of the same size.

Because a set of perfectly consistent judgments produces a consistency index of zero, the consistency ratio will also be zero. A consistency ratio of one indicates consistency akin to that which would be achieved if judgments were not made intelligently but, rather, at random.

Saaty states that it is reasonable, even desirable to allow for some inconsistency; for if we demanded perfect consistency in all of our judgments, we would be dogmatic to the point of refusing to entertain new notions or ideas. From a practical point of view, we know that the real world is very often inconsistent. It is not exceptionally rare in professional sports, for example, for team A to have a better record against team B, for team B to have a better record against team C, and for team C to have a better record against team A.

Saaty argues that a consistency ratio of 0.1 or less (i.e., a consistency index of 10% or less than that obtained from random judgments) is reasonable.

It may be that an inconsistent judgment is due to a clerical error, such as pressing the wrong key on the computer keyboard or entering just the inverse of what the decision maker really had in mind. Such clerical errors are easy to identify and correct. It may be that the decision maker's mind wandered a bit when making the judgments. Or it may be that the decision maker perceives an inconsistency in the real world, in which case the judgments would be left as is.

It is important to emphasize that the objective is to make "good" decisions, not to minimize the inconsistency ratio. Good decisions are most often based on consistent judgments, but the converse is not necessarily true. It is easy to make perfectly consistent judgments that are nonsensical and result in terrible decisions.

Validation

To be credible, this new approach (the natural pair-wise ratio scale and the mathematical technique used to average judgments) should work in areas where we already know the unit of measurement. In fact, it has been vali-

TABLE 2 Light Source Experiment

Chair	Estimate Experiment Group 1	Estimate Experiment Group 2	Results for Applying Inverse Square Law
1	0.61	0.62	0.61
2	0.24	0.22	0.22
3	0.10	0.10	0.11
4	0.05	0.06	0.06

dated in hundreds of experiments that the method *does* indeed generate results conforming to classic ratio scale measurement in physics, economics, and other fields where standard measures already exist.

In one experiment conducted by Saaty, chairs were placed at various distances (9, 15, 21, and 28 yards) from a light source to see if people, standing at the light source, could judge the relative brightness of the chairs. The experiment was conducted with two groups of people. Neither group was familiar with the inverse square law of optics, which says that relative brightness is inversely proportional to the square of the distance of the object from the light source. The results achieved with the AHP approach were in very close agreement with the inverse square law, as can be seen in Table 2.

Synthesis

An important contribution of AHP is that it enables decision makers to structure complex problems in the form of a hierarchy and concentrate their attention on each part of the hierarchy, in turn. Judgments can be made about the importance of criteria relative to the goal; then about the importance of each set of subcriteria relative to the criteria; then about the relative importance of the sub-subcriteria relative to each subcriteria, and so on, until judgments are made about the relative preference of alternatives with respect to the lowest level of subcriteria.

Once this is done, the results must be synthesized to arrive at an overall solution. The synthesis used in AHP will be illustrated in the following case study.

CASE STUDY

The Mitre Corporation, acting as a contractor for Environmental Protection Agency, was assigned the task of evaluating potential hazards to the environment. The results of their study were published in the Federal Register on July 16, 1982. Although this study was performed prior to the development of Expert Choice, a microcomputer software adaptation of AHP [10], we will use the criteria, subcriteria, and alternatives to illustrate how well suited AHP is to complex real-world problems.

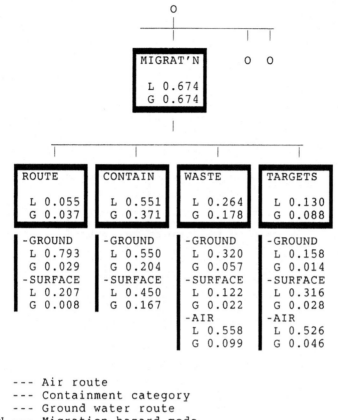

AIR   --- Air route
CONTAIN   --- Containment category
GROUND   --- Ground water route
MIGRAT'N --- Migration hazard mode
ROUTE   --- Route characteristics category
SURFACE   --- Surface water route
TARGETS   --- Targets category
WASTE   --- Waste characteristics category

L   --- LOCAL PRIORITY: PRIORITY RELATIVE TO PARENT
G   --- GLOBAL PRIORITY: PRIORITY RELATIVE TO GOAL

FIGURE 2 Evaluate potential hazards to the environment—MIGRATION.

Expert Choice Model

Figure 1 illustrates an Expert Choice model to evaluate potential hazards
to the environment. This model has three main criteria representing the
mode of the potential hazard: migration, fire and exposure hazard mode,
and direct contact. Each of these criteria have subcriteria. Figure 1 illustrates the first three levels of the hierarchy. Using Expert Choice (EC)
terminology, it shows the first three levels of the EC tree. The goal is at
level 0, the criteria are at level 1, and the subcriteria are at level 2.

Each element in the EC tree is called a node. The numbers next to the
"L" in each node of the model are called "local" priorities and represent
the weights derived from the decision makers' judgments. These judgments
are entered into the model using either EC's verbal or numerical compari-

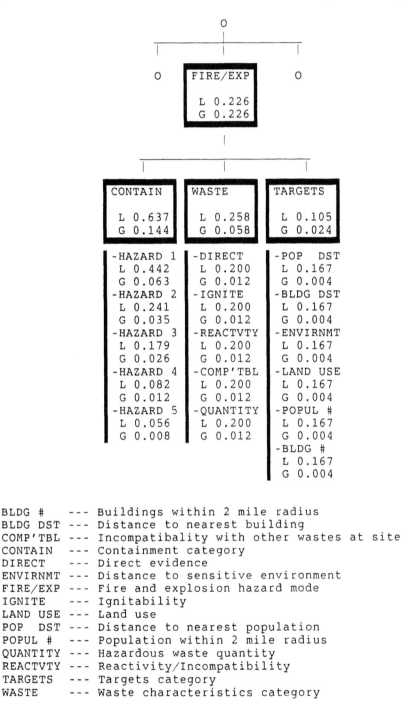

```
BLDG #     --- Buildings within 2 mile radius
BLDG DST --- Distance to nearest building
COMP'TBL --- Incompatibality with other wastes at site
CONTAIN  --- Containment category
DIRECT   --- Direct evidence
ENVIRNMT --- Distance to sensitive environment
FIRE/EXP --- Fire and explosion hazard mode
IGNITE   --- Ignitability
LAND USE --- Land use
POP  DST --- Distance to nearest population
POPUL #  --- Population within 2 mile radius
QUANTITY --- Hazardous waste quantity
REACTVTY --- Reactivity/Incompatibility
TARGETS  --- Targets category
WASTE    --- Waste characteristics category

L        --- LOCAL PRIORITY: PRIORITY RELATIVE TO PARENT
G        --- GLOBAL PRIORITY: PRIORITY RELATIVE TO GOAL
```

FIGURE 3 Evaluate potential hazards to the environment —FIRE/EXP.

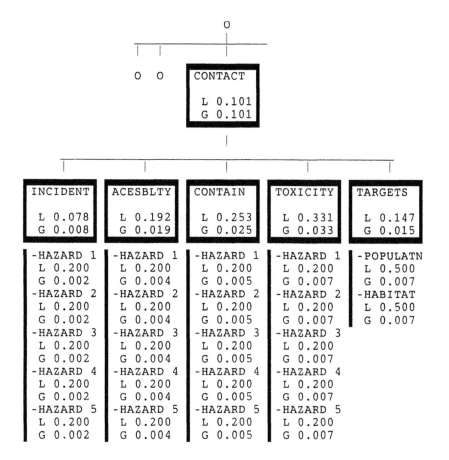

ACESBLTY --- Accessibility of hazardous substances
CONTACT   --- Direct contact mode
CONTAIN   --- Containment category
HABITAT   --- Distance to a critical habitat
INCIDENT --- Observed incident
POPULATN --- Population within 1 mile radius
TARGETS   --- Targets category
TOXICITY --- Toxicity/persistence

L   --- LOCAL PRIORITY: PRIORITY RELATIVE TO PARENT
G   --- GLOBAL PRIORITY: PRIORITY RELATIVE TO GOAL

FIGURE 4 Evaluate potential hazards to the environment—CONTACT.

son modes, as will be shown shortly. The glossary at the bottom of the figure contains the meanings of the node names.

The numbers next to the "G" in each node are called "global" priorities and are found by taking the product of the local priority of a node by the global priority of its parent node.

An EC tree can be redrawn about any node to show lower levels of the model. Figure 2 shows the model redrawn about the migration node.

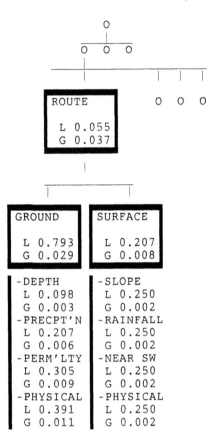

```
DEPTH      --- Depth
GROUND     --- Ground water route
NEAR SW    --- Near surface water
PERM'LTY   --- Permeability
PHYSICAL   --- Physical state
PRECPT'N   --- Net precipitation
RAINFALL   --- Rainfall
ROUTE      --- Route characteristics category
SLOPE      --- Facility slope and intervening terain
SURFACE    --- Surface water route

L          --- LOCAL PRIORITY: PRIORITY RELATIVE TO PARENT
G          --- GLOBAL PRIORITY: PRIORITY RELATIVE TO GOAL
```

FIGURE 5 Evaluate potential hazards to the environment—ROUTE.

Notice that the siblings and ancestry of the migration node are shown in skeletal form. Also notice that each subcriterion has other factors or subcriteria of its own. For example, the waste subcriterion has ground, surface, and air factors (level 4 of the tree).

Figure 3 shows the model redrawn about the fire and exposure mode node. Notice the subcriteria appearing below the waste and targets nodes.

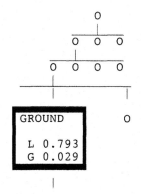

FIGURE 6 Evaluate potential hazards to the environment—GROUND.

DEPTH ---	Depth		
GROUND ---	Ground water route		
PERM'LTY ---	Permeability		
PHYSICAL ---	Physical state		
PRECPT'N ---	Net precipitation		

L   --- LOCAL PRIORITY: PRIORITY RELATIVE TO PARENT
G   --- GLOBAL PRIORITY: PRIORITY RELATIVE TO GOAL

Because the containment node does not have any criteria, the alternative hazards that are to be evaluated appear below the containment node. If we were to look further down below the waste or target nodes, we would find these same alternatives. Thus, the EC tree model need not be "balanced."

```
            MIGRAT'N   FIRE/EXP   CONTACT
MIGRAT'N                 4.0        5.0
FIRE/EXP                            3.0
CONTACT
```

Matrix entry indicates that ROW element is ___
   1 EQUALLY   3 MODERATELY   5 STRONGLY   7 VERY STRONGLY   9 EXTREMELY
more IMPORTANT than COLUMN element
      unless enclosed in parenthesis.

MIGRAT'N :Migration hazard mode
FIRE/EXP :Fire and explosion hazard mode
CONTACT :Direct contact mode

0.674
MIGRAT'N ██

0.226
FIRE/EXP ████████████████

0.101
CONTACT ████████

                    INCONSISTENCY RATIO = 0.074

FIGURE 7 Priorities with respect to GOAL to evaluate potential hazards to environment.

Figures 4 through 6 contain more views of this model to evaluate environmental hazards. Although this model is rather detailed, most complex problems are modeled using only two or three levels below the goal.

Judgments and Priorities

Figures 7 through 9 show some of the judgments made with this model. Each entry in the matrix represents a judgment (about the row/column items) entered by the decision maker(s) (see glossary in Fig. 7 for meaning of entries). Typically, judgments are entered in a verbal mode, but displaying judgments in this numerical fashion is more concise.

Figure 10(A, B) shows the results of the synthesis, and Figure 11 shows the final results—hazard 2 was determined to be the most deterimental attribute to the environment.

A histogram of the weights or priorities derived from the judgments follows the judgment matrix. Each figure also shows the inconsistency ratio. Because the larger the value of this ratio, the more inconsistent are the judgments, EC refers to this ratio as the "inconsistency ratio." The value of this inconcsistency ratio for the judgments about the relative importance of the main criteria is .074, as shown in Figure 7. This is certainly less than 0.1 and is quite acceptable. If it had been greater than 0.1, one would usually ask EC to identify which judgments were most inconsistent.

	ROUTE	CONTAIN	WASTE	TARGETS
ROUTE		(6.0)	(5.0)	(4.0)
CONTAIN			3.0	5.0
WASTE				3.0
TARGETS				

Matrix entry indicates that ROW element is ___
  1 EQUALLY   3 MODERATELY   5 STRONGLY   7 VERY STRONGLY   9 EXTREMELY
more IMPORTANT than COLUMN element
     unless enclosed in parenthesis.

ROUTE   :Route characteristics category
CONTAIN   :Containment category
WASTE   :Waste characteristics category
TARGETS   :Targets category

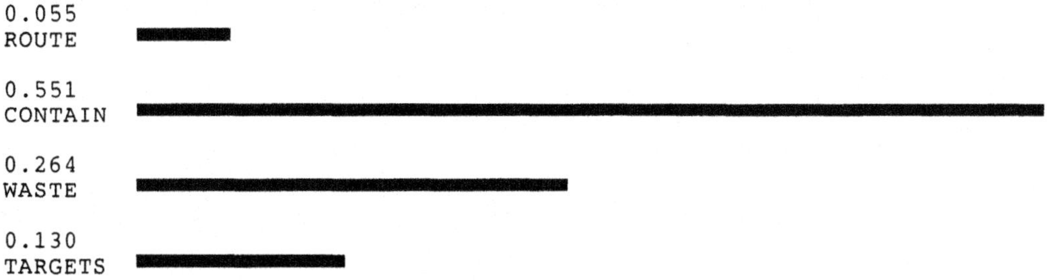

0.055
ROUTE   ▃▃▃▃

0.551
CONTAIN ▃▃

0.264
WASTE   ▃▃▃▃▃▃▃▃▃▃▃▃▃▃▃▃▃▃▃▃

0.130
TARGETS ▃▃▃▃▃▃▃▃▃▃

INCONSISTENCY RATIO = 0.080

FIGURE 8 Judgments and priorities with respect to MIGRATION < GOAL.

Synthesis

Figure 10(A, B) shows the details and the synthesis, and Figure 11 the final results. The synthesis details are sorted by priority, so that the most important factors and subfactors are listed first. The numbers in the synthesis represent the global priorities. For each alternative, the sum of the global priorities with respect to the lowest level subcriteria is the overall priority for that alternative, as shown in a histogram in Figure 11. For example, the overall priority of hazard 2, the hazard that received the highest overall priority in this model, is as follows:

	0.110	with respect to MIGRATION < CONTAIN < GROUND
plus		
	0.033	with respect to MIGRATION < CONTAIN < SURFACE
plus		
	0.035	with respect to MIGRATION < WASTE < AIR < TOXICITY
plus		
	0.003	with respect to MIGRATION < WASTE < AIR < REACTIVITY
etc.	___	
	0.526	

```
            TOXICITY  QUANTITY  REACTVTY
TOXICITY              5.0       4.0
QUANTITY                        (3.0)
REACTVTY
```

Matrix entry indicates that ROW element is ___
  1 EQUALLY   3 MODERATELY   5 STRONGLY   7 VERY STRONGLY   9 EXTREMELY
more IMPORTANT than COLUMN element
     unless enclosed in parenthesis.

TOXICITY :Toxicity/persistence
QUANTITY :Hazardous waste quantity
REACTVTY :Reactivity/Incompatibility

0.674
TOXICITY ██

0.101
QUANTITY █████████

0.226
REACTVTY ██████████████████

                 INCONSISTENCY RATIO = 0.074

FIGURE 9 Judgments and priorities with respect to AIR < WASTE
< MIGRATION < GOAL.

COMMUNICATING RESULTS

Communicating the rationale for a decision about a complex problem is an
important problem in and of itself. The AHP results are ideally suited for
such communication.

   Consider a problem where a consultant performs the analysis and makes
a recommendation to a client. Without the use of AHP, a typical consultant's
report would consist of appendices containing the pertinent information,
the body of the report, and an executive summary of one or two pages.
The executive summary is in recognition that the client will not read the
entire report, much less the appendices. However, the client *does* want
to examine some of the detail in the report and the appendices. The problem is that there is no way of anticipating what detail the client will be interested in seeing.

   In contrast to this reporting mechanism, the AHP can provide an indexed "road map" of the analysis leading up to the recommendation. The
results of a decision analysis using AHP contains information about

   • What criteria were used in making the recommendation.
   • Which criteria were considered most important.
   • What likelihoods were attributed to uncertainties.
   • Which alternatives were considered preferable, relative to each cri-
     terion.

```
LEVEL 1          LEVEL 2          LEVEL 3          LEVEL 4          LEVEL 5
-------          -------          -------          -------          -------

MIGRAT'N =0.674
.                CONTAIN  =0.371
.                .                GROUND   =0.204
.                .                .                HAZARD 2 =0.110
.                .                .                HAZARD 1 =0.042
.                .                .                HAZARD 4 =0.033
.                .                .                HAZARD 3 =0.017
.                .                .                HAZARD 5 =0.002
.                .                SURFACE  =0.167
.                .                .                HAZARD 3 =0.067
.                .                .                HAZARD 5 =0.034
.                .                .                HAZARD 2 =0.033
.                .                .                HAZARD 1 =0.018
.                .                .                HAZARD 4 =0.016
.                WASTE    =0.178
.                .                AIR      =0.099
.                .                .                TOXICITY =0.067
.                .                .                .                HAZARD 2 =0.035
.                .                .                .                HAZARD 1 =0.014
.                .                .                .                HAZARD 3 =0.009
.                .                .                .                HAZARD 4 =0.005
.                .                .                .                HAZARD 5 =0.004
.                .                .                REACTVTY =0.022
.                .                .                .                HAZARD 4 =0.006
.                .                .                .                HAZARD 5 =0.005
.                .                .                .                HAZARD 3 =0.005
.                .                .                .                HAZARD 2 =0.003
.                .                .                .                HAZARD 1 =0.003
.                .                .                QUANTITY =0.010
.                .                .                .                HAZARD 1 =0.002
.                .                .                .                HAZARD 2 =0.002
.                .                .                .                HAZARD 3 =0.002
.                .                .                .                HAZARD 4 =0.002
.                .                .                .                HAZARD 5 =0.002
.                .                GROUND   =0.057
.                .                .                TOXICITY =0.028
.                .                .                .                HAZARD 1 =0.006
.                .                .                .                HAZARD 2 =0.006
.                .                .                .                HAZARD 3 =0.006
.                .                .                .                HAZARD 4 =0.006
.                .                .                .                HAZARD 5 =0.006
.                .                .                QUANTITY =0.028
.                .                .                .                HAZARD 1 =0.006
.                .                .                .                HAZARD 2 =0.006
.                .                .                .                HAZARD 3 =0.006
.                .                .                .                HAZARD 4 =0.006
.                .                .                .                HAZARD 5 =0.006
.                .                SURFACE  =0.022
.                .                .                TOXICITY =0.011
.                .                .                .                HAZARD 1 =0.002
.                .                .                .                HAZARD 2 =0.002
.                .                .                .                HAZARD 3 =0.002
```

FIGURE 10 Evaluate potential hazards to environment—
Tally for synthesis of leaf nodes with respect to GOAL.

```
LEVEL 1          LEVEL 2          LEVEL 3          LEVEL 4          LEVEL 5
-------          -------          -------          -------          -------

  .                .                .                .              HAZARD 4 =0.002
  .                .                .                .              HAZARD 5 =0.002
  .                .                .              QUANTITY =0.011
  .                .                .                .              HAZARD 1 =0.002
  .                .                .                .              HAZARD 2 =0.002
  .                .                .                .              HAZARD 3 =0.002
  .                .                .                .              HAZARD 4 =0.002
  .                .                .                .              HAZARD 5 =0.002
  .              TARGETS =0.088
  .                .              AIR      =0.046
  .                .                .              USE      =0.015
  .                .                .                .              HAZARD 1 =0.003
  .                .                .                .              HAZARD 2 =0.003
  .                .                .                .              HAZARD 3 =0.003
  .                .                .                .              HAZARD 4 =0.003
  .                .                .                .              HAZARD 5 =0.003
  .                .                .              D ENV.   =0.015
  .                .                .                .              HAZARD 1 =0.003
  .                .                .                .              HAZARD 2 =0.003
  .                .                .                .              HAZARD 3 =0.003
  .                .                .                .              HAZARD 4 =0.003
  .                .                .                .              HAZARD 5 =0.003
  .                .                .              POPULATN =0.015
  .                .                .                .              HAZARD 1 =0.003
  .                .                .                .              HAZARD 2 =0.003
  .                .                .                .              HAZARD 3 =0.003
  .                .                .                .              HAZARD 4 =0.003
  .                .                .                .              HAZARD 5 =0.003
  .                .              SURFACE  =0.028
  .                .                .              USE      =0.009
  .                .                .                .              HAZARD 1 =0.002
  .                .                .                .              HAZARD 2 =0.002
  .                .                .                .              HAZARD 3 =0.002
  .                .                .                .              HAZARD 4 =0.002
  .                .                .                .              HAZARD 5 =0.002
  .                .                .              D ENV.   =0.009
  .                .                .                .              HAZARD 1 =0.002
  .                .                .                .              HAZARD 2 =0.002
  .                .                .                .              HAZARD 3 =0.002
  .                .                .                .              HAZARD 4 =0.002
  .                .                .                .              HAZARD 5 =0.002
  .                .                .              POPULATN =0.009
  .                .                .                .              HAZARD 1 =0.002
  .                .                .                .              HAZARD 2 =0.002
  .                .                .                .              HAZARD 3 =0.002
  .                .                .                .              HAZARD 4 =0.002
  .                .                .                .              HAZARD 5 =0.002
  .                .              GROUND   =0.014
  .                .                .              WATERUSE =0.007
  .                .                .                .              HAZARD 1 =0.001
  .                .                .                .              HAZARD 2 =0.001
  .                .                .                .              HAZARD 3 =0.001
```

FIGURE 10   (continued)

OVERALL INCONSISTENCY INDEX = 0.03

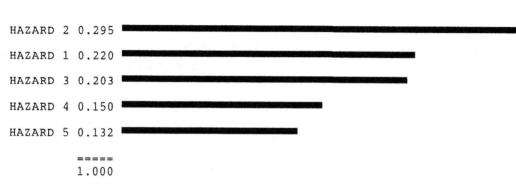

HAZARD 2 0.295

HAZARD 1 0.220

HAZARD 3 0.203

HAZARD 4 0.150

HAZARD 5 0.132

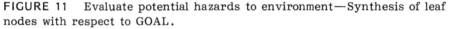

=====
1.000

FIGURE 11   Evaluate potential hazards to environment—Synthesis of leaf nodes with respect to GOAL.

The client can then easily pinpoint the most critical or questionable priorities, likelihoods, or preferences and ask for more detail. This detail is at hand in the form of the pair-wise comparisons for the relevant aspect of the problem being questioned.

Finally, the client may ask, Why did you make this particular judgment? The consultant can then either refer to the proper background information contained in one of the appendices or remind the client that the consultant was hired as an expert and that was his or her expert judgment.

SUMMARY

The AHP, with its microcomputer implementation called Expert Choice, combine to provide decision makers with "an expert support system" that

- Is capable of supporting decisions involving several alternatives.
- Is capable of addressing several (often competing) criteria or factors.
- Allows the decision maker(s) to incorporate subjective as well as objective factors.
- Is capable of accommodating the decision makers' expert judgments about the relative importance of these factors.
- Incorporates the decision makers' expertise.
- Allows the decision maker to synthesize or combine judgments made relative to the many facets of a complex problem.
- Does *not* make, or pretend to make, any decisions. (The decision maker(s) must be able to structure the problem as they see it, provide *their* judgments, request the decision support system to help synthesize their judgments, examine the results of the synthesis, restructure the problem if they think it necessary, and eventually arrive at *their* decision.)
- Supports group decision making.
- Has a theoretically sound foundation.

In his early work, called *The New Science of Management Decision*, Herbert Simon observed that "...decision making involves three principal phases: finding occasions for making a decision; finding possible courses of action; and choosing among courses of action." Simon called these three phases intelligence, design, and choice [8]. Executive decisions are unstructured decisions in that all three phases are not fully understood and therefore cannot be programmed.

Luconi et al. [11] have identified the limits of current expert systems and decision support systems technology. The domain of decision support systems does not encompass the strategic aspect (principally choice) of decisions, whereas the knowledge that can be feasibly encoded in an expert system is not sufficient to make satisfactory decisions by itself. Luconi et al. [11] state that the next logical step should involve systems that aid rather than replace human decision makers and have called these "expert *support* systems."

Simon observed that "When we ask how executives in organizations make nonprogrammed decisions, we are generally told that they 'exercise judgment,' and that this judgment depends, in some undefined way, upon experience, insight, and intuition." Simon took issue with such an explanation when he remarked, "To name a phenomenon is not to explain it. Saying that nonprogrammed decisions are made by exercising judgment *names* that phenomenon but does not explain it" [8].

In contrast, the AHP makes a significant contribution toward understanding this important phenomenon of complex, nonprogrammed decisions. By allowing decision makers to model a complex problem into a structure that shows the relationships of goals, criteria, uncertainties, and alternatives, it allows for the application of experience, insight, and intuition in a logical and thorough way.

REFERENCES

1. R. L. Cook and K. R. Hammond, "Interpersonal Learning and Interpersonal Conflict Reduction in Decision-Making Groups," in *Improving Group Decision Making in Organizations: Approaches from Theory and Research*, Academic Press, New York, 1982.
2. Lyn Jones, *Decision Analysis*, The Open University Press, Milton Keynes, Great Britain, 1975.
3. C. H. Kepner and B. B. Tregoe, *The Rational Manager: A Systematic Approach to Problem Solving and Decision Making*, McGraw-Hill, New York, 1965.
4. James Martin, *Design of Man-Computer Dialogues*, Prentice-Hall, Englewood Cliffs, NJ, 1973.
5. G. A. Miller, "The Magical Number Seven, Plus or Minus Two: Some Limits on Our Capacity for Information Processing," *Psychol. Rev.*, 63(2), 81−97 (March 1956).
6. Thomas L. Saaty, *Decision Making for Leaders*, Lifetime Learning Publications, division of Wadsworth, Inc., Belmont, CA, 1982.
7. L. L. Whyte, *Hierarchical Structures*, American Elsevier, New York, 1969.

8. Herbert A. Simon, *The New Science of Management Decision*, Harper and Brothers, New York, 1960, pp. 40–43.
9. Thomas L. Saaty, *The Analytic Hierarchy Process*, McGraw-Hill, New York, 1980.
10. Ernest H. Forman, Thomas L. Saaty, Mary Ann Selly, and Rozann Waldron, *Expert Choice*, Decision Support Software, McLean, VA, 1983.
11. F. L. Luconi, T. W. Malone, and M. S. Scott-Morton, "Expert Systems and Expert Support Systems: The Next Challenge for Management," Sloan WP No. 1630-85, Center for Information Systems Research, Massachusetts Institute of Technology, Cambridge, MA, 1985.

ERNEST H. FORMAN

MARY ANN SELLY

AUTOMATIC TEXT GENERATION—THE SUBSCRIPTED D-ALGORITHM

INTRODUCTION

"Gang testing" is an automatic test-pattern generation (ATPG) procedure in which one attempts to constructively find a single test pattern that tests a large number (as many as possible) of gates. Gang testing can accelerate the rate of test-pattern generation by attempting to find patterns that control and observe these trageted gates simultaneously. In the process of trying to sensitize many paths simultaneously, conflicts arise when different signals converge at the same gate. To accelerate the algorithm and reduce the number of conflicts, we permit the merging of observation paths at various gates. This generates denser test patterns, as one pattern is able, in most cases, to test more than one faulty gate. The test pattern generated by each iteration of the algorithm is formed from flexible signals. A flexible signal is one that can be set to either 1 or 0 as the need arises. This flexible test pattern is used to create fixed-value test patterns that will completely test the faulty gate. The fixed-value test pattern is generated by giving the value 0 or 1 to the flexible input signals of the flexible test pattern.

The employment of many independent simultaneously sensitized paths requires the use of a subscript to distinguish each one. This gives rise to the name of the algorithm, the subscripted D-algorithm (DALG).

This method is shown to effectively reduce the number of test patterns required to achieve complete fault coverage and is shown to be faster than the Path-Oriented Decision-Making (PODEM) Algorithm and the ordinary D-algorithm.

The problem of test generation has emerged as critical in recent years with the advent of very large-scale integration (VLSI) technology. As the logic circuits under test grow larger, generating tests becomes more difficult. The generation of a test for a gate embedded in a complex circuit involves the assignment of signals to the inputs and outputs of the circuit's gates. Conflicts can occur when the program generating the tests attempts to assign two different signal values to the same line because of the need to satisfy several requirements simultaneously. The number of conflicts increases drastically with the circuit size, and this becomes the main limiting factor in testing techniques.

A greater amount of research on testing has concentrated on the problem of reducing CPU times [1–4]. Greater CPU times are needed for test generation when many conflicts occur, causing excessive backtracking. The algorithm backtracks to retrieve the original signals and tries an alternative to the signal assignment causing the conflict. Depending on the size of the circuit and the frequency of the backtrack occurrences, most of the CPU time spent on a test generation can be consumed trying to resolve conflicts and retrieve salvageable signals.

To reduce the CPU time and accelerate the algorithm, the number of conflicts has to be limited sharply and the processing time between backtracks shortened. Many conflicts are avoided by allowing mergers of observation paths. This is done in a manner so as to preserve the independent identities of the merged paths. The identities of the merging paths are preserved by denoting the merged path (output of the convergent gate) signal by a subscripted D signal (DJ: flexible signal) and by allowing no mergers of the control paths generating these merging (incoming) paths. The CPU time necessary for test generation is reduced further by testing as many gates as possible with the same test pattern. This latter method is called gang testing and results in a compaction of the test patterns. Both methods help to reduce the CPU time involved in the test generation process and yield denser test-pattern sets.

The reductions in both CPU time and number of test patterns is corroborated by the experimental results. This approach is very different from the dynamic test compaction phase [5—7] PODEM, which essentially tries to make good use of the "don't care" (X) states of a conventional test pattern. Because the gang test is aggressively constructed at the outset to test a large number of gates, one is not simply attempting to use the Xs inadvertently produced by PODEM or DALG while testing one gate.

THE SUBSCRIPTED D-ALGORITHM

In this paper, we consider multi-input and multi-output combinational circuits composed of AND, OR, NAND, NOR, and NOT gates. The type of fault model assumed is the standard stuck fault. In other words, all faults can be modeled by lines that are stuck at logical 0 (s-a-0) or stuck at logical 1 (s-a-1).

Based on multiple simultaneous path sensitizations, the subscripted DALG [8—11] sensitizes all control and observation paths for a gate. As compared to Roth's DALG, the subscripted DALG assigns flexible signals to these paths. As mentioned, the flexible value signal can be set to 0 or 1. These flexible signals are denoted symbolically by subscripted Ds, from which the algorithm derives its name. The algorithm is also known as the Absorption Algorithm (AALG) because of the manner in which it absorbs conflicts.

To be more specific, for an N input gate G, we assign $D1,, D2, \cdots DN$ to the N inputs and $D0$ to the output of the gate. The signals $D1, D2, \cdots,$ DN are the control signals, and $D0$ is the observation signal (Fig. 1). The set of these flexible signals is called a control cube. This control cube represents a large set of singular cubes, as defined by Roth [3]. Because all signals are flexible, all input combinations and any singluar cube of the gate G can be obtained by assigning appropriate logical values (0 or 1) to $D1, D2, \cdots, DN$ and $D0$. From this control cube, fixed-value test patterns can be generated to test for all the faults of gate G. By avoiding the repetitious work of generating a test for each fault of gate G, the subscripted DALG has been shown to have better CPU times than PODEM and DALG [2, 3, 9—11].

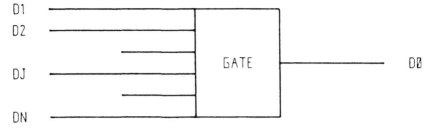

FIGURE 1 Fault assignment.

The basic subscripted DALG consists of three stages:

1. D0 drive to the circuit's outputs.
2. DJ drive to the circuit's inputs.
3. Consistency operation.

The flowchart of Figure 2 provides a high-level description of the AALG.

D0 PROPAGATION

A failure at one of the gate's lines (input or output) is detected if the fault can be propagated and made observable at one of the circuit's outputs. The algorithm constructs a control cube of the gate by assigning flexible signals $D1,\cdots,DN$ to the inputs and D0 to the outputs of the gate. This step of the algorithm establishes a sensitized path from the fault's site to a primary output. This process is similar to Roth's D propagation, but rather than identifying a specific fault, D0 is flexible. The flexible signal D0 can represent any fault that can be set by the flexible signals $D1, D2, \cdots, DN$ at the inputs of the gate. The existence of these flexible signals at the gate's inputs depends on the DJ propagation step of the algorithm.

In generating a test, the algorithm creates a decision tree in which there is more than one choice available at each decision node. A decision node is defined when alternate choices for justifying the output signal of a gate are available. During the execution of the algorithm, it may be necessary to return and try another choice. This is called a backtrack. To accelerate the algorithm, it is necessary to reduce the number of back-tracks, shorten the process time between backtracks, and attempt to control and observe as many gates as possible at one time (gang testing). In the process of trying to sensitize many paths simultaneously, conflicts arise when different signals converge to the same gate. To reduce the number of conflicts and speed up the algorithm, we permit the mergers of observation paths at various gates. This is done in such a manner as to preserve the individual identities of the merged paths. The identities of the incoming merged paths are preserved by denoting the signal of the outgoing path (output of the convergent gate) by a subscripted D0 signal that will differentiate it from the signals of the merged paths. The incoming paths originate from the outputs of the gates under test. To further preserve the identities of the merged paths, the control paths of each gate under test are kept independent and are not allowed to merge with any control or

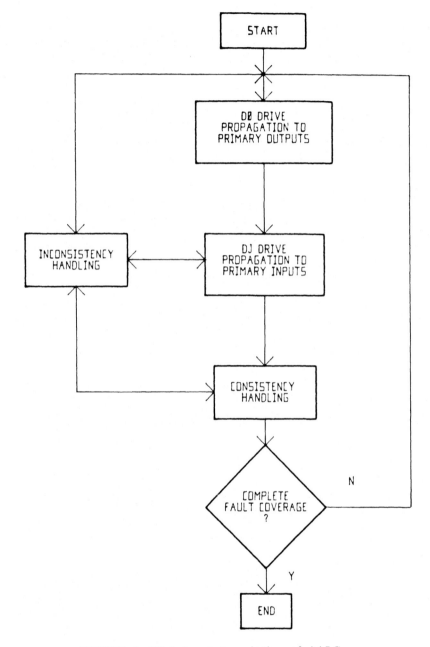

FIGURE 2 High-level description of AALG.

observation path during the first two phases of the algorithm. This latter
merger is allowed in the consistency phase and will be explained shortly.

A further benefit is the reduction of the number of gates on the D0
frontier (the D0 frontier is the set of gates whose outputs have a D0 signal),
which follows the mergers of the observation paths. After the flexible paths
converge to the gate, only one gate is left on the D0 frontier. A third
benefit results during the inconsistency-handling phase of the algorithm.
When a conflict arises, the sensitized path causing the inconsistency is not
completely destroyed. Segments of partially completed sensitized paths that
would have been destroyed through backtracking are now merged with existing paths. This reduces the effort required to control a gate, as it is no
longer necessary to completely construct an independent observation path
for each individual gate. Further conflicts are avoided by carefully choosing the gates and allowing path mergers only for gates on the same level.
A gate is on level i if there are, at most, i gates between the output of
the gate and an output of the circuit. A flexible signal D0 is propagated
through a gate by setting enable signals on all the other inputs of the
gate. Hence, by merging gates from the same level, only inputs that will
not be used for D0 propagation by any of the gates are enabled. Figure
3 provides a more detailed flowchart of the D0 drive phase. To keep the
D0 frontier on one level, the D0 propagation proceeds as follows:

1. Choose a gate on level i whose faults are not yet detected.
2. Set signals $D1, D2, \cdots, DN, D0$ on its inputs and output.
3. Take the next gate.
    a. If the gate is on level i go to a.
    b. Otherwise, propagate the D0 frontier to level $i - 1$.
4. If the whole D0 frontier is at the circuit's output, go to the DJ
    propagation step. Else $i = i - 1$, and then go to a.

To enhance the chances of mergers of observation paths and to increase the number of gates taken in gang testing, the above steps are
applied starting from the highest level (i.e., circuit's input gates). This
will have an impact on the DJ propagation phase and will be explained
shortly.

A gate that has a fault still not detected is selected for testing if all
its input and output are unassigned and if the gate has not been flagged.
A gate is flagged if it is impossible, during the current test generation, to
assign it a DJ (flexible signal) or if a previous propagation of a DJ through
it caused an inconsistency. Because the gate does not make any distinction
between control $(D1, \cdots, DN)$ and observation (D0) signals, the gate is
flagged to remove it from all flexible signal paths. This reduces the number
of conflicts, as a D0 propagation is not allowed to go through a flagged
gate.

DJ PROPAGATION

To preserve the independent identities of the merged paths, control of
each faulty gate is required. Thus, the control paths are kept independent
in order to have individual control of each faulty gate's output. To allow
for the greatest control of the gate, all the gate's inputs whose faults are
not detected are set to a DJ signal. This step of the algorithm will propa-

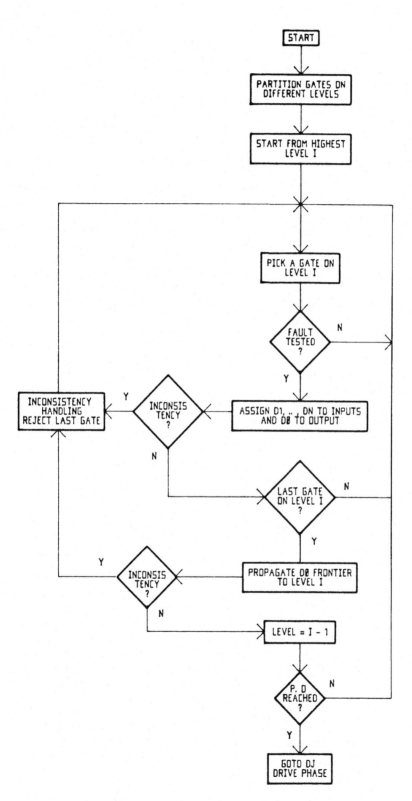

FIGURE 3 Flowchart of D0 drive phase.

gate all the DJ signals of all the faulty gates to the circuit's inputs. Because the output of a gate is completely controlled with one flexible input (while all the other inputs are enabled), this phase of the algorithm will retain only one copy of the flexible signals after backward propagating them to the inputs as was done in the previous versions of the subscripted DALG [9–11]. Because the circuit's gates are being gang tested starting with the levels closest to the circuit's inputs, all gates between those under test and the primary inputs will have been tested already. The replicating of the flexible signals (DJ) to increase the area covered by sensitized paths in front of the level being tested will therefore not increase the fault coverage of the test pattern that will be generated.

The retention of only one DJ path to the inputs of the circuit leaves many of the other inputs as possible alternate routes. These are stored in the decision tree as alternatives for DJ propagation through that gate. The DJ propagation starts with the highest lasar number gate whose output has a DJ signal. A lasar number is the index number given to a gate or a primary input in the data base defining the circuit. An output of a gate will have a higher lasar number than any of its inputs. Thus, the higher the lasar number of the gate, the farther it is from the primary inputs. The backward propagation is done breadth first. This allows for shorter backtracking in case of conflict between two DJ signals because these two signals will have backward propagated through fewer gates, as compared to the number of gates they will have gone through in the depth-first propagation method.

Conflicts can arise in this phase of the algorithm when two (or more) different flexible signals converge to the same gate. This occurs either at the output of the gate (the two DJ signals are coming on different branches of the fan out of the gate) (Fig. 4A), or DI will be trying to backward propagate from the gate's output while the gate's input will already have a DJ (the DJ can be caused by the forward propagation of a fan out gate signal assignment) (Fig. 4B). These conflicts are resolved by pushing one of the flexible signals (DJ or DI) on an alternate route. The alternate paths are offered by the other inputs of the gate through which the signal has propagated. It has been observed, however, that reconvergent DJs cause acute problems only in a small area surrounding the gates under test. In this region, sensitized paths reconverge more often because of the small number of potential paths available. As the sensitized paths diverge after crossing the critical region, conflicts arise more rarely.

To accelerate the handling of inconsistencies, a careful study of all signals that can occur during the execution of the algorithm has been realized. Certain signal situations are not allowed because of the potential for conflicts they will generate at a later time. A conflict can occur because of the undefined status of a signal occurring from the merger of two (or more) DJ control signals. Because the DJs are flexible, the merger signal is undefined at the time it is propagated and cannot be handled. This merger case will be seen as an inconsistency and will be avoided by the algorithm. Another undefined signal is generated when control (DJ) and observation (D0) signals are allowed to merge through a reconvergent gate. This situation will also be handled as an inconsistency and not allowed to occur.

A /

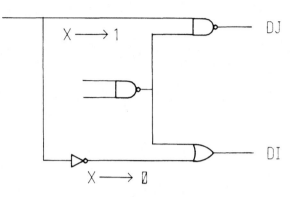

B /

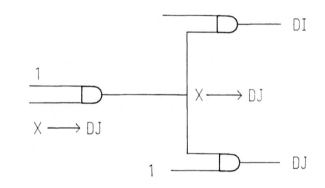

FIGURE 4   Possible DJ conflict.

CONSISTENCY OPERATION

This step of the algorithm calls for a systematic analysis of each gate assigned a 0 or a 1 in order to justify that signal assignment. At this stage
of execution, the subscripted algorithm has made the complete propagation
of observation paths to the primary outputs and the propagation of control
paths to the primary inputs. The justification of a fixed signal at the output of a given gate is done by assigning the correct fixed signals at the
inputs of the gate. The complete implication of these assignments is made
immediately. This might generate an enable signal to some convergent gate
that will merge the D0,DJ or DJ,DI combination at its inputs (Fig. 5). The
justification of gate 10 by assigning a 1 to input 6 will cause a merger of
D1 (gate 9) and D01 (gate 11). This will cause a situation that was not
allowed during the first two steps of the algorithm. At this stage, with
D0 and DJ propagation successfully completed, the situation of Figure 5 will
cause mergers of only "stray" flexible signals that are not taken into consideration by any of the two previous phases.
   Hence, to avoid a burdensome and time-consuming inconsistency-handling process, the merger of those signals is allowed and the output will be

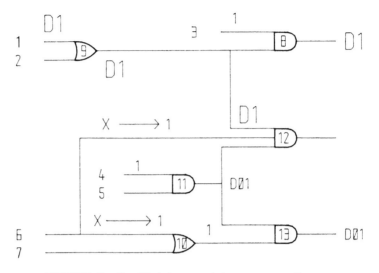

FIGURE 5   Conflict in consistency operation.

assigned a DJ. The consistency process continues until completion or until
a more substantial inconsistency occurs. At this point, a critical inconsistency occurs when we are unable to assign a fixed signal to a gate. During
the backup occurring after the inconsistency detection, the previous signal
of the merger gate (gate 12 in Fig. 5) is retrieved and assigned back to
the output of the gate. When an inconsistency is detected, the algorithm
will try to justify the signal at the gate by using one of the alternatives
stored in the decision array. For a N input AND gate, there will be N
single signal assignment alternatives to justify a 0 at the output of the gate.
If the gate cannot be justified after exhausting all of its alternative input
assignments, the algorithm immediately backs up through the decision tree
to the entry corresponding to the output signal assignment for that gate.
This method is somewhat drastic, as the inconsistency might be resolved by
taking an alternative for the previously justified gates.

After numerous examples, it was discovered that the loss caused by
the full backup is small and negligible in the case where an alternative for
another gate could have solved the case. A gate whose output assignment
cannot be justified by any of its present input signal alternatives is completely unjustifiable by the present signal assignment to the circuit. Hence,
the immediate backing up to the gate entry in the decision tree is the
correct move. The experimental results that follow show clearly the correct-
ness of our decision. After the successful completion of this phase, the
circuit is analyzed for fault coverage. Figure 6 shows a detailed flowchart
of the current phase.

EXAMPLE

Assuming that the reader is familiar with the D and the PODEM algorithms,
we will use some terminology such as D drive, implication, backtrace, etc.,
without definitions (for definitions, see Refs. 1–4). We will define a stray
signal as one that is created when a flexible signal crosses a fan-out gate.

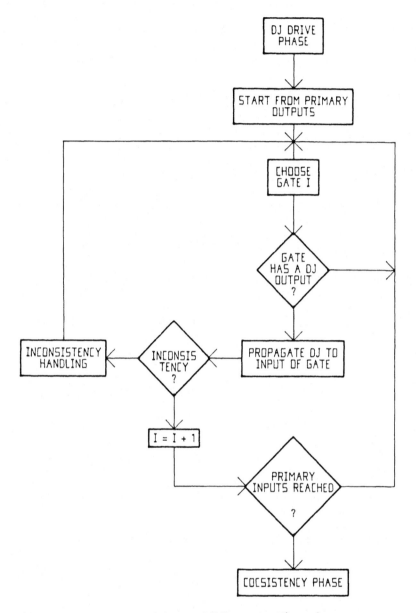

FIGURE 6 Flowchart of DJ propagation phase.

The DJ drive of a flexible signal DJ from a fan out will generate as many signals as there are fan-out branches. During the forward DJ propagation, one signal will be propagated and the others will be considered as alternatives. These unused DJ signals will be defined as stray signals. We will also define the D frontier as the set of gates whose output values are DJs and have to be propagated at the next step of the DJ propagation for the faults to be observed. Note that the D frontier contains none of the gates with a stray signal. These signals will be forward-propagated by any enabling combinations of signals at the inputs of the gates they enter, as was explained in the DJ propagation section above (Fig. 6).

The algorithm begins by finding all the gates on a given level whose faults are still undetected. A gate is selected for detection if its inputs and output are "free" of DJ signals, i.e., are either assigned an enable or a don't care signal. This allows better control of the gate and generates less conflicts during the execution of the algorithm. Figure are used to help the reader understand the explanations on the execution of the algorithm. Sensitized DJ paths are shown as thicker lines in the figures for better grasp of the concepts. In Figure 7, gates have been found and their faults activated. Note that for gate 10, the control and the observation path are the same. This will simplify the control of that gate, as there is no backward DJ propagation for it. Gates 10, 29, and 31 are entered as the D frontier, and their signals will be propagated next. Because they are on the same level, these signals will be propagated simultaneously and be allowed to merge if they converge to the same gate. Although mergers are allowed, the algorithm first attempts to have individual observation paths for each gate. The mergers are done in such a manner as to preserve the individual identities of the merged paths. This is accomplished by denoting the signal output of the merger gate with a DJ different from those of the merged paths.

The propagation of D1 is first tried through gate 40 by assigning a logical value 1 to gates 14 and 4. This causes a logical value 1 to be assigned to gate 22 and a logical 0 to gate 30. The 0 output of gate 30 blocks all the other gates and, hence, allows no propagation of observation paths from the other gates of the D frontier (Fig. 8). This will cause an inconsistency when the propagation of the D2 signal is undertaken. The algorithm starts a backtrace and backs up the decision tree. The original signals are retrieved (Fig. 7), and another path is chosen for the propagation of the D1 signal. This step continues until gate 33 is taken into consideration and the merger of D1, D2, and D3 is done, allowing propagation of all three signals at once (Fig. 9). The propagation of the D1 and D2 signals through gate 34 has caused an inconsistency at the DJ propagation (backward propagation of control signals) phase, and a backup has been initiated. The alternative path through gate 33 has been chosen. This is seen in Figure 10 with the signal C1 backward propagation to gate 41 and merging (if a DJ were allowed to propagate on it, an inconsistency would occur) with the signal coming from gate 34.

An interesting point can be made about the PODEM algorithm at this point. This algorithm, which uses dynamic compaction [4], i.e., construction of single patterns to detect more than one fault, has a different method of finding the faults to be tested together. A fault will be activated and completely controlled and observed before the PODEM algorithm searches the fault list for another faulty gate. The propagation of a signal from the output of gate 31−40 causes a logical 0 that will block all the other gates,

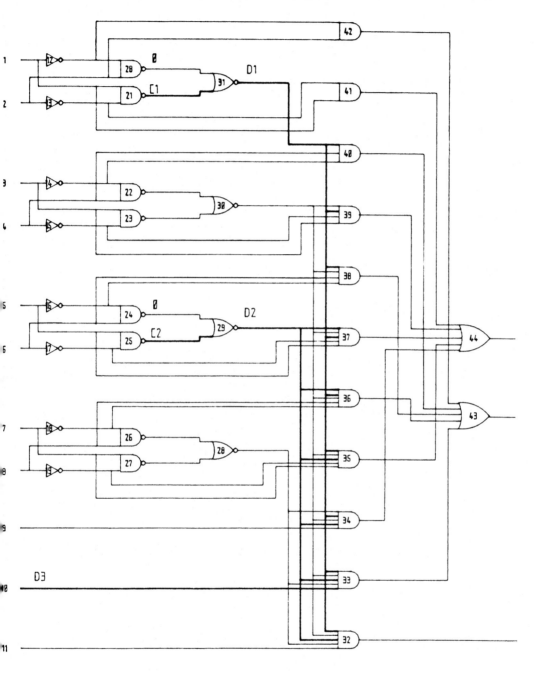

FIGURE 7   D-Frontier gates 10, 29, and 31.

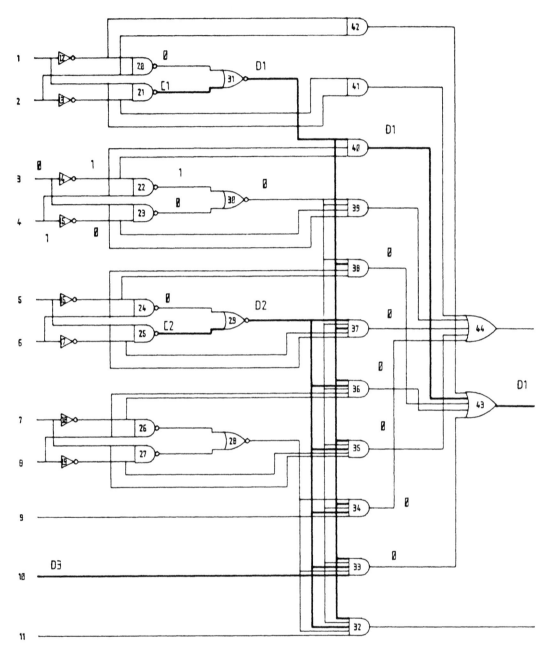

FIGURE 8   Conflict for D2 propagation.

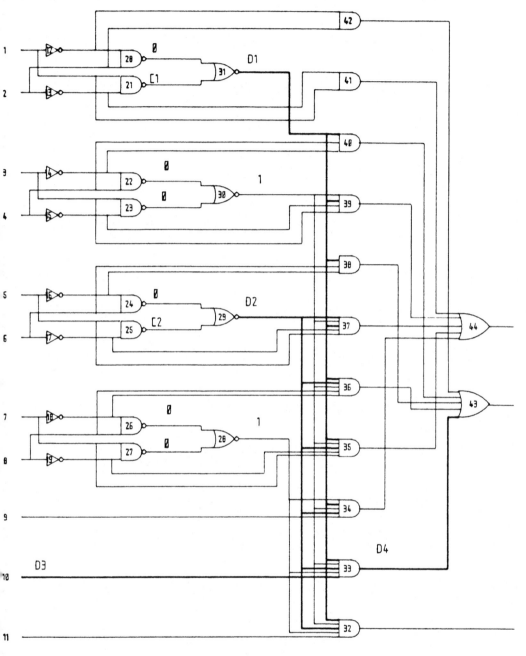

FIGURE 9   D frontier gate 33.

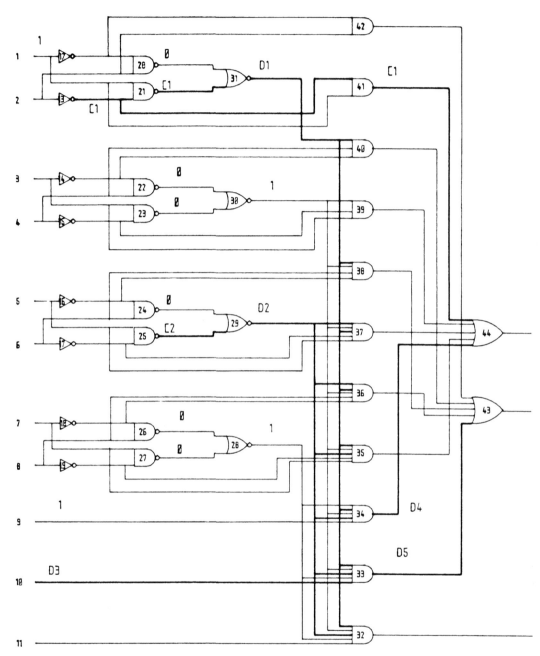

FIGURE 10   Conflict due to the merger of control and observation signals
at gate 44.

hence, destroying all possible paths for the other faulty gates. This is avoided by the subscripted DALG by first collecting all compatible faulty gates in a group and then aggressively trying to propagate all the activated faults to the primary outputs of the circuit. The steps described above show that if the generation of this test is successful, the test set will be denser than the one generated by PODEM or DALG because faults will be detected at gates 29 and 10, along with gate 31. This is not done by PODEM or DALG due to the high fan out of gates 28–31.

The algorithm now continues as follows. The D frontier is constituted by gate 33 only, after the mergers, and it is on a closer level to the primary outputs. The algorithm tries to find more gates to be tested as a group (gang testing). The gates are searched for on the same level as the level on which the D-frontier gates exist. The D drive forward propagation is done on gates that are on the same level to allow for possible mergers. Once a gate is found, its fault is immediately activated, and the implication of the assignment is made. The inputs whose faults have not been detected yet will be assigned a flexible signal. The rest of the inputs are assigned enable signals. The implication of these assignments is undertaken immediately, which might generate an inconsistency and force the algorithm to relinquish part of the control it has over the gate and assign fixed (enable) instead of flexible signals to some inputs. The inconsistency might be important enough to force the algorithm to drop the gate as impossible to test with the current group of gates (Fig. 10). After all possible faulty gates have been collected, the sensitized paths of the D-frontier gates are driven forward one gate closer to the primary outputs.

The steps described above are repeated until all signals on the D frontier have reached a primary output (Fig. 11). A backward propagation of control signals (denoted as CJ signals in the figures) is done after the successful completion of the D drive of observation signals. Many conflicts can occur during this phase. The CJ propagation (called DJ propagation in the previous section) is done breadth first to reduce the effort of backtracking and retrieval of the original signals at an inconsistency occurrence. Two alternate routes, gate 13 and gate 1, are present for the backward propagation of the C1 signal. Either of the paths is chosen, and the other is stored as an alternative. The backward propagation of C1 (C2) causes a stray signal to be generated. This is the signal that did not allow the propagation of the D1,D2 signal through gate 34. The stray signal C1 converges to the same gate (44) as the second stray signal C2 (at gate 37) (Fig. 12). This will have caused an inconsistency in the D-drive phase of the algorithm or in the backward propagation of the control signals. However, in this case, the merger of C1 and C2 is allowed to happen as this generates CK (C3) signal that will propagate through an unused portion of the circuit.

The algorithm backtraces and retrieves the original signals at the next inconsistency. This relaxation of the inconsistency definitions reduces the number of inconsistency occurrences and speeds up the process of test generation because less CPU time is used in retrieving signals and processing backtraces. The mergers of CJ signals are denoted by CK to specify that the signal is a stray one and is unspecified at this point. Only CJ signals propagating backward to primary inputs are essential for the test generation process and are not allowed to merge (for an inconsistency case, see Fig. 5). A consistency and justification phase, where all fixed signals assigned during the first two phases of the algorithm are justified, is done

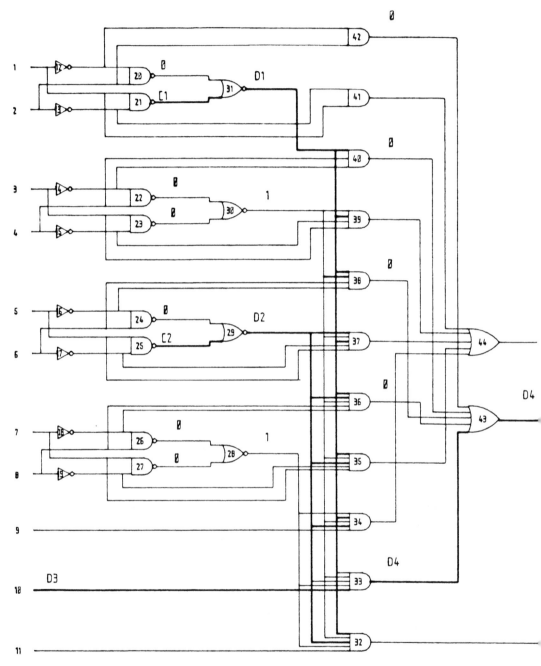

FIGURE 11   D frontier of gate 43.

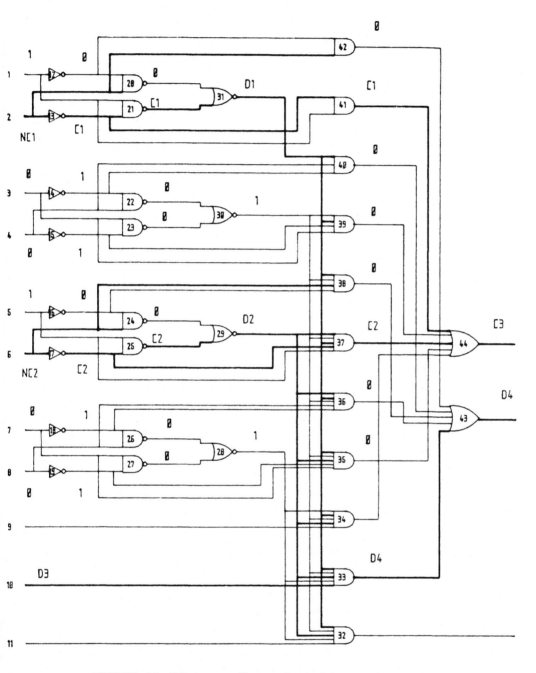

FIGURE 12   DJ propagation and consistency phase.

last. Its successful completion terminates the test generation process, and
a fault detection is done to find all the faults detected by the test pattern.

FAULT COVERAGE

The problem of fault detection is now analyzed. At this stage, all gates
under test are observable and controllable. The flexible test pattern appearing at the primary inputs will be of the form

Inputs:	1	2	3	4	5	6	7	8	9	10	11
Signal:	1	D1	0	0	1	D2	0	0	X	D3	X

where X is a don't care signal. Note that this pattern is the test pattern
of Figure 12 where NC1 and NC2 are replaced by D1 and D2 for consistency
with the preceding sections. The test pattern represents a "recipe" cube
specifying any of $2^{**}N$ (with N being the number of control signals at primary inputs) control input sets, such as

Inputs:	1	2	3	4	5	6	7	8	9	10	11
Signal:	1	1	0	0	1	1	0	0	X	1	X

where $D1 = D2 = D3 = 1$. This pattern tests for gates 10, 29, and 31
s-a-0 and some secondary faults.

Before any test pattern with fixed-signal values is generated, the
program finds and stores all the sensitized observation paths for each gate
under test. The number of sensitized observation paths is found to be
limited and far less than the number of possible observation paths that
exist in the circuit for that same gate. For example, gate 29 has only one
sensitized observation path through gate 33 but possesses many possible
observation paths through gates 32--36. This smaller number of sensitized
observation paths will limit the tree search time drastically and reduce the
CPU time spent constructing the fixed-value test patterns. The test patterns with fixed signal values are found by checking each individual gate
under test and setting the individual control inputs to the fixed values
needed to detect the fault at that particular gate. An immediate implication
is made after the assignment at the gate's inputs. This section will not
cause any inconsistency because the signals will propagate along the already
justified sensitized paths.

The rest of the gates under test are then checked again. If a flexible
signal is found, the gate's fault can be detected by the same pattern after
correct fixed values are assigned to the flexible paths. A sensitized
observation path to the primary output for the fault to be detected is
found before any fixed-value assignments are made. The path might be a
single path to the primary output or be merged with an existing sensitized
path. This can cause some backtracking to be done, but the existence or
nonexistence of the path with that fixed-value pattern is quickly determined.
This is repeated until no more flexible signals are found. This will have
generated a compact test pattern able to detect many faults from the gate
group under test (gang testing). The initial flexible test pattern is used
again to construct another fixed test pattern to test the rest of the undetected faults of the gates of the group.

SUMMARY AND CONCLUSIONS

The main innovation in this new version of the subscripted DALG with gang testing is the provision for the merger of the observation paths. The first benefit is an improved efficiency of test coverage resulting from the constructive compaction of test patterns. The second and most important benefit is the improvement in CPU performance realized when the repetitious construction of complete sensitized paths was avoided and partial paths were merged with complete observation paths. Both of these improvements can be seen clearly in Figures 13—16. The subscripted DALG has been improved recently to handle larger circuits, as shown in Figure 17.

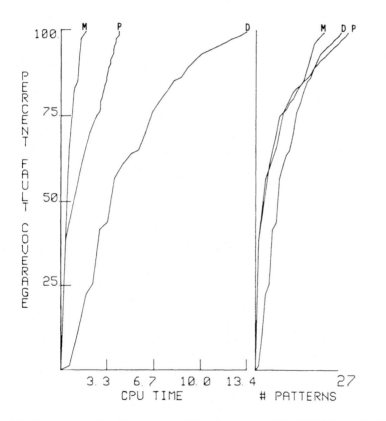

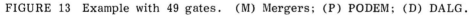

FIGURE 13 Example with 49 gates. (M) Mergers; (P) PODEM; (D) DALG.

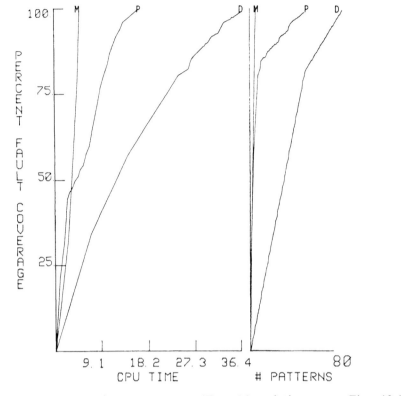

FIGURE 14 Example with 284 gates. (For abbreviations, see Fig. 13.)

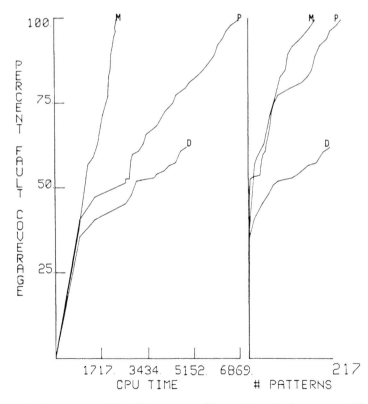

FIGURE 15 Example with 443 gates. (For abbreviations, see Fig. 13.)

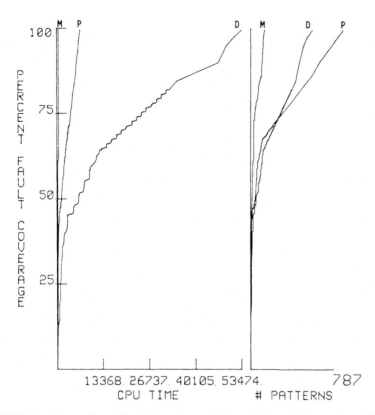

FIGURE 16 Example with 913 gates. (For abbreviations, see Fig. 13.)

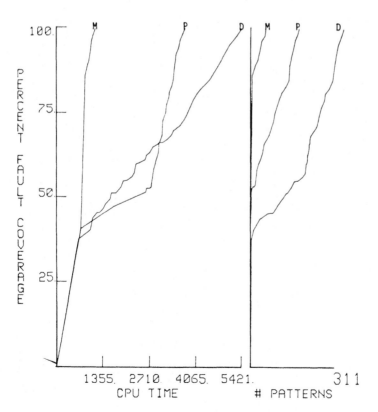

FIGURE 17 Example with 1300 gates. (For abbreviations, see Fig. 13.)

REFERENCES

1. P. Goel, "An Implicit Enumeration Algorithm to generate Tests for Combinational Logic Circuits," in *Proceedings of the 1980 Fault Tolerant Computing Symposium*, October 1980, pp. 145--151.
2. J. P. Roth, W. C. Bouricius, and P. R. Schneider, "Programmed Algorithms to Compute Tests to Detect and Distinguish Between Failures in Logic Circuits," *IEEE Trans. Electron. Comput.*, EC-16 (October 1967).
3. J. P. Roth, "Diagnosis of Automata Failures, a Calculus and a Method," *IBM J. Res. Dev.*, 10, 278–291 (July 1966).
4. P. Goel and B. C. Rosales, "Podem-X: An Automatic Test Generation System for VLSI Logic Structures," in *Eighteenth Design Automation Conference*, 1981, pp. 260--268.
5. P. Goel and B. C. Rosales, "Test Generation and Dynamic Compaction of Tests," in *1979 IEEE Test Conference*, IEEE, Cherry Hill, New Jersey, pp. 189–192.
6. P. Goel and B. C. Rosales, "Dynamic Test Compaction with Fault Selection Using 'Sensitizable' Path Tracing," *IBM Techn. Discl. Bull.*, 23(5) (October 1980).
7. P. Goel, "Dynamic Subsumation Of Test Pattern for LSSD Systems," *IBM Tech. Discl. Bull.*, 21(7) (December 1978).
8. A. N. Airapetian and J. F. McDonald, "Improved Test Set Generation Algorithm for Combinational Circuit Control," in *Proceedings of the Ninth Annual International Symposium on Fault Tolerant Computing*, Madison, WI, June 20–22, 1979, pp. 133–136.
9. C. Benmehrez and J. F. McDonald, "The Subscripted D-Algorithm ATPG with Multiple Independent Control Paths," in *IEEE Automatic Test Program Generation Workshop*, San Francisco, CA, March 15–16, 1983.
10. C. Benmehrez and J. F. McDonald, "Measured Performance of a Programmed Implementation of the Subscripted D-Algorithm," in *Proceedings of the Twentieth Design Automation Conference*, 1983, pp. 308–315.
11. C. Benmehrez and J. F. McDonald, "Test Set Reduction using the Subscripted D-Algorithm," in *Proceedings of the International Test Conference*, 1983, pp. 115–121.

MAHIEDDINE LADJADJ
JOHN F. MCDONALD

COMPUTER-AIDED COMPOSITION

INTRODUCTION

In his comprehensive 1975 article for the *Encyclopedia of Computer Science and Technology*, Arthur Phillips identified eight areas where computers were being used in the composition and presentation of typographic quality text. Such applications ranged from the recording and storage of alphabetic text and numeric data to the intricate manipulation of the format and content of such stored information. In addition, Phillips provided an invaluable history of the printer's font, as well as mechanical and electromechanical typesetting devices. The reader interested in a historical perspective on this subject should refer to Phillips' article.

of composition in two divergent directions. On the one hand, more sophisticated hardware and software have allowed designers of composition systems to redefine the boundaries of computer-aided composition by producing digitized type fonts. On the other hand, microminiaturization of hardware has made possible the expansion of the field to include the following dramatic departures from the state of the art in the early 1970s:

Heavy Reliance on Microcomputers

Used as stand-alone systems, as smart workstations connected to mainframes, or as a part of a distributed, a wide, or local area network, microcomputers have established their worth and versatility in the composition, printing, and publishing market.

Dependence on a Variety of Visual Display Terminals

Video display terminals (VDTs) are currently the most common electronic output device for works in progress that require manipulation of text and graphics before typesetting. Current VDT technology is still highly dependent on cathode-ray tubes (CRTs), but the advent of the luggable and portable computers has increased consumer interest in alternative flat-screen technologies.

Increasing Industry Awareness of End-User Needs

The users' need to concentrate on end-product development rather than to learn to become a computer scientist has, in turn, led to major advances in interface design, with the ultimate aim of making the inner workings of the computer "invisible" to the end user. Current examples of such VDT-based trends include the interface designers' emphasis on WYSIWYG (what you see is what you get) screen output, menu- and icon-based systems, and direct data manipulation techniques.

On-Line Digitization and Manipulation of Color and Graphics

Combined in one system with text processing options, these techniques also place heavy emphasis on the role of intelligent workstations and stand-alone microcomputer environments. Although most of the advances in graphics technology were spurred by high-technology manufacturing concerns using computer-aided design and computer-aided manufacturing (CAD/CAM) processes, the printing and publishing industries were major beneficiaries of these perfected techniques.

Integration of Word, Data, and Graphics

To produce tabular and columnar output, as well as line illustrations within text processing systems, has been a major breakthrough for the prepress industry, saving untold hours of redundant work by the composition staff. In addition, the ability to add halftone artwork to the integrated text and graphics file through input by image scanners is another development that completes the on-line page makeup operation.

Emergence of Image-Scanning Technologies

In addition to existing optical character recognition (OCR) devices and manual keyboard data entry, new image-scanning techniques are expanding the computer's capability to digitize and "recognize" a greater variety and quality of preprinted text and graphics documents.

Expanding Options on Output Media and Greater Versatility in Output Devices

Emerging software and hardware facilities are now capable of producing typeset-quality images on plain paper, resin-coated paper, film, or plate from the same machine-readable base, using identical digital type fonts. This flexibility can reduce preproduction costs during the editing and proofreading stages and present the composition staff with a clear representation of the final product during all of the prepress stages of production. In many instances, the quality of paper output is so high that many users can accept it as the final product, bypassing the film output.

New print output devices such as ink-jet printers and Xerographic-based laser printers have simplified in-house publishing of documents requiring high-quality text and graphics processing.

These technological innovations are being applied in a variety of settings to control the quality of end products, cut costs, and speed up the prepress process. In many instances, the ready availability of these products, combined with their relative low cost and small space requirements, has created new markets in the 1980s. Some of the special features that will be described include those that are of significance to in-house technical publishing, as well as to magazine, newspaper, and book publishing industries. The power of computing once reserved exclusively for mainframe users is now in the microcomputer domain. Unless noted otherwise, the information provided in this article is based on features and facilities available in microcomputer systems.

FRONT-END SYSTEMS IN PUBLISHING

From the moment text or graphics material is captured for electronic storage
and processing in a publishing environment, a variety of hardware and software tools can be used to massage this information in preparation for printing.
Such tools include character and image scanners, word and text processors,
editing systems, graphics design workstations, forms composition systems,
page layout and makeup systems, automatic pagination systems, dictionary
and math packages, and hyphenation and justification systems.

In addition, a multitude of special-purpose application software packages
such as those created for classified advertising, graphics-oriented technical
publishing, and microcomputer-based integrated desktop publishing systems
also fall under the general heading of front-end systems.

As these systems have become more affordable and easier to use, hundreds
of software and hardware companies are vying for a share of this growing
market. Many of the tools being offered are described generically in the
following pages. In addition, a few representative products are also described
for a more in-depth coverage of this field.

DEFINITION OF COMPUTER-AIDED COMPOSITION

Phillips, in the original article on this topic, defined computer-aided composition as "the use of the computer in the preparation of data which will be
printed in the typographic quality and style of hand-set or mechanically
composed printer's type." With the continued growth of computer technology
and a gradual shift in human expectations on the quality and style of printed
matter, the boundaries of "computer-aided composition" may be considered
too vague and too broad.

From the front end of the composition system proper, authors and editors
have now entered the domain once clearly reserved for typesetters alone.
Not only is the computer capturing the author's original keystrokes for
composition purposes, but gradually the author is also being asked to make
text and page formatting decisions as well. Where it was once quite time-
consuming and costly to see preprint copies of text, intermediate results
can now be captured quickly on large-screen VDTs and plain paper, making
it possible for the author/publisher to experiment with the final design without
major time and cost penalties.

From the printing system perspective, recent advances in digital typography (see below), combined with new printing technologies, have allowed the
complete operation to be moved in house under more direct supervision and
control of the author or editor.

EXAMPLE OF A LARGE-SCALE SYSTEM

There is a large common denominator in composition needs that can be met by
generically designed software for general-purpose computers. However, as
with all other software products, large systems invariably require additional
modules or subsystems to meet a given industry's special needs. In addition,
each company within that industry may also require further modification of
given modules. A good example of such a product line can be found in the
field of newspaper publishing.

Among well-established firms offering large-scale composition systems to
the magazine and newspaper publishing industry, Atex offers several products
that are uniquely geared toward the needs of this segment of the marketplace.
Using Atex products as an example also provides the opportunity to look at
large-scale systems that simply cannot be replicated on a microcomputer
because of the sheer volume of work and memory size requirements.

Since the early 1970s, Atex has concentrated on providing specialized
software on its proprietary hardware for publishing applications. Its systems
have evolved gradually from a primarily end-user-oriented text processing
perspective to an integrated electronic publishing system, which incorporates
the following features:

Editorial and News Layout Systems

Apart from providing all generic features of sophisticated word and text
processing systems, Atex software allows editors to track the progress of
stories, write headlines, fit copy, and do page layout and makeup, using
features such as infinite scrolling of text and wire service handling. News
layout grows out of the editorial system in an integrated fashion. Here are
a few other selected functions:

- Stories can be located by the name of the reporter, by subject, or
  by their scheduled page or section designation. Thus, page progress
  can be monitored throughout the production cycle through extensive
  directory capabilities.
- Story space can be reserved and length of unwritten stories can be
  budgeted in advance.
- Space can be reserved for graphics and cut lines, and stories can
  be jumped over any number of pages.
- Items can be moved on a page, and stories reassigned from one page
  to another.
- Type sizes and styles can be mixed and changed on the page, as can
  headline specifications.

A full-page output on the Atex News Layout Pagination System includes
text, headlines, and captions, with space reserved for graphics. The composition coding is performed automatically by the software, generating the
commands needed for text flow from column to column, page to page, around
graphics, or jumping over designated spaces.

Classified Pagination System

This module can be used separately or in conjunction with Atex's Integrated
Advertising System. Classified advertising can be positioned automatically
on a page based on one of the many pagination algorithms available on the
system. As late-coming ads are entered into the system, automatic repagination
takes place and the results can be displayed on a graphics terminal for
review. Several directories, stored in active memory, provide very rapid
access to the status of the pagination process.

This system bypasses the conventional pasteup procedure, eliminating
materials expenditure and reducing layout time dramatically. Ads on a typical
page are arranged in 20 seconds, and the average production time for a
typeset page is approximately $3\frac{1}{2}$ minutes, using an APS-5 typesetter.

Publication Design and Ad Placement

Founded on the Atex Integrated Advertising System and sharing a common advertising data base, this dummying product can retrieve ads and news blocks automatically and assign each to a specific location within the publication. Each newspaper can designate its own design criteria for size, format, and ad placement policies, which will be used as the basis for the system's automatic operation. A sample of such criteria used in the publication design files is as follows:

- Size specifications will designate the number and size of section breaks, as well as the total number of pages in the publication.
- Format information will include the sequence of sections and news hole requirements for each section.
- Ad placement policies take into account the competitive relationships between advertisers and merchandise by offering separation options that include "advertiser avoid advertiser," "merchandise avoid merchandise," and "merchandise avoid advertiser."
- Other special design considerations, such as placement styles and unusual ad grouping, that are assigned priorities for full-page or double-truck ad placement and for color ads are also taken into account.

Once all publication design files are completed and the staff has resolved complex placement and priority problems that are unique to each issue, the system incorporates ads, news, and backup data for the ads to provide a final dummy pass for each page and all sections of the newspaper.

Additional color graphics capabilities were recently added to the Atex system as it began to utilize the sophisticated graphics workstation offered by Eikonix. This system can handle both color and black-and-white photographs, which can be displayed on a VDT for cropping and placement. Color photographs can also be represented in monochrome, leaving the final decision on whether or not to use color with the editor.

PAGE MAKEUP ON A MICROCOMPUTER

One of the most successful page makeup programs available for microcomputers today is Aldus Corporation's PageMaker Desktop Publishing System. Used on an Apple Macintosh, in conjunction with a LaserWriter or ImageWriter printer, Pagemaker offers the following features with a favorable price tag under $11,000 for a complete system (as compared to traditional composition systems, which would cost three times this amount):

- Master page templates for uniform design and formatting independent of text.
- Use of MacDraw and MacPaint utilities through this software, allowing for complete integration of text and graphics, as well as providing access to the full power of these programs to create graphic images within PageMaker.
- Unlimited mixing of type fonts, styles, and sizes, with sizes ranging from 4 to 127 points.
- Up to 10 variable-width columns per page.

- Justified or ragged right, ragged left, and centered columns.
- Proportionally scalable graphic elements.
- Ability to use existing text files created in MacWrite and Microsoft Word documents.
- A built-in library of border designs and fill patterns.

In addition, this software builds upon the Macintosh approach to interface design, making the system easy to understand and use, with a minimum investment in training time.

WORD AND TEXT PROCESSING

Word processing can be considered to be more in the domain of the author and editor than the typesetter. However, electronic manipulation of words can be extended easily to paragraphs, pages, and entire documents. As soon as large segments of text are represented in electronic form, the nature of the medium forces authors to become more sensitive to formatting options.

In a traditional setting, using a pen or pencil and a legal pad, the author may have limited his or her formatting suggestions to an occasional underlining of text for emphasis or indention of portions of text to clarify a concept. More aggressive forms of expression through formatting were likely to be left for the copy editor to suggest and for the typesetter to implement. This is no longer true. As more writers use word processing systems, they make up for the bland and uniform appearance of monochrome text on a VDT screen by using the standard formatting options available on even the least sophisticated word processing software.

Such options include both horizontal and vertical centering of text on a page, underlining, boldface, right justification, as well as left and/or right indention. In addition to such word and page formatting options, text flow can also be controlled within an entire document through automatic pagination and footnoting options, as well as creating running head and feet on each page of the document. More recently released software programs offer a variety of type fonts and sizes that can be mixed on the same page and viewed on the VDT screen as they would appear on the printed page.

A variety of such word processing programs are available on general-purpose microcomputers, as well as on dedicated word processors, minis, and mainframe systems. Many of these programs were designed originally as extensions of dedicated photocomposition/typesetting systems of the late 1960s and early 1970s. Because of the state of hardware technology during that era, the earlier software versions were highly dependent on batch processing techniques and worked within the limits of punch card, paper tape, or teletypewriter output formats. Many of these restrictions were carried over to the early VDT output devices. The most common carryover that has persisted in some systems is the concept of line editing—where corrections can only be made to a single line of text at a time—as opposed to screen or page editing with unrestricted cursor movement, which is the 1980s standard.

As microcomputers became more popular and lower equipment costs placed word processing within the reach of more individuals, software designers began to concentrate on this new market from the point of view of the writer and the typist, not from the perspective of the professional typesetter.

The requirements from this end placed more emphasis on a clean visual display, with fewer composition options but greater emphasis on actual representation of the final product on the screen.

With the maturing of the industry, a merger of ideas took place somewhere halfway between the typesetter and the author. The most cherished options from the two extremes were melded into a variety of software packages. Because each individual's needs for word processing can be unique, the voices from the author's side have been more diluted than those being vocalized by the professional typesetters. However, as much as both sides seem to have benefited from this fusion, the large printing and publishing concerns will undoubtedly continue to have extremely sophisticated electronic composition aids that are clearly distinguishable from the individual or small business word processing operations.

COMPUTER AIDED DESIGN (CAD)

CAD and drafting programs basically handle technical drawings in the same manner that word processing systems handle text.

Just as the basic unit of interaction for a word processing system is an alpha character or symbol, the basic units of work in a CAD system consist of lines, polylines, arcs, circles, and solids. Variations on these basic elements include line-width changes, tapering, automatic curve fitting, and repeats. In addition, certain repeats of objects such as a brick pattern, gear wheels, or computer memory arrays can be generated automatically by the system.

CAD systems allow for the interactive creation and editing of drawings through the use of a variety of input devices such as the mouse, digitizing pads, light or sonar pens, or by "freehand" pointing. Once the drawings have been created and stored, they can be manipulated to meet the requirements of the specific job at hand by changing the vertical or horizontal scale, rotating the drawing to show other dimensions, creating mirror images, copying or repeating all or part of the design, and the like.

In the field of technical publishing, which is heavily dependent on detailed drawings and illustrations, the traditional procedure of cutting and pasting the text and graphics on boards has been replaced by output from these highly efficient graphics workstations. Not only do they help design the actual product, but they can also provide the graphics necessary for the publication of its supporting documentation, such as maintenance and reference manuals. Although the primary output from CAD systems is the detailed specifications for the manufacturing of a product, some workstations are designed specifically to handle the unique needs of technical publishing.

TECHNICAL PUBLISHING IN HOUSE

Any lengthy document that combines text, data, and graphics is a good candidate for testing out the claims of various vendors who supply in-house electronic publishing systems. In the early 1980s, the state of computer technology enabled individual segments of a composition and publishing task to be carried out online. However, there were a number of missing links. First, although graphic output on VDTs was well advanced, it was not as easy to obtain fast and cost-effective high-quality hard copy output. Second, few companies had developed shared data base facilities for all segments of their firm's operations. By the same token, the software system was incapable of linking these isolated segments into an integrated picture. And finally, there were few trained personnel who could retrieve these isolated elements from various computer files and combine them into a meaningful whole, either online or on a pasteup board.

Mid-1980s technology has taken two different approaches to the problem of technical publishing. One concept is based on combining unrelated but fully developed hardware and software systems that have proved their worth independently. Such systems may have come together through the merging of parent companies or the simple merging of existing products within the same company.

For example, Atex text and Kodak graphics were seen as a mutually beneficial combination when Kodak acquired Atex in the early 1980s. Kodak's subsequent acquisition of Eikonix provided yet another link between a highly developed electronic color graphics product and a sophisticated text processing system. Similarly, Versatec (a Xerox company) offers expert CAD software that can be integrated with the Xerox Star text and document processing program through an Ethernet communication network.

The alternative approach has been for newly developed companies to design and produce fully integrated text and graphics software. To acquire a market share in this highly competitive industry, most software developers are now offering programs that convert files developed previously on a competitor's system. One company offering such an integrated technical publishing system is Caddex. This company's complete hardware and software package is intended for use by corporations whose lengthy technical documents include a high percentage of graphics and tables that are likely to go through a great many engineering revisions through a long product life cycle. Its editorial, composition, and publishing tools include:

- A text editor that accommodates multiple users and allows simultaneous work on single or multiple documents, as well as providing a comprehensive array of word and text processing options.
- A composition system that includes a dictionary and algorithmic hyphenation, vertical justification, and column balancing.
- Book administration and format control tools for setting up document and format designs in advance to assure consistency from document to document.
- Table building tools that allow for designing table formats in advance of data entry.
- Illustrating tools that include a 3-D CAD module with a full range of graphics capabilities, as well as a 2-D figure editor for touch-up graphics editing and simple line work.
- Interactive page editing and automatic pagination option that merges text, tables, illustrations, format, and style into its final page form.
- An interface option to external CAD and word processing systems that simplifies the transportation of files from data bases outside the Caddex system.
- A shared relational data base that allows for automatic update of all text and graphics from any access point within the system or through the network. This data base is, in fact, the heart of Caddex in that the system concept revolves around the total integration of all publishing tasks as opposed to accomplishing isolated portions of a task from various workstations.

PAGE DESCRIPTION LANGUAGES
AND STANDARDS

During the 1960s and 1970s the majority of software developers in the text processing business either worked closely with manufacturers of hardware products or produced their own proprietary hardware to ensure a tie-in between the program's capability to produce VDT output and its ability to produce the same output on a typesetter. In either case, their only concern was to communicate a fixed alphanumeric character set between devices.

Two major changes in the late 1970s and 1980s forced the issue of a standard page description language: proliferation of software and hardware and the advent of ink-jet and laser printers. During the 1960s and 1970s, when computer output to typesetters and printers was limited to alphanumeric text, it was sufficient to describe this output in terms of a fixed character set. Document composition languages such as Script (1960), T_EX (1978), and Scribe (1980) were developed to handle this type of composition.

During the early 1980s, graphics-oriented output led to new requirements for page description languages. The advent of nonimpact printing technologies, such as laser printers, had changed the requirements for describing the contents of a page for printing purposes. New printers were no longer limited to a fixed character set. In fact, by this time, the smallest unit to be printed was identified as a tiny dot that could appear anywhere on the page. It was thus necessary for a versatile and sophisticated page description language to define the characteristics of every such dot.

In the absence of industry-wide standards and with widespread competition for a share of the software market, several companies began to concentrate on developing their own page description languages. By the mid-1980s, PostScript from Adobe Systems, Inc., and Interpress from Xerox were among the most highly developed page description languages on the market. By early 1986, PostScript had been chosen by so many application software developers and printer manufacturers that it was declared a de facto industry standard.

This device-independent language provides the user with a standard way of describing any page so that documents can be used interchangeably and printed on a variety of output devices. PostScript may reside in a medium-resolution office printer or a high-resolution typesetter or film recorder, allowing the user to print pages that may have a mixture of text, line art, and halftone graphics. Depending on the printer's capabilities, PostScript software can handle rotated type, textures and patterns, as well as halftones.

Adobe Systems also offers a large selection of typefaces for use with any PostScript printer or typesetter. Each typeface is completely adaptable to any software application that supports PostScript, so that in addition to printer output, screen fonts are also available for word processors and other application programs. Kerning and other typesetting information is also available for the use of professional typesetters.

IMAGE SCANNERS AND OPTICAL CHARACTER
READERS (OCR)

Nonkeyboard input devices for computer-aided composition have shown considerable progress during the past decade. In addition to OCR, which has been used for text input for many years, image scanners have also been developed to digitize graphics for storage, manipulation, and reproduction by computers.

Early versions of OCR machines accepted only specific machine-readable fonts such as IBM's OCR and OCRA font types. Through the years, manufacturers of these products have expanded the number and quality of typefaces that can be read by their machines. However, the majority of these readers are still tied to standard typewriter typefaces. Some will also read computer printouts. But by and large, with the exception of Kurzweil's reading machine, which uses principles of artificial intelligence in pattern recognition to read over 240 typeset as well as typewritten fonts, most machines are limited to fewer than a dozen typefaces.

As with other segments of the composition industry, nonkeyboard data entry systems have been developed for the microcomputer market as well as for mini and mainframe systems. One of the leading manufacturers in this field is DEST Corporation. It offers PC Scan for microcomputer environments, as well as the WorkLess Station for heavier workloads. The latter is capable of reading up to 240 pages of text per hour, with automatic recognition of up to 12 type styles in 10- or 12-pitch type or proportionally spaced text.

Image scanners, on the other hand, have no similar restrictions on the type of material to be digitized. The technique used in digitizing images is called raster image processing (RIP). The processor converts any graphics or text image along each scan line into electrical zeroes and ones that represent the sequence of black-and-white dots making up that line (in effect, creating a bit map for each image). The primary difference among these devices, which are used both for input and output of graphics material, is the number of vertical lines or dots per inch (and number of horizontal dots per inch) that they can represent. The greater the number of dots without excessive overlap, the higher the resolution of the graphics.

Image Processing on Microcomputers

Although sophisticated image processors for mainframe computers can far surpass the capabilities and quality of the microcomputer products, it is still very impressive to review the specifications for a low-cost product developed for small systems.

The ThunderScan scanner from Thunderware, Inc., retails for $175 and is installed in place of a printer ribbon on any Apple ImageWriter dot matrix printer. The program then transforms the printer into an image input device by figuratively putting it in "reverse" mode. Thus, anything that can be rolled through the ImageWriter printer can be turned into a computer graphic.

For every discrete point scanned, Thunderscan can assign one of 32 gray levels (halftones). Either the bit map generated by the software or the halftones can be sent to any PostScript (see Page Description Languages and Standards, above) driven printer, such as the Apple LaserWriter, for output. The user can control screen resolution by selecting scanning magnification from 18 to 288 dots per inch. The printing resolution is dependent on the printer and can range from 75 to 150 dots per inch on the ImageWriter or up to 300 dots per inch on the LaserWriter. This device can be used with page makeup software such as PageMaker (see above) from Aldus Corporation.

DIGITAL TYPOGRAPHY

This technology is based on the computer's ability to translate any alphanumeric character down to its individual picture elements (pixels) along each
scan line of an electron or laser beam (see RIP image scanning above). When
hundreds of these scans are performed for each horizontal inch, every
pixel can be made to fluoresce or to remain dark by turning the light on or
off as appropriate to form a character. In effect, each digitized character
is represented by a series of dots in arrays (a bit map) or their algorithmic
representation. These bit maps are stored in computer memory and used once
again during the printing process. Some of the more sophisticated software
programs producing these fonts can, in turn, drive typesetters, whereas
others will produce images for paper-based printers.

Although bit maps can be a very accurate means of storing font information, their major shortcoming is the large amount of memory they require,
especially if a variety of type fonts and sizes are to be represented. The
most common solutions include storing the "outline" information on each
character (and filling in the details during the printing process) and storing
algorithms representing the straight lines and circular arcs of each character
(and recreating the complete form during output).

A major advantage of digital typography over traditional methods of
typecasting is that for the first time in the history of printing, an accurate
and consistent representation of any character, glyph, or ideogram can be
formed with very little effort. Because electronic keyboards can be reprogrammed to represent any special character or image, digital typography has
opened a new world of communication for ideograph-based languages.

On a lighter note, artists have taken advantage of digital typography,
not only to design new alphanumeric type fonts but also to experiment with
glyphs and ideograms. Figure 1 shows a selected sample of such fonts. Each
symbol is the equivalent of an alpha or numeric character. It can thus be
recreated by a single keystroke on a standard microcomputer keyboard. The
original drawings for each symbol were created freehand, using a mouse
and the Macintosh MacPaint program. The fonts were created using Fontastic
by Altsys Corporation and ArtGrabber by Hayden Software.

ELECTRONIC TYPESETTING EQUIPMENT

The size, cost, operation, and maintenance of the new generation of electronic
printers has had a dramatic effect on the marketplace. The pervasive nature
of the product has not only affected the consumer's general expectation to
receive fast and clean copies of documents, but it has also changed the
public's sense of what constitutes quality typesetting and quality printing.
In very broad terms, three general categories of electronic printers are
marketed today: the low-end impact printers (75 dots per inch); the mid-
range ink-jet printers (300 dots per inch); and the high-resolution laser
printers and typesetters (1,000+ dots per inch).

The same RIP technology, used for capturing graphics images (see Image
Scanners and OCR, above), is also used in conjunction with Xerographic
reproduction technology in the most popular laser printers on the market
today.   The versatility, speed, and quality offered by many high-resolution

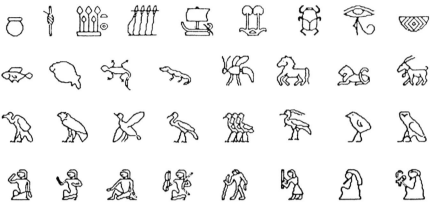

by Barbara Paugh and J. D. Robertson.

FIGURE 1   Selected hieroglyphs from the collection of fonts created by
Barbara Paugh and J. D. Robertson.

laser printers make them ideal candidates for in-house publishing operations.
The Apple LaserWriter is one such printer.

Apple's LaserWriter

This high-resolution laser printer was the first to incorporate a wide range
of sought-after features in a product that is affordable by small publishing
concerns. Its most attractive features are as follows:

- It uses PostScript as its built-in page description language (see
  Page Description languages and Standards, above). Thus, it can be
  driven by any software using PostScript and is not exclusively tied
  in to other Apple products.
- It offers extremely high-quality print at a resolution of 90,000 dots
  per square inch.
- The original LaserWriter offers four families of type for a standard
  "typeset" look, as well as a typewriter look and a set of scientific
  and Greek characters. In addition, LaserWriter Plus offers another
  seven type families, and outside vendors can provide even more
  typefaces for these printers.
- A single character can be printed as small as desired or as large as
  a full sheet of paper.
- Text can be printed in italic, boldface, underline, outline, shadow,
  or a combination of styles.
- Acceptable print media can be plain copier paper, letterhead, labels,
  envelopes, and overhead transparencies.
- Maintenance has been simplified by offering toner cartridges that
  can be replaced by the user and can last for up to 3,000 pages of
  output.

DESKTOP PUBLISHING

Printing is one of the costliest line items in any company's operations budget. Until recently, however, a small or medium-sized business could not afford the capital expenditures required for space and equipment to publish its own materials in house. Microcomputer-based systems can now bring the power of a large print shop to a single "desktop." In addition to businesses, individual authors now have a greater opportunity to publish their own works independent of the established publishers.

One of the major driving forces behind desktop publishing was Apple Computer's introduction of its Macintosh and LaserWriter (see above) in the mid-1980s. The Macintosh's combination of easy-to-use and versatile software, its ability to handle graphics, along with its high-resolution screen and greater storage capacity (20Mb hard disk and 800K external drive), made it an ideal candidate for a desktop publishing arrangement.

Integration of text and graphics from the MacPaint, MacDraw, and Mac-Write series of software products provided the industry with a first glimpse at a new way of "computing" for end-users. Independent software developers were quick to recognize this shift and began to offer a variety of software products that took advantage of Macintosh's new interface design and inherent graphics capabilities.

Aldus's PageMaker (see Page Makeup on a Microcomputer, above) is one example of a sophisticated page composition program written for the Macintosh, which allows the user to design small publications with integrated text and graphics. This complete word and graphics processing, composition, and printing system can be purchased for under $10,000.

DEMAND PUBLISHING

The powerful combination of microcomputers, integrated text and graphics software, and electronic printers has added the momentum necessary to support publishing on demand. The low cost of equipment, maintenance, and operation makes it possible to store original documents on disks and simply produce copies as orders are received. Cost savings associated with reduced inventories are likely to make up for any additional expenses incurred in the low-volume print runs. Demand publishing is especially suitable for replacing a multitude of preprinted company forms, letterheads, and mastheads, as well as for internal reports and documentation.

STANDARDS

As with all other areas of computer technology, lack of standardization has affected several strategic composition functions. Initial incompatibility among various hardware, software, and telecommunication products slowed many networking attempts among authors, editors, and typesetters. Today, ASCII files are considered standard in this industry for transporting alphanumeric text files among application programs and across hardware boundaries.

The Association of American Publishers and the Council on Library Resources have sponsored the development of a standard computer format that allows authors to transmit manuscripts directly to publishers or to typesetters. This standard, created at Aspen Systems Corporation, permits the publication of the manuscript in both print and electronic forms and is an application of the international generic coding standard, Standard Generalized Markup Language.

As noted in the section of Page Description Languages and Standards, it seems that the PostScript page description language has become the de facto industry standard for driving printers and typesetters, although it is likely to take many more years before all software developers adhere to its guidelines.

The rate of change in both the hardware and software segments of the industry make many developers leery of prematurely set standards that can thwart creativity and growth. However, it has become clear from previous experience that even if the industry as a whole cannot come to grips with imposing standards, the sheer chaos created by individuality in a highly interdependent environment will force the survivors to comply with some general guidelines, whether they are compulsory or voluntary in nature.

REFERENCES

Bigelow, Charles, and Donald Day, "Digital Typography," *Sci. Am.*, 249 (2), 106—119 (August 1983).

Borrell, Jerry, "Electronic Publishing Lands on the Desktop," *Mini-Micro Syst.*, 18 (16), 85—92 (December 1985).

Buchanan, David, "Image Processing Enhances Laser Printing," *Mini-Micro Syst.*, 18 (11), 101—109 (August 1985).

Goldstein, Amnon, "Problems Confronting Design of a Typographic Quality Laser Printer," *Graphic Arts Mon.*, 57 (5), 68—74 (May 1985).

Graphic Arts Monthly and the Printing Industry, Prepress Imaging/Computer-Aided Publishing Section.

Kuhn, Larry, and Robert A. Myers, "Ink-Jet Printing," *Sci. Am.*, 240 (4), 162—176 (April 1979).

Phillips, Arthur, "Computer-Aided Composition," *Encyclopedia of Computer Science and Technology,* Marcel Dekker, Inc., New York, 5, 267—374, 1975.

Rubinstein, Richard, *Digital Typography: A Primer,* CHI '86, Human Factors in Computing Systems Conference, Boston, MA, April 1986.

The Seybold Report on Publishing Systems, Seybold Publications, Inc., Media, PA, 1986-1986 reports.

Spencer, David, R., "Typographic Quality Printing on Plain Paper," *Graphic Arts Mon.*, 57 (4), 110—121 (April 1985).

Further Reading

ANPA *R. I. Bulletin* and other reports from the American Newspaper Publishers Association provide comprehensive coverage on new and upcoming developments in hardware and software for the newspaper industry.

Electronic Imaging is a monthly journal dedicated to this field.

Graphic Arts Monthly and the Printing Industry publishes many relevant articles and carries a regular section on Prepress Imaging/Computer-Aided Publishing.

PC World, July 1986 issue is devoted to desktop publishing using microcomputers; the December 1983 issue covers ink-jet printers.

Publisher's Weekly provides regular reports and updates on hardware and software installations in the book publishing trade.

The Seybold Report on Publishing Systems (Seybold Publications, Media, PA) offers comprehensive and timely information on all hardware and software products and manufacturers in this field, with exhaustive coverage of regional, national, and international trade shows and exhibitions. The *Report* is issued 22 times per year.

Weekly newspapers and journals such as *Computerworld, PC Week,* and *ComputerWeekly* cover the computer industry and provide up-to-date information on all facets of computer hardware and software development.

DINEH M. DAVIS

DATABASE DESIGN

INTRODUCTION

Most computer programs store data over time. Typically, a computer program will accept some data values directly from a user and read other data values from some storage file. After processing those data, most programs will display or print some results to the user and write some results back to a storage file.

If a single computer program needs storage files for its exclusive use, it can be written as a file-processing program, so called because the program uses its own data files under its exclusive control. However, if several programs need to share common data, then each can be written as a database processing program [1]. Such programs store data over time through the use of a database management system (DBMS). The names and formats of all data fields are defined through the DBMS; thereafter, all programs use DBMS facilities to concurrently manipulate data values stored within those shared fields.

Database processing can be done in either of two modes: (a) In ad hoc processing, the DBMS software alone is used to manipulate or administer stored data. (b) In programmed processing, the DBMS software is used in conjunction with some conventional programming language like COBOL, FORTRAN, or BASIC to manipulate or administer stored data. Figure 1 illustrates how shared data can be manipulated concurrently through a DBMS.

Database processing provides many advantages: By allowing all users to share common data concurrently, inconsistent or unnecessarily redundant data can be eliminated. The data's integrity over time can be assured through the use of "multistatement transactions" (i.e., treating a series of statements that update separate but address-related records as one all-or-nothing transaction). Data can be secured from unauthorized updates or accesses and protected from system or hardware failures. Storage requirements and response times can be optimized through centralized data administration. Programmer productivity can be increased by the use of labor-saving programming aids provided by the DBMS.

DATABASE MANAGEMENT SYSTEMS

A DBMS always presents an external view of the data to users, called a conceptual schema. A schema is a visual representation of fields within records and relationships between those records. Information provided by a schema not only aids the user's perception of how data are stored by the

---

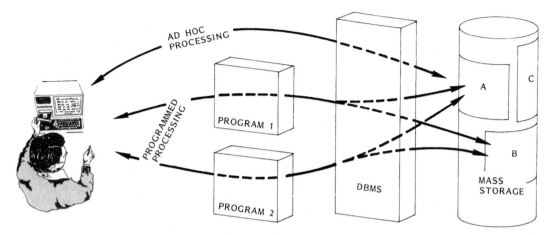

FIGURE 1   Database processing of shared data.

DBMS but also serves to define the physical requirements of the data to
the DBMS software. Most authorities arrange DBMS products into three
families, more or less according to the structure of their conceptual schemas.
Those three DBMS families are hierarchical, network, and relational. (For
an excellent discussion of the history of DBMS families, see Ref. 2).

Commercial DBMS products first began to appear in the mid-1960s.
Based on work done in connection with the Apollo moon-landing program,
Rockwell International developed a DBMS called Information Control System/
Data Language/1 (usually called DL/1) for the IBM System 360 computer.
IBM released its own version of that hierarchical DBMS in 1969, called the
Information Management System/360 (IMS). IMS has evolved into subsequent
versions and remains in wide use today, especially for large applications on
IBM mainframe computers.

The second major DBMS family is the network family. During the 1970s,
the Database Task Group (DBTG) within CODASYL (Conference on Data
Systems Languages)—the group that developed the standards for the COBOL
programming language—developed a database standard specification called
the CODASYL DBTG 1971 Report. Several commercial products have been
developed in reasonably close conformance to the 1971 DBTG standard,
notably UNIVAC's DMS 1100, Cullinane's IDMS, and Honeywell's IDS (Integrated Data Store) [2].

The third major DBMS family is the relational family. In 1970, E. F.
Codd proposed a new "relational model of data" that would protect DBMS
users from disruptive changes to the schema [3]. Considerable research and
development of his relational model was done by computer scientists during
the 1970s. Prototype systems were developed at IBM Research Laboratory,
San Jose, California (SYSTEM R), the University of California, Berkeley
(INGRES), and elsewhere during that time period. Commercial relational
DBMS products first appeared in the late 1970s. Today, there are hundreds
of relational DBMS software packages available for computers of all sizes.
A few examples are IBM's DB2 and SQL/DS, Oracle Inc.'s ORACLE, and
Relational Technology's INGRES.

Hierarchical and network DBMS products have been quite successful in
the marketplace, but significant problems have mitigated that success. The
newer relational DBMS products have overcome problems associated with those

older DBMS types and are now enjoying increasing success; however, relational DBMS products have some resolved problems of their own. The database designer should be aware of the advantages and disadvantages of each DBMS type, especially if given a choice between using one type or another.

Advantages and Disadvantages of Hierarchical and Network Database Management Systems

The conceptual schema of a hierarchical or network DBMS is defined to the DBMS using some kind of data definition language that defines fields within records and links those records with user-visible relationships. The data definition is compiled (assembled), and the object form stored in a system library, ready for use.

Once development of using computer programs has begun, changes to a hierarchical or network schema are usually quite costly to implement because such a change must be defined fully to the DBMS by recompiling the schema. Then, all computer programs that access the changed area must also be recompiled and retested because a schema change to fix one error can unexpectedly cause new errors to appear.

So, as a practical matter, administrators of hierarchical or network DBMS products are quite reluctant to change a schema, even in the early stages of program development. Database design is particularly important when using the hierarchical or network DBMS because the inflexible data structure of those models places a severe requirement on the designer to "get it right the first time."

Programmers who develop database processing programs for either a hierarchical or network DBMS must write "procedural" code that "navigates" from one record to another within the conceptual schema (this will be illustrated later on). Navigational code is quite lengthy, complex to write, and complex to maintain. Although DBMS products were originally touted as products that would improve programming productivity, in reality, neither the hierarchical nor the network DBMS has done so. However, response times of hierarchical and network DBMS products are usually quite satisfactory. Most companies, then, accept the problems of an inflexible schema and lengthy navigational code in order to gain the advantage of quick, concurrent access to shared data under controlled conditions.

Advantages and Disadvantages of Relational Database Management Systems

The newer relational DBMS products have a conceptual schema that is quite flexible. If the composition of the database must be changed or if the database must be accessed in a different manner, such changes can be made quickly without causing revisions or recompilations of the computer programs that access the database. This quality of the relational database is known as "data independence" and is a major advantage of the relational model over older DBMS types. Rather than having to design a near-perfect database from scratch, a relational database designer is encouraged to make a good first-cut design and then revise it as data requirements become better understood.

A relational database is accessed through terse, high-level commands that are translated into executable operations by optimizing algorithms of the

DBMS's back-end processor. This means that relational database processing programs are much shorter than programs that employ hierarchical or network database processing. Furthermore, all relational DBMS products have ad hoc query facilities that are vastly superior to ad hoc facilities of hierarchical or network DBMS products. For these reasons, programmers are much more productive when using a relational DBMS.

On the other hand, response times of most mid-1980s relational DBMS are not as good as that of hierarchical or network DBMS products. That disparity is disappearing, however, as relational back-end optimizers become more efficient and as some or all relational operations are assumed by specialized hardware rather than the DBMS software.

Need for Database Design

An absolute prerequisite to database processing is the need to design a suitable conceptual schema. Someone must determine all data fields required by the application programs that will use the database and arrange those fields into a conceptual schema appropriate to the DBMS being used. A well-designed database eases the work of writing and maintaining application programs significantly. Conversely, a poorly designed database can cause problems that even the best of programmers cannot overcome.

Most authorities describe database design as an intuitive, iterative, cut-and-try process. There are design approaches, however, that will lead the hierarchical or network database designer toward good designs and away from bad designs. Even better procedures are available to the relational database designer.

Most database design procedures have the designer begin by preparing a logical model of data (so called because implementation details are excluded). That model then becomes the basis for preparing a physical model of data appropriate to the hierarchical, network, or relational DBMS product being used.

LOGICAL DATA MODELS

Logical data models, also called semantic models, are a symbolic representation of an organization's data requirements. To illustrate the construction and use of such models, the data requirements of a hypothetical organization called Clinton Tools, Inc., shown in Figure 2, will be used. That same example will be used later on to illustrate how hierarchical, network, and relational databases are designed.

The entity—relationship (E-R) diagram is probably the best known logical data model, so a discussion of it will serve to illustrate the use of such models. An E-R diagram models the real world as entities and relationships, symbolized by rectangular boxes and diamond-shaped boxes, respectively. To illustrate, the E-R diagram that logically models the data requirements of Clinton Tools (Fig. 2) is shown in Figure 3.

Because of its general acceptance as a logical model, useful when designing a hierarchical, network, or relational database, Chen's original symbology has been extended and modified by many subsequent authors. The terminology that follows is taken from Chen's original paper [4], as modified (in this instance) by Ullman [5].

```
┌─────────────────────────────────────────────────────────────┐
│                      Purchase Order                           │
│     CLINTON TOOLS, INC.                  ORDER NO.  561        │
│     9700 Olympic Boulevard                                    │
│     Atlanta, Georgia                                          │
├─────────────────────────────────────────────────────────────┤
│     Morrison Fabricators           Needed:   Mar. 12, 1986    │
│     2112 South Side Road           Terms:    2/10, n/30       │
│     Carthage, Missouri             Ship Via: Overland Trucking,│
│                                              St. Louis, Mo.    │
├──────────┬──────────────┬─────────────────┬──────┬───────────┤
│ Tool No. │ Your Part No.│ Description      │ Quan │ Unit Price│
├──────────┼──────────────┼─────────────────┼──────┼───────────┤
│ P18-103  │ 143J-16L     │ Needle nose pliers│ 200 │    4.50   │
│ A3-101B  │ 34R-3        │ Valve lifter     │  150 │   13.00   │
└──────────┴──────────────┴─────────────────┴──────┴───────────┘
```

FIGURE 2   Clinton Tools, Inc., designs and sells special-purpose hand tools, each identified by tool number and description. Every producer qualified to manufacture a tool assigns their own part number to it. Purchase orders are periodically issued to replenish Clinton Tool's stock of one or more tools.

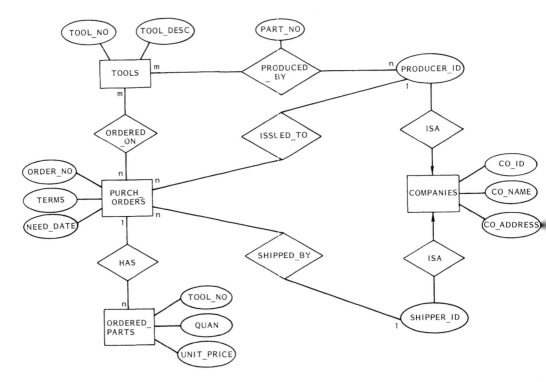

FIGURE 3   E-R diagram of Clinton Tools, Inc.

An entity is an object in the real world, such as a tool, a bank record, or a purchase order. An entity set is a group of similar entities, such as all payroll disbursements, all airline flights, or all salespersons. Associated to each entity set are attributes, shown within circles (or ellipses) connected to the entity. For example (from Fig. 3), the entity set TOOLS has attributes of TOOL-NO and TOOL-DESC.

Entity sets are linked by relationships. In most instances, relationships occur between two entities, but a relationship may be defined on only one entity set or on three or more entity sets. Attributes can be associated to relationships; e.g., the relationship PRODUCED-BY linking TOOLS to PRODUCER-ID in Figure 3 has the attribute PART-NO associated to it.

Because each entity set is different from all others, one or more of its attributes must be the primary key of that entity set. For example, TOOL-NO is the primary key for the entity set TOOLS. As a special case, if an entity set has only one attribute (which must be its primary key), the E-R diagram may use a circle or ellipse to depict that entity set instead of a rectangular box (e.g., PRODUCER-ID in Fig. 3).

The primary key of a relationship comprises the primary key of the involved entities. For example, in Figure 3, the primary key of the relationship ORDERED-ON comprises the fields TOOL-NO and ORDER-NO, the primary keys of entity sets TOOLS and PURCH-ORDERS, respectively.

If the relationship is many to one, the symbols n and 1 are shown by the appropriate entity (e.g., from Fig. 3, a PURCH-ORDERS has many ORDERED-PARTS, whereas an ORDERED-PARTS occurs on only one PURCH-ORDERS). If the relationship is many to many, the symbol m and n are shown by the entities (e.g., TOOLS are ordered on many PURCH-ORDERS, and a PURCH-ORDERS contains many TOOLS.

Some entity sets exist because of their dependence on another entity set; i.e., they are distinguished not by their attributes but by their relationship to entity sets of another type, such as "A is a B," (equivalently, A is a special kind of B). This built-in relationship is called an IS-A. For example, in Fig. 3, PRODUCER-ID IS-A COMPANIES).

HIERARCHICAL DATABASE DESIGN

The conceptual schema of a hierarchical DBMS represents data as an upside-down tree structure of fixed-length or variable-length segments. A single segment at the top of the upside-down tree is called the root segment, and subordinate segments extend from that root as do the branches of a tree. Any segment with subordinate segments is called a parent segment, and its subordinates are called child segments; hence, there is a parent/child linkage between all segments of a hierarchical schema. When processing data within a hierarchical structure, the root segment is accessed first, then one first-level branch segment under that root, then a second-level branch within that first-level branch, etc.

A hierarchical database design can be derived from a logical model like an E-R diagram. This is illustrated by the hierarchical database for Clinton Tools, Inc., shown in Figure 4, that was designed from the E-R diagram of Figure 3. In Figure 4, record segments are represented within blocks; the segment's name is shown on the block's top line, and all fields within a segment are shown on the bottom line (with the sequencing field underlined).

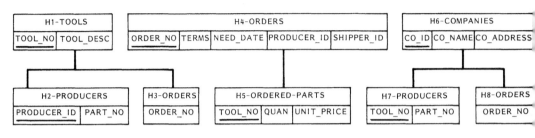

FIGURE 4   Hierarchical database for Clinton Tools, Inc.

One-to-many relationships are modeled as one hierarchy. For example, the one-to-many relationship of PURCH-ORDERS (HAS) ORDERED-PARTS shown on the E-R diagram of Figure 3 is directly modeled in Clinton Tool's hierarchical database by the hierarchy H4-ORDERS to H5-ORDERED-PARTS.

On the other hand, many-to-many relationships are usually modeled by introducing deliberate redundance into the hierarchical database. For example, the many-to-many relationship of TOOLS (PRODUCED-BY) PRODUCER-ID of Figure 3 is modeled using two hierarchies, as shown in Figure 4: H1-TOOLS to H2-PRODUCERS, and H6-COMPANIES to H7-PRODUCERS. The root segment H1-TOOLS is first accessed to find in H2-PRODUCERS all producers of a given tool; alternately, the root segment H6-COMPANIES is first accessed to find in H7-PRODUCERS all tools of a given producer.

Once a conceptual schema has been designed, it is advisable for the designer to desk check the database against the logical model to assure that all requirements of the logical model have been satisfied. For example, a few requirements of Clinton Tool's E-R diagram (Fig. 3) are desk checked against the database of Figure 4 as follows:

- A tool's part number by producer (i.e., from Fig. 3, TOOLS [PRODUCED-BY] PRODUCER-ID): H1-TOOLS is fetched for that TOOL-NO, and each subordinate H2-PRODUCERS is read to obtain H2-PART NO and H2-PRODUCER-ID; an H6-COMPANIES record whose H6-COMPANY-ID matches that H2-PRODUCER-ID is then read to obtain the H6-COMPANY-NAME of that producer.
- A tool's many orders (i.e., TOOLS [ORDERED-NO] PURCH-ORDERS): H1-TOOLS is fetched for that TOOL-NO and all subordinate H3-ORDERS are read to obtain H3-ORDER-NO.
- An order's one producer (i.e., PURCH-ORDERS [ISSUED-TO] PRODUCER-ID): H4-ORDERS is fetched for that ORDER-NO. The H6-COMPANIES record whose H6-COMPANY-ID matches that H4-PRODUCER-ID is obtained, providing H6-COMPANY-NAME.

NETWORK DATABASE DESIGN

The network model's conceptual schema consists of data items, records, and sets. A data item is a field, each given a name and format (e.g., TOOL-ID, PIC X[15]). A record is a collection of data items; repeating groups are allowed (e.g., OCCURS 1 TO 31 TIMES DEPENDING ON 0538-ASSY-CTR). A set is a one-to-many relationship between records. A set can have only one type of record as an owner but can have one or more types of records as its members. A record cannot have two owners in the same set but can have two owners if they are in different sets [1].

Sets are literally one-to-many relationships. For example, given the network schema of Figure 5A, a record named N1-CLUB having one instance of "photography" may have multiple instances of record N2-MEMBER linked to it by set S1, such as instances for club members Jones, Smith, and Brown. However, an N2-MEMBER record for Jones can belong to only one N1-CLUB within set S1. Therefore, Figure 5A is a one-to-many relationship, not a many-to-many relationship. If, in fact, Jones belongs to several clubs, the identity of those clubs can only be determined using the database in Figure 5A by accessing every N1-CLUB record and then seeking a subordinate N2-MEMBER record for Jones within set S1 to determine whether or not Jones belongs to that club.

It is better to model many-to-many relationships (Fig. 5B) by introducing an "intersection" record into the network database. For example, to model "A club can have many members and a member can belong to many clubs," a network database would be designed as shown in Figure 5B, where an "intersection" record named N5-CLUB-MEMBER links many clubs with many members. An N3-CLUB record of Photography and an N4-MEMBER record of Jones could have an N5-CLUB-MEMBER instance of Photography Jones and within sets S2 and S3, respectively. Therefore, one instance of record N5-CLUB-MEMBER would have only one instance within sets S2 and S3. In other words, both sets S2 and S3 are one-to-many relationships, even though the database itself models the many-to-many relationship between clubs and members. The identity of the clubs to which Jones belongs can be determined by fetching the N4-MEMBER record for Jones, seeking every N5-CLUB-MEMBER record within set S3, and for each, seeking the club's name in record N3-CLUB within set S2.

A network database design can be derived from a logical data model like an E-R diagram. This is illustrated by the network database for Clinton Tools, Inc., shown in Figure 6, which was designed from the E-R diagram of Figure 3. In Figure 6, records are represented within blocks. The record's name is shown on the block's top line, and all fields within the record are shown on the bottom line (with the sequencing field underlined). Records that are located by means of a CALC (calculation) key (i.e., the record's primary key is hashed to a specific disk page number) have a "C" in the block's upper right-hand corner; those that are located via a set have an "S" in the upper right-hand corner.

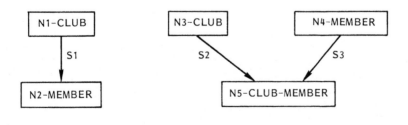

a. One-To-Many   b. Many-To-Many

FIGURE 5 Network DBMS examples.

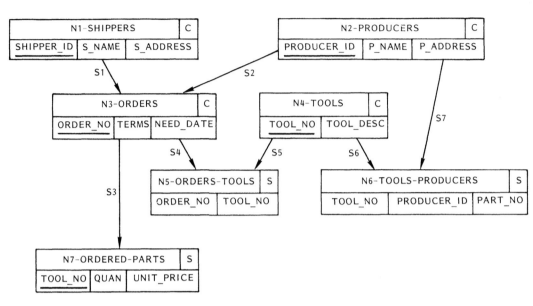

FIGURE 6   Network database for Clinton Tools.

The one-to-many relationship of PURCH-ORDERS (HAS) ORDERED-
PARTS shown on the E-R diagram of Figure 3 is modeled in Clinton Tool's
network database by CALC record N3-ORDERS linked to record N7-
ORDERED-PARTS via set S3.   The many-to-many relationship of TOOLS
(PRODUCED-BY) PRODUCER-ID of Figure 3 is modeled by CALC record
N4-TOOLS linked to intersection record N6-TOOLS-PRODUCERS via set S6
and CALC record N2-PRODUCERS linked to that same intersection record
via set S7.   The other one-to-one and one-to-many relationships of Clinton
Tool's E-R diagram are similarly modeled.

The network database of Figure 6 should be desk checked to assure
that all relationships on the logical model have been satisfied.   For example,

- A tool's part number by producer (i.e., from Figure 3, TOOLS
  [PRODUCED-BY] PRODUCER-ID): N4-TOOLS is fetched for that
  TOOL-NO, and each N6-TOOLS-PRODUCERS in set S6 is read to
  obtain N6-PART-NO and N6-PRODUCER-ID; if desired, that pro-
  ducer's name and address can be obtained from N2-PRODUCERS
  in set S7.
- A tool's many orders (i.e., TOOLS [ORDERED-ON] PURCH-
  ORDERS): N4-TOOLS is fetched for that TOOL-NO, and each
  N5-ORDERS-TOOLS in set S5 is read to obtain N5-ORDER-NO.
- An order's one producer (i.e., PURCH-ORDER [ISSUED-TO]
  PRODUCER-ID): N3-ORDERS is fetched for that ORDER-NO, and
  its owner N2-PRODUCERS is found within set S2 to obtain N2-
  PRODUCER-ID, N2-P-NAME, and N2-P-ADDRESS.

A given database design usually has some advantages and some disadvantages.   For example, the body of a Clinton Tools purchase order (Fig.
2) lists a series of Tool No., Your Part No., Description, Quan, and Unit
Price entries.   Given the schema of Figure 6, the program will print those

data by fetching every N7-ORDERED-PARTS within set S3, but those records do not provide Your Part No. and Description. To get that information, as each N7-ORDERED-PARTS is fetched, the program would CALC to an N4-TOOLS record wherein N4-TOOL-NO matches the current N7-TOOL-NO, obtain Description from N4-TOOL-DESC, and then fetch the N6-TOOLS-PRODUCERS record within set S6 to obtain Your Part No. from N6-PART-NO.

The designer may decide to ease the work of printing purchase orders by adding PART-NO and TOOL-DESC to N7-ORDERED-PARTS, but because duplicate information must be maintained within N7-ORDERED-PARTS, N4-TOOLS, and N6-TOOLS-PRODUCERS, other problems might arise. This illustrates that the database designer is always trading the advantages and disadvantages of one design against those of another design.

THE RELATIONAL DATABASE MANAGEMENT SYSTEM

The originator of the relational model, E. F. Codd, defines this third type of DBMS as a combination of three elements: (*a*) structure, (*b*) operators for manipulating that structure, and (*c*) integrity rules that define permissible states for the structure [3, 6]. This close coupling between the relational model's schema, manipulative language, and integrity rules is in sharp contrast to the ad hoc nature of earlier DBMS types.

Conceptual Schema of the Relational DBMS

The storage structure of the relational model is based upon the *n*-ary relation. To explain, a binary relation between two sets, S1 and S2, is a subset of the ordered pairs in the Cartesian product S1 × S2, as shown in Figure 7A. An *n*-ary relation between *n* sets, S1, S2, ···, Sn, is a subset of the ordered pairs in the Cartesian product S1 × S2 × ···Sn, as shown in Figure 7B.

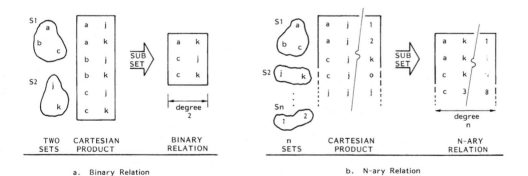

a. Binary Relation   b. N-ary Relation

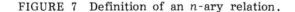

FIGURE 7 Definition of an *n*-ary relation.

So the conceptual schema of the relational model is perceived as a collection of *n*-ary relations (where *n* is the relation's degree, i.e., S1, S2, •••, Sn). The columns of the relation are called attributes, and successive rows of the relation are called tuples. It is irrelevant as to how attributes are ordered left to right within a table or how tuples are ordered top to bottom.

Actual values for attributes are drawn from a domain, defined as "a pool of values, some or all of which may be represented in the data bank at any instant" [3]. If two binary relations each contain an attribute that shares the same domain, those two binary relations can be combined (joined) to form a tertiary relation (i.e., having three attributes) without any loss of information. That is, relations T1 (A, B) and T2 (B, C) can be combined to form relations T3 (A, B, C) because attribute B in both relations is from the same domain. Thus, relations in the relational model are not linked by any predefined parent/child relationship or predefined set relationship, as in the hierarchical or network DBMS types. Instead, relations in the relational model can be linked if attributes from those relations are in the same domain.

Because a data field usually has the same name as its domain, most domains of a database are readily apparent. For example, values for the attribute LIFT-COEF would be drawn from the domain "lift coefficients." On the other hand, it might not be so apparent that values for attributes EMP-NO, DEPT-MGR, and PROJ-LDR (i.e., employee number, department manager, and project leader) are all from the domain "employee number."

The terms relation, attribute, and tuple are usually used when discussing the theoretical relational model (as above), but most software vendors use more comprehensible terms when discussing their relational products: Because an *n*-ary relation looks just like a two-dimensional table, it is commonplace to use the term table instead of relation when discussing relational products. Similarly, the term field or column is used instead of attribute, and row or record instead of tuple. Figure 8 illustrates the relational model's conceptual schema.

Integrity Rules of the Relational Database Management System

Two integrity rules are required by Codd's theoretical relational model [6]: entity integrity and referential integrity.

Entity Integrity: Because a relation is a set and, by definition, sets do not include duplicate elements, no two rows in a table can be duplicates. This is enforced in the relational model by requiring every table to treat one or more of its fields as a primary key: For every record (row) of that table, values within that primary key must be non-null and must be combinatorially (i.e., each combination of fields) unique. For example (see Fig. 8), because fields PROJ-NO and YEAR of table PROJYR comprise that table's primary key, null values are never permitted within those fields and every record (row) of the table must contain values within those fields that are combinatorially unique (e.g., only one record is permitted for project D380 and year 1985).

Referential Integrity: A table may have one or more fields that are foreign keys. If so, a non-null value in a foreign key field must match

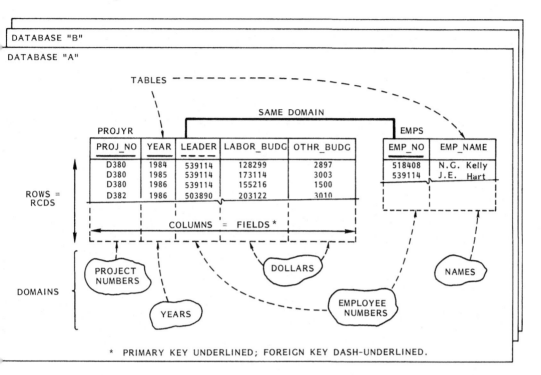

FIGURE 8 Conceptual schema of the relational DBMS.

some value within another table's primary key. For example, if T1 (A, B) is to be joined with T2 (B, C) to form T3 (A, B, C), then B is a foreign key within table T1, and non-null values of B within T1 must match some value of B within T2.

Although few, if any, relational DBMS products support these integrity rules directly, most do have provisions for supporting them indirectly. For example, many products permit tables to be created and used without primary or foreign keys but do make provisions for imposing such keys on the tables if desired. This is usually done through indexes.

Relational data are physically stored in base tables maintained by the DBMS as distinct stored files on mass storage devices. Any field of a table may be used as a search—argument for accessing specific records within the table, thereby providing enormous flexibility to the relational model. If only base table records are available at the time a search—argument is submitted, that argument would be executed as a sequential search of all base table records.

Relational DBMS response times can be improved significantly by establishing index storage structures on selected fields of each table. Because the logical database design expects a table to be accessed by its primary key and foreign keys, it follows that indexes should be established on those keys. Indexing techniques like hash, ISAM (index sequential access method), or B-tree (balanced multi-way tree) are commonly provided by relational DBMS products. When a retrieval is submitted on an indexed field, the index structure quickly points to the correct base table record so that a search of all base table records is not required.

The left-to-right ordering of fields within a composite primary key or foreign key is quite important whenever a B-tree or ISAM storage structure is being used because those indexes work in left-to-right order. When a table is accessed via such keys, the field that is the key's high-order field should be declared first, then its next-highest field, and so on. For example, if a B-tree or ISAM composite key is defined as (A + B), the statement "Retrieve C where A = xxx and B = yyy," will have a fast response because the index will use fields A and B to point to the correct base table records. However, the statement "Retrieve C where B = xxx," will have a slow response; because field A is not mentioned, the index cannot be used, and all base tables must be searched sequentially.

Manipulation of the Relational Database Management System

The relational model uses a high-level language that manipulates entire sets of data rather than individual records. The traditional set operators of union, intersection, difference, and Cartesian product, together with special operators select (or restrict), project, join, and divide, constitute the relational algebra syntax. Also, applied predicate calculus is used as the basis for relational calculus syntax [7]. The manipulative language of many products (like SQL/DS and ORACLE) are based on relational algebra, and many others (like QUEL of INGRES) are based on relational calculus. (Actually, relational DBMS products convert a relational calculus expression to equivalent relational algebra expressions for execution.)

A manipulative language is said to have a relational processing capability if transformations specified by the relational algebra operators select, project, and join can be specified without resorting to commands for iteration or recursion [6].

PROCESSING ANOMALIES AND NORMAL FORM GUIDELINES

The designer of a relational database must, in some manner, assemble tens or hundreds of data fields into a sensible set of tables. The designer should be aware that processing anomalies will be avoided if certain normal form guidelines are followed during that design process.

Processing Anomalies

Persons who write application programs that access a relational database will encounter processing anomalies when adding, changing, or deleting data within that database unless every table within that relational database has been normalized.

To illustrate (using a common example), suppose a series of suppliers stock various parts in specific quantities and each supplier is located in one city. These four fields can be stored within one table, T1 of Figure 9A, with SUPPLIER and PART designated by underlines as unique-address primary key fields. Alternately, these four fields can be stored within two tables, T2 and T3 of Figure 9B, with similarly designated keys.

Processing anomalies will occur if table T1 of Figure 9A is used, but not if tables T2 and T3 of Figure 9B are used.

T1

SUPPLIER	PART	CITY	QUAN
S1	P1	New York	300
S1	P2	New York	200
S1	P5	New York	100
S2	P1	Chicago	300
S2	P2	Chicago	400
S3	P2	Los Angeles	250
S4	P5	Dallas	150

T2

SUPPLIER	PART	QUAN
S1	P1	300
S1	P2	200
S1	P5	100
S2	P1	300
S2	P2	400
S3	P2	250
S4	P5	150

T3

SUPPLIER	CITY
S1	New York
S2	Chicago
S3	Los Angeles
S4	Dallas

a. Alternate One   b. Alternate Two

FIGURE 9   Alternate ways of storing the same data.

Update Anomalies: Suppose SUPPLIER S1 relocates from New York to
Baltimore.   If table T1 is used, the program either must (*a*) find every
existing row for SUPPLIER S1 and change its CITY value from New York to
Baltimore, or (*b*) ignore existing rows for SUPPLIER S1 and show its new
CITY value of Baltimore only for rows that are newly added to table T1.
Both alternatives are unattractive.   But if tables T2 and T3 are used, the
program simply finds SUPPLIER S1 in table T3 and changes its CITY value
from New York to Baltimore.

Insertion Anomalies: Suppose the program must simply allow the user
to enter the fact that new Supplier S5 is located in Miami.   If table T1 is
used, a primary key constraint will be encountered, in that a row cannot
be inserted within T1 unless unique non-null values exist both for SUPPLIER
and PART.   Either the primary key constraints imposed on table T1 must be
removed, or the new supplier cannot be added to the database until they
stock at least one part.   Both alternatives are unattractive.   But if tables
T2 and T3 are used, Supplier S5 can immediately be added to table T3.

Deletion Anomalies: Suppose SUPPLIER S3 ships all 250 units of PART
P2 and is temporarily out of stock.   If table T1 is used, the last row for
that Supplier would be deleted, thereby losing the fact that SUPPLIER S3
is located in Los Angeles.   But if tables T2 and T3 are used, the last row
can be removed from table T2 while retaining the row for SUPPLIER S3 within table T3.

In this case, it is clearly preferable to use tables T2 and T3 as the
database rather than table T1.   But how is a database designer to proceed
in *all* cases?   Is it necessary for the designer to desk check anticipated
updates to all tables of the database in order to anticipate such processing
anomalies?   A major advantage of the relational model, as opposed to the
hierarchical or network model, is that a set of guidelines can be applied to
candidate tables of the proposed database in order to determine whether or
not processing anomalies will be encountered when data are subsequently
added to, changed within, or deleted from that table.   Those guidelines
are called normal form guidelines.

Normal Form Guidelines

Since 1971, computer scientists have postulated circumstances that cause processing anomalies and then stated quidelines for avoiding those circumstances. Such quidelines are first normal form (1NF, [3]), second normal form (2NF, [8]), third normal form (3NF, [8]), Boyce/Codd normal form (BCNF, [9]), fourth normal form (4NF, [10]), and fifth normal form (5NF, [11]).

First Normal Form

First normal form (1NF) means that every attribute (data field) within a relation (table) is atomic, or nondecomposable. For example, if the designer intends the field SAL-HIST to contain a value like 510 20OCT85, where 510 is a salary and 20OCT85 is the effective date of that salary, then that field is not atomic. Instead, the designer should use two fields—SALARY, and SAL-DATE—because the values 510 and 20OCT85 within those fields would be nondecomposable.

Because 1NF restricts the relational model to simple atomic domains, the model can be represented in storage by two-dimensional (n-ary) tables. If nonsimple domains were permitted, a more complicated data structure would be necessary [3]. The practical effect to the designer is that relational DBMS products require tables to be at least in 1NF, whereas higher normal forms are used to avoid processing anomalies.

Second Normal Form

Y is functionally dependent on X if the value of X determines the value of Y, diagramed as X→Y. A 1NF table is in 2NF if every nonkey field of the table is functionally dependent on the complete primary key. Table $\underline{A}$, $\underline{B}$, $\underline{C}$, D, E)—underlines denote fields in the primary key—is in 2NF if a value of D and a value of E is determined by a value of A + B + C.

The illustration used earlier when discussing processing anomalies (Fig. 9) was an example of decomposition to satisfy 2NF.

Third Normal Form

A 2NF table is in 3NF if it has no transitive dependencies. Table T3 ($\underline{A}$, B, C) is not 3NF if A determines B and B determines C, diagramed as A→B, B→C, because the value of C transitions from A through B to C. To avoid processing anomalies, table T3 is decomposed into T3a ($\underline{A}$, B) and T3b ($\underline{B}$, C). All instances of (A + B + C) can always be determined by joining T3a and T3b on common values of B.

For example, table T4 ($\underline{Student}$, Building, Fee) is not 3NF because Student→Building, and Building→Fee. To satisfy the 3NF quideline, T4 is decomposed into T4a ($\underline{Student}$, Building) and T4b ($\underline{Building}$, Fee), both of which satisfy the 3NF guideline. The Fee paid by a given Student can easily be determined by joining tables T4a and T4b on the common attribute (domain) of Building.

Boyce—Codd Normal Form

A 2NF (sic) table is in BCNF if every determinant (a single or composite attribute that determines the value of some other attribute) is a candidate key. Most authorities regard BCNF as a revised definition of 3NF—stronger than the original 3NF guideline because it handles those instances where a table possesses two or more composite and overlapping candidate keys.

Suppose a student in a major has one faculty advisor, (Student-No + Major) → Advisor-Name, and each student has a full name, Student-No → Student-Name. If that information is held in table T5 (Student No, Major, Student-Name, Advisor-Name), T5 satisfies the 3NF guideline given above because it has no transitive dependencies. However, table T5 is not BCNF because determinant Student-No is not the candidate key (i.e., Student-Name is not fully dependent on the complete key of Student-No + Major). To satisfy BCNF and avoid processing anomalies, Table T5 is decomposed into T5a (Student No, Major, Advisor-Name) and T5b (Student No, Student-Name).

Fourth Normal Form

A BCNF table is in 4NF if it has no multivalued independent attributes. If A→→B (read "A multidetermines B") and A→→C, and A, B and C are maintained within table T6 (A, B, C), table T6 is not 4NF because it contains multivalued, independent attributes (actually called "multivalued dependencies" by Fagin [10], whereas Kroenke's definition [1] is used here). To avoid processing anomalies, T6 is decomposed into T6a (A, B) and T6b (A, C).

For example, suppose a student takes many courses and has many hobbies; suppose that those multivalued dependencies are independent (i.e., Student-No→→Course-No, and Student-No→→Hobby); and suppose that the information is held within T7 (Student No, Course No, Hobby). Table T7 is not 4NF because it contains multivalued independent attributes. To avoid processing anomalies, T7 is decomposed into T7a (Student No, Course No) and T7b (Student No, Hobby).

To violate 4NF, the multivalued dependencies within a given table must be independent. For example, suppose a student has many test scores in many courses, i.e., Student-No →→ (Course-No + Test-Score). In such an instance, an all-key table containing those three fields *is* 4NF, e.g., T8 (Student No, Course No, Test Score).

Fifth Normal Form

A 4NF table is 5NF if it cannot be nonloss decomposed into three or more smaller tables with no loss of information. Given T9 (A, B, C), and A→→B, B→→C, and C→→A, table T9 should be decomposed into three smaller tables T9a (A, B), T9b (B, C), and T9c (C, A) because all valid combinations of A, B, and C can be obtained from joins of T9a, T9b, and T9c.

For example, suppose that a user can access many databases and can write many computer programs, and a program accesses one or more databases. If that information is held in table T10 (UserName, DBName, ProgName), T10 should probably be decomposed into T10a (UserName, DBName), T10b (UserName, ProgName), and T10c (ProgName, DBName) because all combinations of users, programs, and databases can be obtained by joins of T10a, T10b, and T10c.

Why "probably?" An important consideration in determining whether or not to decompose a table like T10 is *time*, i.e., what information occurs at the same instant in time? If table T10 is to be used, then a given User-

Name/DBName/ProgName combination must be known at the same point in time, because null values are not permitted within any field of the primary key. On the other hand, if tables T10a, T10b, and T10c are used, then a given UserName/DBName combination, UserName/ProgName combination, or ProgName/DBName combination must be known at the same time. In many instances, the latter cases will be true, not the former.

RELATIONAL DATABASE DESIGN USING NONLOSS DECOMPOSITION

Computer scientists who developed normal form guidelines postulated them in terms of decomposition. If an existing table did not meet a given guideline, that table was decomposed into two (or three, in the case of 5NF) tables that did meet the guideline. That methodology is known as nonloss decomposition. The name nonloss decomposition is derived from this fact: If table n is decomposed into tables $n1$ and $n2$ in order to satisfy some normal form guideline, the original data of table n can always be recovered by a relational join of tables $n1$ and $n2$, with no loss of information.

Nonloss decomposition works like this: Beginning with one or more tables known to be 1NF, the 2NF guideline is applied to every 1NF table, causing each either to be declared 2NF or to be decomposed into two jointly equivalent tables that now satisfy 2NF. The BCNF guideline is then applied to every 2NF table, causing each either to be declared BCNF or to be decomposed into two jointly equivalent tables that now satisfy BCNF. The 4NF guideline is then applied to every BCNF table, causing each either to be declared 4NF or to be decomposed into two jointly equivalent tables that now satisfy 4NF. The 5NF guideline is then applied to every 4NF table, causing each either to be declared 5NF or to be decomposed into three jointly equivalent tables that now satisfy 5NF. At that point, all tables of the database are fully normalized.

During this process of nonloss decomposition, "candidate keys" are confirmed as the primary key of each table, thereby satisfying the entity integrity requirement of the relational model. Foreign keys of each table are identified at the same time in order to satisfy the referential integrity requirement of the relational model.

Normal form guidelines enable the design of relational databases that will not cause update, insertion, or deletion anomalies. However, one or more candidate table must be in hand before those normal form guidelines can be applied. If no more than 20 or 30 fields are involved, the designer can intuitively assign those fields to a few tables and proceed to nonloss decompose each table. But if scores of data fields must be arranged into tables—and that situation is quite common within industry—some rational method of developing candidate tables (or some alternate approach) must be applied.

RELATIONAL DATABASE DESIGN USING LOGICAL MODELS AND NORMAL FORM GUIDELINES

Many authorities recommend these procedural steps when designing a relational database: (*a*) A logical model of the firm's data requirements is developed, using some semantic model like the E-R diagram; (*b*) candidate tables are developed from that logical model; (c) normal form guidelines are applied to every candidate table, assuring that each is fully normalized; and (d) some kind of desk checking is done to assure that all processing require-ments are satisfied; if not, the design is altered and rechecked. To illus-trate this process, consider the earlier example of Clinton Tools, Inc., (Fig. 2) and its logical model, the E-R diagram of Figure 3.

Based on that logical model, candidate tables are developed: First, a candidate table is developed from each entity set of the E-R diagram, con-sisting of all attributes of that entity set (also, the key attributes of any many-to-one relationships associated with that entity set may be added to the table). For example, from the entity sets of Figure 3, these candidate tables are developed (fields of the candidate key are underlined): from TOOLS, T1TOOLS (TOOL-NO, TOOL-DESC); from PURCH-ORDERS, T2OR-DERS (ORDER-NO, TERMS, NEED-DATE, PRODUCER-ID, SHIPPER-ID); from ORDERED-PARTS, T3ORDPARTS (TOOL-NO, QUAN, UNIT-PRICE, ORDER-NO); from COMPANIES, T4COMPANIES (CO-ID , CO-NAME, CO-ADDRESS).

Next, a candidate table is developed from each relationship of the E-R diagram, consisting of the key attributes of the relationship's entity sets, plus any attributes associated with the relationship itself. For example, from these relationships of Figure 3, these candidate tables are developed: from PRODUCED-BY, T5PRODUCEDBY (TOOL-NO, PRODUCER-ID, PART-NO); from ORDERED-ON, T6ORDEREDON (TOOL-NO, ORDER-NO). Rela-tionship HAS was covered earlier when T3ORDPARTS was developed; rela-tionships ISSUED TO and SHIPPED ON were covered earlier when T3-ORDERS was developed.

The designer now checks each candidate table, assuring that every normal form guideline is satisfied and identifying the table's primary key and any foreign keys: T1TOOLS is correct. T2ORDERS is correct, except that fields PRODUCER-ID and SHIPPER-ID are foreign keys because rela-tional joins to T4COMPANIES are expected. The candidate key of T3ORD-PARTS (TOOL-NO) is not the primary key, because QUAN and UNIT-PRICE are functionally dependent on ORDER-NO plus TOOL-NO; therefore, the primary key of T3ORDPARTS is ORDER-NO plus TOOL-NO. T4COMPANIES is correct. T5PRODUCEDBY is correct. "T6ORDEREDON" is eliminated, because it duplicates information provided by T3ORDPARTS.

The finished relational database for Clinton Tools is shown in Figure 10.

T1TOOLS

TOOL_NO	TOOL_DESC

T4COMPANIES

CO_ID	CO_NAME	CO_ADDRESS

T2ORDERS

ORDER_NO	TERMS	NEED_DATE	PRODUCER_ID	SHIPPER_ID

T5PRODUCEDBY

TOOL_NO	PRODUCER_ID	PART_NO

T3ORDPARTS

ORDER_NO	TOOL_NO	QUAN	UNIT_PRICE

FIGURE 10   Relational database for Clinton Tools, Inc.

Using this methodology, the relational database should be desk checked to assure that all requirements of the logical model have been satisfied. For example, some requirements of Clinton Tool's E-R diagram (Fig. 3) are desk checked as follows, using the syntax of QUEL [12] (note that the first two inquiries will cause a set of records to be returned, whereas the third will cause one record to be returned):

- A tool's part number
  by producer:

  range of pb is T5producedby
  range of c is T4companies
  retrieve (pb.part-no, c.co-
     name, c.co-address)
  where pb.tool-no = 'P18-103'
     and pb.producer-id = c.co-
     id

- A tool's many orders:

  range of op is T3ordparts
  retrieve (op.order-no)
     where op.tool-no = 'P18-103'

- An order's one producer:

  range of o is T2orders
  retrieve (c.co-name, c.co-
     address)
  where o.order-no = '561' and
     o.producer-id = c.co-id

RELATIONAL DATABASE DESIGN USING RIGOROUS DEPENDENCY DIAGRAM AND ASSOCIATED DEPENDENCY LIST

A more direct methodology can be used to design a relational database [13]. In this methodology, a logical/physical model of the firm's data requirements is developed as a rigorous dependency diagram (RDD) with an associated dependency list (DL). Because fully normalized tables can be recognized by inspection on an RDD, including each table's primary key and foreign keys, the RDD serves both as a logical and physical model of data. When development of the RDD is complete, normalized tables are composed from it and depicted on a schema drawing.

Design reviews by associates and managers can readily be conducted while the database is being designed, because the RDD and DL provide excellent documentation of all design decisions. Completed RDDs and DLs make good deliverable products, either to clients or company management.

Single-Valued and Multivalued Dependence

The RDD and its associated DL logically model real-world single-valued and multivalued dependencies between data fields. Definitions of those terms (A and B are single or composite data fields) follow:

There exists a single-valued dependence from A to B, diagramed as A→B, if, at any point in time, a value of A determines one value of B. As key field(s), every value of A must be non-null and combinatorially unique. As nonkey field(s), B may contain null or duplicate values. To illustrate single-valued dependence, "An EMP-NO employee number has one EMP-NAME name and one EMP-SPOUSE spouse's name." This is diagramed as EMP-NO → (EMP-NAME + EMP-SPOUSE).

There exists a multivalued dependence from A to B, diagramed as A↠B, if, at any point in time, a value of A determines multiple values of B. Both A and B are key fields, so every value within A and B must be non-null and combinatorially unique. To illustrate multivalued dependence, "An EMP-NO may have many SKILL-NO skills practiced at a SKILL-PROF proficiency," diagramed as EMP-NO ↠ (SKILL-NO + SKILL-PROF).

It must be recognized that the above definition of multivalued dependence is different from that commonly used to explain 4NF. In the usual explanation of 4NF, Fagin's term multivalued dependence [10] describes a 3NF table that has three or more fields, e.g., T1 (A, B, C), and a multivalued dependence between two of them (e.g., A↠B), without regard for the other fields of the table. To avoid processing anomalies, that 3NF table with "multivalued dependence" must be decomposed into two tables that now satisfy 4NF. The explanation of 4NF used earlier in this article used Kroenke's more understandable term "multivalued independent attributes" [1].

Preparing Database Design Documentation

A DL is a numbered list of statements about data fields and their dependencies. An RDD is an unambiguous depiction of those same dependencies. As each DL statement is written, its fields and dependencies are diagramed on the RDD. An RDD is never prepared without preparing a DL concurrently.

The Dependency List

A DL comprises a series of statements, each identified with a number. Every statement should be rather short, but several lines may be required for those statements where one field or set of fields determines the value(s) of a long series of additional fields.

In getting started, the designer should take advantage of the fact that all applications have a few centrally important data fields, usually, "address" fields like PROJECT-NUMBER, TEST-NUMBER, or ACCOUNT-NUMBER. Beginning with the most important such field(s), the designer documents it and all related fields whose value(s) it determines. Some of those related fields will determine the value(s) of additional fields, so those dependencies are documented in more DL statements. This process continues until the designer has documented all data requirements of the system being modeled.

Every field defined within a DL statement must be atomic or nondecomposable, so that the provisions of 1NF (defined earlier) are automatically satisfied. In wording each DL statement, the designer should

- Assign one name to each data field. Names are used that satisfy all rules of the computer software that will use the database. For clarity, the name is emphasized within DL statements by typing it in capital letters, e.g., AIRPORT-ID.
- Define each field if its assigned name is too cryptic to be understood easily (e.g., "an XMAC mean aerodynamic chord"). Although necessary, this practice can produce strange-sounding sentences in DL statements, e.g., "a PROJ project number."
- Illustrate the field's usage with examples, so that all readers will thoroughly understand what's being modeled (e.g., "a TYPE-PT code, where A = Assembly, I = Installation, D = Detail part, and S = Standard part").
- Define single-valued and multivalued dependencies between data fields. For example, "A MODEL-ID wind tunnel model has one MODEL-DESC description, and several PORT-STA scanivalve port stations."

The Rigorous Dependency Diagram

As each DL statement is written, the designer posts those field names to an RDD and diagrams single-valued and multivalued dependencies between those fields, using arrows and bubbles. *A given field must appear only once in an RDD.* Fields that have a dependency on one another should be near each other on the diagram. For cross-reference purposes, DL statement numbers are noted alongside relevant dependency arrows on the RDD.

As successive DL statements are written and diagramed on the RDD, the application's overall data requirements will become clearer to the designer. Usually, revisions to previous DL statements and to the RDD itself will become necessary.

The rigorous diagraming conventions used in preparing the RDD are presented below. A universal convention is that arrowheads are shown only at one end of a line connecting field(s), never at both ends.

Single-valued dependence, prime-keys, and targets: As shown in Figure 11A, a single-headed arrow from field(s) M to N means that M to N is a single-valued dependence, as defined previously. M is called a prime-key bubble because it (totally or partially) determines the value of N; N is called a target bubble. As will be explained, other arrows may point to a prime-key bubble. It is irrelevant as to whether or not arrows point from a target bubble.

When many fields occur within one target bubble, the RDD may be simplified by showing only one or two of those fields within the target bubble and cross-referencing the others using the relevant DL statement number (Fig. 11B).

If a prime-key bubble has several target bubbles, the RDD may be simplified by combining those target bubbles into one target bubble (Fig. 11C).

If the DL states single-valued facts in such a way that they are diagramed as A→B, B→C, A→C, that A→C dependence is an unacceptable transitive dependence [8]. To avoid processing anomalies (explained earlier in the 3NF guideline), that transitive dependence of A→C must be erased from the RDD (Fig. 11D), and the DL statement altered accordingly.

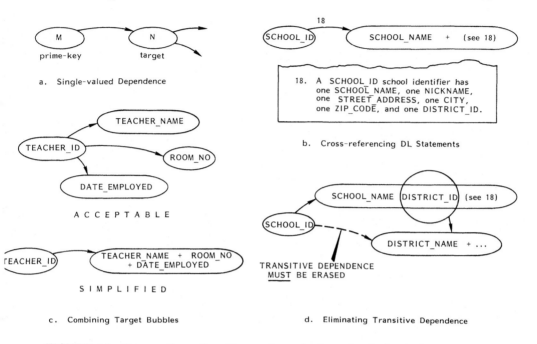

FIGURE 11   Conventions for diagraming single-valued dependence.

Multivalued Dependence, End-Keys, and Uplink Keys: As shown in Figure 12A, a double-headed arrow from field(s) Y to Z means that Y to Z is a multivalued dependence, as defined earlier.   Y of the multivalued dependence Y↠Z is called a prime-key bubble because it (totally or partially) determines the values of Z.   Z is called an end-key bubble if a double-headed arrow points to it and no arrows point from it; in such specific cases (i.e., no arrow from Z), Y↠Z is called an end-key dependence.

If a double-headed arrow points to a prime-key bubble, e.g., W↠X→ Y, bubble W is called an uplink key.   Note: *Only one double-headed arrow can point to a prime-key or uplink-key bubble.*   Uplink keys are used to show a series of keys, as in "values of W and X determine the value of Y and values of Z" (Fig. 12B).   Furthermore, an entire series of uplink-key bubbles may be linked to a prime-key bubble, as in "values of M, N, O, and P determine the value of Q" (Fig. 12C).   If desired, fields within uplink-key and prime-key bubbles may be combined into one prime-key bubble, as in Figure 12D (although it is not necessarily preferable to do so).

Isolated Bubbles: If one or more fields having a multivalued dependence from one to another are enclosed within one bubble, and if that bubble ultimately has no arrows pointing to or from it, then that bubble is called an isolated bubble.   An isolated bubble is equivalent to an end-key dependence, as shown in Figure 13.

Double Bubbles: Double bubbles are defined as two or more bubbles encompassing the same field or fields.   As stated earlier, a given field can appear only once on an RDD, and only one double-headed arrow can point to a prime-key or uplink-key bubble.   These necessary rules cause dia-

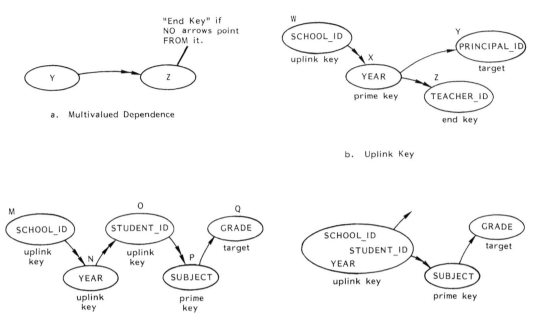

FIGURE 12 Conventions for diagraming multivalued dependence.

graming conflicts if a given field(s) is involved in more than one dependency. Conflicts are resolved by enclosing that field(s) with double bubbles.

For example, given that "W determines values of X; X-only determines the value of Y and the values of Z," a double bubble around X specifies that two sets of dependence linkages involve fields X, as shown in Figure 14A. Or, if A→B and B→C (Fig. 14B), a double bubble around B would show that field(s) B is both a target of A and a prime key of C (although single-headed arrows pointing to and from B are perfectly acceptable).

Domain Flags: As shown in Figure 15, if differently named fields share the same domain (defined earlier), the name of that domain is specified alongside a domain flag at the bottom of the RDD. That domain flag is then placed within the RDD alongside each field name that shares the domain.

FIGURE 13 Isolated bubble is equivalent to an end-key dependence.

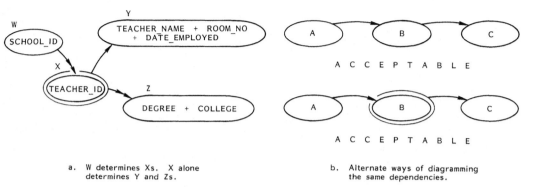

a. W determines Xs. X alone determines Y and Zs.

b. Alternate ways of diagramming the same dependencies.

FIGURE 14 Double bubbles show several dependencies through the same field(s): (A) W determines Xs. X alone determines Y and Zs. (B) Alternate ways of diagraming the same dependencies.

Composing Tables From a Completed RDD

The rigorous diagraming conventions used when preparing an RDD enable fully normalized tables to be directly composed from a completed RDD [13]. This will be demonstrated by composing tables from the illustrative RDD of Figure 16. (Note that in practice, tables are not composed from an RDD until it has been made "practicable." That procedure cannot be explained, however, without first explaining how to compose normalized tables from an RDD.)

Single-Valued Dependence Composed into Normalized Tables: A single-valued dependence is defined as a single-headed arrow connecting a prime-key bubble to a target bubble. Fields within bubbles linked to a single-valued dependence are composed into one table.

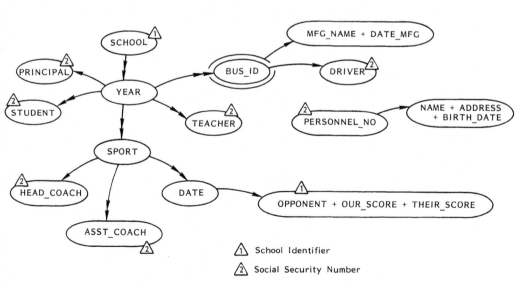

FIGURE 15 Domain flags denote that differently names fields share the domains of (1) School identifier, and (2) Social Security number.

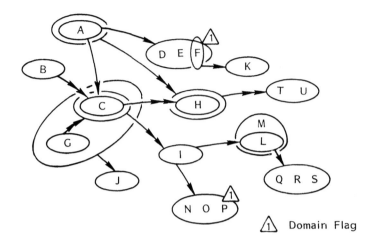

FIGURE 16   Illustrative RDD from which normalized tables are to be composed.

Field(s) within any/all uplink key bubbles of that dependence, plus field(s) within the prime key bubble of that dependence, become the primary key of that table.   A solid underline is drawn under the primary key's fields.

Fields within the target bubble of that single-valued dependence, plus all other target bubbles linked to that prime-key bubble, become the remaining fields of the table.   Field(s) from a target bubble become a foreign key if that field (a) was also enclosed within some uplink key, prime key, or end-key bubble on the RDD or (b) had a domain flag alongside it.   A dashed underline is drawn under a foreign key's fields.

These procedures are illustrated in Figure 17.   As each single-valued dependence is composed into a table, it is crossed-off on the RDD as "worked," e.g., ⊣⊢→.

End-Key Dependence Composed into Normalized Tables: An end-key dependence is defined as a double-headed arrow from a prime-key bubble to an end-key bubble (end-key because a double-headed arrow points to it and no arrows point from it).   Fields within all bubbles linked to an end-key dependence are composed into one all-primary-key table.   That is, fields within any/all uplink key bubbles of that dependence, plus fields within the prime key bubble, plus fields within the end-key bubble become the primary key of one table.   Note that each end-key dependence must be composed into a separate table.

These procedures are illustrated in Figure 18.   As each end-key dependence is composed into a table, it is crossed off on the RDD as "worked," e.g., ⊣⊢→⤜ .

Isolated Bubbles Composed into Normalized Tables: An isolated bubble is defined as a bubble having no arrows pointing either to or from it. Fields within an isolated bubble are composed into one all-primary-key table, as shown in Figure 19.   When finished, the bubble itself is crossed off as "worked."

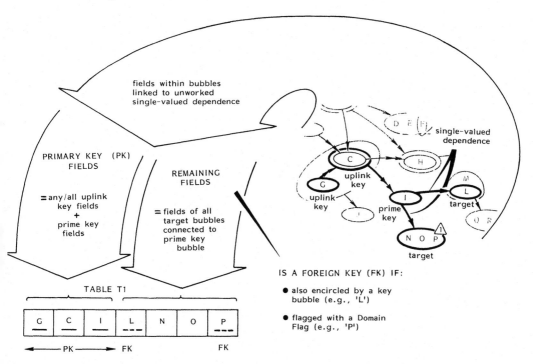

FIGURE 17 Composing a normalized table from a single-valued dependence.

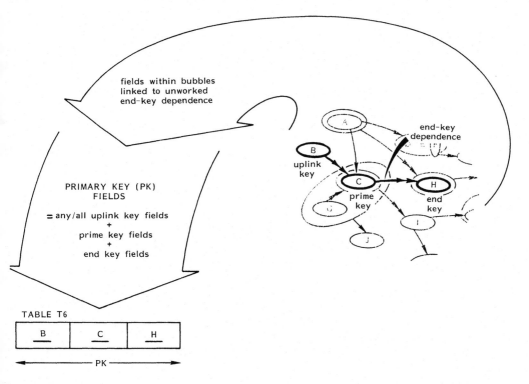

FIGURE 18 Composing a normalized table from an end-key dependence.

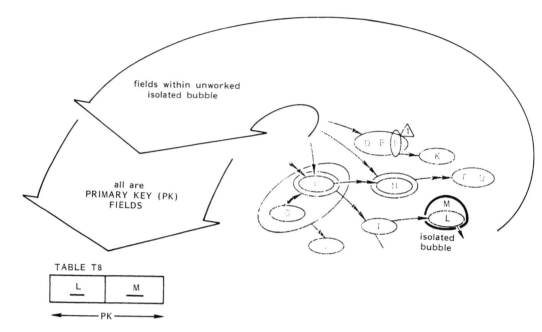

fields within unworked
isolated bubble

all are
PRIMARY KEY (PK)
FIELDS

isolated
bubble

TABLE T8

L	M

◄────── PK ──────►

FIGURE 19   Composing normalized tables from an isolated bubble.

Overnormalization: A word of caution is in order: If data will routinely be added to, changed within, or deleted from tables of the database,
full normalization is necessary in order to avoid processing anomalies.

However, if data are periodically bulk loaded into the tables and thereafter used only in response to some query (i.e., retrieves only), full
normalization is not a good idea.   Instead, response times will be significantly improved if the dependency diagram is used to compose tables in
unnormalized (but at least 1NF) formats that maximize single-table operations
and minimize multitable joins.

Making the RDD Practicable

If a table's primary key is too wide (measured in bytes), unnecessary redundance will increase storage requirements and degrade disk access times.   To
avoid this, the interlinked set of RDD key bubbles that comprise the too-
long primary key is broken by inserting a surrogate key, causing two tables
to be composed rather than one.   The surrogate key will become a foreign
key of the first table and a primary key (or a portion thereof) of the
second table.   That is, suppose the linked dependence $(A+B) \twoheadrightarrow C \twoheadrightarrow D \rightarrow (E+F+G)$ that composes to T1 ($\underline{A}$, $\underline{B}$, $\underline{C}$, $\underline{D}$, E, F, G) would have too long a
primary key.   To resolve this a $S\overline{U}ROG1$ surrogate key is inserted into the
chain as a target of C and an uplink key of D, as shown in Figure 20.
This causes two tables to be composed, both of which have fewer fields
within the primary key.   PK-width guidelines are specific to particular RDB
software and hardware products.

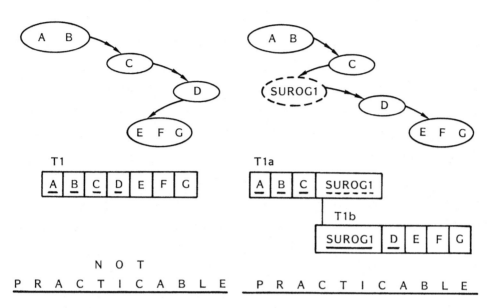

FIGURE 20 Surrogate keys added to original RDD (if necessary) to make a practicable RDD.

Preparing Final Tables and Conceptual Schema

Suppose that the RDD of Figure 16 is not practicable because the dependence linkage A↠H↠(T+U) would compose into a table with too many bytes within the primary key. To resolve that, a SUROG1 surrogate is inserted into that chain, making A↠H→SUROG1, and SUROG1↠(T+U). The now practicable RDD is shown in Figure 21A.

Once a practicable RDD has been prepared from the original RDD (both are valuable documentation and should be saved), the final set of normalized tables is composed from the practicable RDD using the procedures described above. When all single-valued dependences, all end-key dependences, and all isolated bubbles on the practicable RDD have been marked as "worked" on the RDD, all required tables will have been composed.

Each table is then assigned to a database. Because relational operations between tables are easier if those tables are within the same database, associated tables should be assigned to one database. The complete set of tables is arranged on a conceptual schema drawing, with each table's primary key and foreign keys shown with a solid underline and a dashed underline, respectively. The tables should be arranged on the drawing so as to facilitate drawing lines between fields that share the same domain. To illustrate these conventions, all tables composed from the practicable RDD of Figure 21A are shown on the schema drawing of Figure 21B.

Relational Database for Clinton Tools, Inc.

An RDD and DL comprise a nonambiguous logical and physical model of data. This means that physical issues (e.g., too many relational joins—excessive fields in the primary key) can be considered at the same time that logical requirements are being modeled. It is a fact that any organization's data

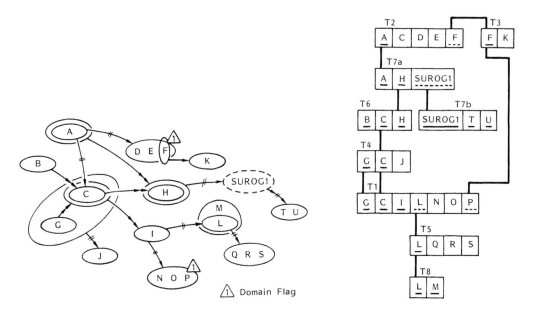

a. Practicable RDD (From Fig. 16)

b. Normalized Tables

FIGURE 21 Practicable RDD, and normalized tables on a schema drawing.

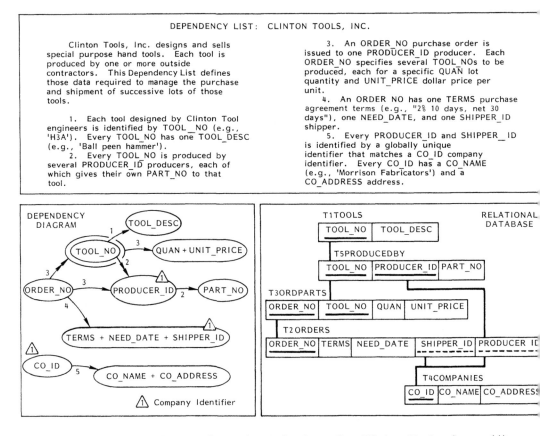

DEPENDENCY LIST: CLINTON TOOLS, INC.

Clinton Tools, Inc. designs and sells special purpose hand tools. Each tool is produced by one or more outside contractors. This Dependency List defines those data required to manage the purchase and shipment of successive lots of those tools.

1. Each tool designed by Clinton Tool engineers is identified by TOOL _NO (e.g., 'H3A'). Every TOOL_NO has one TOOL_DESC (e.g., 'Ball peen hammer').
2. Every TOOL_NO is produced by several PRODUCER_ID producers, each of which gives their own PART_NO to that tool.

3. An ORDER_NO purchase order is issued to one PRODUCER_ID producer. Each ORDER_NO specifies several TOOL_NOs to be produced, each for a specific QUAN lot quantity and UNIT_PRICE dollar price per unit.
4. An ORDER NO has one TERMS purchase agreement terms (e.g., "2% 10 days, net 30 days"), one NEED_DATE, and one SHIPPER_ID shipper.
5. Every PRODUCER_ID and SHIPPER_ ID is identified by a globally unique identifier that matches a CO_ID company identifier. Every CO_ID has a CO_NAME (e.g., 'Morrison Fabricators') and a CO_ADDRESS address.

FIGURE 22 DL, RDD, and relational database for Clinton Tools, Inc. (1) Company identifier.

requirements can always be modeled in different ways (e.g., "A part is made from one material," or "A material can be used by many parts"). Using an RDD and DL, the designer can logically model portions of the data one way or another while simultaneously deciding which alternative results in the best-performing physical database.

Although the DL, RDD, and schema drawing are working documents used to design a relational database, they also completely document a relational database and all premises underlying its design. To illustrate this, consider again the example of Clinton Tools, Inc. In Figure 22, the data requirements of Clinton Tools (given earlier in Fig. 2) are stated on a DL and diagramed on an RDD. After determining that the RDD is practicable, normalized tables are composed from it and arranged on a schema drawing. Primary and foreign key fields that share the same domain are connected by lines, so that users of the database can perceive implied linkages built into the database by the designer.

REFERENCES

1. D. M. Kroenke, *Database Processing: Fundamentals, Design, Implementation*, 2nd ed., Science Research Assoc., Inc., Chicago, IL, 1983, pp. 169–398; 491–496.

2. J. P. Fry and E. H. Sibley, "Evolution of Database Management Systems," *ACM Comput. Surv.*, *8*(1) (March 1976).

3. E. F. Codd, "A Relational Model of Data for Large Shared Databanks," *Commun. ACM*, *13*(6) (June 1970).

4. P. P. Chen, "The Entity-Relationship Model: Toward A Unified View of Data," *ACM Trans. Database Syst.*, *1*(1) (March 1976).

5. J. D. Ullman, *Principles of Database Systems*, 2nd ed., Computer Science Press, Rockville, MD, 1982, pp.11–35.

6. E. F. Codd, "Relational Database: A Practical Foundation for Productivity," The 1981 Turing Award Lecture, *Comm. ACM 25*(2) (February 1982).

7. C. J. Date, *An Introduction to Database Systems*, 3rd ed., Addison-Wesley, Reading, MA, 1981, pp. 3–93; 203–265.

8. E. F. Codd, "Further Normalization of the Database Relational Model," in *Courant Computer Science Symposia*, Vol. 6, Database Systems. Prentice-Hall, Englewood Cliffs, NJ, 1971.

9. E. F. Codd, "Recent Investigations into Relational Database Systems," in *Information Processing 74, Proceedings IFIP Congress*, Vol. 5, North-Holland, Amsterdam, August 1974.

10. R. Fagin, "Multivalued Dependencies and a New Normal Form for Relational Databases," *ACM Trans. Database Syst.*, *2*(3) (September 1977).

11. R. Fagin, "Normal Forms and Relational Database Operators," in *Proceedings of the ACM-SIGMOD International Conference on Management of Data*, ACM, Boston, MA, May 30–June 1, New York, 1979.

12. M. R. Stonebraker, E. Wong, and P. Krebs, "The Design and Implementation of INGRES," *ACM Trans. Database Syst.*, *1*(3) (September 1976).

13. H. C. Smith, "Database Design: Composing Fully Normalized Tables from a Rigorous Dependency Diagram," *Commun. ACM*, *28*(8) (August 1985).

HENRY C. SMITH

DECISION SUPPORT SYSTEMS:
DEVELOPMENT AND TRENDS

INTRODUCTION

The development of the decision support system (DSS) is perhaps the most significant achievement of the research efforts in the fields of decision science and computer technology. The DSS that aims to support the decision maker in a complex problem-solving environment represents a radical departure in the application of the computer and information to the decision-making process in organizations. The origin of the systems is considered to have begun in the early 1970s with contributions from Scott Morton [1], who developed the "management decision system," in 1971, and Gerrity [2], who designed a system to support "portfolio management" in the same year. These early systems evolved from the two main areas of research: (a) the theoretical studies on organizational decision making done at the Carnegie Institute of Technology at Pittsburgh during the late 1950s and early 1960s and (b) the technical work on interactive computer systems mainly carried out at MIT in the late 1960s, which made possible a literal dialogue between the system and the user [3].

The recent literature on management science (MS), management information system (MIS), and computer science including artificial intelligence (AI) reports significant contributions, highlighting the benefits and virtues of the DSS. It is claimed that instead of producing lengthy periodic reports on ongoing problems, as is being done by the MIS, the DSS emphasizes direct support to the decision-making processes of the decision makers/ managers.

The support provided by the DSS entails the use of a computer system to access to facts or data retrieval and to provide filtering and pattern recognition ability to the data retrieved, as well as the generous computational facility to the data for comparison and projection [4]. The system permits the manager to explore, analyze, and examine complex decision problems of nonroutine nature where the judgment of the manager is vital. The system enhances the cognitive ability of managers and serves as a stimulus that improves the decision-making process and, hence, their efficiency and effectiveness [5]. Accordingly, the concept of the DSS challenges the assumption that the computer is valuable mainly for data processing and producing periodic reports or handling routine types of tasks. However, some critics consider the current interest in the DSS as merely a repetition of the enthusiastic reception given to the MIS concept a decade ago, which was followed by disenchantment. The current use of the term DSS is considered by critics as merely a "buzz word" [6]. Some have maintained that DSS is little more than a label applied to various software products in an effort to take advantage of the term's fashionability [7].

DECISION SUPPORT SYSTEMS

For there to be a full appreciation of the concept of DSS, as well as understanding of the question whether or not the DSS is merely a repetition of the MIS, it is useful to examine each individual term in the phrase decision support system and the underlying concepts.

Decision

Although DSS and MIS are both concerned with information processing within the decision-making environment in organizations, the difference between the two is that the former is typically concerned with the information-processing activity that constitutes a decision process [8]. DSS differs fundamentally from MIS in that the former is always oriented to the particular kind of decision that is categorized as unstructured (ill structured), in which there is sufficient scope of the role of computer and analytical aids as well as where the manager's judgment is essential [9]. A DSS is designed and developed to support managers in structuring the unstructured decision problems, in building models of the problem, and in specifying criteria and sets of alternatives before making a final choice. The system enables the manager to elicit preferences within the framework of the assigned structure (determination of criteria relations, alternative estimates, etc.) [10]. However, a full appreciation of the role of DSS as a supportive tool to the decision-making processes requires a clear understanding of the term decision and the underlying concept.

Forrester [11] argues that a decision involves three things. First, the creation of a concept of a desired state of affairs. What would we like the system to be? What are we striving for? What are the goals and objectives of this decision point? Second, there is the apparent state of actual condition. Our available information leads us to certain observations that we believe represent the present state of the system. The third involves the generation of the kind of action to be taken in accordance with the discrepancy between the desired and actual states. In general, the kind of action taken involves selecting the appropriate information and converting it into action that may eliminate the discrepancy between the desired and actual states. This process of conversion of information into the proposed action is decision making. The success of a decision depends primarily on what information is chosen and how conversion is executed.

What is information and how does it affect decision making? There are far too many definitions and meanings of the word information. However, only those clear statements that appear to be more relevant to the context of decision making are discussed here. George Miller [12] suggests that "information is something we need when we face a choice. Whatever amount of information is required depends on the complexity of the choice. If we face a wide range of equally likely alternatives, if anything can happen, we need more information than if we face a simple choice between only a few alternatives." Cherry [13] believes that "information aids the decision maker by narrowing his range of viable alternatives." Yovits et al. [14] state that (a) information is data of value in decision making; and (b) information gives rise to observable effects. In the opinion of Davis [15] and Johnson et al. [16], data are potential information, but when data actually are used (processed), they are called information.

Information process is viewed as the transformation of data into information. Information as the output of the information process highlights the "purpose" of information, rather than the "processing" aspect. In a general sense, the purpose of information processing is to reduce uncertainty. Information, therefore, can be viewed as data which, after transformation via the information process, reduces uncertainty related to the outcome of a particular problem, event, or activity [17]. Uncertainty exists in a choice situation when it is not possible to determine precisely the probability distribution of various states of nature. In some cases, uncertain choices may be assessed as if under risk by introducing subjective probabilities for the state of nature. Such a difference lies in the degree of knowledge of the probability distributions in the future states. Uncertainty is, therefore, that state of nature of which we have no knowledge. We reduce our uncertainty by expanding our knowledge, that is by gaining more knowledge [18]. Knowledge is gained from the processing of information. As information about a problem, an event or activity, or a system increases, uncertainty about it decreases, and so information is the negative of uncertainty [19]. According to Galbraith [20], the greater the uncertainty, the greater the amount of information that must be processed among decision makers during the execution of a task in order to achieve a given level of performance.

Thompson and Tuden [21] view the relationship between information and decision making in the organizational setting as a distinction between uncertainty (or disagreement) over organizational objectives and uncertainty over cause and effect relationship embedded in particular organizational actions. When objectives are clear and undisputed and cause and effect are certain, the decision making is pursued by computation, that is, where algorithm, formula, and decision rules could be used for defining problems and their solution. In other words, problems are of routine nature, repetitive and structured so that decision rules can be predefined for them. Maximizing modes of decision making, such as operations research (OR) and other analytical techniques, are useful in solving problems. They can be easily delegated to the computer. Organizations established MIS to produce information to support solving this category of decision problems.

Decision problems with clear objectives but uncertain cause−effect relationships tend to be unstructured, nonroutine, and complex, involving many more variables with intricate relationships. Such problems require the decision maker to explore, analyze, and dig for facts to look into the relationship among the variables involved. Nevertheless, tracing the cause-effect relationship that links decisions to actions may be a difficult task. Such decision problems defy standard mathematical tools, such as OR, and no decision rules can be applied in their case. Therefore, these cannot be delegated to the computer [22].

Informational demand of such decision problems exceeds the information-processing capacity of the individual decision maker, resulting in the breakdown of his cognitive process. As a result, the decision maker acts rationally only within the boundaries of his perception of the problem, and these boundaries generally have been found to be quite narrow when compared to the scope of complexity of such problems [23].

This perspective in the administrative decision process emphasizes that the decision tools should allow the decision maker to examine the key issues of the problem under investigation and define and select information easily that can reduce uncertainty about the cause−effect relationship, thereby improving his boundaries of perception of the problem. The DSS makes it

possible for the decision maker to retrieve information from its data base
according to the nature and complexity of the problem, as well as his own
perception, so that he is able to integrate computer output (objectivity)
with his own judgment (subjectivity), which is necessary for producing
meaningful information that reduces uncertainty of causation [24].

Support

The computer system of a DSS is conceived of as a tool to support the
decision maker within the decision-making process. The system provides
support in the form of extending the cognitive ability of the decision maker.
It permits him to replicate the model of the problem under investigation,
to analyze the problem by examining its different parts (variables) and,
finally, to examine various alternatives in order to find the one with the
highest expected return. This kind of support is extremely valuable in
finding quick and pragmatic solutions to a wide range of problems that
currently defy effective solution.

The support provided by a DSS in the form of data retrieval tailored
according to the needs and scope of the problem is of great importance.
The greater size and complexity of modern organizations with denser communication networks generally bring about greater demand for and wider
uses of information. Finding relevant data in a large mass of raw data for
decision making is itself a difficult task. The data storage and retrieval
facility of the DSS permits the decision maker to access and filter data
according to the problem to be addressed, as well as to manipulate the
data retrieved in iterative and interactive mode [25].

Due to limited cognitive ability to select and categorize data for
processing, decision makers typically use a few broad categories of data
even when such broad cetegorization suppresses important information [26].
They attempt to reduce the input (data) from the environment to a manage-
able quantity by selecting and filtering. A DSS serves as a backup to the
cognitive process and provides pattern recognition ability to the data
retrieved. This kind of support is important because even for those who
follow a random process in their decision making, some pattern exists in
their categorization of data [27]. The DSS provides support in the form
of graphic summaries of reports or time—series analysis, which help the
decision maker to categorize all rich information in order to find relevant
data that sharpens or refines his understanding of the problem and that
reduces dispersion in the various probability distributions.

In modern organizations, decision problems have become highly complex,
requiring high analytical ability to evaluate problems and look for alternatives
from a myriad of data derived from internal and external sources. The DSS
supports the decision-making process by providing computational facilities
to all decision makers, who can be categorized as either high analytical
(field independent) or low analytical (field dependent) [28]. With the
support of a DSS, the decision maker is able to reduce data to simple
computation, comparison, projection, and so on, according to his own
cognitive style—intellectual and perceptual abilities [29].

The modeling facility of the DSS enables the decision maker to build
models of the real-world problem by piecing together all of its different
parts (variables). This support is significant because decision makers
usually make decisions by constructing a mental model of a problem based

on only a few parts (variables) that are foremost in their minds at the time of decision making while neglecting other variables that may also be equally important [30].

System

The third term, system, refers to both man and the machine. A basic feature of the DSS is the man—machine interface. Machine, here, refers to the computer system that incorporates a data base, a data base management system, and a modeling facility, as well as dialogue generation and management software. These features enable a DSS to work in a manner that loosely resembles the human faculties of memory and reasoning. Certain data base management systems provide the ability to retrieve information in a manner in which meaningful patterns and correlations may be discerned, and in a manner that augments the memory and reasoning power of the individual decision maker. A DSS using simulation techniques can extend the decision maker's reasoning ability. The system permits the construction of models of a business environment with which the decision maker can experiment in an interactive and exploratory mode in order to (a) project future business trends, (b) identify and select a best course of action from among several alternatives, and (c) foresee consequences of the proposed action. The decision maker controls the system and tailors data queries, display mode, and other system characteristics according to individual preferences, cognitive style, intellectual ability, and perception of the problem [31]. The computer system reflects the way the decision maker thinks and serves as stimulus to his "knowledgeable behavior" by providing support with its representation of knowledge of a problem domain— a combination of data structures and interpretation procedures [32]. The system is flexible and adaptive through ease of modification and evolves to meet the changing needs, knowledge, and situations with which an individual decision maker is confronted. The decision maker will not use the system lacking these attributes [33].

The DSS as a field is interdisciplinary in nature, drawing upon work in data base management, language processing, OR and modeling, AI, formal logic, cognitive psychology, and other disciplines [34]. The applicability of these disciplines becomes obvious from the study into the genesis and development of the DSS. Furthermore, a full appreciation of the possibilities of the support rendered by the DSS will depend on a clear understanding of the design assumptions and the methods of its construction.

DEVELOPMENT OF INFORMATION SYSTEMS

The importance of information and concern toward information processing in organizational decisiom making is certainly not new. Organizations from the earliest times have been concerned with processing of information to define goals and to guide their operations so as to bring about effective and harmonious achievements of their goals. However, until recent times, organizations were fewer in number, smaller in scale, and less complex. Their information needs were simple, and information processing for the support of decision making was of manual—mental nature. Information generally found to be useful emanates from internal sources and is handled on a word-of-mouth basis.

During the last 25 years, the role of organizational information and the formalized use and processing of information have expanded at a phenomenal rate. The reasons for such expansion are (a) the rapid growth in size and complexity of organizations and their environment, (b) proliferation of staff groups within large organizations, (c) improvements in planning and control techniques, and (d) increasing use of technology [35]. As organizations have increased in size and complexity, their communication networks have become denser. As a result, communications can no longer be handled on a word-of-mouth basis. Rather, comprehensive formal arrangements have become necessary to process vast amounts of information for effective communication. At the same time, proliferation of staff groups in large organizations has led to departmentalization and specialization. This has resulted in more people participating in the decision-making process which, in turn, has accelerated the demand for information. In the changing competitive and complex environment, there is a growing concern in organizations to improve planning and control techniques so as to achieve greater accomplishment. Planning has become decentralized, involving more prople in the process. This, in turn, has reinforced the need to process more information in organizations.

Perhaps the greatest impact on organizations in recent years has been that of technology, which has radically transformed the production process, diversified product lines, and decentralized production and distribution operations geographically. This, in turn, has altered the structure and behavior of organizations. They are now a complex web of interrelated decisions, functions, activities, and resource flows. As a result of such complexity, organizations have required matching sophistication in methods of decision making. Two issues have become preeminently important: first, precise control and speedy flow of data for better decision to improve productivity, efficiency, and effectiveness; and second, a reduction of operating costs. In modern business organizations, decision making is a continuing struggle for increased productivity, creating more and more economic value per unit of human effort and invested capital, including that spent on technology. The continued and mounting pressure to improve productivity, efficiency, and effectiveness against the background of ever-rising costs has led the organizations to employ information technology to support the decision-making process of managers. As a result, organizations can no longer remain predominantly a human system. A present-day organization is best characterized as a man—machine system in both its material processing and information processing aspects [36].

INFORMATION SYSTEMS IN ORGANIZATIONS

The natural evolutionary advancement of information technology and its use in the organizational context has led to the development of information systems in organizations, progressing from electronic data processing (EDP), to MIS, and to the current DSS. During the early 1950s, when the first-generation digital computers such as the IBM 650 were introduced, they were used successfully to carry out certain basic accounting operations such as payroll processing, record keeping, and the production of summary reports for managers. These computer activities known as EDP were large-scale "paper-pushing" operations. The focus was primarily on automating clerical and routine work. Managers were concerned mainly with the output of the

activities. Obviously, these early efforts did not aim at directly supporting the decision-making process of managers [37].

Further developments in the digital computer systems expanded the
scope of their applications in organizational information activities. In the
late 1950s, the second-generation computers, such as the IBM 1401, became
available, designed primarily for business applications. These computers
were capable of handling a large volume of data input and information output. They were fitted with high-speed printers capable of producing large
quantities of printed information, facilitating the production of standardized
reports and documents. Organizations began to use one or more of the
second-generation computers to produce massive quantities of information.
As a result, it became possible to focus on a new level of the information
needs of organizations. The new focus elevated the EDP to the MIS [38].

According to Voich et al. [39], in the mid-1960s, the third-generation
computers, such as the IBM 360, were introduced and quickly became the
nucleus of MIS. In addition to being considerably larger and faster than
earlier machines, these computers provided a time-sharing capability, enabling simultaneous sharing of time on a single computer by different users,
usually from remote locations. Whereas the second-generation computers
permitted processing of information in batch mode one at a time, the third-
generation computers enabled organizations to process greater volumes of
information more or less simultaneously and continuously on a variety of
functions for staff groups and to other managers in the organization in
order to facilitate the performance of management functions.

LIMITATIONS OF INFORMATION SYSTEMS

After computers were installed in organizations for managerial use, rumbles
of dissatisfaction began to be heard. There was some critism regarding
viability of services provided by such information systems, which focused
on the types of information produced, the cost of information processing,
and the management of the information systems. The major criticism was
that MIS had commonly failed to provide information useful to support the
decision-making process of managers with respect to unstructured, complex
problems that defy standard decision techniques for solution. In his classic
article, Ackoff [40] drew attention to the lack of payoff from information
systems and pointed out what were, in his opinion, inappropriate design
assimptions. According to Argyris [41], a recurring theme in the literature
of management science is that the MIS was disappointing in so far as it
commonly had failed to meet expectations. Keen and Wagner [42] have
observed that EDP/MIS, OR/MS, and other analytical disciplines needed to
bridge the gap between their specialized world and that of the managers.

The limitations of MIS are attributed to the MIS professionals who did
not pay attention to the needs, attitudes, and cognitive styles of decision
makers and to the question of how best to support them in the context of
important decisions, many of which are unstructured (ill structured). The
critical element in unstructured decisions is the decision maker (in contrast
to the structured decisions) whose judgment is essential in defining data
requirements and in formulating strategy for decisions. To make the information system meaningful, it is necessary for the designers of information
systems to consider more carefully the way decision makers acquire and
use information [43].

Many MIS designers failed to take into account the cognitive styles while designing the information systems obviously because they lacked an understanding of the subject and human information processing behavior. From evidence accumulated in the course of more than 20 years of research at different centers, Witkin et al. [44] have reported that all individuals have characteristic modes of functioning that reflect throughout their perceptual and intellectual activities in a highly consistent and pervasive way. These modes of functioning are called cognitive styles.

COGNITIVE STYLES

To assure the success of MIS, the focus on cognitive styles of decision makers is of unquestionable significance. In their empirical study, Churchman and Schainblatt [45] concluded that individuals will simply ignore information that is presented in a format incompatible with their own style. Doktor and Hamilton [46] have examined the effects of cognitive styles on the acceptance of MS recommendations. They have concluded that the differences in acceptance rate were not only due to differences in cognitive style but also to differences in the subject population. Each individual is unique and focuses on personalized abilities and strategies. While addressing the issue in MIS design, Mason and Mitroff [47] observed that "what is information for one type of decision maker will definitely not be information for another. Thus, as designers of MIS, our job is not to get (or force) all types to conform to one but give each type the kind of information he is psychologically attuned to and will use most effectively." Huysman [48] has investigated the impact of cognitive style differences between management scientists and managers on the managerial implementation of recommendations. He distinguished between analytics, involving a planned, model-based quantitative approach, and heuristics, involving intuition and search for analogies and feedback. Schroeder and others [49] have characterized individuals as abstract versus concrete types, where abstract-type individuals are able to handle and integrate more information cues than concrete type and have an advantage in complex and novel problem solutions. While developing the measure of cognitive style, Witkin and associates [50] distinguished between field-independent and field-dependent subjects on the basis of their ability to differentiate an object from its context. The cognitive style, as envisaged in their measurement, refers to a self-consistent way of functioning that an individual exhibits across perceptual and intellectual activities. They have observed that "at one extreme is the tendency for experience to be global; the organization of field as a whole dictates the way in which its parts are experienced. At the other extreme, the tendency is for experience to be delineated and structured; parts of a field are experienced as discrete and the field as a whole is structured." Hence, according to their assessment, subjects can be classified as having a propensity to be either high analytic (field independent) or low analytic (field dependent).

COGNITIVE STYLE MODELS

A broad generalization on the impact of cognitive styles based on the findings of this limited number of experimental studies is, however, difficult to
derive. Nevertheless, the findings of these studies support the differences
in cognitive styles and hypothesize in theoretical models, which are discussed
next. These models are approached psychologically and physiologically,
which provide an insight into the human thinking process and problem-
solving behavior.

Thinking—Feeling Approach

Carl Jung's [51] model of cognitive style provides a psychological basis of
the human information processing system (HIPS). The model identifies two
dimensions of HIPS, which seem to be directly related to right and left
brain activity:

   1. Perception (gathering data and information) is acheived by either
      sensing (S) or intuition (N).
   2. Judgment (processing information) is achieved by either thinking
      (T) or feeling (F).

Pairing a mode of perception with a mode of judgment yields four basic
human information processing styles:

   ST: Sensation/thinking
   NT: Intuition/thinking
   SF: Sensation/feeling
   NF: Intuition/feeling

The four HIPS styles are arranged in sequence from left to right, in
terms of brain hemisphere activities; and each type depicts a different
decision-making process. Individuals differ according to these psychological
traits and may adopt various ways of thinking in solving different problems.
Physiologically, individuals are categorized on the basis of left and right
hemispheres of the brain. An understanding of the left and right hemispheres indicates the distinctive processing characteristics of the two
hemispheres. Whereas the left hemisphere is the logical and sequential
processor, the right hemisphere processes nonlogically and simultaneously.
Whereas the left hemisphere is casual and analytical in its perception and
judgment of a situation, the right is holistic. The left hemisphere has a
structured processing orientation, whereas the right has a nonstructured
outlook. These skills complement each other to provide an integral processing style for individuals that develop their abilities to exercise the
range of right and left brain skills [52].

McKenney and Keen Model

McKenney and Keen [53] proposed a model of cognitive behavior based on
the dual premise that modes of thought develop through training and
experience and that these modes can be classified along two dimensions:
(*a*) information gathering and (*b*) information evaluation. Information

INFORMATION GATHERING

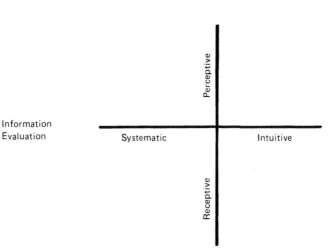

FIGURE 1   Model of cognitive style (McKenney and Keen [53]).

gathering refers to the perceptual processes by which the mind organizes
the diffuse verbal and visual stimuli it encounters.   Essentially information
gathering involves rejecting some of the data encountered and summarizing
and categorizing the rest.   The two polar modes of information gathering
are perceptive and receptive.   Perceptive individuals tend to generalize
about the environment.   They recognize forms and relationships.   Receptive
individuals tend to build images of the environment from the details and
exact attributes of data.

Information evaluation refers to the activities of design and choices in
problem solving.   Not only do individuals differ in their methods of gathering data but also in their methods and sequences of analyzing data.   On
the basis of this difference, individuals range from systematic to intuitive
thinkers.   Systematic individuals tend to approach a problem by structuring
it in terms of a method which, if followed through, leads to a likely solution.
Intuitive or heuristic individuals prefer trial and error.   They rely on
unverbalized, informal cues and are more sensitive to common-sense solutions [54] (Fig. 1).

RATIONAL VIEW

The designers of MIS have been concerned traditionally with the rational
approach to decision making in organizations [55].   This approach emphasizes that the decision makers must have access to all information pertaining
to a decision problem.   It tends to favor a mode of thinking based on the
left hemisphere of the brain.   The decision maker is viewed as an ideal-
seeking individual, technically competent, explicit, and consistent in his
assessments.   His approach to decision making is determined by economic
factors, where an analytic definition of the variables involved in the
decisions is needed together with a precise, objective criterion for the

choice of the course of action with the greatest expected value. The decision maker is a rational individual who makes a decision on the basis of [56]

1. A known set of relevant alternatives with corresponding outcomes
2. An established rule or set of relationships that produces a preferred ordering of alternatives
3. Maximizing the preferences or utilities

The rational concept of administrative decision making is one of the earliest and dominates activities in organizations. the concept has emerged from microeconomics in which emphasis is placed on information support for entrepreneurial or managerial decision making at the extremum with holistic choice problems. It is highly normative, is based on theorems, and focuses on the logic of optimal choice. The ideal it promotes is the complete and explicit knowledge of cause and effect relationships with rationality at its center. This concept of rationality has played a major role in the development and refinement of analytic methods of decisions such as OR, systems analysis, planning program—budgeting system (PPBS), and cost-benefit analysis. MS has concentrated its efforts on developing models of decision making aiming at optimization—the goal of the rational viewpoint [57].

BEHAVIORISTIC VIEW

The rational concept in administrative decision making invoked sharp criticism from the "behavioristic school" of March—Cyert—Simon as being unrealistic. Simon [58] made an in-depth analysis of the rational approach and demolished the concept of the "rational man" that endows the decision maker with perfect knowledge, no cognitive limitations, and adherence to the logic of optimal choice. Simon's main argument is that it is impractical to generate all of the relevant alternatives necessary for a rational decision. Cognitive limitations prohibit human beings from selecting and assimilating information pertaining to the variables of all possible alternatives. As a result, a decision maker cannot always select alternatives that may lead to optimal goal achievement, the ideal of rationality. Therefore, rationality falls short of its goal. Newell and Simon [59] have presented a model of human beings as decision makers that explains how finite cognitive capabilities result in constrained rationality.

HUMAN INFORMATION PROCESSING SYSTEM

Newell and Simon [59] have suggested that the thinking process of human beings in the decision-making activity can best be explained in the same way as we describe information processing in a computer. This means that the visible behavior of the thinking person can be explained by abstracting internal nonobservable processes in a model of symbol processing. This model, however, does not pay attention to sensory and motor skills, perceptions, learning, or motivation personality variables as emphasized by other behavioristic models. The model of HIPS became the central framework of subsequent studies and theory building in decision science. Apparently, the reasons were that (*a*) this model better represents the decisions of present-day organizations facing moderately difficult and complex problems of symbolic nature, and (*b*) the model is embedded in the best concept of information processing. It provides an analytic approach to the cognitive processes.

According to the model proposed by Newell and Simon [59], the major subsystems of the HIPS, which tell us how the human mind processes information, consist of the following (Fig. 2, HIPS):

- The perceptual subsystem, comprising receptors and buffer memories
- The cognitive processor
- The internal memory, comprising the short-term memory (STM) and the long-term memory (LTM)
- The motor subsystem

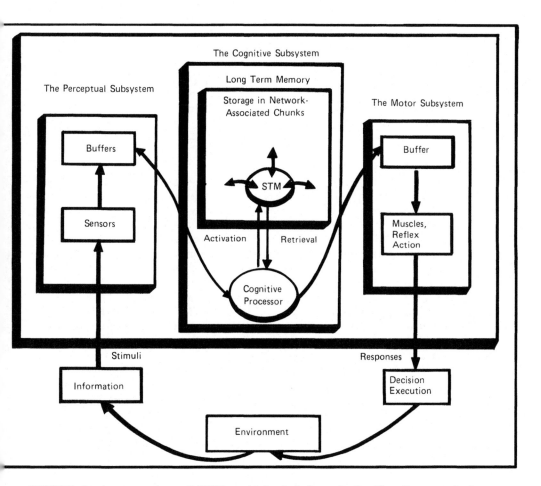

FIGURE 2 An overview of HIPS. (Adapted from Ref. 60. By permission of the copyright owner: John Wiley & Sons, Inc., New York)

The Perceptual Subsystem

The perceptual subsystem consists of receptors and buffer memories.
Receptors are sensors such as eyes and ears and serve as input devices
that receive stimuli from the outside world and transmit to buffer memories.
The incoming stimuli are temporarily stored in buffer memories awaiting
transfer by the cognitive processor to the STM for processing. The perceptual subsystem has an access time on the order of 100 milliseconds.

The Cognitive Processor

The cognitive processor, which works in "recognize—act" cycles analogous
to the "fetch—execute" cycle of computers, forms the basic quantum of
cognitive processing. It scans and filters the percepts (stimuli) stored in
buffer memories and encodes in symbols for transferring to the STM. The
process of selecting percepts from the sensory buffer memories and transferring to the STM (working memory) is paying attention. The cognitive
processor, like the central processing unit (CPU) of the computer, cycles
periodically as it fetches data (symbols or sensory referrants) from buffer
memories and transfers them to the STM. It is estimated that each cognitive processing cycle takes approximately 70 milliseconds [60].

After the symbols are transformed into information through processing
by the STM, the cognitive processor transfers information to other buffer
memories and then to the motor subsystem for execution. In simple tasks
the cognitive processor simply transfers information from the sensory inputs
to the motor subsystem for execution. Habitual tasks that require no deep
thinking fall into this category.

Short-Term Memory

The STM, permanently accessible to the cognitive processor, acts like the
arithmetic logic unit (ALU) of the computer. It processes very few symbols
at a time, perhaps one or two, and can store only a few symbols due to its
very small capacity. According to Miller's [61] experiment, only five to
seven symbols can be stored at a time. On the other hand, senses that
receive input from the environment constantly store a huge amount of incoming sensory referrants (percepts) in buffer memories awaiting transfer by
the cognitive processor to the STM for processing.

Limited capacity of the STM for storing symbols sets the limit for
parallel-processing capability. Symbols in the STM decay quickly and need
a rehearsal process. This accounts for individual differences in rates of
the problem-solving process. A more reliable STM might permit a problem
solver to work faster.

Processing in the STM is serial, executing one elementary process at
a time. But the rapid switch from one task to another makes it appear to
be parallel processing. The STM works in association with the LTM.
Associativity is achieved through comparing and evaluating symbols already
stroed in the LTM. The STM is conceptualized by many as only a small
portion of the LTM, which is activated at any point in time by the symbols
from the perceptual subsystem.

Long-Term Memory

The LTM stores symbols in network structures, each consisting of a set of symbols connected by a relationship. As new symbols representing new knowledge are stored in the LTM, they are designated by symbols from the potential vocabulary. Through learning, the stimuli or patterns of stimuli received by the input channels of senses designated by particular symbols become recognizable. The recognizable stimulus patterns are called "chunks." The LTM consists of a cluster of chunks. A chunk is a collection of symbols associated with a set or pattern of stimuli chunks that are hierarchically organized collections of still smaller chunks. In this conception, the LTM is a vast network of chunks. Learning and remembering occur as linkages between chunks are established and revised.

The LTM that holds an individual's mass of accumulated knowledge, related in some kind of complex network, sets no limit to the amount of symbols to be stored in it. The time required to read a symbol to recall from the LTM is on the order of a few hundred milliseconds. The writing time is much longer. It takes an average of 7 seconds per chunk to assure that the fact is properly linked into the LTM. In practice, it takes some 50–100 seconds to memorize a 10-digit number and some one tenth of a second to recall it.

Human Information Processing System Activity

The HIPS activity consists of executing sequences of elementary information processes performed by the cognitive processor, such as "compare and replace." Problem solving results in the integration of the sequences. The cognitive processor consists of three parts: the elementary processes, the STM (working memory), and the interpreter-containing mechanisms to activate a program stored in the memory and to provide integration. The program is the set of rules that describes the sequence of elementary processes. The program organization has three important aspects:

1. Conceptualizing a model of a problem in symbolic terms, which is referred to as a problem space.
2. Structuring of a problem space like a program consisting of patterns of elements or symbols, each representing a state or way that the task situation may occur. Each configuration of symbols is a state of the problem.
3. Linking between elements/symbols corresponding to the operations that can change one state to another. Operations are logical moves that cause one state to change to another.

The Problem Space

Problem solving implies that a problem exists and has been recognized. A process takes place to determine a problem space (modeling a problem) within the limits set by the task environment and the basic structure of the HIPS. The problem space is the abstraction of the task environment as conceived by the HIPS in order to work on it. The problem-solving activity takes place by a search in the problem space to determine the problem program, that is, method(s) to be used in problem solving. The program is structured as a production program, that is, a program where the next step is taken if some condition is satisfied. Each of the conditional statements is the production. The condition for evocation of the production is the sequence of appropriate symbols in the STM [62].

In this model, problem space is configured as a network of knowledge state nodes. Reasoning is a serach through the network until a desired knowledge state is reached, mostly moving incrementally from one state to the next. The search involves backup that is return to the old knowledge state. A knowledge state is typically in sizes of a few hundred sumbols at most, and more generally a few dozen. The problem solver remains within a given problem space for a time on the order of at least tens of minutes [63].

An important feature of the problem space is its structure. Structure is equivalent to redundancy. By virtue of redundancy, information present in one part of the space becomes predictive, at least heuristically, of properties in another part of the space [64].

Motor Subsystem

The cognitive processor sends instructions to the motor subsystem after recognize—act cycles—scanning and searching memories. The motor subsystem then initiates actions of muscles and their internal system, resulting in the observable actions.

Synthesis of the Human Information Processing System

The basic features of HIPS can be summarized as follows:

1. HIPS processes symbols that are sensory referrants or a combination of other symbols.
2. HIPS utilizes two levels of internal memory, STM and LTM, for information processing. The STM is fast but has a very small capacity (five to seven symbols) and needs rehearsal to retain symbols. The ability to recall in the STM tends to decline as storage load is increased. STM features serial processing of symbols with elementary processing times on the order of about 70 milliseconds.
3. The LTM has unlimited capacity but takes a relatively long period of time in storing information (about 7 seconds). However, it can be accessed by the STM at a much faster rate in each 70-millisecond cycle. This asymmetry is of great importance in understanding how the human mind works. Sophisticated performance at a rapid rate is not uncommon among humans, but the rapid storage of new information for long-term use is very rare.
4. HIPS conceives of a problem space within the limits set by the task environment and the basic structure of the HIPS in order to work on it.

COGNITIVE LIMITATIONS OF HUMAN BEINGS

Human beings as information processors exhibit limitations due to the small capacity of STM, sequential processing of data, slow storing process of data in LTM, and reduction and simplification of the real world abstracted in the form of problem space. These cognitive limitations result in a breakdown of the decision maker's cognitive process, which occurs when the informational demand of a decision problem exceeds his information-processing capacity. As a result, decision makers cannot make a rational decision.

BOUNDED RATIONALITY

The inability of decision makers to make rational decisions owing to cognitive limitations led March and Simon [65] to the concept of bounded rationality. According to this concept, human decision makers act rationally only within the boundaries of their perception of the problem, and these boundaries generally have been found to be quite narrow when compared to the scope of complexity typifying most organizational problems. In theories of administrative decision making, it is this notion of bounded rationality that commonly serves as the basis for explaining departures from rationality (e.g., use of other than a maximizing mode)[66].

The concept of bounded rationality has led Simon [67] to suggest the strategy of "satisficing" in decision making. In a satisficing mode, the decision maker sets up a feasible aspiration level and searches for solutions until he finds one that achieves this level. As soon as a satisficing solution is found, he terminates his search and selects that alternative. Thus, satisficing implies that a decision maker will settle for a decision that will satisfice rather than optimize. The main assumptions of the theory of satisficing as given by Simon are summarized as follows:

> In the real world human beings usually do not have a choice between satisfactory and optimal solutions, because only rarely is there a method of finding the optimum. The problem solver cannot, within practicable computational limits, generate all the admissible alternatives and compare their relative merits, because there is not a way to recognize the best alternative, until all of them have been examined. We satisfice by looking for alternatives in such a way that an acceptable one is found after only moderate search.

HEURISTICS AND DECISION SUPPORT SYSTEM

Problem-solving strategy for satisficing follows a heuristics mode of decision making. Heuristics are rules of thumb, an ad hoc mode of decision making or simplification that reduces or limits search in a large problem space. Unlike algorithms, heuristics do not guarantee correct solutions at all times. Heuristics reflect bounded rationality. They are, thus, a compromise between the demands of the problem and the decision maker's cognitive capabilities and his commitments [68].

Keen and Scott Morton [69] have suggested that heuristics can be improved more cheaply and acceptably in terms of relieving the cognitive strain of the decision maker with the aid of DSS, which may enable him to manage the information overload of the problem under investigation.

Development of the Decision Support System

The major forces that have made it possible for the development of DSS to improve heuristics are [70]

- An understanding of the organizational decision problems leading to the development of taxonomies of decisions.
- Advances in hardware and software, broadening the domain of applications of the computer within the decision-making processes.

The "rational view" of decision making envisages that each decision problem requires essentially the same strategy for its solution. Simon [71] refuted this concept on the ground that problem-solving strategy adopted by a decision maker is determined by the nature of the decision problem. Because decision making is information intensive, the demand for information and its type will be determined by the nature of the decision problem and the strategy to be followed for the solution. An information system, therefore, must be designed and developed according to the characteristics of managerial functions in terms of the types of decision problems involved. This concept led Gorry and Scott Morton [72] to develop a two-dimensional taxonomy of decisions encountered in organizations, by synthesizing Anthony's [73] classification of management functions and Simon's [74] typology of organizational decisions. Their synthesis is based on the assessment that in the ideas of Anthony and Simon, there are two different ways of looking at the managerial functions within an organization. Anthony's classification is based on the purpose of management functions, whereas Simon's typology is based on the ways in which managers deal with problems that they confront.

Anthony's Classification of Managerial Functions

Anthony's [75] classification of the major decision problems that organizations regularly face consists of

1. Strategic planning, which is the process of deciding on objectives of the organization, on changes in these objectives, on the resources used to attain these objectives, and on the policies that are to govern the acquisition, use, and disposition of these resources.
2. Management control, which is the process by which managers assure that resources are obtained and used efficiently and effectively in the accomplishment of the organization's objectives.
3. Operational control, which is the process of assuring that specific tasks are carried out efficiently and effectively.

The strategic planning focuses on two major issues. First, emphasis is on the choice of objectives for the organization and on the activities as well as means acquired to achieve these objectives. As a result, a major problem in the area is predicting the future of the organization and the environment in which it will operate. Second, the strategic planning process typically involves a small number of high-level people in an organization who operate in a nonrepetitive and often very creative way. The complex nature of the planning problems and the nonroutine manner in which they are handled make it quite difficult for the decision maker to appraise their quality and predefine the decision rules [76].

In the management control area, three elements are involved: First, interpersonal interaction to ensure the use of resources efficiently and effectively in the accomplishment of the organization's objectives; second, this interaction takes place within the context of the policies and objectives developed at the strategic planning level; and third, ensuring effective and efficient performance at the operational level. The decision makers at this level are concerned with major functional areas, such as production planning and quality control [77].

Operational control differs from management control in that the former is often concerned with the specific tasks to be carried out efficiently and effectively, whereas the latter is concerned with people who are responsible for carrying out the tasks. There is much less judgment to be exercised in operational control because the tasks, goals, and resources have been carefully identified and defined as well as procedures have been carefully worked out at the management control level [78].

Although the boundaries between these three categories of organizational activities are often not clear, they are found to be useful in the analysis of information requirements to support them. One is very different from the other in terms of information requirements. The difference is not simply a matter of aggregation but of the fundamental character of the information needed by the decision makers in these areas [79].

Simon's Typology of Organizational Decisions

Simon [80] categorized organizational decisions based on the manner in which decision makers solve problems, regardless of their position in an organization. Although very little operational definition of the types of decisions as proposed by Simon has been provided, these types, which have been identified as "programmed" and "nonprogrammed," have served as the basis for developing the two-dimensional taxonomy of decisions.

Decisions are programmed to the extent that they are repetitive and routine, to the extent that a definite procedure has been worked out for handling them so that they don't have to be treated de novo each time they occur. Decisions are nonprogrammed to the extent that they are novel, unstructured, and consequential. There is no clear-cut method for handling the problem because it has not arisen before, because its precise nature and structure are elusive or complex, or because it is so important that it deserves a custom-tailored treatment [81].

Theoretically, a programmed task is one for which clear rules, potentially a computer program, can be defined, replacing the judgment of a decision maker. The precise nature and the components of the task can be clearly identified and defined. A decision task is nonprogrammed—no specific procedure can be outlined for it—it must fall back on whatever general capacity there is for an intelligent, adaptive, problem-oriented action. In other words, the task that does not yield to algorithmic solution so that it can be programmed is unstructured. The objectives, trade-offs, relevant information, and methodology for analysis of the task cannot be predetermined [82].

In their taxonomy, Gorry and Scott Morton [83] used the terms "structured" and "unstructured" for Simon's programmed and nonprogrammed terms, because these terms (introduced by them) imply less dependence on the basic character of the problem-solving activity. They added a "semistructured" category on the continuum between the structured and unstructured (ill-structured) tasks. Semistructured tasks are hard to routinize, perhaps because of the size of the problems or the computational complexity and the precision needed to solve them. The models of management science and the reports generated by the MIS are inadequate to support the decision-making process of semistructured tasks because the solution involves some judgment and subjective analysis.

A Framework for the Decision Support System

The two-dimensional taxonomy of decisions provides a framework useful to identify the decision problems and define their information needs. The taxonomy is helpful in the analysis of the decision characteristics and in assessing the purpose and relevance of information to particular types of decisions within the decision-making process. Although this taxonomy is broad and incomplete in certain respects, it is useful in delineating the role of information provided by classical MIS versus DSS in support of the organizational decision-making process. It also provides a mechanism by which an organization can check its current position with respect to information systems in general. It is, however, not a theory but a simple scheme for classifying decisions in relation to information and the support needed from the information systems.

The matrix given in Table 1, adapted from Keen and Scott Morton [22], shows the two-dimensional taxonomy of decisions and the information system support needed for decision making.

Decisions and Information Requirements

The usefulness of the taxonomy in categorizing decisions and their information needs is clear from the following [84].

Structured Operational Control

The decision tasks are usually routine and repetive and require little analysis or judgment. The use of information is communicative in nature. It is needed for ensuring that the operations of the organization are carried out as planned, which include coordination of efforts of those individuals who are involved in group task, regulation of resources, and work flow. Information serves both as a process activator by communicating requirements to each group and as a feedback mechanism by providing a basis upon which to determine that requirements are received, understood, and carried out.

Information requirements are well defined, narrow in scope, and detailed. They are obtained from internal sources and are required very frequently because the decision process is of an ongoing nature. Output from MIS is useful to support the decision tasks.

Semistructured Operational Control

Decision tasks in this category cannot be automated because of their inability to be quantified in any useful way. This is due to their complex nature, involving large numbers of variables that may change at any point in time. The complexity of decision tasks is made up of a variety of autonomous

TABLE 1   A Framework for Information Systems[a]

Topology of Decisions	Managerial Activity			
	Operational Control	Management Control	Strategic Planning	Information System/ Support Needed
Structured	Routine and repetitive tasks	Budgetary allocation, cost-benefit analysis	Factory location, departments, branch locations	Clerical/MIS/MS
Semistructured	Scheduling of operations, work flow, decision analysis	Forecasting, service promotions, resource control, estimate tracking, quantity of personnel	Environmental analysis, resource allocation, centralization, decentralization, technology assessment	DSS
Unstructured	Group behavior, determining needs, quality of personnel, personnel training and development, advertisement	Hiring staff, motivation, payoffs in social and political returns, revising subgoals and plans standard performance	Planning, goals and objectives, research and development	Human intuition

[a]Adapted from Keen and Scott Morton [22].

elements, integrated in an elaborate network of relations constantly interacting with its own environment. Information may be needed for planning
appropriate means--ends relations; designing conditions of work performance,
by organizing relations between means and ends; and modifying developed
relationships in response to the feedback obtained by monitoring the behavior
of conceptual relations in operational practices in an organization.

    Computer support in terms of information retrieval, analytical models,
or data manipulation may be valuable, but managers' judgment may be the
best resource for the solution of problems. Therefore, the DSS may be
useful for providing support to this category of decision tasks.

Unstructured Operational Control

The stochastic nature of decision problems in this category makes it difficult
for the decision maker to explore, analyze, and determine the factors crucial
in their solution. Decisions are affected by uncontrolled external and
seasonal factors. They rarely yield to algorithmic solution and may require
guesswork or intuitive judgment for their solutions rather than fixed rules.

    Information is the means of determining resource-allocation patterns
and policies in light of external factors and changes in environment. The
decision maker might need information about such uncontrolled factors as
users apprehension, concerning products, consumers' likes and dislikes,
changing needs. He might need information that improves his judgment.

Structured Management Control

Decision tasks are mostly related with increasing the rate of productivity
and better resource allocations. Information is required for analysis of past
operations and performance on a periodic, rather than on a continuous basis.
It is used to measure and evaluate operational performance and management
control in relation to an organization's goals, plans, budgets, and standards
of performance. This type of information may result in corrective action
and replanning.

    Decision techniques of MS such as linear programming or simulation
modeling are useful for producing information as a raw material to support
the decision-making process. The manager's subjective judgment or
preferences are not critical. Much of the information needed is obtained
through such studies as cost-benefit analysis.

Semistructured Management Control

The decision tasks possess characteristics that require both the defining of
decision rules and the subjective judgment of the manager. Information is
needed to reduce uncertainity encountered in the control and coordination
of human and physical variables along with organizational objectives. The
manager is concerned with the basic triad made up of people, organization,
and the environment, managing the conflicts and the relationship among
these three. Information must be useful for design, communication, and
analytical purposes within the search for causes of problems, which usually
means, in effect, searching for negative relations. The DSS is useful
because the manager is able to explore the implications of various courses
of action using information produced by the system's computer after analyzing various aspects of the problem and then applying his own judgment.

Unstructured Management Control

In general, decisions involving personnel, such as hiring managers or motivation of staff, fall into this category. The problems of the personnel department require the use of intuitive judgment as to which person to hire or which experienced applicant would be suitable for a job. The manager spells out the responsibilities and ensures that the people who are assigned the responsibility are capable of carrying it out. The information regarding the person to be hired and the job to be assigned will support the judgment of the decision maker, which will be the basis for his decision.

Structured Strategic Planning

The decisions are dominated by economic considerations with emphasis on commitment of resources to achieve the organization's objectives. The overall purpose is to achieve the optimum balance between demand for products and services and the organization's capacity to produce them efficiently. The decisions are reflected in revised objectives, forecasts, budgets estimates, work statements and schedules, quality specifications, as well as resource acquisitions.

The MIS is useful in providing information for planning in areas of demand analysis, resources capacity analysis, and budgeting. Although subjective judgment plays a decisive role, the report from output of cost-benefit analysis, demand analysis, and resource capacity analysis are vital to support the decision-making processes.

Semistructured Strategic Planning

Planning decisions of this category are concerned with questions of organizational structure, commensurate with goals and objectives, such as centralization versus decentralization, evaluation of long-term investment, and the introduction of new products and services. The decisions are concerned with forecasting. How will the future treat the organization? What must it do now to meet challenges ahead? How can it best exploit changes that are to its advantage? Obviously, such planning decisions cannot be handed over exclusively to the computer, as the judgment of the decision maker will be critical. The DSS is useful as it permits modeling the changes likely to affect the organization's future structure, objectives, plans, and procedures, and the decision maker is able to integrate his own judgment with the output of DSS for planning and problem solving.

Unstructured Strategic Planning

Decision tasks in this category are concerned mostly with redefining the future of the organization—its goals and objectives—in relation to its environment. In the turbulent and threatening environment in which organizations operate, it is difficult to define clearly boundary conditions that influence various alternative courses of action that the organization can pursue based on its capacity to perform. There is a great deal more uncertainty in an actual planning process and in setting organizational goals and priorities, as these involve a large number of variables and are influenced by exogenous factors. The assumptions are made concerning constraints, and decision criteria are reviewed and evaluated to develop feasible product and service objectives. Emphasis is placed on research and development. It is difficult to predefine decision rules in such cases so that they cannot be handed over to the computer. The intuitive judgment of the decision maker plays a major role in resolving the issues involved in the planning process.

DECISION-MAKING PROCESS AND THE DECISION SUPPORT SYSTEM

Research efforts directed toward the use of the computer as a tool to support the decision-making process in the realm of semi- and unstructured (ill-structured) decisions where objectivity (computer output) and subjectivity (manager's judgment) are critical, led the development of DSS—a man—machine system. For a full appreciation of the use of DSS as a supportive tool in the decision process, it is necessary to understand which aspects of information processing are performed by the machine (computer) element of the DSS and which remain with the system's human element. These questions can be answered to the extent that we understand the aspects of the decision-making process.

Simon [85] has presented a model of the decision-making process, which can be broken down into three phases:

Intelligence: The first phase in the decision process is intelligence, which means searching the environment for conditions calling for decisions. At this phase, raw data are collected, processed, and analyzed for cues that may help to identify the problem.

Design: The second phase, design, involves the process of inventing, developing, and analyzing possible courses of action. At this phase, an attempt is made to understand the problem, to generate potential solutions, and to test them for "reasonableness."

Choice: The third phase, choice, involves selecting a course of action from those available. This also includes implementation after the choice is made. Although the choice phase in Simon's model includes implementation, many believe that implementation is significant enough to be shown separately [86].

The decision process is a complex activity. Intelligence activity precedes design, and design activity precedes choice. There is a cycle of activity. The design phase, for example, may call for new intelligence activities. Problems at any given level generate subproblems that, in turn, have their intelligence, design, and choice phases. These phases can be clearly identified as the organizational decision process unfolds, similar to John Dewey's [87] problem-solving strategies: What is the problem? What are alternatives? Which alternative is the best?

This model is useful in delineating the role of EDP/MIS, DSS, and MS techniques, such as OR, in the decision-making process. EDP/MIS is useful for the intelligence phase in which the decision maker obtains data, processes them, examines cues from the processing of data, and identifies problems. According to Bonczek et al. [36], the present-day DSS typically exhibits some combination of information collection, problem recognition, and analysis abilities. At the very least, these are involved in the intelligence phase of the decision process, and some of these abilities may also be used during the design phase.

The information-collection ability usually manifests itself as the gathering of information from the DSS user and from some repository of information about the application area stored in the system's computer. A typical DSS helps recognize the problem (or some aspect of it) that needs to be solved. A DSS permits the user interfacing of the collected information with a model, through a modeling facility of the computer to generate some predictions, beliefs, or expectations. The DSS is always specifically oriented toward that kind of information-processing activity, which constitutes a decision process. It can contribute to all the phases of the decision-making processes [86] (see Fig. 3).

A DSS is not merely concerned with data compilation and reporting as is done in traditional MIS, nor do users serve essentially as operators directing the system, but the system provides support more in the sense that it achieves a coupling of an individual's intellectual resources with those of the machine (computer). A DSS can be categorized as corresponding loosely to the faculties of memory and reasoning. For example, certain data base management systems, providing the ability to retrieve information in such a way that meaningful patterns and correlations may be discerned,

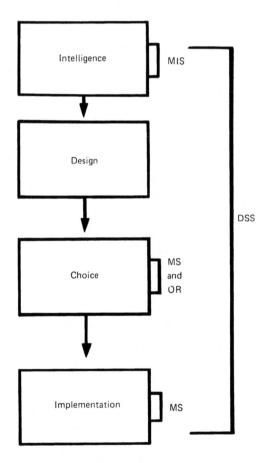

FIGURE 3 Phases of the decision-making process. (Adapted from Ref. 86, by permission of the copyright owner: Pergmon Press, Inc., New York)

augment the memory. A simulation-based system can be seen as extensions of an executive's reasoning powers. Models of business environment help an executive envision possibilities for the future, foresee consequences, and identify and select alternative solutions [88].

The basic characteristics that distinguish DSS from MIS are that a DSS should be able to reflect the way managers think, be flexible and adaptive through ease of modification, support managers in the complex process of exploration and learning, and evolve to meet changing needs, knowledge, and situations [89].

DECISION SUPPORT SYSTEMS: DEFINITIONS

At present there is a lack of a unified approach to the definition of DSS as in other developing disciplines. From an analysis of definitions of DSS offered in recent years, it will be evident that each definition represents the special interest of the author proposing it. However, Ginzberg and Stohr [90] believe that all of these definitions must reflect the central concern of the DSS field in the support and improvement of decision making in organizations.

Michael S. Scott Morton [1], who presented the earliest of the definitions and termed the system as "management decision system" defined it as "an interactive computer-based system that helps decision makers utilize data and models to solve unstructured problems."

Gorry and Scott Morton [72] defined DSS as "a system to support managerial decision makers in semistructured and unstructured decision situations." The key concepts in the definition are support and semi- and unstructured decisions. The term support conveys the notion of providing aid to the decision maker in his efforts toward solving the decision problems that are unspecified, nonrepetitive, and incapable of being automated.

Little [91] characterized DSS as a model-based set of procedures, data, and judgment to assist a manager in his decision-making tasks. The author believed that in order to be successful, such a system must be simple, robust, and easy to communicate with. The author views a DSS to be a computer-based interactive system that will serve as an extension of the user's problem-solving capabilities.

Instead of suggesting any definition, Alter [92], has identified characteristics that distinguish DSS from traditional EDP/MIS in five dimensions:

1. *Use:* Active (DSS) versus passive (EDP)
2. *User:* Line, staff, and management (DSS) versus clerk (EDP)
3. *Goal:* Overall effectiveness (DSS) versus past (EDP)
4. *Time horizon:* Present and future (DSS) versus past (EDP)
5. *Objective:* Flexibility (DSS) versus consistency (EDP)

Moore and Chang [93] defined DSS as an "extensive system capable of supporting ad hoc data analysis and decision modeling, oriented towards future planning and used at irregular unplanned intervals."

Bonczek et al. [36] characterized DSS as a computer-based interactive system consisting of three interacting components, which form a genetic framework of the DSS constitution. These components are (*a*) a language system (LS)—a mechanism to provide communication between the user and other components of the DSS; (b) a knowledge system (KS)—the repository of problem domain knowledge embodied in the DSS, either as data or as procedures; and (c) a problem-processing system (PPS)—the link between the other two components, containing one or more of the general problem-manipulation capabilities required for decision making.

Keen [94] viewed DSS as a tool for providing access to information and analytic models directly to decision makers in order to support decision tasks that blend the use of both intuitive judgment and analytical methods. This challenges the assumption that computers are mainly valuable for data processing operations or the creation of standardized information systems.

Ginzberg and Stohr [95] characterized DSS as a computer-based information system used to support decision-making activities in situations where it is not possible or desirable to have an automated system perform the entire decision process.

Thierauf [96] described DSS as the system that allows the decision maker to combine his or her judgment with computer output in a human—machine interface for producing meaningful information to support the decision-making process. The system aids in solving all types of problems (structured, semistructured, and unstructured) and uses query capabilities to obtain information by request. As deemed appropriate, it utilizes mathematical and statistical models, as well as data base elements, for solving problems under study.

Keen and Morton [97] believed that in a DSS, (a) the impact is on decisions in which there is sufficient structure for computer and analytical aid to be of value but where a manager's judgment is essential; (b) the payoff is in extending the range and capability of the manager's decision process to help improve effectiveness; and (c) the relevance for the mamager is the creation of a supportive tool, which does not attempt to automate the decision process, predefine objectives, or impose solutions.

From these definitions, it is obvious that different approaches have been employed to define DSS. As a result, difference in emphasis on characteristics that help to define the system is inevitable. Gorry and Scott Morton emphasized the problem type and support aspects of the system. Little stressed the functional and interface aspects. Moore and Chang focused on the use pattern and task domain. Bonczek et al. defined the DSS from a structural point of view that serves as a unique approach for devising a generative mechanism for DSS theory. Keen emphasized evolutionary characteristics of the DSS that must assure feedback. Ginzberg and Stohr stressed the support aspect of DSS. Thierauf presented a comprehensive description of DSS covering the elements that distinguish DSS from MIS. Keen and Scott Morton highlighted the support aspect of the DSS and its orientation toward the individual decision maker and decision process.

Despite the differences of approach in defining the DSS, it is, however, explicit that the existence of an a priori relationship between information systems and effective decision process has been recognized. The perspective that the authors have attempted to seek is concerned with a broader appreciation of the structure of decision tasks and the need for supporting and improving the decision process. Focus is on cognitive style and unstructured decisions for which relevant data and the solution process are difficult to define in advance and where judgment of the decision maker is critical. As it is implied from the definitions, a DSS aims at providing an optimal integration of decision tasks, people, and technology. A close fit between the user and the computerized system is regarded as particularly important. The kind of support expected from a DSS is suitable for those decision makers who follow the heuristic mode of decision making and who should be able to explore scenarios from the task environment to generate cues and test solutions. The system permits the decision maker to shift between levels of details and generality. It helps to develop a new insight into the problems that a decision maker faces in complex situations. It is flexible, adaptive, and accommodates improved insight into the problems. The system is deemed to be user driven and allows the decision maker to tailor data queries, display modes, and other system characteristics in tune with his cognitive style and task environment.

HARDWARE AND SOFTWARE OF THE DECISION SUPPORT SYSTEM

Recent advances in computer hardware, the CPU, increased memory size and speed, distributed data base facility, the data base, and data base management system (DBMS) together provide building blocks for DSS from the decision-making perspective ranging from structured to more sophisticated heuristics. Developments in graphics, voice recognition, and voice synthesis have made possible user interfaces, enabling DSS to be more adaptable.

Software in DSS is used for managing the data base and tnterpreting user queries. The query facility typically permits ad hoc (nonroutine, nonstructured) queries for retrieval and, in some cases, enables ad hoc analysis. The DSS differs from MIS in relation to the management of software in the following respects [98].

   1.   DSS incorporates models into the information system software.
   2.   It provides useful information for high-level management to support comparatively unstructured decisions.
   3.   It furnishes the system users with powerful yet easy-to-use languages for problem solving.

CLASSIFICATION OF THE DECISION SUPPORT SYSTEM

DSS has been categorized variously by different authors on the basis of the characteristics of software used. Alter [99] has divided DSS into seven types on the basis of functions performed by the software. Of these, three types are data oriented, and their software provides facility for performing data retrieval and data analysis. The remaining four types are model oriented. Their software contains simulation capability and an optimization or computation facility for generating an answer to a problem. An example of the former type is IRIS, a transaction-based DSS for human resource management, which utilizes a high-level interactive query language and data base techniques [100]. An example of a model-oriented DSS is hierachical integration of production planning and scheduling (HIPPS), which combines optimization and heuristics capabilities [101].

Donovan and Madrick [102] divided DSS into institutional and ad hoc categories on the basis of the nature of the decision situations that they are designed to support. The institutional DSS addresses recurring

decisions. For example, the portfolio management system (PMS) has been
in use at several large banks to support investment management [2]. This
caterogy of DSS may be developed and refined over a number of years,
along with the growing understanding of the problems. Ad hoc DSS deals
with specific problems that are neither anticipated nor recurring. It uses
general-purpose software for information retrieval, data analysis, and
modeling, which can quickly be customized for a specific application [95].
An example is NEEMIS (New England Energy Management Information System),
which was developed to deal with the energy crisis of 1973–1974 [103].
When the crisis was over, the system was converted to support such new
problems arising out of economic factors as fluctuations in the price of
energy, conservation of fuel, analysis of impacts of tariffs, and decontrol
of natural gas and oil prices.

Sprague [104] has identified three categories of DSS based on each of
the levels of hardware and software. These are specific DSS, DSS generators, and DSS tools. Specific DSS contains hardware and software that
allow a decision maker to deal with specific sets of related problems. An
example is the Police-Beat Allocation System used by the San Jose Police
Department in California. The system allows a police officer to display a
map outline and call up data by geographical zones, showing police calls
for service activity levels, service time, and so on. The DSS generator is
a "package" of related hardware and software that provides a set of
capabilities to build a specific DSS quickly and easily. For example,
Geodata Analysis and Display System (GADS) is a DSS generator that has
been used over a number of years to create a series of specific DSS, for
a variety of nonprogrammers. The DSS generators have evolutionary
characteristics that come from special-purpose languages. In fact, most of
the software systems that might be used as DSS generators are evolving
from enhanced planning languages or modeling languages with report
generation and graphic display capabilities. DSS generators facilitate the
generation of specific DSS. They use a special-purpose language, a query
language, color graphics, and supporting software. GADS is an example
of this type as well. It is written in FORTRAN and uses an experimental
graphic subroutine package as the primary dialogue handling software and
a laboratory-enhanced roster scan color monitor.

Bonczek et al. [105] categorized the DSS on the basis of procedurality
and nonprocedurality of data retrieval and modeling languages. Procedural
languages require a step-by-step specification of how data are to be
retrieved or a computation is to be performed. Nonprocedural languages
require the user to specify only what is required. An intermediate level of
procedurality uses a command language that allows the user to specify the
name of a prespecified report or model. Based on these three levels of
procedurality, Bonczek et al. [105] have identified three components of
DSS: LS, KS, and PPS. A user states a problem for a DSS to solve by
using a LS. The KS holds facts about application areas that are relevant
to solving problems that may arise in the application area. The PPS, the
main component of a DSS, accepts problems represented in the form of strings
of symbols organized according to its LS syntax and acquires strings of
symbols organized according to its KS representation. Excercising its other
abilities, the PPS generates some information for presentation to a user.
Given a problem (stated with the LS) and problem–domain knowledge

(represented in the KS), the PPS software attempts to derive a solution that supports (enhances, facilitiates, or makes possible) a decision-making process.

It is obvious that there is a wide range of diversity in the software components of DSS. Ginzberg and Stohr [106] have stated that "no DSS that we know of contains all the previously discussed components, though most contain at least some of them." Several of these components can be found in EDP and MIS, as well. However, the model management system (MMS), knowledge base, inference, and control procedures are unique to DSS. Thus far, the development of DSS is distinguished by employment of more flexible and sophisticated data bases and DBMS. A unique feature of DSS is that it can be developed through an adaptive process of learning and evolution. The prototyping or adaptive design approach is, therefore, typical to the DSS [107].

STRUCTURE OF A DECISION SUPPORT SYSTEM

Sprague and Carlson [108] used a "black box" approach to explain the mechanism of the DSS. Opening the DSS black box reveals a data base, a model base, and a complex software system for linking the user to each of them. The data base and model base are interrelated. The software system has three sets of capabilities: DBMS, model base management system (MBMS), and software for managing the interface between the user and the system, which might by called dialogue generation and management system (DGMS). The three components provide a schema for the structure of a DSS (see Fig. 4).

Dialogue Subsystem

The dialogue subsystem is an extremely valuable component of the DSS, which provides capability to the use to interface with data base and permits the use of the system in an interactive and iterative mode. The DSS draws its characteristics of user friendliness and flexibility from the dialogue system in which the capabilities of the system are articulated and implemented. According to Bennet [109], a dialogue system includes the user, the terminal, and the software components. The dialogue experience is divided into the following three parts:

1. *The action language:* What the user can do in communicating with the system. It comprises such options as the availability of a regular keyboard, function keys, touch panels, joystick, voice command, and so on.
2. *The display or presentation language:* What the user sees. The display language includes such options as a character or line printer, a display screen, graphics, color, plotters, and audio output.
3. *The knowledge base:* What the user must know. The knowledge base consists of what the user needs to bring to the session with the system to use it effectively. The knowledge may be in the user's head, on a reference card or an instruction sheet, in a user's manual, or in a series of "help" commands available in the system upon request.

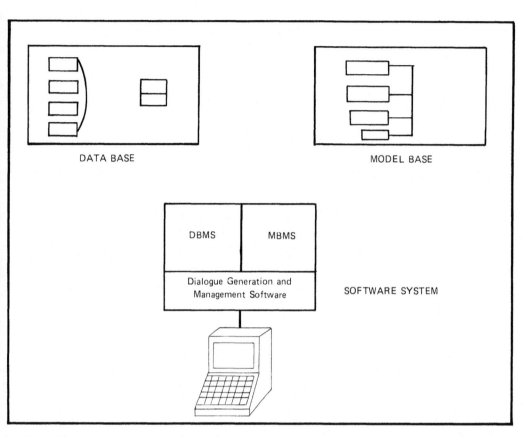

DATA BASE

MODEL BASE

DBMS

MBMS

Dialogue Generation and
Management Software

SOFTWARE SYSTEM

FIGURE 4 Components of the decision support system. (Adapted from Ref.
6. By permission of the copyright owner: Prentice-Hall, Inc., Englewood
Cliffs, New Jersey)

The dialogue system should have the following characteristics [110]:

1. Ability to handle a variety of dialogue styles, perhaps with the
   ability to shift among them at the user's choice
2. Ability to accommodate user actions with a variety of input devices
3. Ability to present data with a variety of formats and output devices
4. Ability to provide flexible support for the user's knowledge base

Dialogue Styles

Dialogue styles describe the nature of interface bewteen the system and the
user. The following dialogue styles are used in existing DSS [111].

Question—Answer Dialogue

Question—answer (Q A) dialogue may use natural language and may provide
multiple choices to produce answers. The usefulness of the Q A dialogue
is evident in case of inexperienced or infrequent users, who are unfamiliar
with the problem to be solved. However, this style is not considered to

be highly effective for sophisticated and frequent users who are irked by the necessity to proceed through the questions. Nevertheless, to accommodate both frequent and infrequent users, Q A dialogue may provide more than one mode of use, for example, a full sentence and an abbreviated mode, or it may provide default answers. The Q A dialogue leads to awkward use patterns if the user needs to modify answers to previous questions during dialogue.

Command Language

Several existing versions of DSS use a command style of dialogue that includes verb—noun pairs (e.g., PLOT SALE) with short spellings in six to eight characters for the nouns and verbs. For simple applications, a command language can easily become a programming language, thereby requiring more skill to use. It is also possible to develop a "layered" command language, which consists of simple commands for simple or frequently used functions. These can be combined with other, more complicated commands for complex infrequently used functions.

Menu Dialogue

Menu dialogue consists of a number of alternatives such as report names or computation commands. Instead of requiring the user commands, a menu dialogue utilizes a CRT terminal and permits the user to select from a menu of alternatives through a keyboard or a "picking device" such as a light pen. The user is thus able to select the type of report to be displayed by the DSS.

Menu dialogue seems to be quite effective for inexperienced or infrequent users who are familiar with the problem to be solved. In the DSS that provides a large number of functions, a menu dialogue system permits the user to structure queries in a menu according to the items to be examined.

Input—Output Form Dialogue

This dialogue provides input forms on which the user enters commands and data and output forms on which the DSS produces responses. After viewing the output form, the user can fill in another input form to continue the dialogue. This system allows asking questions in Q A style with an input form corresponding to a set of questions and an output form corresponding to a set of answers. From the user's cognitive point of view, this system is found to be even more useful if there is correspondence between the input—output forms in the DSS and paper forms or thought patterns of the user. For example, an input form can correspond to an existing checklist or it can be arranged to group items that a decision maker is likely to think about together.

Input-in-Context-of-Output Dialogue

This style utilizes a combination of input—output form in which user inputs are always given in the context of the previous output from the DSS. The DSS represents an output, for example, a table, graph, or a list, within which the user may fill in or select inputs that will either modify the current output or result in a different output. For instance, a skeletal report giving sample or standard data can be used as an input form if the user can write new data names or selection criteria on the report for subsequent use as inputs to the DSS.

The Data Base and Data Base Management System

DSS and MIS both depend upon the use and management of data. However, in DSS, the purpose for which data are used is different from that of MIS. In MIS, data are used for the support of repetitive and routine tasks for which decision rules can easily be defined and simple algorithms can be used. In DSS, data are used to support the manager by permitting him to pose ad hoc, exploratory questions and to factor the problem in order to see its parts and their interactions so that the manager may be able to combine his judgment about the problem (subjectivity) with the computer's output (objectivity) in order to select the best possible alternative.

Characteristics of Data and Data Base

For a DSS, the data and DBMS are important requirements. Data represent certain parts of the real or conceptual problem domain—in other words, a problem space in symbolic form. A data base is a collection of data stored in a computer to be used for analysis and interpretation of the problems being investigated. The data base must have a defined structure, with the data elements properly identified and interrelated. Activities involving data collection, maintenance, access, update, and protection of data are referred to as the DBMS. In DSS, the DBMS facilitates access and manipulation of data to create an initial state and search through the problem space in order to identify the sequence of operations or activities that will lead to a desired goal.

Data for a DSS must come from internal as well as external sources. For strategic planning, data are collected from external sources on matters relating to economic conditions, technological developments, competitive reactions, and on such other environmental factors that assume paramount importance in planning and goal setting. Data captured are broad rather than detailed, and they must be able to provide an approximate indication of future trends rather than exact statements of the past or present. For managerial control, data are collected from both external and internal sources. In case of operational control, the sources of data are largely within the organization as the data concern the activities that are carried out by operating personnel when performing day-to-day operations [112].

DSS also differs in the process of data capture and extraction from the wider sets of data sources. The system requires that the extraction process and DBMS be flexible enough to allow rapid additions and alterations in response to unanticipated user requirements. Sprague and Carlson [108] have identified a partial set of capabilities required for the data base:

1. Ability to capture a variety of data sources through a data capture and extraction process
2. Ability to add and delete sources quickly and easily
3. Ability to portray a logical data structure in user terms so that the user understands what is available and can specify needed additions and alterations

4. Ability to handle personal and unofficial data so that the user can experiment with alternatives based on personal judgment
5. Ability to manage this wide variety of data with a full range of data management functions

DATA BASE REQUIREMENTS FOR THE DECISION SUPPORT SYSTEM

It is difficult to present a comprehensive account of data base requirements for a DSS. A basic reason for this is a limited understanding of the theories of decision making, bounded rationality versus optimization. However, Sprague and Carlson [113] have given a broad assessment of data base requirements for the DSS on the basis of the studies of existing systems and on the theoretical basis of their development:

Data Reduction: Studies indicate that data use in DSS involves reduction/abstraction of data from large amounts of data. This consists of subsetting, combination, and aggregation of records and fields in a data base.

Support for memories: A DSS may require data base support for four kinds of memorizing aids—work space for intermediate results, libraries for saving work spaces, links (indices) among data, and triggers to remind the decision makers of the operations to be performed or the data to be used.

Varying levels of detail: Often a detailed data base is required for a DSS, allowing decision makers to examine comprehensive data instead of aggregate data.

Varying amounts of data: The amount of data to be used in a DSS may vary over time during the decision process. The amount of data may also vary according to the complexity of the problem to be resolved and the cognitive capability of the decision maker.

Multiple sources: Data for the DSS are collected from both internal and external sources. Evidently, because of emphasis on support to the decision-making process, data requirements in the DSS vary considerably according to the decision tasks being supported.

Catalog of sources: Because a DSS uses a variety of sources for comprising data and supports a part of the decision process that involves "intelligence" gathering, a catalog of data sources is a valuable aid for the data base.

Wide time frame: A DSS usually requires data from the past and data projecting the future. Therefore, several master files of the past and present data, as well as alternative master files of data projecting the future, are likely to be needed.

Varying degree of accuracy: In view of the aggregate data often used in a DSS, absolute accuracy of the data is necessary. If errors are found in a data base, they will reduce the level of confidence of the decision maker. If more than 1% error is found in the data base, the decision maker will spend his time looking for additional errors and correcting them if found rather than making decisions. Recent data should be used in DSS, especially where decisions are based on time—series data, which covers several years.

Set operations: A data base of a DSS often includes records on sets of events or set operations, as well as time—series data.

Random access: In the DSS environment, decision makers generally do not proceed through a set of data in a sequential or other predetermined order. Rather, new insights or questions based on one set of data may lead them to the desire for accessing new data that they did not expect at the onset or data that are not being currently used in terms of storage location or access keys.

Support for relationships and views: In the process of decision making in interactive and iterative mode, data stored in the data base must permit new insight by looking at data in new ways or by establishing new relationships among data stored in the DSS.

Performance: For a successful DSS, performance of the data base is measured in terms of response time. However, good response times are relative to the time frame of the decision task being resolved and the time constraints and expectations of the decision maker. The increasing popularity of the interactive DSS indicates that data base performance is likely to become an important requirement.

End user interface: Because the DSS user will tend to have low programming skills, the data base management component of the DSS should allow interfacing the system with the user at the external level rather than at the internal level. This means that users do not have to know the details of how data are stored and how operations on the data are performed.

DATA BASE MODEL FOR THE DECISION SUPPORT SYSTEM

A data base model is a method of representing organizing, storing, and handling data in a computer. Codd [114] has identified three constituents of a data base model:

1. A collection of data structures, which includes lists, tables, relations, hierarchies, and networks.
2. A collection of operations that can be applied (usually by DBMS) to the data structures. Retrieval, update, combination, and summation are some of the operations.
3. A collection of integrity rules that define the "legal" states (set of values) or changes of state (operations on values) for the data structures.

Data models are of different levels: external, conceptual, and internal. The external model is used in the application program and thus is closest to the user. The conceptual model is an integrating or a global model that encompasses several external models for different applications. The internal model describes how the conceptual model is presented in storage. The relationships between models are achieved through mapping, which describes the transformation needed to obtain one model through another. The conceptual model is most important because it makes possible the integration of the data base which, in turn, provides data for use in several specific versions of DSS. As a result, a decision maker is able to use data in them. This means that a conceptual model is appropriate for the DSS generator, and the external model is useful for specific DSS. The data models through data structures, operations, and integrity constraints influence the representations and operations of a DSS and extend the user's understanding of the memory functions of the system. A simple and consistent data model can often be a strong unifying and simplifying factor for helping users to understand a DSS [115].

DATA MODEL FEATURES

A data model is described as a set of objects. These objects can be either values or relationships among values. Generally, values are represented in a data model by "fields." Relationships are represented by collections of fields called "records" or by values that link fields. The basic features of a data model are summarized as follows [116]:

1. Data structures define fields and records allowed in the data base.
2. Operations define the allowed manipulations of these fields and records.
3. Integrity defines the constraints of the fields and records to be preserved by the operations.

TYPES OF DATA MODEL

A DSS uses one or more of the following types of data model [117].

Record model
Relational model
Hierachical model
Network model
Rule model

Record model: The record model is the oldest and most common data model, with the most varied structures and the least well-defined operations and integrity constraints. It is a set of records, and each set consists of a set of fields. If there is more than one type of record, one field usually contains a value that indicates what other fields are in the record. This sort of model is very common in DSS and uses time series data.

Relational model: The relational model limits the data structures of the record model, provides a mathematical basis for a set operations on records, and defines integrity constraints that require the operations to leave the data base in any of a variety of "consistent" states. The data structures in the relational model consist only of relations. A relation is a set of "tuples" or "records." Each relation can be thought of as a table and each row in the table is a tuple. Each column in each row is a field. The columns are often called "attributes." Another important aspect of the data structures for the relational model is that each field has a domain that defines the set of values allowed for that field. Many fields can have the same domain.

Hierarchical model: The hierarchical model contains several descendant records. For any record there may be several instances of descendents. It may be in a tree form, where records stating from a root (a base record) rise to any level in the hierarchy permitting data to be represented in a hierarchical structure.

Network model: The network model consists of sets of records and links. Links are explicit, named representations of relationships. Unlike the hierarchical model, a record can have several relationships. It also has two main structural differences from the hierarchical model. First, some fields in the hierarchical model are replaced by relationships in the network model. Second, the relationships are explicit and may be represented in more than one way.

Rule model: The rule model is seldom used in traditional information systems, but it is common in AI systems where it is known as a "production rule." The rule data model is most common in so-called knowledge-based DSS or expert system/knowledge system, where part of decision making involves drawing inferences from the manipulation of data.

SELECTING A MODEL

For the selection of an appropriate model for DSS, emphasis is not so much on the representation of the data but on the operation and integrity constraints. For a given set of data, there is a representation of data in any of the five models. The selection of a model will be based on the consideration of whether the relationships are explicit or implicit, what operations are possible given the representation of data, and what constraints are placed on the representation. A DSS may use one or more data models and may impose restrictions on the data structures, operations, and constraints in addition to those that are inherent in the models.

The choice of a data model is also influenced by such factors as the users, the decisions, and the capabilities of the DBMS. A DBMS usually supports only one data model and provides an operational system to create, maintain, and access one or more data bases that conform to the model to be used. The operations provided by the DBMS include dictionary, creation, deletion, update, query (retrieval), views, protection, sharing, recovering, and optimization. The successful application of a DBMS depends on the operations provided by it, costs involved, and the suitability of the data model [118].

DATA MANAGEMENT FACILITIES

According to Sprague and Carlson [118], data management can be performed at several levels in an organization. On the lowest level, data are highly personalized, with one individual responsible for capturing the data and entering them into the system. The data are stored for personal use only. This is called personal data management (PDM), which was typical in the early stages of DSS implementation where data files were model specific and usually small.

A specific DSS may be designed with enhanced data-retrieval capabilities that can take advantage of data already captured and stored in files or data gathered from outside the organization. Access may be provided to data files of other application systems (e.g., accounting information systems), to the organizational data bases, and to the external on-line data bases.

Accessing, aggregating, and reformatting data to fit individual models use a technique known as "data extraction." Entering data into a DSS by means of data extraction techniques is called external data management (EDM).

Data extracted from other sources may be pooled into a single data base and shared among several users. These data are managed by a DSS DBMS and may be available to both users and models by an interface language.

Data stored in the data base are normally structured and formulated into fields, records, and files. As the needs of many systems user's may not be in this form, sometimes data are also presented in the form of a free text contained in documents. Documents can also be stored in files according to the content and searched for key words or context words. Maps, pictures, diagrams, and figures are also stored in the data bases so that they are available to systems users if and when required.

MODELING AND MODEL MANAGEMENT SYSTEM

The modeling component is an important feature of a DSS, which provides the decision maker with the capability to describe and analyze existing problems as well as to generate and compare alternative solutions. In fact, it is the integration of models into the information system that moves forward the MIS to the DSS. The modeling facility of a DSS improves the cognitive capability of a decision maker. According to Ackoff [119], human beings approach the problem solution tasks by developing appropriate mental models of the problem to work on. Mintzberg [120] found that the managers collect and piece together various scraps of information until patterns begin to form a mental model of a problem. The modeling facility of the DSS enables a decision maker to replicate his mental model of the phenomenon under study, often in mathematical terms. By manipulating the model in the computer, the decision maker is able to obtain both new knowledge of the modeled phenomenon and of the model itself, without the cost, inconvenience, or danger of manipulation of the real phenomenon.

An important aspect of the modeling component of a DSS from the decision-making point of view is that it allows feedback and provides inter-action between the user and the system, permitting the user to examine cues that may help in identifying problems and in inventing, developing, and analyzing the possible courses of action. The main activities of the modeling component have been summarized as follows [121]:

    Projection
    Deduction
    Analysis
    Creation of alternatives (suggestions)
    Comparison of alternatives
    Optimization
    Simulation

These operational procedures offered by the modeling component of a DSS are possible because of the facility of on-line interactive computer terminals that permit users to insert their own assumptions into the model.

Barbosa and Herko [122] described the characteristics and uses of modeling facility as the following:

1. *Inference:*
   a. The user should be able to work in a problem-solving environment without unnecessary distractions and should not have to interrupt this process just to supply control parameters before continuing.
   b. The control parameters should be expressed in terms with which the user will be familiar. A person should be able to think about only those parameters that have a direct bearing on the problem-solving process.
2. *Control:*
   a. The user should be given a spectrum of control. If possible, the system should support manual, as well as fully automated, operation. This permits the user to select the level of algorithmic operation that seems most suitable. It also enables users to learn more easily by allowing each one to proceed at the pace desired.
   b. The control mechanism should allow the user to introduce subjective information as demanded by the problem solution process. It should not require the user to specify all constraints a priori. Direct human control of the solution process can make up for deficiencies in the algorithm and will often permit the system to utilize a simpler algorithm, frequently resulting in a smaller information burden on the user.
3. *Flexibility:* The algorithmic and manual operations should be interchangeable in the sense that the user is able to develop part of a solution via manual methods and then continue with the algorithm, or vice versa. This statement implies that the range of all operations should be contained in the domain of the operations, that is, the result of one operation can be used as input to another operation. In this way, the sequence of operations can be selected arbitrarily by the user. Both flexibility and control allow the user to construct a solution process that best suits the problem. This idea of interchangeability of operations is deceptively simple, but it has far-reaching implications. This is the manner by which flexibility and control are achieved, that is, an arbitrary solution process can be composed of a sequence of primitive subprocesses.
4. *Feedback:*
   a. The system should provide sufficient feedback so that the user is fully cognizant of the state of the solution generation process at all times. This feedback is essential for supporting human control of the process.
   b. The design process itself should make use of feedback. Valuable information can be derived from introduction of the initial system or prototype to the user. Feedback should be especially meaningful in the area of usability.

SYSTEMS REQUIREMENTS

A DSS requires a set of modeling capabilities in order to meet the following functional needs [123]:

- A model base and a set of software functions to manage it (MBMS)
- Integration of the modeling component with the dialogue component
- Integration of the modeling component with the data component

Model Base

The model base, which is analogous to a data base, is comprised of a library of models that may contain the following:

1. The variety of models available in the library: The "types of models" are defined here in terms of levels of aggregation.
   - Primitives, which are operators to perform more complex mathematical/logical operations
   - Functions, which combine primitives to perform more complex mathematical/logical operations
   - Macros, which are similar to functions but are used for nonstandard operations
   - Subroutines
   - Analysis models
   - Procedures (execution of command models)
2. The library should have the ability to maintain, catalog, and integrate:
   - Prewritten or "canned" models
   - User-built models that become permanent
   - User-built models that are temporary or ad hoc
3. The extent of the canned library varies so that in addition to most models, there will be subroutine or analysis models, as well as other levels of models. A variety of analysis modeling types (LP, regression, correlation, etc.), or modeling approaches such as simulation, Monte Carlo, and goal seeking may be included.

The strength of the model base will depend on the ability to provide support for creating and building models of all types quickly and easily. This is a collection of capabilities, known as a "model definition language," which may include the abilities to

1. Specify mathematical relationships between data variables
2. Specify mathematical relationships between model types
3. Specify data required for a model
4. Integrate canned models and user-built models into composite models

The model base should have the ability to support manipulation and operation of these models. This ability is achieved through a model manipulation language that may have the following capabilities:

1. Run and rerun models
2. Test performance—sensitivity over a range of data

3. Run a base model that may include a set of "what if" questions, and compare the output from several runs
4. Perform the goal-seeking activity
5. Store and encode permanent models to permit more efficient runs
6. Update models that are based on data in a predefined way
7. Play an active role in the analysis and decision-making process by supplying some guidance to the user
8. Support heuristic search with models that require a strong link with dialogue capabilities

Model Base Management System

As a result of the research to provide facility for both the development of models and their subsequent use for decision support in the DSS, the concept of MBMS has evolved with the following functions:

1. *Generate:* A flexible mechanism for building or generating models, perhaps through a type of model definition language.
2. *Restructure:* A method of redefining or restructuring a model in response to changes in the model situation such as a change in the basic form of the model.
3. *Update:* A procedure for updating a model in response to changes in data, for instance, a revised parameter estimate without a change in structure.
4. *Report generation inquiry:* Operation of the model to obtain the decision support desired. This may include the following alternatives:
   a. Periodic run of a well-established model
   b. Special results from an ad hoc model
   c. Use of the data analysis model
   d. Iterative rerun of a model or set of models
   e. Sequential run of a set of interrelated models according to a predefined procedure

Integration of the Model Base with Other Components

The MBMS provides the ability to integrate a model base with the dialogue base and data base directly. As a result of the direct integration of the model base with the dialogue component, a user is able to exercise direct control over the operation, manipulation, and use of models. It is this link that provides the user with the ability to interact with modeling. Integration of a model base with the data base permits users to run model segments in a variety of sequences, to change parameters, and even to change objective functions in response to intermediate results, if necessary, or to interrupt a model when required.

MODELING FACILITY IN THE DECISION SUPPORT SYSTEM AND THE GENERAL PROBLEM SOLVER

The utility of the modeling facility cannot be overemphasized. The role of models in the decision-making process can be well understood within the framework of the problem-solving model presented by Simon [124], which

is a fairly general and abstract approach to problem solving. The model
is the General Problem Solver (GPS).

Bonczek et al. [125] have succinctly described the implications of the
GPS model in relation to the modeling facility in a decision support environment. The GPS is concerned with three basic elements: states, operators,
and goals. A state is simply a situation. Operators permit a decision maker
to move from one state to another state, that is, to transform one situation
into another situation. A goal is a desired state. A problem is described
in terms of an existing initial state and a goal state. The GPS approach to
problem solving consists of selecting a series of operators that will successively move the problem from its initial state. Given any state, it is assumed
that a difference can be determined between the state and the goal state.
Operators are selected to reduce the difference between that state and the
goal state. The selection of operators will depend on the knowledge and
experience of the particular problem domain in question. Knowledge of the
task and experience provide an idea of the given and desired states and of
the kind of operators that may be relevant for transforming one state to
another. In other words, GPS is a program that permits reasoning of both
ends and means. It provides the capability of defining ends and seeking
means to attain them, and in the process of doing so, it can permit defining
new subsidiary ends, or subgoals, related to the ultimate goal. The concept
of posing a problem for solution and setting a goal leads to the creation of
subproblems, and the solution of each subproblem, in turn, becomes an
immediate goal. This implies that problem solving involves a series of
subproblems, sub-subproblems, and so on, in an organized, often hierarchical fashion.

The GPS approach can be used recursively and includes a collection of
information about the states and the formulation of models that represent
sequences of operators. States can be used in the sense of the state of
information stored in the form of data in the data base of a DSS, and
operators can be taken as modules. The modules representing subproblems
enable the decision maker to move from one information state (input of data)
to another (output) in incremental steps. The modules of a DSS enable the
decision maker to solve problems of a complex nature by factoring them into
a familiar structured elements.

CURRENT PROBLEMS IN MODELING AND DATA STRUCTURE

Modeling and data structure in the DSS currently encounter three major
problems. First, models are not easily combined. They are not developed
as modules that can be combined to form other models as the need arises.
Thus, current modeling facility does not permit flaxibility in creating models
dealing with new, unanticipated problems. Second, an established data
base structure that a model can use recursively has not yet been developed.
Data must be repeatedly collected and organized for each run of the model.
And last, it is difficult to update a model and modify it in the ways models
can be used. Sprague and Carlson [126] have identified the following
requirements for the modeling component in a DSS:

- Ability to catalog and maintain a wide range of models supporting
  all levels of management

- Ability to interrelate these models with appropriate linkage through the data base
- Ability to manage the model base with software management functions analogous to data base management functions such as a language for easy creation and modification of models, along with a mechanism for storing, cataloging, linking, and accessing models

KNOWLEDGE-BASED SYSTEMS

In the field of AI, an interdisciplinary field of computer science and cognitive psychology, early research efforts focused on generality, which was seen as a keystone of human intelligence; intelligence appeared to reside in a small collection of domain-independent problem-solving methods. Programs based on such methods displayed encouraging success [127].

However, subsequent research in the field of AI found that although the early methods were useful, they were inadequate to deal with complex real-world problems. Performance in such problems seemed to require large stores of domain-specific knowledge and process that knowledge in a more humanlike fashion than conventional methods do [128]. As a result, systems have been developed that can model human expertise of a well-defined field and offer intelligent support (not replacement) to a practitioner. These are commonly referred to as knowledge-based expert systems or knowledge systems.

Are these systems different or simply additions to the DSS arsenal? According to Basden [129], the expert system techniques are not more readily accepted among practitioners of conventional computing, but among the end users, especially those who have perhaps viewed computers as useful but believe that they cannot solve any real problems, because real problems involve a lot of judgment. Bonczek et al. [130] have claimed that "although builders of expert systems do not generally refer to their creations as decision support systems, expert systems fit the generic DSS framework very nicely, and the works in the DSS field can benefit from the study of the techniques used to implement these systems."

DEFINITION OF AN EXPERT SYSTEM

Feigenbaum [131] has defined an expert system as "an intelligent computer program that uses knowledge and inference procedures to solve problems that are difficult enough to require significant human expertise for their solutions." Knowledge necessary to perform at such a level plus the inference procedure used can be thought of as a model of the expertise of the best practitioners of the field.

The knowledge of an expert system consists of facts and heuristics. The facts constitute a body of information that is widely shared, publically available, and generally agreed upon by experts in a field. The heuristics are mostly private, little discussed rules of good judgment (rules of plausible reasoning, rules of good guessing) that characterize expert-level decision making in the field. The performance level of an expert system is primarily a function of the size and the quality of the knowledge base it possesses.

Feigbaum calls those who build knowledge-based expert systems "knowledge engineers" [131] and refers to their technology as knowledge engineering.

Knowledge engineers focus on replicating the behavior of an expert of a specific field engaged in solving a narrowly defined problem to develop computer systems that will produce results that are normally associated with human intelligence.

A brief description of the structure of expert systems has been presented in order to give an idea how knowledge engineers work for their construction.

STRUCTURE OF EXPERT SYSTEMS

The HIPS model of Newell and Simon describes how cognitive systems works. Events in the world produce stimuli that impinge upon human senses. Human beings receive stimuli through senses and store them in buffer memories. Some stimuli are transferred to STM (working memory). The transferred stimuli activate the IF portion of a production rule. The THEN portion of the production from the LTM indicates appropriate actions, which are executed by the motor system and are observed as responses [132].

The HIPS model led the AI researchers to focus their attention on the role that IF—THEN rules play in human cognition. They created a programming language called "production system." The production system is based on the basic idea that the data base consists of rules called productions, in the form of condition—action pairs: "IF this condition arises, THEN take this action." The system consists of two parts: (*a*) production rules of IF—THEN statements, and (*b*) a working memory. To put it in another way, a production rule is an instruction for recognize—act processor. Production rules (or simply production) are applied to working memory. If they succeed, they ordinarily contribute some new information to memory. This very basic concept led the AI researchers to develop expert systems or knowledge systems to help decision makers improve their heuristics [133].

An expert system is built using the production rule derived from the HIPS model. It consists of two major parts: (*a*) the knowledge base including the working memory, and (*b*) the inference engine (see Fig. 5).

Experts solve problems by employing a large number of task-specific facts and heuristics. An expert is "an individual who is widely recognized as being able to solve a particular type of problem that most other people cannot solve nearly as efficiently or effectively" [134]. Experts perform well because they have a large amount of complied, task-specific knowledge stored in LTM. It is estimated that a world-class expert, such as a Nobel laureate in chemistry, has 50,000 to 100,000 chunks of heuristic information about his speciality. Each chunk with its myriad associations can be retrieved, examined, and utilized at will. Psychologists believe that it takes at least 10 years to acquire 50,000 chunks. This estimate is based on the constraints that our mental hardware places on our ability to enter information into the LTM [135].

If a person succeeds in becoming an expert, he/she arranges the knowledge in the LTM so that he/she can respond to problem situations by using heuristics and task-specific theories. The knowledge stored in the LTM takes two forms: firstly, principles and general theories of a profession acquired through schooling and formal informational channels such as books,

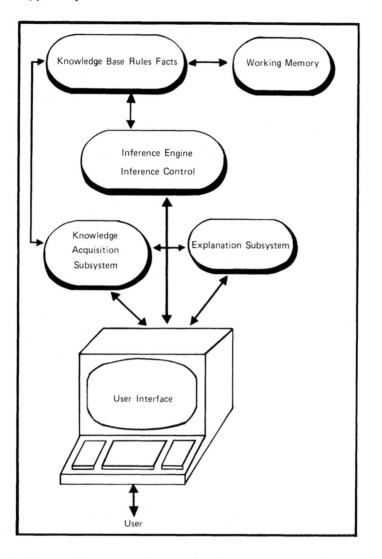

FIGURE 5 The architecture of knowledge-based expert systems. (Adapted from Ref. 60. By permission of the copyright owner: John Wiley & Sons, Inc., New York)

and second, heuristics and task-specific knowledge acquired through experience and practices in the profession as well as from mentors.

Knowledge engineers build the knowledge base by capturing the knowledge of a human expert. It is typical for knowledge engineers to talk with an expert and ask him/her to describe various aspects of his/her domain. The knowledge engineers thus collect elements or objects, identify characteristics of each of the objects, and analyze and establish relationships linking objects (concrete or conceptual) that constitute knowledge stored in the expert's LTM. After analyzing the knowledge of an expert, the knowledge engineers represent that knowledge in the software to be used in an expert system.

METHODS OF KNOWLEDGE REPRESENTATION

The basic element in the construction of an expert system is representation of knowledge itself. Knowledge representation research in AI has been concerned with the syntax and semantics of the representation of knowledge [136], unlike data base research which tends to focue solely on syntax [137]. The basic idea behind the focus on semantics is that in order to be of use in real life, knowledge representation must be able to provide processing with things, phenomena, and concepts, as well as with relations between them in the surrounding world. Man collects this kind of information, known as semantic knowledge, through his own senses and by receiving information on the perception of others. Research efforts in AI are concerned with constructing knowledge in the computer in the same way [138].

A variety of methods have been developed by the AI researchers to represent knowledge in the computer with a shift toward semantics. These include [139]:

- Semantic networks
- Object—attribute--value (O-A-V) triplets
- Rules
- Frame
- Logical expression

Semantic Networks

The scheme of semantic networks was first proposed by Quillian [140] and evolved rapidly to become a major concept in knowledge representation. Semantic networks are a collection of objects called nodes. Nodes are connected together by arcs or links. Ordinarily, both the links and the nodes are labeled. The nodes and links are described and named as the following [141]:

1. Nodes are used to represent objects and descriptors.
   - Physical entities that can be seen and touched (objects).
   - Conceptual entities such as acts, events, or abstract categories (objects).
   - Descriptors provide additional information about objects.
2. Links relate objects and descriptors. A link may represent any relationship. Common links include the following:
   - "Is a" link is often used to represent the class/instance relationship.
   - "Has a" link is a second common relationship. This identifies nodes that are properties of other nodes.
   - Some links are definitional.
   - Links that capture heuristic knowledge enrich the network by providing additional paths.

The semantic network scheme possesses two distinct advantages, namely, flexibility and inheritance. Flexibility permits the user to define new nodes and links as needed. Inheritance refers to the ability of one node to "inherit" the characteristics of other nodes. "Is a" link defines taxonomic relations and the inheritance of attributes from higher nodes (superconcepts) to lower nodes (subconcepts) in the hierarchy.

The scheme of semantic networks to represent knowledge in the form of nodes, links, and inheritance hierarchies is related to research into how humans store knowledge. The scheme provides a flexible syntax and a layered set of semantic primitives in which to represent knowledge.

Object—Attribute—Value

Another method of representing knowledge is O-A-V triplets [142]. In this scheme, object (O) may be a physical or a conceptual entity; attributes (A) may be general characteristics or properties associated with objects; value (V) in the scheme represents the specific nature of an attribute in a particular situation. The O-A-V triplets scheme is a specialized form of semantic network approach.

In some cases, the scheme may be used to represent just two relationship: O ⟶ A link, and A ⟶ V link, representing an "is a" link.

The O-A-V triplets scheme has three salient features: First, the scheme can represent knowledge either in static or dynamic state. Objects that have generic attributes and that do not change with the change of situation represent static knowledge. Objects that have attributes that change from case to case represent dynamic knowledge.

The knowledge in the form of facts and rules stored in the knowledge base of an expert system represents static knowledge. When the practitioner interfaces with the knowledge base and determines values of various attributes relative to the particular situation, he generates dynamic knowledge. The system stores this dynamic knowledge in its working memory for reasoning. The process of determining specific values for the attributes stored in a static knowledge base is often called instantiation.

Second, the scheme offers a methodology of ordering objects and establishing links with one another. The possible ordering of objects is in the form of a tree. The top object is called the "root" and is used as a starting point for reasoning and acquiring information. The objects of the tree are static. The objects may also have multiple instances with values that are not abstract values but that represent a dynamic form of an object tree.

The objects may have linkages in the form of whole and part, as well as in an irregular form—subordinate objects may be related to more than one higher level object. This implies that in certain cases, a subordinate object will inherit properties from more than one higher level object. The tree of objects having irregular linkage is called "tangled."

Third, the O-A-V triplet scheme is a procedure for handling uncertainty. Triplets can be modified by a certainty factor. Certainty factors represent the confidence that one may have in a piece of evidence. Certainty factors are not probabilities but they are an information measure of confidence or certainty for a piece of evidence. They represent the degree to which one believes that evidence is, in fact, true. Certainty factors can be represented in a number of ways.

Some systems may be built around a single object, or they may not formally represent multiple objects. In such cases, the system will represent facts in terms of A ⟶ V, (A-V) pairs rather than triplets. This scheme of pairs works like the O-A-V triplets, except because it cannot represent multiple objects, it cannot take advantage of inheritance hierarchies.

Rules

The rules-based scheme of knowledge representation is one of the most common and easily understood approaches. The basic premise of the scheme is that for each type of problem, a set of rules exists that solve it. A rule condition is specific enough to identify the problem and generate a search space. The rules are equivalent to search operators [143].

The most common approach of the rules scheme is productions. The basic idea behind the production system is that the data base consists of rules, called productions, in the form of condition—action pairs. "IF this condition arises, THEN take this action." Rules are thus represented in the form of IF, THEN, AND, and OR logical operators. A sample rule from the system MYCIN, developed for diagnosing infectious diseases, is shown below. MYCIN's knowledge base is composed of some 500 rules [144].

> IF the infection is primarily in the blood stream and the culture was obtained from a narrowly sterile site, and the suspected portal of entry of the organism is the gastrointestinal tract, THEN there is suggestive evidence (.8) that the identity of the organism is bacteroids.

Rules can also be used with A-V, or O-A-V representation. Rules can be simple or quite complex. Certainty factors can also be attached to rules in the same way as with facts. In case of moderately certain facts, indefinite relationships can be represented by attaching a certainty factor. Uncertain rules represent values that are less than definite. The method of handling uncertain facts and relationships is through the use of IF-THEN logical operators. Some knowledge systems use rules that incorporate "pattern-matching variables." The variable rules allow the system to substitute many different facts into the same general format.

Frame

In 1975, Minsky [145] introduced the concept of frame for knowledge representation. A frame partitions a semantic network into easily identifiable concepts. It represents knowledge in the form of a description of an object that contains slots for all of the information associated with the object. Slots, like attributes, may store values. Slots may also contain default values, pointers to other frames, or sets of rules or procedures by which values may be obtained. These additional features make frames different from the O-A-V triplets scheme. Frames permit the richer representation of knowledge, however, they are far more complex and more difficult to develop than O-A-V triplets and rules systems.

Frame's knowledge structure includes declarative and procedural information in a predetermined internal relation. A declarative representation of a fact is simply an assertion that "the fact is true." A procedural representation of a fact is a set of instructions that, when carried out, arrive at a result consistent with the fact. Thus, declarative and procedural representations are alternative strategies that achieve the same results [146].

An important feature of the frame scheme is its ability to determine whether it is applicable in a given situation. The idea is that the frame tries to match itself to the data it describes.

Logical Expressions

Logic provides another way of representing factual and representational knowledge [147]. Of several logical forms of knowledge representations, two are most common: propositional logic and predicate calculus.

Propositional logic systems contain statements that are either true or false. Propositions that are linked together with connectives such as AND, OR, NOT, IMPLIES, and EQUIVALENT are called compound statements. Propositional logic is concerned with the truthfulness of compound statements. There are rules for propagating the truthfulness of statements, depending on connectives.

Procedural calculus is an extension of propositional logic. The elementary unit in predicate logic is an object. Statements about objects are called predicates. In the predicate, logic assertion is either true or false; for example, the statement "is-red ball" expresses the assertion that a ball is red. Predicates can address more than one object.

Logical expressions represent knowledge in a different manner than the preceding three approaches. Logic provides a powerful tool to build knowledge representation. However, most of the knowledge systems built to date use semantic networks and O-A-V triplets schemes. The rules are, for the most part, quite simple methods of representing knowledge. The frame system is becoming more popular as complex systems are being built.

INFERENCE ENGINE

The knowledge base is roughly a collection of assertions (rules) about a collection of subjects. To use this knowledge, it is necessary to adopt an inference mechanism (or engine). Some of these angines are used only as deduction machines, whereas a few have been proposed that also have generating capabilities [148].

The inference engine of an expert system stands between the user and the knowledge base and performs two major tasks: (a) it examines existing facts and rules and adds new facts when possible; (b) it decides the order in which inferences are made. Thus, it formulates strategies used to draw inferences and control the reasoning process. Inference and control strategies guide a knowledge system as it uses the facts and rules stored in its knowledge base and the information it acquires from the user [149].

An inference engine contains inference and control mechanisms that direct the system in its use of facts and rules contained in the knowledge base. The inference and control mechanisms are based on the following subsystems:

Inference:
- Modus ponens
- Reasoning about uncertainty
- Resolution

Control:
- Forward and backward chaining
- Depth-first versus breadh-first search
- Monotonic verses nonmonotonic reasoning

Inference

Modus ponens, is the most common logical rule for deriving new facts from rules and known facts. It is a simple, intuitively appealing way to conduct reasoning. The rule envisages that when premises of a rule are true, conclusions can be believed to be true. The rule has two important implications for knowledge system. First, the rule is simple, so reasoning based on it is easily understood. Second, not all possible valid inferences can be drawn using just this rule.

Reasoning about uncertainty, the inference engine of an expert system is able to handle incomplete information just as consultants and advisors typically deal with cases for which some information is missing. Unknown information is handled by allowing rules to fail when information necessary to evaluate the premises of these rules is simply unavailable. Unknown information is handled by logical rules: AND, OR, IF-THEN.

Resolution is a set of logical statements to discover whether a new fact is valid. The resolution strategy is derived from applying operations such as (a) the ability to write IF-THEN and AND-OR statements; and (b) the ability to combine OR statements. Most knowledge systems using logical systems prefer resolution strategy.

Control

The control mechanism of an inference engine addresses two problems faced while interfacing a knowledge system: (a) the way to decide where the reasoning process is to begin; (b) resolving conflicts that occur when alternative lines of reasoning emerge. To address these problems, the following alternative rules are followed.

The most common form of reasoning used in the inference engine is the rules to reason either forward, from observations to conclusions or, backward, from a hypothesis back toward observations that might support or refute the hypothesis [150].

The system that reasons forward starts with data supplied by the user and applies all rules whose IF part are satisfied. The system is useful where the number of possible outcomes is large. In this case, the goal is constructed or possible solutions are assembled first. Given the information on hand, premises of the rules are examined to see whether or not they are true. If so, the conclusions are added to the lists of facts known to be true, and the system examines the rules again. The forward-chaining system is sometimes called a data-driven system.

The system that reasons backward starts with a goal and works backward through the subgoals in an effort to choose an answer. Each premise of the rule retrieved becomes a new goal, in turn, and rules relevant to those goals are retrieved. Reasoning backward from the initial goal toward more primitive data continues until the system encounters topics for which there are no rules. At that point, information is requested from the user. The backward chaining strategy is also referred to as a "goal-directed" system. This system is efficient if the possible outcome (i.e., the values of goal attributes) is known, and if the attributes are reasonably small in number. Most existing systems use this strategy.

Spreadsheets are useful to reason forward, working from input data toward results. It is also useful to work backward on the same model [151].

Depth-first search strategy permits inferring subgoals as well as searching for details in depth, from "action," to "means," and to "distance." Searching for details first is the theme of back-chaining in a depth-first manner. A breadth-first search examines all premises in a rule before searching for greater detail. This search strategy will be more efficient if one rule succeeds and the goal attribute's value is obtained.

Most expert systems employ the depth-first search, which permits analysis of details at a deeper level and, by following a chain of rules, directs questions that the knowledge system asks in a meaningful way.

Some systems use monotonic and some use nonmonotonic reasoning strategies. In monotonic reasoning strategy, all values concluded for an attribute remain true for the duration of the consultation session. Facts that become true remain true, and the amount of true information in the system grows steadily or monotonically.

In a nonmonotonic reasoning strategy, facts that are true may be retracted; for example, in the early stages of a planning problem, it may make sense to proceed in a certain way. Later, as information continues to accumulate, it may turn out that an early decision was wrong. Decisions and their consequences need to be retracted. Although most expert systems use monotonic reasoning strategy, the rest allow only carefully controlled types of nonmonotonic reasoning procedures.

AI LANGUAGES

Efforts to build knowledge-based systems have led to the development of AI programs. AI programs commonly use high-level (AI) languages such as list-processing (LISP) language and programming language for logic (PROLOG) [152]. LISP consists of operators that facilitate the creation of programs that manipulate lists. The list can be used to represent relations between the things represented by the symbols. Manipulation of these list structures can deduce implicit relations. Programs can use lists to build structures of unpredictable sizes and shapes during execution without predetermined or artificial limits.

McCarthy has described the salient features of LISP as follows [153]:

1. Computing with symbolic expressions rather than numbers, that is, bit patterns in a computer's memory and registers can stand for arbitrary symbols, not just those of arithmetic
2. List processing, that is, representing data as linked-list structures in the machine and as multilevel lists on paper
3. Control structure based on the composition of functions to form more complex functions
4. Recursion as a way to describe processes and problems
5. Representation of LISP programs internally as linked lists and externally as multilevel lists, that is, in the same form as all data are represented
6. The function of EVAL written in LISP itself, serves as an interpreter for LISP and as a format definition of the language

Because there is not an essential difference between data and programs in LISP, one LISP program can use another LISP program as data. LISP is highly recursive, and data as well as programs are both represented as lists. The list can be nested, one within another within another. It does not always make for easily read syntax, but it allows for very elegant solutions to complex problems that are very difficult to solve in various programming languages.

Developed in 1972 by A. Colmerauer and P. Roussel at the University of Marseilles, PROLOG is a programming language that implements a simplified version of predicate calculus, although it cannot begin to handle all the deductions that are theoretically possible in predicate calculus. It contains constructs that make it easy to write programs that manipulate logical expressions. It is designed for symbolic rather than simply for numerical computation. PROLOG is very efficient at list processing. Similarly, PROLOG is an interpreted language and thus responds to any query by attempting to return an answer immediately [154].

Programming in PROLOG involves the following:

1. Specifies some facts about objects and relationships
2. Specifies rules about objects and relationships
3. Asks questions about objects and relationships

PROLOG has two programming styles: a declarative style and a procedural style. In the declarative programming style, one focuses on telling the system what it should know and relies on the system to handle the procedure. In procedural programming, one considers the specific problem-solving behavior the computer will exhibit. Most expert systems use procedural style.

An advantage of using PROLOG is that new rules can be added easily to modify the system behavior. The system will perform exhaustive searches with all the rules and all clauses from the data base to find appropriate bindings for input parameters that are unspecified.

TOOLS FOR BUILDING EXPERT SYSTEMS

Tools have been designed to facilitate the rapid development of expert systems. These tools contain elementary constructs for modeling a system. They offer two advantages [155].

1. They provide for rapid system development by furnishing a substantial amount of computer code that would otherwise need to be written, tested, debugged, and maintained.
2. Tools provide specific techniques for holding knowledge representation, inference, and control, which help knowledge engineers to model the salient characteristics of a particular class of problems.

The framework for tools initially emerged from an expert system designed at Stanford for medical diagnosis, MYCIN. The developers realized that there were two distinct parts to their system: (a) the knowledge base, which was specific to the area of medical diagnosis; and (b) the inference strategy system, which was a general-purpose back-chaining rule evaluator. The distinction led to building an "empty" MYCIN or EMYCIN, without a knowledge case, (Fig. 6).

EMYCIN [156] is a tool for building MYCIN-like consultant systems. It requires only knowledge to be represented as objects, attributes, values, and rules in much the same way as that of a spreadsheet program in which data are represented in rows and columns. EMYCIN is a knowledge system without domain knowledge. It is a tool and not a computing language.

Similar to EMYCIN, a number of other expert systems led to the development of tools. PROSPECTOR led to a tool called Knowledge Acquisition Systems (KAS) [157]. HEARSAY I led to HEARSAY 11, and AGE and UNITS led to KEE. Each of these software tools provides a different means for representing and reasoning out knowledge. Each provides power for programmers by creating an environment in which the building blocks for machine problem solving are readily available and well integrated.

In addition, there are a number of knowledge system building tools available commercially. It is reported that several AI companies are engaged in developing and marketing minicomputer- and microprocessor-based large and small knowledge system tools [158].

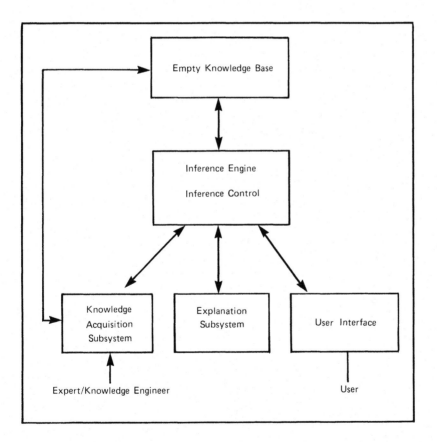

FIGURE 6 The architecture of EMYCIN. (Adapted from Ref. 152. By permission of the copyright owner: John Wiley & Sons, Inc., New York)

RESEARCH TRENDS

The research trends in computer science and technology, including AI, focus on eliminating the hardware and software limitations. Currently, computers are unable to process enough knowledge fast enough to allow the building of workable systems that can deal with many types of complex problems simultaneously. The increasing complexity in organizational decision problems that requires matching sophistication in the decision-making process places demands on computers with capabilities of processing large amounts of rules simultaneously, so that knowledge-based systems can be developed to support the problem-solving process concerning decisions requiring vast amounts of data to be processed. It is reported that the Japanese are building fifth-generation computers that will be capable of knowledge processing based on innovative theories and techniques that can offer advanced functions expected to be required in the next decades, overcoming the technical limitations of conventional computers. The fifth-generation computer may provide building blocks for DSS/expert system and permit parallel processing of a large amount of data [159].

The software systems currently available are inadequate to handle complex logical manipulation. They handle nonmonotonic problems with considerable difficulty. Many significant problems require that the data be constantly reevaluated to take ongoing changes into account [160]. To support managers on an ongoing basis, DSS/ES must be able to learn from its own experience and update its own knowledge base (data representing specific problem domains) constantly. In other words, systems must possess self-evolving characteristics. Currently, the question of designing systems that can learn from their own experience, which is normally referred to as machine learning, is faced with a number of difficult problems that researchers are only beginning to realize [161].

As an organization grows in size and complexity, the information needs for decision making at the different managerial levels grow correspondingly. As a result, the number of decision support systems/knowledge-based systems may increase in an organization to fulfill the growing demand for information processing by the decision makers. This may press for demand to represent knowledge in a flexible manner, which may be able to respond to varying decision tasks so that the expensive task of replicating or creating new knowledge bases can be avoided. To meet this demand in the future, current research efforts in the field of knowledge representation focus on providing flaxible syntax and a layered set of semantic primitives in which to represent knowledge enabling systems to be built that may permit sharing of the knowledge [162].

The current research efforts in AI focus on developing methodology to incorporate strategies in the knowledge base necessary for the solution of problems. As strategies for problem solving are domain dependent, knowledge-based systems must include the kind of knowledge that may be useful in selecting a strategy appropriate to the solution of the problem at hand. That strategy must then guide the application of knowledge in the original knowledge base. The problem to be tackled in this respect is discovering the strategies that can be used to solve problems and developing knowledge representation languages that are both expressive and efficient to construct the knowledge base with a built-in mechanism to formulate strategies for problem solving [163].

Another issue that is currently drawing attention is the approach to reasoning, which needs to be further refined. The focus of research is to enhance the capability of the knowledge base and the inference engine to identify and establish cause—effect relationships and explanations to causality. Such explanations will enhance the power of reasoning, broadening the scope of the system's performance [164].

The present research directions in AI will ultimately enhance the computer capabilities, enabling it to adapt to specifics of the HIPS, eventually allowing the creation of genuine amplifiers of the decision maker's intelligence [165,166].

REFERENCES

1. Michael S. Scott Morton, "Management Decision System: Computer-Based Support for Decision Making," Graduate School of Business Administration, Harvard University, Cambridge, MA, 1971.
2. T. P. Gerrity, Jr., "Design of Man-Machine Decision Systems: An Application to Portfolio Management," *Sloan Manage. Rev.*, 12(2), 59—75 (1971).
3. Herbert A. Simon, "Forward," in *Foundations of Decision Support Systems* (Robert H. Bonczek et al. eds.), Academic Press, New York, 1981.
4. Kyosti Pulkkinen, " The phases of Development of an Organization and Knowledge Representation within DSS," in *Knowledge Representation for Decision Support Systems* (L. B. Methlie and R. H. Spragno, Jr., eds.), Elsevier Science (North Holland), New York, 1985, p. 43.
5. Peter G. W. Keen, "Decision Support Systems: Translating Analytic Technique into Useful Tools," *Sloan Manage. Rev.*, 33 (Spring 1980).
6. Ralph H. Sprague, Jr., and Eric D. Carlson, *Building Effective Decision Support Systems*, Prentice-Hall, Englewood Cliffs, NJ, 1982, pp. 2,4.
7. Robert H. Bonczek et al., "Development in Decision Support Systems," in *Advances in Computers*, Academic Press, New York, 1984, vol. 23.
8. Ref. 7, p. 145.
9. Peter G. W. Keen, "Decision Support Systems: A Research Perspective," in *Decision Support Systems: Issues and Challanges* (Gordon Fick and Ralph H. Sprague, Jr., eds.), Pergamon, New York, 1980, pp. 23—44.
10. O. I. Larichev, "Problem of Man-Machine Interaction in Decision Support Systems," in *Knowledge Representation for Decision Support Systems* (L. B. Methlie and R. H. Sprague, Jr., eds.), Elsevier Sciences (North-Holland), New York, 1985, p. 28.
11. Jay W. Forrester, "Managerial Decision Making," in *Management and the Computer of the Future* (Martin Greenberger, ed.), MIT Press, Cambridge, MA, 1962, pp. 37—38.
12. George Miller, *Essays on Communication*, Penguin Books, New York, 1972.
13. C. Cherry, *On Human Communication*, MIT Press, Cambridge, MA, 1966.
14. Marshal C. Yovits et al., "Information Flow and Analysis," *J. Am. Soc. Inf. Sci.*, 32, 1987 (May 1981).
15. G. B. Davis, *Management Information Systems: Concept Foundations. Structure and Development*, McGraw-Hill, New York, 1977.
16. R. A. Johnson et al., *The Theory and Management of Systems*, 2nd ed., McGraw-Hill, New York, 1967, pp. 235—236.

17. Dan Voich, Jr., et al., *Information Systems for Operational and Management*, South-Western Publishing, Cincinnati, Ohio, 1975, p. 6.

18. J. D. Thompson and A. Tuden, "Strategies, Structures and Processes of Organizational Decision," in *Comparative Studies in Administration* (J. D. Thompson et al., eds.), University of Pittsburgh, Pittsburgh, PA, 1959, pp. 57−59.

19. Gordon Pask, *An Approach to Cybernetics*, Hutchinson & Co., London, 1961, pp. 26−27.

20. Jay Galbraith, *Organization Design*, Addison-Wesley, Reading MA, 1977, pp. 38−39.

21. Ref. *18*, pp. 11−12.

22. Peter G. W. Keen and Michael S. Scott Morton, *Decision Support Systems: An Organizational Perspective*, Addison-Wesley, Reading, MA, 1978.

23. Ronald N. Taylor, "Psychological Aspects of Planning," *Long Range Planning, 9*, 66−74 (April 1976).

24. Ref. *22*, pp. 4−5.

25. A. Burns and M. A. Rathwell, "Distributed Decision-Making and Democratic System Design," in *International On-Line Information*, Learned Information, Inc., Medford, NJ, 1982, pp. 387−396.

26. J. S. Brumer et al., *A Study of Thinking*, Science Editions, New York, 1956.

27. J. Feldman, "Simulation of Behavior in the Binard Choice Experiments," *Computer and Thought* (E. A. Feigenbaum and J. Feldman, eds.), McGraw-Hill, New York, 1963, pp. 329−346.

28. H. A. Witkin, "Origin of Cognitive Style," in *Cognition, Theory, Research, Promise* (Constance Scheere, ed.), Harper and Row, New York, 1964.

29. Ref. *22*, p. 58.

30. Henry Mintzberg, "The Myths of MIS," *Calif. Manage. Rev., 19*, 92−97 (Fall 1972).

31. J. R. Wagner, "Optimizing Decision Support Systems," *Datamation, 26*, 209 (May 1980).

32. Barr Avron et al., *The Handbook of Artificial Intelligence*, William Kaufman, Los Altos, CA, 1981, vol. 1, p. 143.

33. Peter G. W. Keen and J. R. Wagner, "DSS: An Executive Mind-Support System," *Datamation, 25*, 118 (November 1979).

34. Ref. *7*, p. 142.

35. Ref. *17*, p. 11.

36. Robert H. Bonczek et al., *Foundations of Decision Support Systems*, Academic Press, New York, 1981, pp. 11−13.

37. Ref. *22*, pp. 2−3.

38. Ref. *17*, pp. 15−16.

39. Ref. *17*, p. 22.

40. Russel L. Ackoff, "Management Mis-information Systems," *Manage. Sci., 14*, 147−156 (1967).

41. Chris Argyris, "Organizational Learning and Management Systems," *Acc. Organ. Soc., 2*, 113−123 (November 1977).

42. Ref. *33*, p. 122.

43. Izak Banbasat, "Cognitive Style Considerations in DSS design," *Data Base, 8*, 37−38 (Winter 1977).

44. H. A. Witkin et al., *Psychological Differentiation*, Wiley, New York, 1962.

45. C. W. Churchman and A. H. Schainblatt, "The Researcher and the Manager: A Dialectic of Implementation," *Manage. Sci.*, 7, 31–38 (Fall 1964).

46. R. H. Doktor and W. F. Hamilton, "Cognitive Style and the Acceptance of Management Science Recommendations," *Manage. Sci.*, 19, 884–894 (April 1973).

47. R. O. Mason and I. Mitroff, "A Program for Research on Management Information Systems," *Manage. Sci.*, 19, 475–487 (January 1973).

48. J. H. B. M. Huysman, "The Effectiveness of the Cognitive Style Constraints in Implementing Operations Research Proposals," *Manage. Sci.*, 17, 92–104 (1970).

49. H. M. Schroeder et al., *Human Information Processing*, Holt Rinehart and Wiston, New York, 1967.

50. Ref. *28*, pp. 172–205.

51. Carl Jung, *Psychological Types* (translated by R. F. C. Hall), Princeton University, Princeton, NJ, 1971.

52. Pentti Kerola and William Taggart, "Human Information Processing Systems Development Process," in *Evolutionary Information Systems* (J. Hawgood, ed.), North-Holland, New York, 1982, pp. 64–65.

53. J. L. McKenney and P. G. W. Keen, "How Manager's Mind Work," *Har. Bus. Rev.*, 52, 99–90 (May–June 1974).

54. Phillipe J. Dumas, "Management Information Systems: A Dialectic Theory and the Evaluation Issue," (unpublished Ph. D. Dissertation), University of Texas at Austin, 1978.

55. Chris Argyris, "Management Information Systems: The challenge to Rationality and Emotionality," *Manage. Sci.*, 17, B275–B292 (February 1971).

56. Ref. *22*, pp. 64–65.

57. E. S. Quade and W. I. Boucher, eds., *Systems Analysis and Policy Planning: Applications in Defense*, Elsevier, New York, 1968.

58. Herbert A. Simon, "A Behavioral Model of Rational Choice," in *Models of Man: Social and Rational*, Wiley, New York, 1957, pp. 241–260.

59. A. Newell and Herbert A. Simon, *Human Problem Solving*, Prentice-Hall, Englewood Cliffs, NJ 1972.

60. Paul Harmon and David King, *Expert Systems: Artificial Intelligence in Business*, Wiley, New York, 1985, p. 23.

61. G. A. Miller, "The Magical Number Seven, Plus or Minus Two: Some Limits on out capacity for Processing Information," *Psychol. Rev.*, 63, 107–112 (March 1967).

62. Ref. *59*, pp. 806–809.

63. Ref. *59*, p. 811.

64. Ref. *59*, p. 825.

65. James G. March and Herbert A. Simon, *Organizations*, Wiley, New York, 1958.

66. Ronald N. Taylor, "Psychological Aspects of Planning," *Long-Range Planning*, 9, 66–74 (April 1976).

67. Herbert A. Simon, *The Science of Artificial*, MIT Press, Cambridge, MA, 1969, p. 64.

68. Ref. *60*, p. 260.

69. Ref. *22*, p. 66.

70. Ref. *3*, pp. VII–IX.

71. Herbert A. Simon, *The New Science of Management Decision*, Harper and Brothers, New York, 1960.

72. G. Anthony Gorry and Michael S. Scott Morton, "A Framework for Management Information Systems," *Sloan Manage. Rev.*, 3, 55—70, (Fall 1971).

73. R. N. Anthony, *Planning and Control Systems: A Framework for Analysis*, Harvard University, Graduate School of Public Administration, Cambridge, MA, 1965.

74. Ref. 71, pp. 9—20.

75. Ref. 73, pp. 24—27.

76. Ref. 22, p. 59.

77. Ref. 22, pp. 60—72.

78. Ref. 22, pp. 73—81.

79. Ref. 22, pp. 82—83.

80. Ref. 71, pp. 4—20.

81. Ref. 71, pp. 5—6.

82. Ref. 71, p. 6.

83. Ref. 72, pp. 57—60.

84. Ref. 22, pp. 82—93.

85. Ref. 71, pp. 1—4.

86. Ralph H. Sprague, Jr., "A Framework for Research on Decision Support Systems," in *Decision Support Systems: Issues and Challenges* (Guran Fick and Ralph H. Sprague, Jr., eds.), Pergmon, New York, 1980, pp. 12—13.

87. John Dewey, *How We Think*, D. C. Heath, New York, 1910, Chapter 8.

88. Ref. 31, p. 209.

89. Peter G. W. Keen and G. R. Wagner, "DSS: An Executive Mind-Support System," *Datamation*, 117—122 (November 1979).

90. Michael J. Ginzberg and Edward A. Stohr, "Decision Support Systems. Issues and Perspectives," in *Decision Support System* (M. J. Ginzberg and W. Reitman, eds.), Elsevier, New York, 1982, p. 9.

91. John D. C. Little, "Model and Managers: The Concept of a Decision Calculus," *Manage. Sci.*, 16, 13406—13485 (April 1970).

92. S. L. Alter, *Decision Support Systems. Current Practice and Continuing Challenges*, Addison-Wesley, Reading, MA, 1980.

93. J. H. Moore and M. G. Chang, "Design of Decision Support Systems," *Data Base*, 12, 8—14 (Fall 1980).

94. Peter G. W. Keen, "Adaptive Design for Decision Support Systems," *Data Base*, 12, 15—25 (Fall 1980).

95. Ref. 92, p. 13.

96. Robert J. Thierauf, *Decision Support Systems for Effective Planning and Control: A Case Study Approach*, Prentice-Hall, Englewood Cliffs, NJ 1982, pp. 85—100.

97. Ref. 22, p. 2.

98. Ref. 92, pp. 22—25.

99. S. L. Alter, "Taxonomy of Decision Support Systems," *Sloan Manage. Rev.*, 19, 39—56 (Fall 1977).

100. Paul Berger and Franz Edelman, "IRIS: A Transaction-Based DSS for Human Resources Management," *Data Base*, 22–29.
101. A. C. Max and H. C. Meal, "Heirarachial Integration of Production Planning and Scheduling," in *Studies in the Management Sciences* (M. A. Geisler, ed.), North-Holland, New York, 1975.
102. J. J. Donovan and S. E. Madrick, "Institutional and Ad-Hoc Decision Support Systems and their Effective Use," *Data Base*, 8, 78–88 (Winter 1977).
103. J. J. Donovan, "Data Base System Approach to Management Decision Support," *Trans. Data Base Syst.*, 1, 344–369 (December 1976).
104. R. H. Sprague, Jr., "A Framework for the Development of Decision Support System," *MIS Q*, 4, 1–26 (December 1980).
105. Robert H. Bonczek et al., "Evolution from MIS to DSS: Extension of Data Management to Model Management," in *Decision Support Systems* (Michael J. Ginzberg et al., eds.), North-Holland, New York, 1982, pp. 61–78.
106. Ref. *92*, p. 18.
107. J. C. Henderson and R. S. Ingrahm, "Prototyping for DSS: A Critical Appraisal," in *Decision Support Systems* (M. J. Ginzberg et al., eds.), North-Holland, New York, 1982.
108. Ref. *6*, p. 28.
109. J. Bennett, "User Oriented Graphics: Systems for Decision Support in Unstructured Tests," in *User Oriented Design of Interactive Graphics Systems* (S. Tren, ed.), Association of Computing Machinery, New York, 1970, pp. 3–11.
110. Ref. *6*, p. 62.
111. J. Martin, *Design of Man-Computer Dialogue*, Prentice-Hall, Englewood Cliffs, NJ, 1973.
112. Ref. *36*, p. 63.
113. Ref. *6*, pp. 240–243.
114. E. F. Codd, "Data Models in Data Base Management," Addison-Wesley, Reading, MA, 1977.
115. Ref. *6*, p. 225.
116. Ref. *6*, p. 226.
117. Ref. *6*, pp. 234–235.
118. Ref. *6*, p. 236.
119. Russel L. Ackoff, "A Concept of Corporate Planning," *Long Range Planning*, 3, 3 (1970).
120. Henry Mintzberg, *The Nature of Managerial Work*, Harper and Row, New York, 1973.
121. Ref. *6*, p. 260.
122. L. C. Barbosa and R. C. Herko, "Integration of Algorithmic Aids into Decision Support Systems," *MIS Q*, 4, 1–12 (March 1980).
123. Ref. *6*, p. 261.
124. Herbert A. Simon, "Simulation of Human Thinking," in *Management and the Computer of the Future* (Martin Greenberger, ed.), MIT Press, Cambridge, MA, 1962, pp. 94–118.
125. Ref. *36*, pp. 58–78.
126. Ref. *6*, p. 273.
127. Randall Davis, "Knowledge-Based Systems," *Science*, 231, 957 (February 28, 1986).

128. B. G. Buchanan and E. A. Feigenbaum, "DENDRAL and Meta-DENDRAL: Their Applications, Dimensions," *Artif. Intell.*, *11*, 5−24 (1978).

129. A. Basden, "On the Application of Expert Systems," in *Development in Expert Systems* (M. J. Coombs, ed.), Academic Press, New York, 1984, p. 61.

130. Ref. 7, p. 167.

131. E. A. Feigenbaum, "Lecture Notes, November 10, 1983," in *Expert Systems: Artificial Intelligence in Business* (Paul Hermen and David King, eds.), Wiley, New York, 1985, p. 5.

132. Ref. *60*, p. 25.

133. Ref. *60*, p. 26.

134. Ref. *60*, p. 31.

135. Ref. *60*, p. 32.

136. R. J. Brachman, "On the Epistemological Status of Semantic Network," in *Associative Networks: Representation and Use of Knowledge by Computers* (N. V. Findler, ed.), Academic Press, New York, 1979, pp. 3−5.

137. Mark S. Fox, "Knowledge Representation for Decision Support," in *Knowledge Representation for Decision Support Systems* (L. B. Methlie and Ralph H. Sprague, Jr., eds.), Elsevier Science, New York, 1985, p. 3.

138. Ref. 4, pp. 3−4.

139. Ref. *60*, pp. 34−60.

140. M. R. Quillian, "Semantic Memory," (Ph. D. thesis), Carnegie-Mellon University, Pittsburgh, PA, 1966.

141. Ref. *60*, pp. 35−36.

142. Ref. *60*, pp. 36−42.

143. B. G. Buchnan and E. H. Short-liffe, *Rule-Based Expert Systems*, Addison-Wesley, Reading, MA, 1984.

144. Ref. *136*, p. 958.

145. M. Minsky, "A Framework for Representing Knowledge," in *The Psychology of Computer Vision* (P. Winston, ed.), McGraw-Hill, New York, 1975.

146. Ref. *60*, pp. 44−46.

147. Ref. *60*, pp. 46−47.

148. Y. Vassilien et al., "Access to specific Declarative Knowledge by Expert Systems: The Impact of Logic Programming," Research Report, New York University, 1983.

149. Ref. *60*, pp. 49−60.

150. Ref. *60*, pp. 55−58.

151. Ref. *136*, p. 959.

152. Ref. *60*, pp. 82−89.

153. J. McCarthy, "History of LISP," in *The Handbook of Artificial Intelligence* (A. Barr et al., eds.), William Kaufmann, Los Altos, CA, 1981, vol. 2, p. 15.

154. W. F. Clockstin and C. S. Mellish, Programming in PROLOG. Springer-Verlag, Berlin, Germany, 1981.

155. Ref. *60*, pp. 80−81.

156. F. Haye-Roth et al., eds., *Building Expert Systems*, Addison-Wesley, Reading, MA, 1983.

157. Richard O. Duda and Rene Reboh, "AI and Decision-making: The PROSPECTOR Experience," in *Artificial Intelligence* (Walter Reitman, ed.), Alex Publishing, Norwood, NJ, 1984.

158. P. H. Winston and K. A. Prendergaser, eds., *The AI Business: The Commercial Use of Artificial Intelligence*, MIT Press, Cambridge, MA, 1984.

159. G. L. Simons, *Toward Fifth-Generation Computers*, NCC Publication, Manchester, England, 1983.

160. R. David, "Expert Systems: Where Are We? And Where Do We Go from Here?" *AI Mag.*, 2 (1982).

161. R. S. Michalski et al., eds., *Machine Learning: An Artificial Intelligence Approach*, Tioga Press, Palo Alto, CA, 1983.

162. Ref. *171*, pp. 3—26.

163. Randall Davis, "Meta-rules: Reasoning about Control," *Artif. Intell.*, 15(3), 179—222 (December 1980); "Content Reference: Reasoning about Rules," *Artif. Intell.*, 15(3), 223—239 (December 1980).

164. W. J. Clancey, "The Epistemology of a Rule-Based Expert System: A framework for explanation," *Artif. Intell.*, 20(3), 215—251 (January 1983).

165. A. Pepper, "The Paradox of Machine Intelligence," *Electrotechnology*, 9(1), 25—126 (1981).

166. Ref. *10*, p. 37.

YOGENDRA P. DUBEY

FIFTH GENERATION COMPUTER SYSTEMS PROJECT

DEVELOPMENT PLANS

Aims

The ultimate goal of the Fifth-Generation Computer Systems (FGCS) Project is the realization of a computer system possessing a wide range of intelligent capabilities, making feasible its use in the new applications of the 1990s.

A new world of applications will be opened up by the FGCS. The form that the new type of information processing will take is referred to as "knowledge information processing (KIP)". A large part of the technology for realizing knowledge information processing systems (KIPS) will make use of the results of artificial intelligence (AI) research. To integrate these results into a single system, it will be necessary to selectively combine results to form a consistent whole while augmenting underdeveloped parts of AI technologies.

KIP programs will be very large and complex. It would be difficult or impossible to try to implement such programs in presently existing programming environments. To overcome such problems it has become necessary to introduce an entirely new type of programming language, based on entirely new principles. A programming environment that reduces the cognitive demands on human beings will be created. Under such an environment, it is hoped that people with no expert knowledge will be able to write programs with ease on the foundation of this new programming language by efficiently using the capabilities of the computer system.

Of course, it is understood that programming is a type of intelligent human activity itself. Thus, by making programming the object of KIP, much of the burden may be transferred to the computer. This has already been taken up as a goal of AI and forms the field of research known as automatic programming; however, efforts based on existing computer systems make it rather difficult to produce results that can be practically applied. Hopes are thus placed in FGCS to make such practical applications possible as well. If such extremely voluminous and complex programs should become possible, the remaining task is to build a computer powerful enough to execute them.

Judging from the past results of AI research, it appears necessary to make the operating speeds of fifth-generation machines faster than those of existing computer systems by about two orders of magnitude. To realize such tremendous processing speeds, the concept of highly parallel processing must be introduced, in which several hundred processors are employed simultaneously to execute a single program.

Fortunately, thanks to advances in very large-scale integration (VLSI) technology, the use of a large number of processors will probably not lead to serious cost problems. However, highly parallel processing is not applicable to all programs. An appropriate programming language must be chosen, and an architecture suited to the language must be developed.

Approaches to FGCS

The first task to be performed in concretely defining the goals of the FGCS project is the discovery of a programming language suitable for describing the intelligent activities to be executed by the computer. To this end, it is essential to understand the principles underlying the intelligent activities that the language is to express. In contrast, existing computer architectures embody the basic arithmetic operations, which form the underlying principles of numerical calculations.

For the FGCS, logic and predicate logic, in particular, has been adopted as best expressing the principles underlying intelligent activity. Logic is generally regarded as the universal law governing reasoning processes. There are various forms of logic, and predicate logic is the form that is most closely related to natural language. Thus, aside from the initial apprehension we all feel toward anything so strict and rigid, such logic can be manipulated by anyone.

Although predicate logic alone is not capable of handling all intelligent activities, there is no doubt that it is the most powerful means available in terms of description.

Inference is the mechanism fundamental to logic; by the rigid procedure of inference, knowledge is used to extract from known information what was previously not known explicitly. When human beings attempt to understand the meaning of something, whether they are conscious of it or not, inference plays a central role in the process. The possession of knowledge and the execution of inference procedures together comprise the fundamental conditions for intelligent activity.

Inference is carried out according to a set of inference rules. The most basic of these rules are syllogisms, in which $A \longrightarrow B$ and $B \longrightarrow C$ leads to $A \longrightarrow C$. One method by which computers may be made to reason by inference is to build such inference rules into the hardware in order to make automatic execution possible. This is, in fact, the approach taken in research on the FGCS.

The method by which programs are expressed in logical form and executed with inference functions is called logic programming. Such programs correspond to, say, the expression of an arithmetic problem as a system of simultaneous linear equations. Inference operations would then correspond to solving such a problem by cancellation. Thus, a large part of the program consists of the knowledge that is to be used in the inference operation.

Assuming that such logic programming is employed, much of the knowledge accumulated within the computer system must be expressed in the form of predicate logic. This format may be made to correspond almost exactly with the relational descriptions in existing relational data bases. Thus, in constructing a knowledge base, existing relational data base technologies may be directly utilized as a springboard.

In addition, parallel processing of programs employing predicate logic is possible. This is similar to solving in parallel for each unknown of a system of linear equations.

Configuration of the FGCS

Figure 1 presents the targeted configuration of the FGCS. With the programming language (Kernel language) at the center of the figure acting as interfaces, the FGCS software unfolds upward, and the hardware downward.

In terms of present software levels, the software scheme consists of a demonstration system for basic software and the basic software system, with very high-level programming languages intervening between the two.

The demonstration system for basic software consists of a number of application-oriented systems constructed to test KIP concepts. Once the FGCS is completed, it is expected that a large number of full-scale application systems will be developed by commercial vendors.

The basic software system is the most important element in the software hierarchy, forming as it does the basis for KIP. The problem-solving and inference software module is, in terms of existing computer systems, the operating system. It makes possible effective use of the inference machine by constructing higher-order inferences from simple syllogisms and ensuring that a variety of different types of problems may be solved efficiently in a manner convenient to users. The knowledge base management software module corresponds in principle to data base management systems, but because it handles knowledge instead of data, far greater intelligent functions will be required of it. One example of this might be a learning function, by which the module could determine whether information was significant. The system could accumulate knowledge based on such decisions.

Simply put, the intelligent interface software module will make it possible for the computer to understand human language: to "speak" and "hear" and to converse through figures. The intelligent programming software module will employ advanced software engineering technology to reduce to the absolute minimum the burden imposed on human programmers, with the ultimate goal of automatic programming.

The hardware of the FGCS will consist of three subsystems; in the future, however, an integration of these in one form or another is anticipated.

Using basic functions, such as those for syllogisms, the inference machine directly executes programs written in Kernel Language.

The knowledge base machine (KBM) carries out high-level processing of knowledge expressed in a variety of complex forms.

The intelligent interface hardware is in charge of executing basic functions for speech and image processing. All of these make use of advanced parallel processing technology, the goal of which is ultra-high-speed performance. In element technology, VLSI device technology will be employed.

Steps in the Development of the FGCS

Because research and development (R & D) on the FGCS incurs a high level of risk, involving as it does a large number of unknowns, a relatively long period—10 years—has been allotted for the project. This 10-year period will be divided into several stages: 3 years for the initial stage, 4 years for the intermediate stage, and 3 years for the final stage.

The initial stage of R & D was conducted with emphasis placed on the fundamental technology elements required to build a FGCS.

In the intermediate stage, the algorithms and basic architecture to be used in subsystems that will constitute the foundation of the FGCS will be

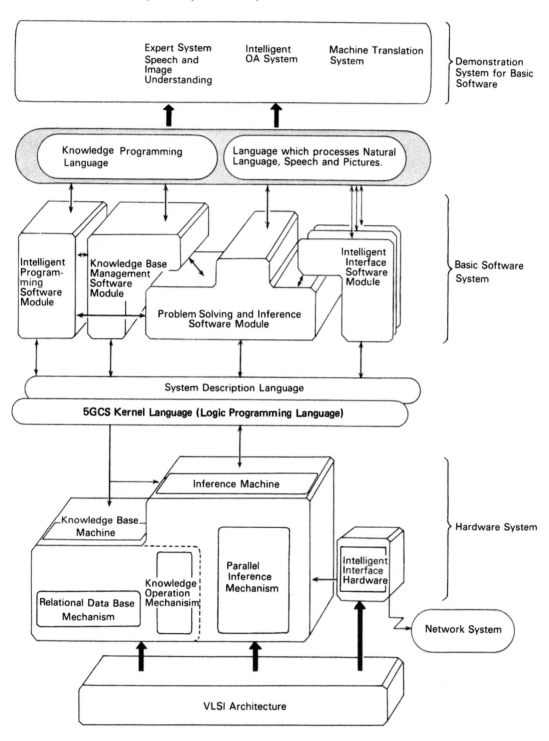

FIGURE 1 Basic configuration image of the FGCS.

determined based on the results of the initial stage. Following this, a small-to medium-scale system will be developed using various subsystems as components.

The final stage of R & D has as its goal the completion of a FGCS prototype, completely integrating all the results of research performed up to this point.

In addition, a primary objective of this project is the in-house development of R & D tools; this work will be carried out from the initial through the intermediate stages. Because the FGCS will be based on revolutionary new programming languages, software development could not be expected to proceed efficiently using conventional computer systems. Existing technology is being employed in the development of these high-performance tools for software development in order to complete the project in a short time (see Fig. 2).

RESEARCH AND DEVELOPMENT THEMES AND STATE OF PROGRESS

The Initial Stage

A summary of the R & D areas of the initial 3-year stage, as well as the interrelations between them, is presented in Figure 3.

The four basic areas for R & D are listed below; each of these is further subdivided into research themes (see Table 1).

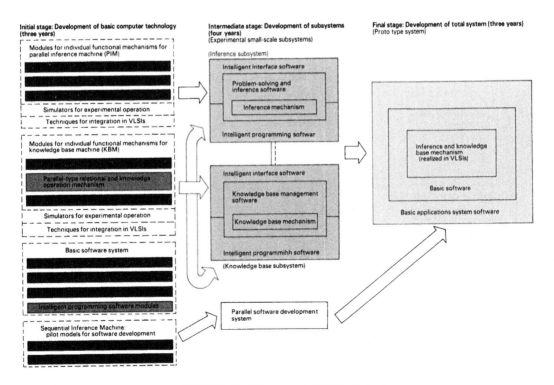

FIGURE 2   Stages of FGCS R & D.

TABLE 1   Research and Development Subjects in the Initial Stage (1982–1984)

R & D Subject	Details
Parallel inference machine (PIM)	The PIM, together with the KBM, forms the nucleus of the FGCS hardware. In the initial stage, an evaluation will be made of the basic inference module configuration. This module will consist of the following: 1. A parallel inference basic mechanism to manage the parallel execution of inference operations. 2. A data flow mechanism to execute inference operations and rapidly determine solutions. 3. An abstract data-type mechanism to consolidate detailed inference operations into several groups and control them by group.
Modules for individual functional mechanisms for PIM	The parallel inference basic mechanism, data flow mechanism, and abstract data-type mechanism each consist of functional submodules. Initially, prototypes of these submodules will be constructed and integrated to construct a prototype module for each of the three functional mechanisms.
Simulators for experimental operation	Prototype simulators for experimental operation will be built to simulate module configurations, using different combinations of submodules. They will also be used to determine the optimum configuration of the modules for the three functional mechanisms and the inference basic module, which these submodules will constitute.
Techniques for integration in VLSIs	Prototype software will be developed to evaluate VLSI convertibility for each of the submodule circuits designed.
KBM	The KBM, together with the PIM, forms the nucleus of the FGCS hardware. In the initial stage, an evaluative study will be made on the configuration of the basic knowledge base module, which will consist of the following: 1. A basic knowledge base mechanism to provide overall management of the execution of knowledge base operations. 2. A parallel relation and knowledge operation mechanism to streamline knowledge accumulation, retrieval and updating, data, conversion, etc. 3. A relational data base mechanism to provide large-capacity knowledge accumulation, storage and management.

(continued)

TABLE 1   Continued

R & D Subject	Details
Modules for individual KBM functional mechanisms	The basic knowledge base mechanism, parallel relation and knowledge operation mechanism, and relational data base mechanism each consist of functional submodules. Prototypes of these submodules will be constructed in the initial stage. These prototype submodules will be subsequently combined to produce a prototype module for each of the three functional mechanisms.
Simulators for experimental operation	Prototype simulators for operational testing will be built to simulate module configuration using different numbers and combinations of submodules. They will also be used to determine the optimum configuration of the modules for the three functional mechanisms and for the basic knowledge base module, which these sub-modules will constitute.
Techniques for integration in VLSIs	Prototype software will be developed to evaluate VLSI convertibility for each of the submodules circuits designed.

Basic software system	The basic software system forms the nucleus of the FGCS software and is composed of the following four software modules for KIP:
	
	    1. Problem-solving and inference software module.
	    2. Knowledge base management software module.
	    3. Intelligent interface software module.
	    4. Intelligent programming software module.
	
	An extended FGCS Kernel Language, required for the intermediate stage, will be developed by organizing the knowledge, obtained through designing and breadboarding the basic software system. A prototype software system will be created to test the specifications and to validate their accuracy.

FGCS Kernel Language	The FGCS Kernel Language, the base language for all other modules, will define interfaces between FGCS hardware and software. Development and evaluation of prototype KL0, (based on PROLOG), is planned for the initial stage of the project. This will be followed by specification design and development of prototype KL1 oriented to parallel execution.
Problem-solving and inference software module	The problem-solving and inference software module has capabilities for deductive inference, inductive inference (including conjecture based on incomplete knowledge), and inference by mutual complementation of knowledge. The development of prototype basic parallel inference software is planned for the initial stage for use in

TABLE 1 Continued

R & D Subject	Details
	high-speed execution of deductive inference and basic software for problem solving to determine efficient solutions to problems.
Knowledge base management software module	The knowledge base management software module has capabilities for knowledge accumulation, distributed knowledge source utilization, and knowledge acquisition. The development of a prototype knowledge representation system is planned for the initial stage in order to define knowledge representation methods. A large-scale relational data base management program is also planned to accumulate and manage a large volume of data represented as knowledge.
Intelligent interface software module	The intelligent interface software module is for flexible interaction between humans and computers. The development of a prototype of an advanced syntactic analysis program is planned for the initial stage. The aim is to achieve high-speed syntactic analysis and simplified algorithms for natural language understanding, which is critical to man—machine interaction. Basic techniques for semantic analysis and a pilot model of a dictionary system will also be developed.
Intelligent programming software module	The intelligent programming software module will automatically convert a given problem into an efficient computer program (at the Kernel Language level). A program module management system capable of extracting component modules and verifying program facilities is planned for development in the initial stage. Here, the aim is to establish modular programming, which is basic to intelligent programming, extraction of the necessary program, and program verification.
SIMs: Pilot models for software development	Pilot models (prototype SIM) will be implemented for efficient development of software for the FGCS. These models will be developed by modifying a selected language suitable for inference and by partly modifying existing von Neumann architecture.

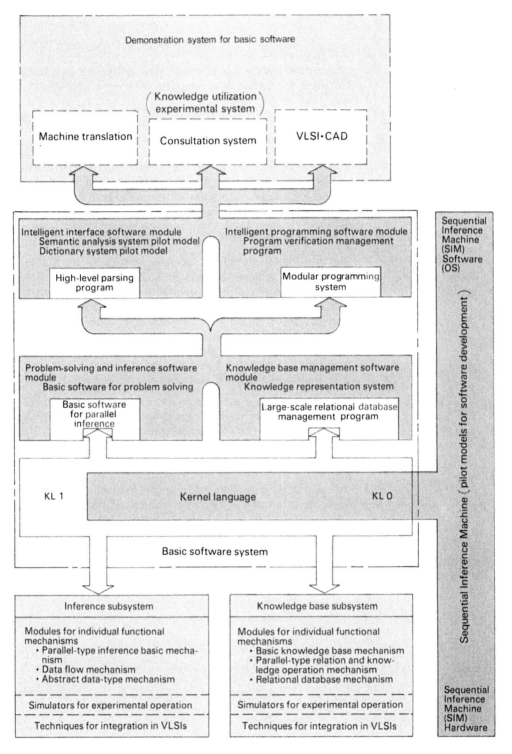

FIGURE 3   Overview of R & D in the initial stage.

1. Inference subsystem.
2. Knowledge base subsystem.
3. Basic software system.
4. Pilot models for software development.

The demonstration system for basic software shown in Figure 3 is not, however, taken up directly in the initial stage.

Major Results of the Initial Stage

The major results of R & D anticipated in the initial stage may be listed as follows (see Table 1):

1. Inference subsystem.
    a. Investigation of various parallel inference schemes (data flow scheme, reduction scheme, clause unit scheme, complete copying scheme).
    b. Trial fabrication of hardware simulators.
    c. Accumulation and evaluation of design data.
2. Knowledge base system.
    a. Development of a parallel-type relational data base machine (Delta).
    b. Establishment of specifications for tightly coupled interface with the inference machine.
3. Basic software system.
    a. Establishment of parallel-type logic programming language (KL1) specifications.
    b. Development of the basic specifications for a knowledge programming language (Mandala).
    c. Development of a large-scale relational data base program (KAISER).
    d. Partial prototyping of a knowledge utilization system (Japanese proofreader support system, etc.).
    e. Development of an advanced syntactic analysis program (Bottom up parser).
    f. Prototype creation of an experimental semantic analysis program.
    g. Development of a module programming system (for use with sequential inference machines [SIMs]).
    h. Prototype creation of an experimental software verification management program.
4. Pilot models for software development.
    a. Development of sequential logic programming languages (KL0, ESP).
    b. Development of SIM hardware (PSI).
    c. Development of SIM software (SIMPOS).

The Intermediate Stage

In the intermediate stage, while development at the subsystem level is being carried out based on the results of the initial 3-year stage, R & D results will be verified in terms of practical utilization. This stage may be regarded as a period crucial to determining the final outcome of the FGCS Project as a whole.

The central area for R & D in the intermediate stage will be the development and prototype fabrication of two subsystems with problem-solving and inference functions and a knowledge base management function.

KIP technology will be applied to real-world situations to attempt to verify related research results. The results of these applications will be evaluated and fed back into the project for use in work on each of the research themes. At the same time, a demonstration system for basic software will be constructed. Also, in order to support R & D on software technology based on parallel processing, work on a machine for parallel software development will be carried out.

The objectives of each R & D area are as follows (for details, see Table 2):

1. *Inference subsystem.* The architecture of a parallel inference macchine (with about 100 processing elements) capable of efficient execution of programs written in Kernel Language version 1 (KL1) will be established, and experimental hardware will be fabricated.

2. *Knowledge base subsystem.* When clarifying the technology for implementing the type of knowledge operations that will be required by KBMs, as well as establishing the parallel architecture specifications for the KBM, concrete details of the hardware will also be determined.

3. *Basic software system.*
   a. FGCS Kernel Language. Themes include improvement of KL1, raising the system processing speed and determining the specifications of Kernel Language version 2 (KL2).
   b. Problem-solving and inference software module. In a parallel processing environment (with a parallelism factor of about 100), attempts will be made to realize higher-level inference functions, such as those for inductive reasoning and analogy and to implement cooperative problem-solving functions.
   c. Knowledge base management software module. Central themes for research are a distributed knowledge base and a knowledge representation language.
   d. Intelligent interfaces software module. Research themes include an experimental semantic analysis system, electronic dictionaries and an experimental interactive speech processing system.
   e. Intelligent programming software module. Themes include design of a specification description language and an experimental design support system.
   f. Demonstration system for basic software. To evaluate the validity of R & D results, an integrated evaluation system employing each of the basic software modules will be created.

4. *Development support system.* To increase R & D efficiency, a system for developing parallel software will be implemented. This system will employ several closely coupled PSIs. A local area network will also be implemented.

TABLE 2 Proposed Research and Development Subjectives for the Intermediate Stage

R & D Subjective	Details
Hardware systems	The two subsystems that will form the nucleus of the FGCS hardware will be trial fabricated. 1. To effectively execute programs written in KL1, about 100 processing element modules will be linked to form a prototype inference subsystem. 2. Knowledge processing implementation schemes will be investigated, and a number of processing element modules incorporating knowledge operation mechanisms will be linked to form a knowledge base subsystem.
Inference subsystem	To implement the inference subsystem, R&D on the following items will be carried out. 1. The dynamic characteristics of the PIM will be analyzed and evaluated, and the PIM architecture will be determined by means of simulations. 2. Prototypes of data flow, reduction, and other mechanisms will be developed based on component modules. Each will make use of the highly parallel execution of KL1 programs. 3. A parallel inference machine architecture will be developed from about 100 processing elements linked in a network to form an experimental PIM. 4. R&D of a software system controlling, testing, and evaluating the PIM architecture and component modules. 5. In preparation for scaling up the PIM (to about 1000 processing elements), studies will be made of large-scale PIM architecture, including fusion with machine models, VLSI architecture, and KBMs.
Knowledge base subsystem	To implement a knowledge base subsystem, R&D will be performed on the following items: 1. Analysis and evaluation of the dynamic characteristics of KBMs and development of a knowledge base model to determine the architecture. 2. Further improvement and miniaturization of relational data base machines (RDBMs), through adoption of VLSI components and development of a KBM architecture to form the nucleus of the KBM.

(continued)

TABLE 2   Continued

R & D Subjective	Details
	3. Establishment of technology for configuring a distributed RDBM, centered on models of distributed RDBMs and control algorithms.
	4. Investigation of schemes for integrating inference engines within RDBMs, establishment of connection mechanisms for such schemes, and trial construction; also, research on knowledge base parallel control mechanisms to support parallel processing in KBMs and the realization of knowledge operations.
	5. In preparation for large-scale KBMs, research will be conducted on large-scale KBM architecture, with a view toward implementation of machine models, VLSI architecture, and knowledge acquisition and systemization mechanisms.
Basic software system	The basic software systems will form the nucleus of the FGCS and will be composed of the following modules for knowledge information processing:
	1. Problem-solving and inference software module.
	2. Knowledge base management software module.
	3. Intelligent interface software module.
	4. Intelligent programming software module.
	5. Demonstration system for basic software.
	Through the design and prototype creation of the basic software system, the results gained will be consolidated and, based on these, KL2 will be specified for the final stage. In addition, software for use in actual verification of specifications will be created, experiments performed, and the specifications clarified further.
FGCS Kernel language	The FGCS Kernel Language, the base language for all other modules, will define interfaces between FGCS hardware and software. In the intermediate stage, design of specifications for KL2, which will become the language of the FGCS prototype system, will be completed. The processor and programming system of KL1, the specifications of which were determined in the initial stage, will be prototyped.
Problem-solving and inference software modules	The problem-solving and inference software module has capabilities for deductive inference, inductive inference (including conjecture based on incomplete knowledge), and inference by mutual complementation of knowledge. In the intermediate stage, the following four kinds of software will be developed.

TABLE 2 Continued

R & D Subjective	Details
	1. Parallel inference software that operates on the basis of an advanced parallel processing algorithm to perform high-speed deductive inference and problem solving.
	2. Basic high-level inference software, i.e., experimental software that performs advanced inferences such as those for induction and analogy, and basic software for studying a learning function.
	3. Basic cooperative problem-solving software, i.e., experimental software in which a number of problem-solving programs are made to co-operate to realize an inference function through mutual complementation of knowledge.
	4. Demonstrative problem-solving and inference software, by which the results of R&D may be applied directly to actual fields of application to verify the validity of the results and also as a means for testing by feeding back evaluation results into the development of each type of software.
Knowledge base management software module	The knowledge base management software module has capabilities for knowledge accumulation, distributed knowledge source utilization, and knowledge acquisition. In the intermediate stage, prototypes of the following kinds of software will be created.
	1. A knowledge representation system, which not only includes functions for representation and accumulation of knowledge and for effective use of knowledge gained using appropriate inference facilities but also contains tools for construction and support of knowledge bases.
	2. Basic knowledge acquisition software, experimental software based on inductive inference, equipped with functions for acquiring knowledge.
	3. Basic software for distributed knowledge base management, which manages a number of knowledge bases as a logically unified whole.
	4. Demonstrative knowledge base management software, by which the results of R&D may be applied directly to actual fields of application, to verify the validity of the results, and also as a means for testing by feeding back evaluation results into the development of each type of software.

(continued)

TABLE 2   Continued

R & D Subjective	Details
Intelligent interface software module	The intelligent interface software module is for flexible interaction between humans and computers. In the intermediate stage, prototypes of the following kinds of software will be created.

    1. A semantic dictionary/semantic analysis system: Analyzes meanings using a thesaurus (of Japanese, English, etc.) in knowledge base form.

    2. Basic software for sentence analysis and synthesis: Experimental software that has sentence analysis and synthesis functions, which are basic to text understanding.

    3. A conversational system pilot model: An experimental system offering comprehensive functions for smooth interaction via natural language.

    4. A pilot model for an interactive speech processing system to be created by studying techniques for analysis and understanding of conversational language, containing a large number of ellipses and depending greatly on context, and based on technology for speech understanding and synthesis.

    5. A pilot model for an interactive graphics and image-processing system. Studies will center on techniques for representation of graphic and image data and on unification with natural language. An experimental system will be created based on functions for graphic/image understanding and synthesis, in which large amounts of information are to be exchanged.

    6. Demonstrative intelligent interface software, by which the results of R&D may be applied directly to actual fields of application, to verify the validity of the results, and also as a means for testing by feeding back evaluation results into the development of each type of software.

| Intelligent programming software module | Goals for the intelligent programming software module include automation of the basic operations involved in writing programs, developing and maintaining software, and the realization of integrated high-level support for all processes. In the intermediate stage, the following kinds of software will be developed. |

    1. A specification description and verification system, in which high-level specification des-

TABLE 2 Continued

R & D Subjective	Details

	criptions using natural or formal languages, as well as advanced program testing based on this, are performed.
2.	A software knowledge management system that organizes various programs developed on SIMs into knowledge bases and provides intelligent program development support.
3.	Basic software for program transformation, verification, and synthesis, experimental software that transforms programs with logical strictness using optimization and other factors as a measure, verifies the correctness of the transformation, and synthesizes software based on the transformation.
4.	Experimental software for pilot model of a software design, production, and maintenance system by which all processes from software development through maintenance are consistently managed and supported.
5.	Demonstrative intelligent programming software, by which the results of R&D may be applied directly to actual fields of application to verify the validity of the results and also as a means for testing by feeding back evaluation results into the development of each type of software.

| Demonstration system for basic software | A demonstration system for basic software will be developed, by which results of each R&D subject may be applied directly to actual fields of application, to verify the validity of the results, and also as a means for testing by feeding back evaluation results into the development of each type of software. |

| Development support system | In any advanced R&D project, appropriate development support systems are essential; in the initial stage, the SIM is being developed for use as a software development tool. In the intermediate stage, to facilitate R&D efforts, the following two systems will be developed: |

| | 1. A pilot model machine for parallel software development. |
| | 2. A network system for development support. |

| Pilot model for parallel software development | The following will be developed for use in the system for parallel software development. |

| | 1. A machine for parallel software development, |

(continued)

TABLE 2   Continued

R & D Subjective	Details
	which will be capable of efficient development of parallel software, such as software for processing parallel KL1 programs and other parallel inference software. 2. A SIM (improved version), to be implemented by miniaturization and improvement of the hardware of the SIM developed in the initial stage and for enhancing software functions.
Network system for development support	A network system for supporting development efforts to use R&D results efficiently.

SUMMARY OF THE ORGANIZATION OF THE INSTITUTE FOR NEW GENERATION COMPUTER TECHNOLOGY

Establishment and Organization

The Institute for New Generation Computer Technology (ICOT) was established in April of 1982 as the central organization responsible for promoting the FGCS Project. Its research center was opened for operation in June of the same year.

ICOT is divided into research laboratories and general affairs offices (Fig. 4). At present, approximately 70 researchers and 10 administrative staff are employed at the institute.

Activities

Research and Development on the FGCS

R & D activities on the FGCS are being carried out under the auspices of the Ministry of International Trade and Industry, with funds alloted to the project amounting to 400 million yen in 1982, 2.7 billion yen in 1983, 5.1 billion yen in 1984, and 4.7 billion yen in 1985.

The work on basic technology for the FGCS is performed by project teams consisting of members of the ICOT laboratories. In addition, a project promotion committee and working groups including acknowledged outside authorities have been formed to give advice on the project and to exchange opinions with the ICOT research teams.

Project Promotion Committee

Parallel inference machine and multi-PSI
KBM
Parallel software
Natural language processing system
Japanese generalized phrase structure grammer
Speech-understanding system

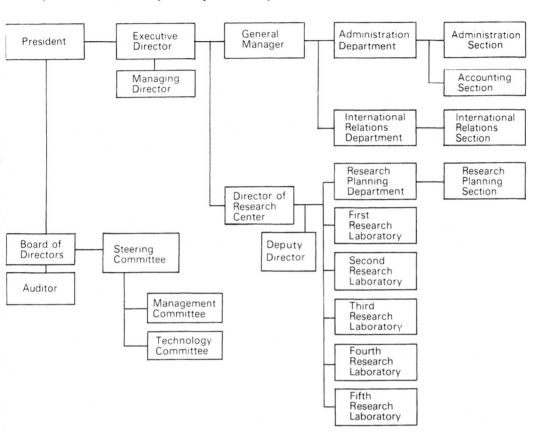

FIGURE 4   ICOT organization.

Foundation for AI
Computer Go and Shogi
Computer-Aided proof
Term rewriting system
Japanese specification language
Intelligent programming system
Machine-readable dictionary

As the present R & D effort has as its object advanced technology, research workers are sent to advanced research organizations in the United States and Europe to survey the latest technology and to exchange opinions. Experts from other countries are invited to Japan for short periods of time for purposes of research exchange.

Survey Studies Related to Advanced Computers

As one step toward promoting R & D on the FGCS, survey studies are being conducted on trends in related technology both in Japan and abroad.   These surveys, conducted by committees of experts from various fields, seek to identify promising areas for FGCS applications and to evaluate the impact of new developments.

Promotion of International Cooperation on FGCS

To facilitate international exchanges related to R & D, the following activities
are being executed.

1. Dispatch of university and other researchers and specialists to the
   United States and Europe.
2. Preparation and distribution of English-language technical journals
   (such as the *ICOT Journal* and various technical reports).

Propagation and Publication of Project Results

ICOT sponsors a symposium each year to announce and explain the results
of project R & D. In addition, ICOT issues a number of publications, such
as the ICOT technical reports, technical memos, and the *ICOT Journal* and,
through these, makes positive efforts to transmit the results of its research.

Sponsorship of International Conferences on FGCS

In October of 1981, the International Conference on Fifth Generation Computer
Systems was held in Tokyo, with approximately 300 persons attending from
Japan and abroad; enthusiastic discussions of technical possibilities and problems took place. In November 1984, the third year of the initial R & D
stage, an international conference called FGCS'84, was held by ICOT for a
period of 4 days (November 6-9). The conference was attended by some
1,100 participants from 29 countries.

   Through these international conferences on FGCS we at ICOT hope for
fruitful exchange of opinions on the significance, goals, and results of
advanced technical development in this promising field. This paper was
written in July, 1986.

KAZUHIRO FUCHI

INTEL CORPORATION

INTRODUCTION

Intel Corporation is an industry leader in the design and manufacture of VLSI (very large-scale integrated) circuits and system-level products based on those circuits. Founded in 1968 in Mountain View, California, Intel's emergence occurred at a key time and place in electronic history, when the phenomenon of Silicon Valley—today the acknowledged center of the world's semiconductor industry—was beginning to take shape. The corporation currently employs roughly 20,000 people at its domestic and international sites spread throughout 6 countries and territories. Annualized revenues for the most recent fiscal year were roughly $2 billion.

Intel is responsible for two of the major postwar innovations in microelectronics that have made today's computer revolution possible—large-scale integrated (LSI) memory and the microprocessor. These developments established the corporation as a technology leader in the vanguard of microelectronics and an important producer of what the media soon came to dub the "microchip," an innovation that has revolutionized the way people live.

The wide range of Intel's component, board, system, and software products is positioned at the leading edge of advanced technology, concentrating on high-end volume applications. The bulk of the corporation's customer base is comprised of original equipment manufacturers (OEMs), which incorporate Intel's products into their own systems geared for the end-user market.

Currently, Intel is a recognized market-share leader in microprocessors, microcontrollers, EPROMs (erasable programmable read-only memories), bus architecture, development systems, and real-time operating systems, Many of Intel's products have become industry standards; the corporation continues to work closely with many other leading companies—electronic and otherwise—to establish future standards that all of industry can use to develop or implement microelectronic products.

PRE-INTEL HISTORY

Intel's roots stretch back some 12 years prior to the founding of the corporation, when Robert N. Noyce and Gordon E. Moore joined Shockley Semiconductor Laboratory in Palo Alto, California, in 1956. William Shockley had been working on a device for electrical amplification and switching as an alternative to the vacuum tube since 1939. Along with John Bardeen and Walter Brattain, he developed the junction transistor while at Bell Laboratories. The three men were awarded the Nobel Prize in 1956 for their efforts.

Shockley decided to pursue the commercial potential of semiconductor devices and opened his laboratory in 1956, attracting many of the bright young minds emerging from university electronics programs. Noyce had received his Ph.D. in physical electronics and solid-state physics from the Massachusetts Institute of Technology in 1953 and had gone on to do research at Philco Corporation. Moore had earned his Ph.D. in chemistry and physics from the California Institute of Technology in 1954 and had joined the technical staff of the Applied Physics Laboratory at Johns Hopkins University, where he did basic research in chemical physics.

Both men traveled west to work on semiconductor process technology with Shockley. They discovered a unique environment ripe for the developments that would eventually lead to the creation of Silicon Valley. Successful electronic firms such as Hewlett–Packard and Varian Associates were already established in the San Francisco Bay area, and Stanford University was active in encouraging engineering firms to locate near Palo Alto to take advantage of its research facilities. These factors, along with a climate featuring nearly ideal living conditions, were drawing leading talent to the area and encouraging a budding entrepreneurial spirit within the engineering community.

Noyce and Moore soon realized they shared a common goal: to find an economical way to manufacture and use transistors. After gaining the support of Fairchild Camera and Instruments Corporation, they left Shockley Laboratory in 1957 with six other colleagues to establish their own laboratory in Mountain View, California. The new Fairchild Semiconductor Company expanded rapidly, thanks in large part to Noyce's coinvention of the integrated circuit (Jack Kilby of Texas Instruments, working independently of Noyce, was also credited with the breakthrough). Noyce served as Fairchild's vice president and general manager and was responsible for initial development of the firm's silicon mesa and planar transistor product lines. As Fairchild's director of research and development, Moore was a key figure in the production of the first commercial integrated circuit.

Despite Fairchild's continued success, instability within the organization led Noyce and Moore to resign in 1968. Once again the two men joined forces and, cognizant of opportunities in the semiconductor market and spurred by the goal of making LSI technology a practical reality, they founded Intel (an acronym for integrated electronics) Corporation in July 1968. They were joined by Andrew S. Grove, who had worked at Fairchild following his Ph.D. in 1963 from the University of California, Berkeley, and had risen to the position of the corporation's assistant director of research and development in 1967. This triumvirate of founding fathers remains intact at Intel today.

The logistics surrounding the founding of Intel are noteworthy because they characterize the entrepreneurial methods that form the foundation upon which Silicon Valley rests. Noyce and Moore talked to Arthur Rock, a San Francisco venture capitalist who had helped start Fairchild Semiconductor, Teledyne, and Scientific Data Systems, among others. The business plan consisted of a single typewritten page stating that the company was going into the development of LSI circuits. The strength of the idea and the reputation of the founders was enough to enable Rock to raise several million dollars by arranging for the sale of convertible debentures, mostly to individual investors. A similar amount was realized in private placements over the next 2 years. Intel went public in 1971.

Between 1968 and 1973, over 50 other companies sprang up under similar circumstances. Armed with ideas to push the frontiers of commercial microelectronics forward, alumni of established firms such as Fairchild struck out on their own to found companies within the growing semiconductor field, transforming the Santa Clara Valley into the capital of a new industry. Today, 20 years later, the name Silicon Valley has become a familiar term in the lexicon of modern society.

THE EARLY YEARS

Intel's first charter was to explore emerging LSI technology—the placement of thousands of microminiature electronic devices on a tiny silicon chip. The initial target was computer memory. At that time, nearly all computer memories utilized magnetic cores, which were 10 times cheaper than equivalent semiconductor devices. The goal was to use LSI to make semiconductor memories the most cost-effective form of solid-state memory for the growing computer market.

Initial efforst were directed at bipolar and MOS (metal-oxide semiconductor) memories. Intel's first successful product was the 3101 Schottky bipolar memory, a 64-bit, high-speed static random access memory (SRAM) introduced in 1969. Bipolar memories were not new, but Intel was able to successfully implement an innovation called Schottky bipolar technology (named for the German physicist, Walter Schottky).

This success helped support the development of the silicon-gate MOS chip, a device that allowed greater density and performance at a lower price. At first, the MOS project encountered many obstacles in perfecting the technique for putting polysilicon on top of the oxide. The biggest problem was combating "drift" on MOS devices, a phenomenon whereby a chip's electrical threshold does not hold constant due to contamination. After a year of development, the first commercial use of LSI MOS silicon-gate technology occurred with the introduction of Intel's 1101 256-bit SRAM in 1969. It was the emergence shortly afterward of the 1103, the world's first 1K bit dynamic RAM (DRAM), that signaled a breakthrough: For the first time, significant amounts of information could be stored on a single chip. The 1103 began to replace core memories and soon became an industry standard. By 1972, it was the largest selling semiconductor memory in the world.

These efforts in the memory field led Intel to the invention of the EPROM in 1971. Research into the silicon-gate MOS process made Intel engineers conclude that disconnected or floating gates could be the cause of device failures. This realization produced another discovery: that the floating gate phenomenon might be the basis for a programmable and erasable memory. Soon a novel floating-gate memory was created that stored charges permanently. Previously, devices had required a constant power supply to maintain memory functions; if power was lost, the devices had to be reprogrammed. When it was determined that memory in the new device could be erased by applying ultraviolet rays, a glass window was placed on the chip to allow the erasure, and the 1701 2K bit EPROM was born.

At the time, the industry was unsure how this technology could be applied. The EPROM was viewed initially as a prototyping device to be employed in research and development, and many customers who purchased the chip were reluctant to use it in their commercial systems because of unanswered questions relating to the long-term reliability of the device. It was with the advent of the microprocessor that same year—another Intel invention—that the real significance of the EPROM was realized. The microprocessor and the EPROM developed a symbiotic relationship with each other: The ability of the EPROM to be reprogrammed to meet specific application needs allowed the microprocessor to act as a general-purpose processor to handle the logic functions of a virtually unlimited range of applications.

THE MICROPROCESSOR

Despite the heavy emphasis on LSI memories, it was Intel's invention and introduction of the microprocessor—a logic device—that was, perhaps, the single factor most responsible for establishing the corporation as a technology leader. Known as a "computer on a chip," the microprocessor is a general-purpose information processor that can be modified for specific uses by programs stored in memory.

The invention of this device revolutionized the way computers are designed and applied. It put intelligence into "dumb" machines and distributed processing capability into previously undreamed of applications. The advent of intelligent machines based on microprocessors changed the way information is gathered and communicated, reshaping the contours of the modern workplace. Today, 17 years after its introduction, it remains the heart of the microelectronics revolution.

The development of the microprocessor began in 1969, when Busicom, a now-defunct Japanese calculator manufacturer, asked Intel to design a set of chips for a family of high-performance programmable calculators. The original design called for at least five chips, but Intel engineer and project leader Marcian E. "Ted" Hoff considered this configuration too complex to be cost-effective. His solution was to create a general-purpose data processor by reducing the complexity of the instructions and storing the program for a specific application in semiconductor memory.

The initial design involved four chips: a central processing unit (CPU), a read-only memory (ROM) for custom application programs, a RAM for processing data, and a shift register for input/output (I/O) tasks. The CPU chip eventually came to be called a microprocessor.

Measuring 1/8 inch wide by 1/6 inch long and made up of 2,300 MOS transistors, Intel's first microprocessor was equal in computing power to the first electronic computer, ENIAC, which filled 3,000 cubic feet with 18,000 vacuum tubes when it was built in 1946. Intel's 4004 4-bit microprocessor could execute 60,000 operations in 1 second—primitive by today's standards, but a major breakthrough at the time.

Suspecting the market potential for such a product, Intel secured the rights to the microprocessor designs and the rights to market the device for noncalculator applications. This allowed the corporation to extend its commitment to memories; the potential of the EPROM when used with the microprocessor then brought the former device into focus. Designers could change their systems simply by reprogramming the microprocessor via an EPROM rather than employing fixed ROMs with it. In addition, it became necessary to supply customers with development aids—elementary programming tools—to use the first microprocessors more easily. This need gave birth to development systems, a market in which Intel remains strong today.

The microprocessor also spawned a number of other products that form the backbone of Intel's business. Software was developed for microprocessors, which gave engineers the ability to conduct modular software design through the generation of linkable, relocatable object code modules. All of the software aids developed during the first 5 years of the microprocessor's existence fostered the development of supporting hardware, such as microcontrollers, single-board computers, peripheral chips, and coprocessors. These will be discussed later in this article.

The 4004 was introduced at the end of 1971, followed by the 8-bit 8008 the next year. Aside from the number of bits, the 8008 differed from its predecessor in its orientation to data/character manipulation rather than arithmetic orientation.

It was with the introduction of the 8-bit 8080 in 1974 that the microprocessor became firmly ensconced in the industry. The 8080 was much more highly integrated than its predecessors, offering over five times the performance, executing nearly 290,000 operations per second, and addressing 46 Kbytes of memory. Both the 4004 and 8008 utilized P-channel MOS (PMOS) technology, whereas the 8080 used an innovative N-channel MOS (NMOS) process, yielding vast gains in speed, power, capacity, and density. The device required only 6 support chips for operation, as opposed to 20 with the 8008. Armed with these advantages, the 8080 soon became an industry standard. It was followed closely by the 8-bit 8085, which operated on a single 5-volt power supply, was faster, and integrated more functions onto the chip.

The next step was producing a 16-bit architecture. The decision was made to build a microprocessor that offered complete compatibility with the application software used with Intel's 8-bit family of microprocessors. This led to the development of the 16-bit 8086, introduced in 1978. It offered power, speed, and features far beyond the capabilities of the second-generation 8-bit microprocessors. Throughput increased an order of magnitude over the 8080, memory space was 16 times greater (1 Mbyte vs. 64 bytes), and I/O addressability grew from 256 bytes in the 8080 to 64 Kbytes in the 8086. Other features included efficient high-level language addressing, interruptible string manipulation, and full decimal arithmetic—all executed in 29K transistors on a die only 27% larger than the 8080.

In 1979, Intel introduced the 8088 microprocessor, featuring the same internal 16-bit architecture as the 8086. Whereas the latter offered a 16-bit bus interface, the 8088 was configured with an 8-bit bus interface, opening it up to the large market of 8-bit designs. The move proved propitious; IBM chose the 8088 as the microprocessor for its new line of personal computers, a decision that helped to establish Intel's 8086/88 architecture as the undisputed industry leaders.

The next step in Intel's microprocessor evolution was to expand its 16-bit product line by developing function and performance gains. Two new microprocessors were introduced in 1982, the 80186 and the 80286. The former is now used primarily to control data in embedded applications.

The 80286 is aimed at the high end of the 16-bit market, featuring on-chip memory management that allows it to support users performing several different tasks at the same time. The 80286 handles sophisticated program languages, program management, multitasking operating systems, computer graphics, and high-speed telecommunications tied to personal computers. It is six times faster than the 8086 or 8088, yet it maintains full compatibility with all the operating systems and application software programs originally designed for the 8086.

According to Dataquest, a San Jose, California, market research firm, by the end of 1984, Intel's 16-bit architecture had captured over 83% of the 16-bit microprocessor market. The next challenge to build on this success lay in the 32-bit arena. In late 1985, Intel introduced the 80386, the highest-performance commercial microprocessor ever built. A look at its features reveals how far technology has progressed since the microprocessor's first appearance in 1971. The 80386 has over 275,000 transistors on chip, executes 3 to 4 million instructions per second (MIPS), and offers both paged and segmented addressing. It addresses 4 gigabytes (giga = billion) of physical memory and 64 terabytes (tera = trillion) of virtual memory. It is currently the only 32-bit microprocessor available that allows simultaneous processing of applications running under different operating systems.

These advanced features have made the 80386 the dominant player in three diverse segments of the computing market. As the only 32-bit microprocessor that can tap into the existing $10 billion base of application software written for the 8086 and 80286 16-bit architectures, the 80386 provides the perfect upgrade for existing high performance 16-bit microsystems. And with performance comparable to that of a VAX minicomputer, the 80386 provides a cost-effective replacement to the current closed, proprietary minicomputer architectures. Finally, features such as multitasking, on-chip MMU, virtual memory with paging, software protection and large address space mark the 80386 as the ideal chip for a host of entirely new (and in some cases, still undeveloped) applications.

By the end of 1987, the 80386 had become an enormous success: design wins for the chip exceeded 400 and more than 100 of those 80386 based products had been brought to market. Many of the products go beyond the traditional personal computing applications: In 1987, the 80386 was designed into engineering workstations and parallel processing systems as well as artificial intelligence, telecommunications, and military applications.

The microprocessor has had an enormous impact on the fabric of everyday life; its immense performance capabilities, coupled with its tiny size, has allowed it to be used in everything from automobiles to automated teller machines, radar to robots, and personal computers to process control systems. It is the core around which Intel's business is built.

PROCESS TECHNOLOGY

A key step in making integrated circuit (IC) memories practical was achieving a breakthrough in process technology. Starting in 1968, Intel chose to develop two relatively new technological approaches that had previously only been used to make laboratory devices. One was the silicon-gate MOS process, which substituted a film of polycrystalline silicon for the aluminum used previously; the other was a variation of the bipolar technology known as the Schottky TTL process.

The latter developed quickly, but the MOS process proved to be a formidable challenge. Intel's earliest MOS technology was P-channel (positively charged), which was used on the corporation's first SRAM and DRAM in the early 1970s. PMOS, however, had speed limitations, compelling Intel to develop an N-channel (negatively charged) MOS process in 1974. This was followed by a high-density, high-performance technology that became known as HMOS (high-performance MOS). HMOS involved scaling the transistors and using positive photoresist and projection printing, leading to shrink technology and the application of the HMOS process to microprocessors.

Since its inception, HMOS has continued to evolve, allowing Intel to produce ever denser, smaller, and higher-performing devices. In 1983, Intel introduced the third generation of this technology, HMOS-III, which produces devices up to 40% smaller than previously possible.

Next came the development of an advanced CMOS (complementary MOS) process. Traditional CMOS was first developed by RCA in the 1950s and later gained success in many portable microelectronic applications; the advantage of CMOS was that it used far less energy and generated much less heat than comparable NMOS devices. The problem with this process, however, was that it was difficult to use in high-density and high-performance configurations and was considered too complicated and expensive for most VLSI applications.

Intel's solution was to combine the high performance and density of HMOS with the low power of CMOS in a process known as CHMOS (complementary high-performance MOS). With the relatively straightforward addition of an N-well in the same high resistivity substrate used in HMOS, a CMOS process was obtained. Intel has developed both P-well and N-well CHMOS to meet the requirements of SRAMs and microprocessors (P-well) on the one hand, and microcontrollers and EPROMs (N-well) on the other.

The biggest hurdle for CHMOS was overcoming latch up problems, a traditional nemesis of CMOS. Given the presence of parasitic structures within every bulk CMOS chip, a current pulse of sufficient magnitude occurring either internally or externally to the chip is capable of causing catastrophic latch up. Intel avoided this problem by using epitaxial substrates for its entire line of CHMOS technology. The episubstrate brings the same benefits to all product lines, in many cases providing additional advantages, such as improved surface lifetimes and reduced dc resistance.

Double-layer metal has become an important element of the CHMOS process, allowing an efficient layout of random logic. The second layer of metal is advantageous to long-distance routing and power busing. Intel has converted many of its HMOS products to CHMOS; by 1988, 37% of the company's manufacturing activities were being done in CHMOS. Intel is also doing the bulk of its production on 1.5 micron technologies, which allows a larger number of components to be packed on a chip of silicon. This trend will continue into sub-micron technologies.

PRODUCTS

Intel's products cover a wide range of component, board, system, and software offerings. Here is a brief look at each of the corporation's major product families.

Memories

As noted earlier, Intel began as a supplier of LSI memory, and that course
has lead the company to virtually every corner of the memory market. At
various times during the past 20 years, Intel has produced EPROMs, EEPROMs,
SRAMs, nonvolatile RAMs (NVRAMs), DRAMs, bubble memories and flash
memories. Today, Intel has chosen to focus its resources exclusively on
EPROM and flash technology.

EPROMs

The advent of the microprocessor created a huge market for EPROMs; as
mentioned previously, Intel invented both devices in 1971. With each new
generation of ROMs cramming more and more memory onto a single chip,
Intel introduced denser EPROMs in the mid-1970s which built on the success
of its earliest devices, beginning with the 8K 2708 in 1975. The 16K 2716,
introduced in 1977, became an industry standard. Featuring a 5-volt power
supply, it was compatible with any microprocessor system, greatly broadening its application potential.

Intel has continued to introduce next-generation EPROMs; the latest
example is a 4-megabit CMOS EPROM—the world's first 256K x 16 memory
device—introduced in 1988. Intel remains the recognized world leader in
EPROM market share and technology.

Flash Memories

Introduced in 1988, Intel's flash memories were heralded as the future of
non-volatile memory. Flash memories combine the reliability and low cost
of EPROM with the electrical erasibility of EEPROM. They can be erased
and reprogrammed in less than five seconds using standard EPROM reprogramming methods—such as PROM programmers/testers of "edge connectors"
for on-board programming—or by using the local CPU to in-system write
functions. Currently, Intel's line of flash memory products consists of the
64-Kbit 27F64 and the 256-Kbit 27F256 and 28F256.

DRAMs

DRAMs were one of the important cornerstones of Intel's business in its
early years. As already noted, the development in 1970 of the world's
first 1K DRAM, the 1103, was a vital step in establishing Intel as a technology leader. Intel continued to add density and performance gains to new
generations of DRAMs and began to produce these devices with CHMOS technology in the 1980s. These efforts culminated with the introduction of the
world's first CMOS 256K DRAM in 1984. In 1985, however, the lack of
adequate profit margins in this marketplace led the corporation to announce
its withdrawal from the DRAM business. Currently, the company markets
DRAMs produced by Micron Technologies and Samsung under the Intel name.

Logic Devices

Embedded Controllers

Embedded controllers are highly-integrated, commodity price-driven, micro-
computer chips—typically microprocessors or more often, microcontrollers.
They differ from Intel's traditional microprocessor in two important ways.
First, an embedded controller's lifecycle is dependent on its mix of on-chip

features—more memory, I/O or application-specific functions, for instance—
rather than MIPS (millions of instructions per second). Second, unlike the
microprocessors in PCs and workstations, embedded controllers are not
reprogrammable through applications software. Instead, they are prepro-
grammed by product designers for specific functions.

Intel has a long history in the embedded control market. The company
invented the industry's first EPROM microcontroller—the 8748—in 1976.
The 8-bit 8048 was introduced two years later, and the 8-bit 8051 followed
in 1981. A year later, Intel introduced its 16-bit 8096, and in 1987 the
company came out with the 80C196KA, a more powerful, CMOS version of
the 8096. Along with these microcontrollers, a number of Intel's 8086 family
of microprocessors—most notably, the 80186, its new CMOS version, the
80C186, and the recently introduced 80376 architecture, an 80386-based
device—are targeted at embedded control applications. The 80960, a new
32-bit architecture aimed at high-end embedded control applications, was
also introduced in 1988.

In addition to its standard controllers, Intel now offers versions customized for the requirements of a particular application or customer. This
ability to customize from a standard chip "core" is an important part of
Intel's push to serve the embedded controller market more effectively with
Application Specific Standard Products (ASSPs).

Peripheral Components

The invention of the microprocessor created a need for peripheral controllers
that interface with the CPU to perform various functions. Among the early
devices Intel introduced in 1975 were a series of programmable chips, followed
soon after by the 8275 CRT controller and the 8271 floppy disk controller.

It was Intel's introduction of the 8087 coprocessor in 1980 that brought
the peripheral marketplace into the spotlight. Coprocessors act as extensions of the host CPU, offloading specialized tasks that they can handle
more effectively than the microprocessor. The 8087, for example, can solve
difficult mathematical problems on 8086- and 8088-based systems, which
formerly had to be solved on larger higher-cost minicomputers or mainframes.
The 8087 computes about 100 times faster than equivalent numeric software
running directly on the microprocessor.

The 8087 also established the technology for the coprocessors that
would follow to provide even greater software integration; it paved the way,
for example, for the 80287, Intel's coprocessor that runs with the 16-bit
80286 microprocessor. Other devices include the 82586 and 82588 for network data communications, the 82716 for video storage and display, the
82730 text processor, and the 82786 graphics coprocessor. In 1987, Intel
announced three new peripherals designed to run with the 80386: The 8230
for DMA control, the 80387 numeric coprocessor, and the 82385 cache controller.

Systems and Software

The success of Intel's early component products soon led to the development
of a systems business. The case of the 1103 1K DRAM offers a good
example. Because Intel was producing leading-edge semiconductor memories
that were ahead of their time, it became obvious that many customers did
not have the technical capability or the financial resources to implement
these devices properly. This realization spawned a memory systems opera-

tion at Intel, which began by putting components together on demonstration boards to show customers how such devices could be used. The first product in 1971 was the IN-10, a memory board with peripheral components to support the 1103. The next step came in 1972 with the development of add-on memories for IBM mainframes.

The IBM add-on business and the memory boards flourished until the late 1970s. By that time, Intel's memory products had become easier to use, and as customers became increasingly sophisticated, more and more of them began buying at the component level. The memory systems operation was sold in 1983, but a strong precedent had been set by then, which resulted in a number of other system products.

Development Systems

Intel found itself in a position similar to the memory systems dilemma when the 4004 microprocessor was introduced in 1971. A market need for design and development aids soon revealed itself, prompting Intel to build simulator boards to help customers use the new microprocessor. The SIM4-01 and SIM4-02 were introduced in 1972 as kit boards containing a 4004, which could be hooked to an I/O device and users' EPROMs. The generation of a simple assembler, along with monitors to debug software, allowed customers to develop their own application programs.

Simulator boards began to generate healthy profits and were soon joined in 1973 by the Intellec 4 and Intellec 8 software development tools, which added cross assemblers and other features to the basic simulator boards. The design aids became the key to Intel's microprocessor sales; they were so popular that their revenues soon exceeded the sales of microprocessors. It was not until 1978, in fact, that component sales would overtake those of systems.

Intel's next advance in development aids came in 1975 with the introduction of the ICE^{TM}-80 in-circuit emulator—an industry first. ICE modules were devices that could be substituted for the microprocessors that were actually used in customers' systems. They provided design engineers with a window through which they could look inside the component to see what was going on in the system. These aids proved invaluable in developing and debugging microprocessor-based systems.

All of these innovations established Intel as the industry leader in development systems, a position it still holds today. The corporation's latest contribution, the "open development environment," now allows Intel hardware and software development tools to be used on a wide variety of host development systems and networking equipment found in established design engineering environments. In addition to employing the Intellec system as a host, engineers can now use Intel development tools with a multitude of operating systems. The open development environment, for examples, enables design work to be done on a VAX or an IBM PC, options that had not been available previously.

Bus Architecture

Bus architecture comprises the conceptual foundations that define systems architecture and the physical interconnections that tie the elements of those systems together. In 1975, Intel introduced its MULTIBUS® specification, so named because it was designed to deal with multiprocessing configurations. As an 8/16-bit bus architecture, MULTIBUS allowed auxiliary boards and extension modules with microprocessors on them to be hooked into the main system and perform functions at very high speeds.

The rapid acceptance of the MULTIBUS architecture resulted in the adoption of this specification by the IEEE as an industry standard (IEEE 796). By 1986, more than one million installed CPU boards were based on the MULTIBUS architecture. Next in line was the MULTIBUS II architecture, a 32-bit BUS architecture built on the foundation of MULTIBUS I and designed to connect 32-bit systems modules together.

Another Intel innovation, the BITBUS^{TM} architecture, was developed in 1984 as an open serial interconnect standard designed to provide real-time communications among single-board computers, their microcontrollers, and other VLSI devices. The BITBUS architecture offers an inexpensive and fast alternative to other networks at the process and sensor levels in industrial applications. Process-level controllers and their sensors/actuators can now communicate via a twisted-pair set of wires at the rate of over 1,000 messages per second.

Single-Board Computers

The development of in-circuit emulators and the MULTIBUS architecture led Intel into a market that has proved profitable for the corporation since its first products were introduced: single-board computers. Many companies soon realized that their best business approach was to buy more highly integrated board-level systems to use in their end products rather than spend the time and money necessary to design board modules themselves. This strategy allows them to spend their resources on building applications software to make their products more desirable to the market.

In 1976, Intel introduced the industry's first single-board computer, the iSBC 80/10. Based on the 8080 microprocessor and MULTIBUS architecture, the board had 4K bytes of memory. The iSBC 80/10 met with immediate success, spawning the development over the years of many new board-level products in the iSBC family, which have provided multiple levels of expansion and design flexibility for OEMs. Single-board computers allow for the addition of large amounts of high speed memory, low-cost modular I/O, and math expsnsion, among other features. There are now more than 100 MULTIBUS-based boards on the market from Intel—ample testimony to Intel's position as an industry leader in the single-board computer market-place.

Operating Systems

Intel first developed operating systems to go along with some of its early development tools. As demand increased for higher levels of integration in board-level products, Intel developed its first real-time operating system in 1978—the iRMX® 80. Real time refers to the processing of transactions as they occur rather than the sequential processing used in batch-mode applications. Real-time operating systems are particularly useful in industrial applications, for example, where fast response times to events are required.

The iRMX 80 was first targeted to be used with the 8-bit iSBC® 80 single-board computer. It was followed by the 16-bit iRMX 86 multitasking operating system in 1980, which soon became an industry standard. iRMX 86 provides a number of standard interfaces that allow applications to take advantage of industry-standard device controllers, hardware components, and a multitude of software packages developed by independent software

vendors (ISVs). In 1987, iRMX 286 Release 2.0 was introduced, extending
iRMX support to the 80286 and the 80386 microprocessors.

Personal Computer Enhancement Products

Its success in OEM boards and operating systems targeted at computer
builders prompted Intel to look into board market opportunities for computer
users. Several years ago, Intel created a personal computer enhancement
business to meet the needs of PC users. By offering customers PC-bus
modules—such as memory expansion boards that plug easily into existing
IBM PCs and compatibles—Intel has expanded its board-level influence
beyond the OEM computer-builder base. These products, in fact, may be
purchased at a large number of retail outlets—a notable diversion from
Intel's traditional sales and distribution channels.

Microcomputer Systems

Once it was successful with its boards, the next step in Intel's systems
evolution was to provide completely integrated systems. The first move in
this direction was the introduction of the System 86/330, based on the 8086,
in 1981. Packaged in a chassis, the System 330 combined SBCs, memory
boards, disks, power supply and systems software, including the operating
system. Many customers found it a cost-effective alternative to building
their own systems.

In 1983, Intel introduced the System 286/310, based on the high-
performance 80286 16-bit microprocessor. System 310 combines the microprocessor, a numeric coprocessor, an enhanced MULTIBUS architecture, and
a new systems software. Next came the APEX (advanced processor extension) series. Based on the 80286, this series makes use of multiple (up to
four) microprocessors, allowing it to deliver minicomputer power at a fraction of typical minicomputer costs.

Today, Intel's System 300 series, as it is now known, has thousands
of installations in various configurations, and has penetrated a wide variety
of applications, including robotics, environmental control, networking hosts
and engineering workstations. In 1988, Intel introduced the latest members
of this family: The System 301 and System 302 incorporate the power of the
32-bit 80386 into a PC AT-compatible design.

Scientific Computers

In 1985, Intel developed the world's first commercially supported concurrent
computer. The iPSC® family was designed and priced to put concurrent
computers into the hands of individual researchers and scientific groups in
laboratory environments who could not afford these types of machines previously. The concept of concurrency is to distribute the workload of
processing a problem among as many as several hundred CPUs. Each of
these CPUs is an individual computer that operates concurrently on a portion
of the problem.

Based on a "hypercube" topology first developed at Cal Tech, each
iPSC system can be upgraded to larger, higher-performance models by
modular expansion of the number of computational units. Three iPSC models
are currently available, consisting of 32, 64, or 128 processing nodes. In
1987, Intel introduced the 80386-based iPSC/2 system, its second generation
hypercude. The iPSC/2 system is available in configurations from 16 to 128
processing nodes and is easier to program and up to 10 times faster than its
predecessor.

Microcommunications Products

The development of microelectronic storage (memory) and computational (logic) products over the years has created a need for communications products that connect the diverse array of systems now on the market and allow them to interoperate. The emerging microcommunications market reflects the merging of telecommunications and data communications, areas where Intel has already made key contributions. The corporation now offers products on both the component and systems levels, marking it as a major participant in microcommunications technology.

Components

Telecommunications: Intel was the first major domestic semiconductor manufacturer to enter the telecommunications marketplace, beginning with the introduction of the 2910 codec chip in 1977. Intel's codecs, line filters, and combo chips function as special—purpose A/D (analog-to-digital) and D/A converters for use in line circuits in telephony switching and transmission systems. Their wide dynamic range and minimal conversion time make them ideal for such other applications as voice storage, digital echo cancelers, secure communications systems, and satellite earth stations.

These early telephony components soon became industry standards and were followed in 1984 by a family of advanced line-interface circuit components to provide OEMs with an evolutionary growth path toward an all-digital network. The first members of this family, the 29C51 Feature Control Combo and the 2952 Integrated Line Gard Controller, handle analog elements of the telephone system and provide for A/D conversion. With the introduction of the 82502 transceiver chip in 1986, Intel eliminated the need for several active and passive components used in Ethernet LAN systems. The company's latest contribution to data communications is the 83C152 universal communications controller, introduced in 1987, a semi-custom chip designed for embedded control applications that require both serial communications and real-time microcontroller capabilities.

Date Communications: LANs are becoming the backbone of data communications in the office, laboratory and factory environments. Intel's family of LAN system building blocks allows users to achieve early market entry with MULTIBUS-compatible Ethernet controllers, network software and Ethernet cluster modules. Its 82586, introduced in 1982, was the industry's first LAN coprocessor. This device was followed by the introduction of the 82588 in 1984, a single-chip LAN controller that allows for low-cost networking. In 1986, Intel introduced the 29C53 transceiver chip, a digital-loop controller that connects telephones, personal computers and facsimile machines in accordance with the all-digital Integrated Services Digital Network (ISDN). It was accompanied by the 29C48, a converter chip that switches telephone voice to digital and vice versa. All Intel telecom products are in accordance with ISDN standards. These devices are supported by an array of single-board computers optimized for various network communications functions.

Networking Products

Intel has played a leading role in the standardization and development of networking hardware and software. In 1981, in conjunction with DEC and Xerox, Intel pioneered the development of the Ethernet local area network

(LAN), which enabled a number of computers to communicate. This high performance network has since become an industry standard. In 1985, Intel introduced its OpenNET^{TM} networking strategy, which allowed different computers and operating systems to work together. This was followed by the MultiSERVER^{TM} Department Service Network, an Ethernet-based LAN that lets large PC network users share resources, communicate with mini-computers and mainframes and access files without interfering with each others work.

Intel has also been a major player in the MAP (Manufacturing Area Protocol) standardization effort, and offers a strong array of MAP network-ing products for the factory floor. Most recently, Intel has addressed the connectivity needs of microcomputer and minicomputer users who need to tie into mainframes. Its FASTPATH^{TM} connectivity platform provides an economical means to accomplish these functions while conforming to industry-standard protocols.

OPEN SYSTEMS AND STANDARDS

All of Intel's systems products subscribe to the corporation's "open systems" philosophy, a concept geared to protect established hardware and software investments by ensuring that new products can be integrated easily into existing systems without having to face compatibility issues. By adopting and driving industry-wide standards, Intel spares its customers from wrestling with the costly and time-consuming problem of dealing with a maze of proprietary systems. The modular approach to product implementation allows OEMs to employ Intel products as "building blocks," which can be replaced or upgraded without forcing the complete redesign of systems. Every new Intel product is geared for compatibility with its predecessors, allowing the entire product line to function as a related family of solutions.

To support this philosophy, Intel remains active in implementing industry standards. Many of its products have become de facto standards due to their widespread acceptance in the marketplace, whereas others have been adopted by the IEEE as official standards. Intel's adherence to stand-ards allows its products to function efficiently with those of other vendors also observing these standards, providing customers with the flexibility to mix and match their purchases to achieve the best results for the specific needs of their applications.

CORPORATE CULTURE

One of the most significant features of Intel is its unique corporate culture, a set of values that defines its working environment. Many of the tenets of this culture have been adopted over time by other Silicon Valley firms, creating an atmosphere that is markedly different from most traditional corporate structures.

In its early days, when the corporation was still very small in size, Intel's offices were characterized by an informal atmosphere, where ideas were exchanges freely and employees had access to all levels of manage-ment. As Intel grew rapidly, it became necessary to define a set of guide-lines that would preserve these approaches. The "open door" policy re-mains an integral part of the cluture, epitomized by modular offices known as cubicles. These structures are five-foot-high partitions built without doors, allowing for an easy and efficient exchange of ideas. Even the highest levels of management work in cubicles, providing accessibility and a close working relationship with all employees. None of the other traditional perquisities of old-line corporations exist at Intel; for example, there are no executive dining rooms or assigned parking spaces. The working atmosphere is also characterized by a lack of any dress codes, and employees usually come to work in casual attire.

Employees meet with their managers in "one-on-ones," which allow them to discuss important problems and issues directly and on a regular basis. It is the right of all employees to schedule one-on-ones with anyone in the corporation if the need for such meetings arises.

Another concept known as "constructive confrontation" is practiced. This allows employees to get to the root of problems quickly by being encouraged to voice their ideas without fear of ridicule; politicking or closed lobbying for personal gain is not tolerated. Intel encourages decision making at the lowest possible levels and expects its employees to deal directly with problems in a straightforward manner.

The technique of "management by objective" is practiced at Intel, where individual and group objectives are defined carefully on a quarterly and monthly basis and then later evaluated to determine if results have been met. Risk taking is encouraged, and the corporation rewards its employees based on a "meritocracy," where promotions are based on achievements rather than on seniority or other criteria.

Adoption of these innovative techniques has been a major factor in Intel's success and growth. By tearing down many of the traditional practices of corporate business, Intel has been able to solve problems and develop new technologies and products with a minimum of bureaucracy; as noted, many of these innovative management techniques have spilled over to other Silicon Valley microelectronic concerns. As a result, Intel was included in both editions of *The 100 Best Companies To Work For in America*, published in 1984 and 1985 by the New American Library. The company's performance in 1987 earned it similar acclaim from *Electronics Business* and the *San Francisco Chronicle*.

SUMMARY

Intel is firm in its conviction to remain in the forefront of microelectronic technologies. To maintain this position, the corporation will continue to concentrate on leading-edge products and strategies. As the VLSI explosion proliferates, markets such as factory automation and microcommunications are opening their doors to microelectronic innovations as never before.

The evolution of the corporation reflects the changes that have occurred in high technology over the past two decades. As microelectronics has grown, a greater emphasis is being placed on meeting quality and reliability standards and offering extensive customer services. It is no longer enough to merely provide the market with products; Intel's large and well-trained sales and support force positions it as a leader in meeting customer needs after sales have been made, a vital factor that will allow the corporation to maintain its leadership position in the industry.

This article has covered many of the inventions and industry firsts that Intel has pioneered. These developments would be significant for any corporation, but they are particularly impressive in light of Intel's relatively short period of existence— 20 years, as of this writing. As an established market share and technology leader in many areas, the corporation stands on a solid foundation to extend its legacy of leadership into the future.

INTEL CORPORATE COMMUNICATIONS

LOCAL AREA NETWORKS

DEFINITION

Local area networks (LANs) are a phenomenon that began in the 1970s. In the late 1970s the Institute of Electrical and Electronics Engineers (IEEE) began to formulate standards for various types of LANs, and they adopted the following definition [1]:

> A data communications system which allows a number of independent data devices to communicate with each other.... A local network is distinguished from other types of data networks in that the communication is confined to a moderate sized geographic area such as a single office building, a warehouse, or a campus. The network can generally depend on a physical communications channel of moderate to high data rate, which has consistently low error rate.

IMPETUS

For our purposes, it is useful to comment further on the causes and origins of LANs to give more insight into this definition. There are two driving factors behind the growth of LANs: the need for them and the ability to satisfy that need. Both are driven by a signel innovation, the development of the microprocessor, in the period that is now commonly referred to as the microprocessor revolution.

When the cost of computer processing is expensive relative to the cost of communications, as was the case in the 1960s and early 1970s, the result is the sharing of computing by many users via telecommunications access, namely, "timesharing." With the development of the microprocessor, computing became so inexpensive that any desktop can now have its own computer. To be sure, there are still shared expensive computers, but much of the computation that was once done on these central facilities is now done by microprocessor-based dedicated minicomputers and personal computers. These computers have penetrated every conceivable business, educational, and government environment, including offices, factories, and classrooms. The need next arose to interconnect these microprocessors within a facility so that they could share their data bases and results, interact with remaining central facilities, and communicate with other facilities. The communications network that performs this interconnection is called the LAN. Once again, it is the microprocessor that facilitated the building of this LAN to satisfy the very need it created. In a typical LAN configuration (shown in Fig. 1A), the various user micros are interfaced to the network by a network interface unit (NIU), which itself contains an integrated circuit microprocessor.

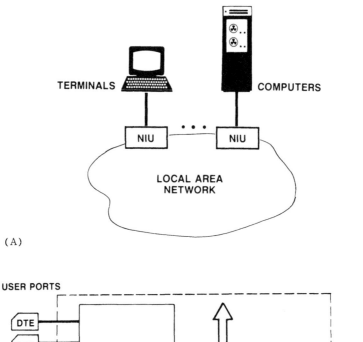

(A)

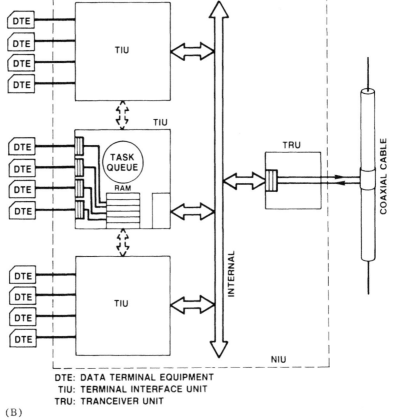

DTE: DATA TERMINAL EQUIPMENT
TIU: TERMINAL INTERFACE UNIT
TRU: TRANCEIVER UNIT

(B)

FIGURE 1   (A) LAN configuration; (B) typical NIU building blocks; (C) typical NIU.   (DTE) Data reminal equipment; (TIU) terminal interface unit; (TRU) transceive unit.

FIGURE 1

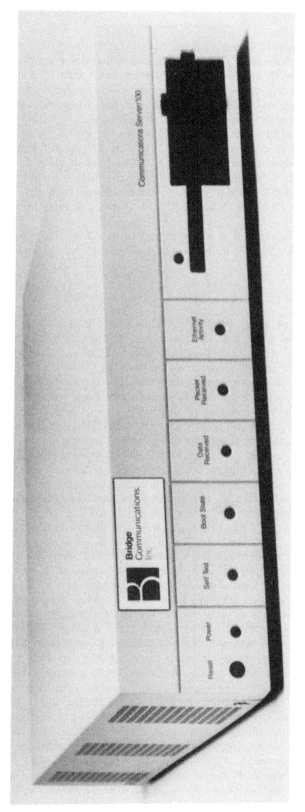

FIGURE 1C

A variety of other names abound for these NIUs. Two common ones are bus interface unit (BIU) and communications interface unit (CIU). A block diagram of a typical NIU is shown in Figure 1B [2]. The NIU connects data terminal equipment (DTE) to user ports on one side and to some transmission medium such as coaxial cable on the other side. Within the NIU are microprocessor-based terminal interface units (TIUs). For different vendors these TIUs may handle 1, 2, 4, or sometimes up to 8 or even 32 ports. NIUs often have multiple TIUs, as shown, to handle even more terminals. As shown inside one of the TIUs, messages and tasks are queued and passed to a high-speed bus within the NIU to other TIUs or to a transceiver unit (TRU), which queues the messages from the DTEs for transmission to other NIUs in the system and then performs the transmission and reception.

A photograph of a commercial NIU is shown in Figure 1C. A typical NIU measures about 3 inches in height and 12 by 12 inches at its base.

ORIGINS

It is a measure of the dynamism of the field of LANs that beyond the IEEE definition, the more detailed functional definitions of LANs are still not agreed upon. It is therefore instructive to examine some of the prehistory of the LAN to try to discern its underlying causes and directions.

In the 1960s, a significant breakthrough occurred in data communications in that users began to separate from their central computers. As Figure 2 indicates, computers originally stood alone with direct physical access to them. The next step was the separation of a single user from his computer by mail or telephone lines, resulting finally in time-shared systems with multiple users. In the 1970s, evolution was greatly speeded by the development, as in Figure 3, of all sorts of devices to save communication costs, e.g., multidrop lines, multiplexers, concentrators, and others.

The culmination of these activities was the development of highly distributed communication systems, of which the Advanced Research Projects Agency Network (ARPANET) [3] was one of the earliest and most significant examples, as shown in Figure 4. Soon after the ARPANET came up, a telling fact was noted at its Network Measurement Center. A significant amount of the traffic on this nationally distributed communication system turned out to be local. Indeed, it tended to stay at a single "packet switch" or interface message processor within a given facility. For example in 1972, there was an average of 1.8 million packets of information per day, and about one fourth of these were within a single facility. At first it was thought that this was strictly a temporary phenomenon having to do with the fact that people were performing local experiments before launching into nationwide transmission. However, as Table 1 shows, the phenomenon changed very little over a period of 9 years. The lesson is that for the first time, a data-switching facility was available within a single location that performed certain intelligent data-switching functions, such as interfacing of hosts and terminals, that other vehicles such as multiplexers and private branch exchanges (PBXs) were not performing. A major need for LANs was uncovered. This need was exploited to some extent by the Advanced Research Projects Agency (ARPA); under its funding a communication system was developed for radio communications, and experiments were performed in applying these techniques to random access transmission cable

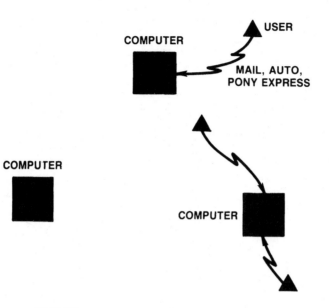

FIGURE 2.   Data nets in the 1960s.

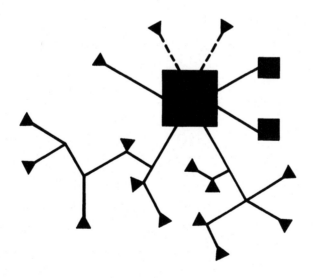

FIGURE 3.   A typical 1970 data net.

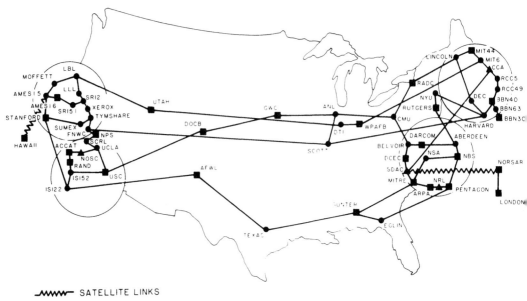

━━ SATELLITE LINKS

● IMP (INTERFACE MESSAGE PROCESSOR TO HOST COMPUTERS)

■ TIP (TERMINAL INTERFACE PROCESSOR)

▲ MULTIPROCESSOR

FIGURE 4.   ARPANET.

TABLE 1.   Representative ARPANET Traffic (thousands of packets/day)

	Intranode	Internode
1972	453	1,357
1973	764	3,016
1974	1,823	3,777
1975	3,774	5,098
1976	3,885	6,990
1977	3,614	8,081
1978	1,977	8,656
1979	2,956	10,737
1980	2,943	11,482

television (CATV) systems [3]. The packet switches performing these functions were initially minicomputers, later multiprocessor minicomputer systems, and ultimately microprocessor systems.

What we see in the pioneering ARPA effort is the beginning of a reversal of the trend in the 1960s. In the 1960s, there was a centralization of intelligence with well-engineered communications to access the central facilities. With LANs we see a redistribution of that intelligence to perform communications processing and to perform higher level functions that can be off-loaded from central host processors. In other words, we see the LAN as part of the phenomenon of distributed intelligence and processing. It is a simple application of the maxim that when computing is expensive relative to communications, processing is centralized, and when computing becomes cheap relative to communications, it becomes distributed.

There are various claims as to the origin and driving force behind LANs. To the extent that these have some bearing on the future direction of LANs, a comment based upon our brief analysis is appropriate. Some people claim that the genesis of LANs is in voice communications, in PBXs, in coaxial cable, or in optical fibers. Without belaboring the point, the simple lesson shown in Figure 5 is that the father of LANs is cheap proces-

FIGURE 5. The genesis of LANs.

sing and the mother is cheap bandwidth. Although it is not apparent from Figure 5, the mother is much older than the father, because coaxial cable has been around for decades. Microprocessors are the true cause and impetus for LANs; their date of availability is almost simultaneous with the development of true LANs.

APPLICATIONS

From its definition and orgins, we can discern some of the areas of application for LANs [4]. They are intended for interactive computer applications. That is, in a typical application a user at a terminal may wish to enter an inquiry to one of several processors and receive a response. He may wish to be logged into several different computers, i.e., establish "virtual circuits" to them and access each as needed. An even more ambitious configuration is shown in Figure 6.

In this architecture, the communications bus and communications resources act as a LAN. The communications resources automatically route an inquiry to an appropriate computer, the "applications resource," or to a backup computer in case the primary computer is down. The network system resources perform functions such as keeping track of routing and repair needs and authorization access. In this configuration, a LAN performs the following functions:

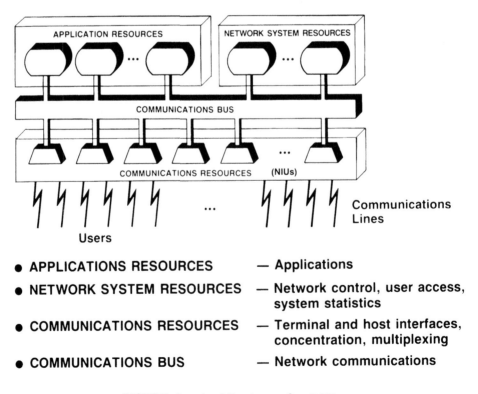

- APPLICATIONS RESOURCES   — Applications
- NETWORK SYSTEM RESOURCES — Network control, user access, system statistics
- COMMUNICATIONS RESOURCES — Terminal and host interfaces, concentration, multiplexing
- COMMUNICATIONS BUS   — Network communications

FIGURE 6. Architecture of a LAN.

- Provides a medium for interactive computing.
- Allows users to share computing resources.
- Allows users to switch among primary and backup resources.
- Provides microprocessor-based NIUs with protocol conversion that allows devices from different vendors to communicate.
- Interconnects computing resources in a facility so that they can communicate with the outside world through telephone lines, satellites, and other media.

THE ISO OSI MODEL

To classify LANs and their applications, we must adopt a more precise terminology. This terminology is provided by a particular standard. The International Standards Organization (ISO) [5] has defined a model to describe communications interfaces and protocols called the Open Systems Interconnect (OSI) model. The essence of the model is illustrated in Figure 7. Its purpose was to define standards for functional layers of communications to establish

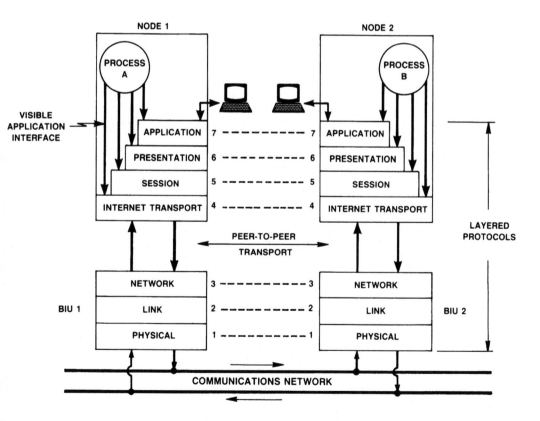

FIGURE 7. OSI Model.

1. Protocols, i.e., rules for communications between equivalent layers
    in different devices.
2. Interfaces, i.e., rules for connecting between different layers in
    the same device.

As a result, hardware and software could be partitioned and designed to
appropriate protocol and interface standards with confidence that they would
be compatible with existing systems and devices.

The reason for introducing the ISO OSI model here is that it enables
us to focus on and classify the contribution and options of LANs within
each layer. Furthermore, it is significant that the evolution of LANs has
followed a path from the lower layers through the higher layers of the model.
The earliest LANs were concerned almost exculsively with the first two
layers of the protocol; namely, establishing a physical electrical connection
and providing some level of reliability by providing link procedures for
requesting, acknowledging, repeating, and correcting messages. Indeed,
the IEEE standard already referred to, deals only with these two layers.
However, even from Figure 7, it is clear that for users, the real services
that they need are at the higher layers. LAN designers are now adding
more of these higher layers to LANs. Since LANs will be described at the
level of each layer, I will first describe each layer briefly.

The Physical Layer

The physical layer is concerned with transmitting raw bits over a communication channel. The design issues have to do with ensuring that when one
side sends a 1 bit, it is received by the other side as a 1 bit, not as a 0
bit. Typical questions are how many volts should be used to represent a
1 bit and how many to represent 0 bit, how many microseconds a bit occupies,
whether transmission may proceed simultaneously in both directions, how the
initial connection is established and how it is torn down when both sides
are finished, how many pins the network connector has, and what each pin
is used for.

The Data Link Layer

The task of the data link layer is to take a raw transmission facility and
transform it into a link that appears free of transmission errors to the
network layer. It accomplishes this task by breaking the input data into
data frames, transmitting the frames sequentially, and processing the
acknowledgment frames sent back by the receiver.

The Network Layer

The network layer, sometimes called the communication subnet layer, controls the operation of the subnet. Among other things, it determines the
chief characteristics of the computer or terminal interface and how packets,
the units of information exchanges in layer 3, are routed within the subnet.

The Transport Layer

The basic function of the transport layer, also known as the host—host
layer, is to accept data from the session layer, split it up into smaller unit,

if need be, pass these to the network layer, and ensure that the pieces all arrive at the other end correctly. Furthermore, all this must be done in the most efficient way possible, and in a way that isolates the session layer from the inevitable changes in the hardware technology.

The Session Layer

The session layer is the user's interface into the network. It is this layer that the user must negotiate to establish a connection with a process on another machine. Once the connection has been established, the session layer can manage the dialog in an orderly manner if the user has requested that service.

The Presentation Layer

The presentation layer deals with the format of the data given to the user in terms of characters, printer speed, size of screens, and so on. The presentation layer in the network performs functions that are requested sufficiently often to warrant finding a general solution for them, rather than letting each user solve the problems. Typical examples of a transformation service that can be performed here are text compression and encryption.

The Application Layer

The application layer deals with the user's actual application—word processing, spread sheets, computer aided design, and so on. The content of the application layer is up to the individual user. In the network industry, specific protocols, such as those for banking or airline reservation, allow computers from different companies to access one another's data bases when needed.

The fundamental distinctions of many LANs are at the physical and link layers, and these layers will be discussed first.

CLASSIFICATION OF LANs—THE PHYSICAL LAYER

The most basic issue for the physical layer is the transmission medium, as illustrated in the decision tree in Figure 8 [6]. Various exotic schemes such as infrared signals or point-to-point unguided microwave have been the subjects of experiments. However, the three primary alternatives are those shown, namely, optical fiber, twisted wire pair, and coaxial cable. In many respects, optical fiber is the most desirable medium. It is light, small in diameter, flexible, easy to install, impervious to most electromagnetic interference and, most important, has a bandwidth that far out lasts the other media, as shown in Table 2. In theory, gigabits (i.e., billions of bits) of data can be sent every second for miles before signals have to be amplified. The only drawback to optical fiber is that as of this writing, it is expensive to tap. That is, the tap, the device that removes that signal from the fiber and routes it to a user terminal, is relatively expensive to make in a reliable replicable form. As a result, when it is used in current systems, the optical fiber is used for "backbone" signaling, as shown in Figure 9, where the nodes are stations that repeat signals and act as a hub for multiple user drops and taps.

TABLE 2. Transmission Media Characteristics[a]

Characteristics	Twisted pair Wire	Coaxial Cable	Fiber Optic Cable
Cost			
Initial	Low	High	Highest
Maintenance	Low	Low	Low
Electromagnetic Susceptibility	Very high	Low	None
Availability	In place or readily available	Off-the-shelf CATV	Developing, available
Bandwidth	1.5Mbit/sec @ 1.5 km 56Kbit/sec @ 5 km	10Mbit/sec 350Mbit/sec aggregate	1Gbit/sec @ 1 km 100Mbit/sec @ 10 km
Maximum no. of Stations	More than 1,000	Many thousands	More than 1,000
Distance	About 2 km	10 to 50 km (with repeaters)	More than 10 km

[a]See Acronyms for abbreviations.

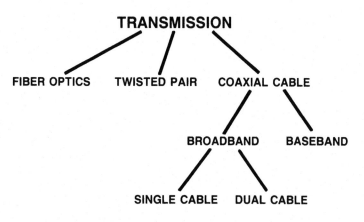

FIGURE 8.   Transmission medium alternatives.

Twisted wire pair has the most limited capability of the media considered.   Twisted wire pairs are simply a pair of telephone wires twisted to prevent interference of signals from different conversations.   Its primary merit is that it is virtually ubiquitous in every organization as the primary mechanism for telephone systems.   On the other hand, many designers are now finding that existing wire pair is often inappropriate for the simple piggybacking of LAN services because these high-speed services are more demanding in terms of physical and electrical characteristics of the wire than is voice communications.   In any case, at its best, wire pair can be pushed to hundreds of kilobits per second or even megabits per second for short distances, with good lines and frequent amplifiers.

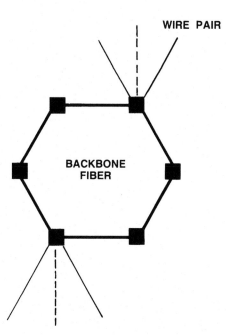

FIGURE 9.   Typical LAN with optical fiber backbone.

In some ways, at present, coaxial cable supplies the most desirable medium, in that it provides a compromise between the shortcomings of optical fiber and wire pair. Throughputs of several hundred megabits per second are possible with amplifiers located a half mile apart.

Within the domain of LANs, it must be pointed out that there are several different types of coaxial cable which, once selected, often make different LANs somewhat incompatible. Coaxial cable consists of an outer cylindrical conductor surrounding a center wire conductor with the two seperated by a nonconducting dielectric material. The electrical energy propagates down the cable within the outer conductor. Depending upon the diameters of the conductors and the dielectric material chosen, the cable has a so-called "characteristic impedance." For CATV systems, 75 ohms (75 Ω) has been selected as the standard characteristic impedance. If one uses 75 Ω systems, off-the-shelf CATV equipment can be used. However, other LANs use a less expensive 50 Ω cable and cannot use CATV equipment. Usually "broad band" systems use 75 Ω, and "base band" systems use 50 Ω. (These terms will be covered in the next section.) Finally, there are hybrids. As one example, existing wire pair may be used to bring signals to a backbone section of the system, which uses coaxial cable or optical fiber.

Base Band and Broad Band Systems

An early and continuing dispute among LAN vendors and users has been concerned with the distinction between, and relative merits of, base band and broad band systems [7].

The data signal on the cable in a broad band system is represented by line voltage shifts. In particular, the data do not modulate a carrier signal. Rather, a line driver is used to impress the voltage variations onto the transmission medium.

Broad band systems employ multiple, high-frequency carrier waves, dispersed across the transmission medium's bandwidth. Each carrier is modulated by the voice, data, or video information it carries. The modulation may be carried out by changing the carrier's amplitude, phase, or frequency. A modulator is used to impress signal changes onto each carrier.

The essential difference (from the user's perspective) between baseband and broad-band systems is that a broad-band system can accommodate several independent transmission channels, whereas a base-band system can handle only one. As an example, a broad-band system can have a channel devoted to a selected group of users, a second channel devoted to another group, a third channel devoted to TV transmission, and so on. A baseband system cannot. In most other aspects, the differences between baseband and broad-band systems depend on the characteristics of the transmission cable, its length, and the line drivers or modulators/demodulators (modems) employed.

The merits of the broad-band system are

1. It can handle multiple channels devoted to different data streams, applications, communities of interest, or modes of communication—such as television and telemetry.
2. It can use standard CATV equipment with CATV amplifiers that can extend system performance for miles.
3. It has good noise immunity.

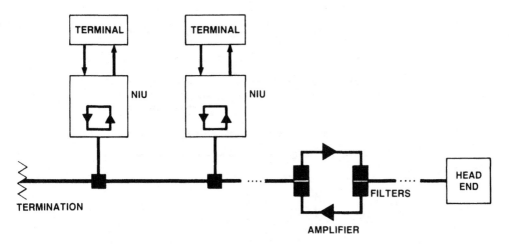

FIGURE 10.   A single-cable configuration.

The merit of the base-band systems is somewhat simpler equipment
with concomitant lower costs than broad band.   In particular, modems are
not required for base-band systems.

For broad-band systems, two types of CATV configurations are used
for transmission in a LAN.   One uses a single coaxial cable, with the forward
and return traffic multiplexed in frequency so that the low half-band (e.g.,
5–110 megahertz [millions of cycles per second]) is used for the return
channels and the upper half-band (e.g., 160–265 megahertz) for the forward
channels.   As shown in Figure 10, a "head end" at one end of the cable is
used to translate the forward channel frequency into the return frequency.
Two-way amplifiers are used to compensate for the signal attenuation.

Another approach uses two parallel cables, one for the outbound and
one for the inbound traffic, as shown in Figure 11.   One-way amplifiers
are used on each cable.

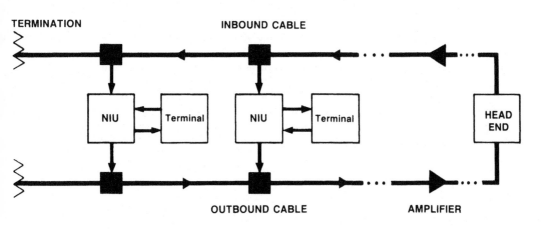

FIGURE 11.   A dual-cable configuration.

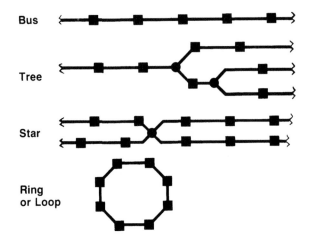

FIGURE 12.   LAN topology.

In many applications, cable cost does not represent a major factor in the total network cost. For such cases, the two-cable configuration can be more advantageous. It provides twice the network capacity and does not use two-way active components, which reduce overall reliability and availability. However, for today's commercial environment, single cable systems provide sufficient performance and flexibility to meet most user needs.

Once a medium is selected, it must be configured in some physical manner, usually referred to as the topology of the system. The standard topologies are shown in Figure 12. The simplest configuration is a linear array shown in Figure 12. In this scheme, every terminal hears every message that is broadcast and acts upon only those addressed to it. A tree, as shown in Figure 12, is made up of a concatenation of buses and usually works in the same way. In some cases, amplification is required where buses are connected together. A special case of a tree is a star in which all buses are connected together at a single point. A ring, as shown in Figure 12, is quite different from the bus and tree architectures in that it is clear that broadcast messages will continue to travel around the ring unless they are removed by some physical device. Accordingly, the mechanisms for operating rings and trees must be very different. Finally, there may be hybrids of the various types of systems.

Usually, a user of LANs does not select a topology but rather installs a system with a topology dictated by the system offered by a vendor. For each vendor, the topology is tied critically to the operation of the system. Thus, as will be shown vendors of PBXs usually select star topologies, with their PBXs at the central location. Similarly, vendors who use CATV equipment usually use tree topologies, consistent with CATV layout.

CLASSIFICATION OF LANs—THE LINK LAYER

The next level of classification is at the link layer. As with the physical layer, there are many issues and options. However, the deepest difference among alternative systems concerns the "access method."

Access Method

There are many ways in which a broad-band channel can be accessed, and many of these methods have been implemented. In Figure 13, we depict the major choices for methods of accessing the transmission medium. The three primary alternatives are dedicated allocation of resources, such as frequency, time, or space division multiplexing; and two more flexible approaches, controlled and random access. The dedicated approach is not promising for LANs because it wastes resources and is inflexible for most office and data processing environments. Both controlled and random access are techniques that permit sharing of a high bandwidth medium by a multiplicity of contending users.

In controlled access, contention is reduced by polling or use of reservations. Roll-call polling assumes that a centralized controller interrogates each subscriber separately and allocates the channel accordingly. In token polling, control is distributed by means of a polling message, called a token, which is passed from subscriber to subscriber and triggers data transmission, if any, by the subscriber who owns the token.

To understand the simplest form of random access, consider Figure 14, where users 1, 2, and 3 are illustrated. Each user transmits its packet of data as soon as he is ready, e.g., a message is completed, and a carriage return is hit or a buffer is filled. Al long as the packets do not overlap in time, they are received correctly. If they collide (in the simplest form), neither is received correctly and neither is acknowledged. In that case, there is a random time out for both packets and they are retransmitted.

Among inherently distributed random access schemes, carrier sense multiple access/collision detect (CSMA/CD) is the most popular. With CSMA/

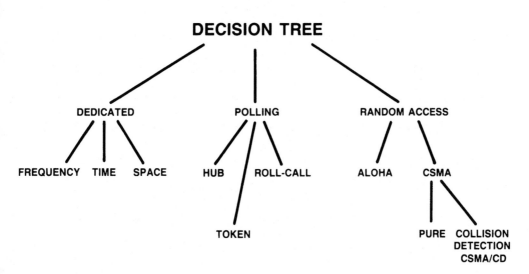

FIGURE 13. Access method alternatives.

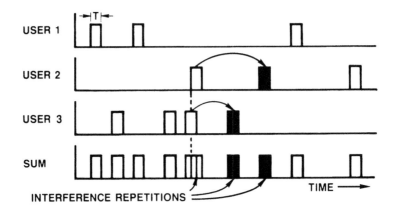

FIGURE 14. Random access packet multiplexing.

CD, a subscriber transmits only when the broadcast medium is sensed idle
(carrier sense) and stops transmitting if a collision occurs (collision detect).
     It should be evident from this discussion that a user has a variety
of system alternatives from which to choose. In Figure 15, we present a
typical trade-off of access delay versus the total network utilization and the
number of connected NIUs. CSMA/CD is relatively insensitive to the number of users below some number. Token passing depends on that number,
because each node introduces a fixed overhead component—the transmission
time of the token. On the other hand, CSMA/CD networks exhibit sharp
saturation at high utilization due to increases of collisions, whereas token
schemes resolve contention in an orderly way and, thus, delay increases
more gradually. The curves tend to show that token polling is more suitable
for a limited number of nodes with heavy traffic (e.g., file transfers), and
CSMA/CD is appropriate for a large number of bursty users (e.g., in an
office and interactive data processing environment). For a large range of
applications, both schemes perform reasonably well and the trade-off is not
that obvious [8].
     However, it should be recognized that the token versus CSMA/CD
controversy is usually beside the point because either will work. The
access delay is usually in the order of milliseconds, whereas the total
end-to-end delay in a message may be a few seconds. The remaining delays
are due to the terminal access lines, the network interface unit handling, and
the transmission times for messages. Transmission time is illustrated in
Figure 16, which shows relative delays due to source port, LAN, and
destination port under mismatched input and output speeds. In either
case, the contribution of the LAN to transmission delay is low because its
channel speed is in the megabit per second (Mbit/sec) range, whereas source
and destination speeds are usually lower.
     From the previous discussion, one can discern that the speed of the
channel used is an important factor in the performance of the LAN. In
particular, in a CSMA/CD system the shorter the packets, the less chance
there is of their collision. For example, in a 1Mbit/sec system, bits are 1
microsecond (μsec) long and a 1000-bit packet would be 1 millisecond (msec)
in duration. On the other hand, in a 10Mbit/sec system, each bit is 0.1
μsec in duration and a 1000-bit packet would be only 100 μsec in duration.

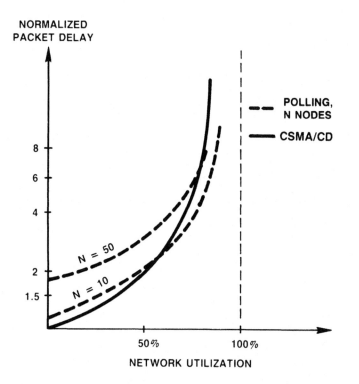

FIGURE 15.   Comparison of CSMA and token polling.

Hence, for a 10Mbit/sec system, there is less chance of two packets overlapping each other and colliding.   Similarly, in a token system, the time
to transmit a token is less for a higher speed system and, hence, performance is better.   Most commercial LANs have 1, 2, 4, 5, and 10Mbit/sec
channels.   At least one system has 128Kbit/sec and at least one has 50Mbit/
sec.

      Two of the factors influencing a designer's selection of channel speed
are cost of appropriate hardware and software.   However, it is also true
that the highest speed is not necessarily the best system.   The performance
of the system for the users depends on factors other than channel speed,
e.g., the length of the system's longest path and the packet size.

      Finally, we noted in Figure 15 that delay is a function of network
utilization.   This, in turn, means that as more users utilize the system,
the performance, or delay, to service each user degrades.   Based upon
curves such as these shown in Figure 15, one can design LANs so that
systems can deliver satisfactory performance to groups of a few dozen to
thousands of users for reasonable costs [9,10].

Link Protocols

The rest of the link layer of protocols is concerned primarily with orderly
delivery of information from one NIU of the LAN to another.   It uses the
services of the physical and access protocol to obtain a share of the network
raw bandwidth by gaining access to the actual communications channel.

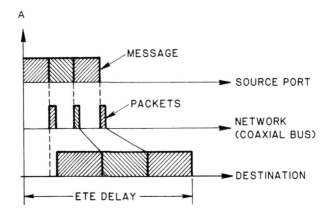

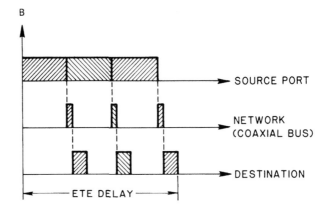

FIGURE 16.   Comparison of transmission delays in a LAN.   (A) Source
port speed > destination port speed; (B) Source port speed < destination
port speed.

The link protocol then deals with addressing, error control, accountability,
sequencing, and flow control.

The link protocols used on LANs are similar to the standard data link
control procedures, such as synchronous data link control (SDLC) or high
level data link control (HDLC) [11].   However, because cable is basically
a broadcast medium, these standard protocols are enhanced in order to take
advantage of the one-to-many or many-to-many capabilities of the LAN.
For example, a broadcast address that can be recognized by all the NIUs
on the cable is very useful for network control messages and should be
included in the link protocol.   On the other hand, the unique characteristics
of cable transmission, such as high data rate and low propagation delay,
allow simplification in protocol design.   For example, the complex buffer
management, flow control, and network congestion control mechanisms, which
are necessary in a long-haul network, can all be replaced by simpler schemes
because the interactions between sender and receiver are almost instantaneous
compared with the nationwide networks.

The basic data unit controlled by the link protocol, called a "frame," is used by most standard protocols, such as HDLC, to indicate a link controlled block. This basic data unit is sometimes called a packet. However, a packet typically represents the units to be routed from source to destination node, through several intermediate nodes, in a packet-switching network. Because in LAN all NIUs on the same cable can exchange such data units directly without intermediate nodes, it is appropriate to call such basic data units frames.

Each frame consists of a header, data (or information), and a trailer and requires a mechanism to indicate the beginning and end of a frame. Various framing mechanisms are employed in different LAN implementations. The IEEE 802 Committee recommends a special frame delimiter that includes illegal bit codes. However, in many LANs, traditional HDLC flags are used to delimit a frame, with data bits enclosed by the leading and trailing flags and subjected to the usual bit-stuffing process in order to provide data transparency. In such a framing mechanism, a single-bit error may cause an entire frame to be delimited incorrectly. Other LANs use a byte count in the frame header to determine the length of a frame. The advantage of using the byte count is that a bit reversal in the middle of the frame will not cause an incorrectly delimited frame, although errors in the byte count field can still cause incorrect frame delimiting.

The addressing scheme supported by the link protocol must be flexible to easily accommodate various LAN equipment configurations. Figure 17 illustrates several possible connections between NIUs and external hosts or terminals. Each of these types of connections should be included in the direct network address in the frame header. To accommodate these needs, LANs use two address fields—the destination address and the source address. The size of the address field varies from one implementation to another; clearly "layered" addresses will allow more flexible addressing schemes, as well as direct addressing to the physical ports or attached devices.

Most LANs provide at least two addressing modes—point to point and broadcasting. Typically, the broadcast address is all ones in the destination address field and is received by all NIUs. Some networks dedicate the first 8 bits to be the NIU address and the second 8 bits for the internal port address or equipment address. Others have implemented the group-addressing capability (i.e., simultaneous transmission to a selected group of NIUs), which is useful when more than one physical destination device can be used to service the particular user request (any printer, host, or port).

Each data frame is protected from transmission errors by an error-detecting code. There are two retransmission strategies in LANs for further error control. In the first approach, no acknowledgment is sent at the link level for correctly received frames, whereas erroneous frames are simply discarded. Higher level protocols then handle the acknowledgment and retransmission functions, only if required by high-level applications. Most LANs have implemented the second approach, namely, a stop-and-wait error control procedure, whereby each frame (or group of frames) has to be acknowledged specifically before the next frame (or group of frames) can be transmitted. Different networks have implemented slightly different versions of stop-and-wait error-control procedures, tailored to their own specific applications. In some implementations, e.g., the retransmission time-out interval is taken from tables. This allows several short interval

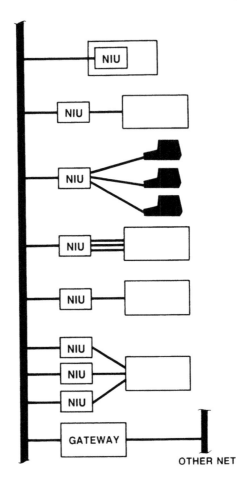

FIGURE 17.   LAN attachment alternatives.

retries followed by longer waits. It also allows fewer retries during the
initial connection stage than in normal data transmission.

Generally speaking, the first approach, which moves the accountability
functions to higher level protocols, has simplified the link protocol design
significantly. This is true because the bulk of a traditional link control
function involves acknowledgement, retransmission, and time-out, to name
a few. Removing the responsibility for reliable communication from the
link transport mechanism also allows the user to tailor reliability to applications and to place error recovery where it will do the most good. However, the success of this approach depends heavily on the assumption that
the transmission medium (such as coaxial cable) provides a reasonably low
bit error rate. Otherwise, the excessive overhead of acknowledgment and
retransmission at the network level of protocol will degrade the overall
system performance severely. Therefore, this approach may not work if
twisted pairs instead of coaxial cables are used as the basic transmission
medium. Such a scheme also deviates significantly from most standard link
control procedures. This may cause compatibility problems when the LANs
are interconnected with other types of communications networks.

On the other hand, the stop-and-wait type error control mechanism must be carefully designed to allow flexible handling of data streams with different error control requirements. For example, the stop-and-wait protocol may not be desirable for certain types of traffic, such as digitized voice or video signals. Because of the severe requirements of the timeliness of these data streams, it is better to receive a frame with a few transmission errors rather than waiting for retransmission of an entire frame. The proper link error control mechanism for a LAN should provide the flexibility to handle both error-controlled and nonerror-controlled traffic. It should also conform as much as possible to the standard link control procedures for easy interface to existing communication systems.

Due to the high data rate of the medium and incompatible input—output rates of user equipment connected to the medium, it is desirable to have a flow control mechanism to prevent buffer overflow. In general, most networks have implemented three stages of flow control procedures: the control of the data flow between sending and receiving user equipment and the NIUs and the control of network data flow between two NIUs. Double data buffers, one for cable interface and one for user equipment interface, are required at NIUs. This decoupling allows independent flow control mechanisms to be tailored.

Each network has implemented an internal flow control mechanism. Some include a buffer status bit in the frame header. Thus, when the receiving buffer is full, a status bit is set in the acknowledgment (ACK) frame, and the sender suspends the transmission until the bit is reset. Others have implemented a special global flow control scheme, analogous to a traffic light operation, to avoid deadlocks or traffic congestion for an entire network. In this method, each NIU maintains a flow control table that records the buffer load of every other NIU on the medium. These flow control tables are constantly updated by ACK, negative acknowledgment (NACK), or ANNOUNCE frames, which are broadcast to all NIUs. When the total buffer load is less than 75%, it is "green light" (all messages are allowed to enter the network). When the total load is between 75% and 85%, it is "yellow light" (encourage expeditious processing). When the total load exceeds 85%, it is "red light" (only an emergency message is allowed to enter the system). The buffer status could be combined with the ACK frame. When ACK is received, it indicates buffer availability. Otherwise, the receiver will withhold the ACK when the buffer is full until it is clear again. However, such a scheme may result in excessive retransmission of data frames. Each of these flow control schemes has its own unique advantages and disadvantages. The "flow control through ACK" scheme is simpler to implement but requires larger buffer space to avoid constant flooding of the bus with repeated retransmissions. On the other hand, the effectiveness of the sophisticated global flow control scheme remains to be seen.

THE IEEE 802 STANDARD

The IEEE has established a committee (designated the IEEE 802 Committee) to develop standards for LANs. The committee's purpose is to establish a standard interface to connected data equipment to bus NIUs of a LAN. Figure 18 indicates that the scope of the IEEE 802 Committee is layers one and two of the ISO protocols, which have been discussed, the physical

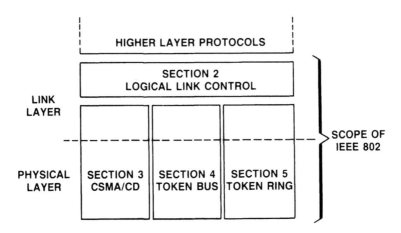

FIGURE 18.   IEEE 802 LAN standards domain.

layer and the link layer.   The standard is concerned with the so-called
media access unit (MAU), as shown in Figure 19.   The specification indicates
that if a vendor has a full standard MAU, the MAU must provide all the
mandatory functions and must operate at one or more of the standard data
rates.   It must also have a standard access unit interface and have one of
the standard media interfaces.   If the device contains only the DTE side of
the access unit interface, the access unit interface must be exposed, the
device must operate at one or more of the standard data rates, and the
device must have the mandatory logical link control capabilities and use one
of the standard media access control methods.   If the device does not have
the access unit interface exposed, all the above requirements must be met
except for those relating to the access unit interface.

     As can be seen from Figure 18, the 802 Committee is concerned with
four standards.   At the physical and lower link layer there are three standards; 802.3 for CSMA/CD bus, 802.4 for token bus, and 802.5 for token

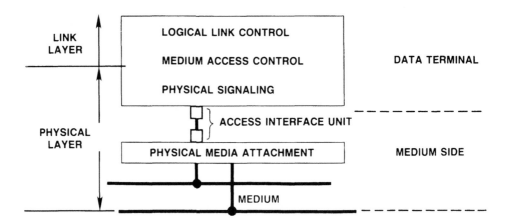

FIGURE 19.   IEEE 802 Standard media access unit (MAU).

ring [1,12,13]. Finally, there is an 802.2 standard being developed for the upper link layer protocol common to all three physical and lower link layer standards.

The standards establish the details to allow a vendor to unambiguously develop equipment that can be connected to the LAN. As an example, the IEEE Standard 802.3 addresses physical layer issues, such as signal level, pin connections, and temperature and humidity requirements. At the link level, the standard describes the details of the CSMA/CD operation. The logical link control protocol 802.2 specifies parameters such as addressing, control fields, packet structure, and acknowledgments.

PBX VS. LAN

Because the issue often arises in practice, the relationship of PBXs and LANs must be discussed. However, to understand this relationship it is necessary first to digress to explain the difference between circuit switching and packet switching.

Circuit switching has been the classical mode for voice communications, whereby an end-to-end path between two telephones is established before communications take place. In packet switching on the other hand, a packet or block of data, receives its address and is then sent to an intermediate relay point where it waits until a next link is available. Packet switching is similar to sending telegrams on a "message-switching" basis except that packets are so short, a few hundred characters, and the line speeds so fast that the packets take only milliseconds to traverse a link. Accordingly, packets from many different sources can share a link. The original intent of packet switching was to lower costs for data communications users by allowing them to share expensive nationwide links. Circuit switching and packet switching differ drastically with regard to almost every technical feature of telecommunications. Only two are illustrated here.

1. *Call setup time:* Circuit switching takes seconds to establish a path for a call. In packet switching, each packet has an address and there is no need for end-to-end signaling.
2. *Flow control:* In circuit switching, there is no flow control to regulate terminal data speeds; the path is transparent. In packet switching, there may be many types of flow control, such as queueing packets at a terminal if there is too much traffic on the system.

To return to the discussion of PBXs versus LANs they are illustrated conceptually in Figures 20 and 21. In its classical form, a telephone switch at a telephone company central office is a circuit switch. A PBX is a telephone-type switch located in a customer's premises but is still a circuit switch in its classical form. The NIUs in a LAN operate in a mode similar to packet switches. However, they are simpler than packet switches in many ways. Most of the differences arise from the fact that a LAN is confined to a building, whereas a packet-switched network is nationwide. Thus, there is no need for intermediate storage in a LAN because links are so short and reliable. If a packet is received incorrectly, it can be retransmitted end to end in a short time. On the other hand, in a packet-switched network, the packet must be stored until it is acknowledged as being cor-

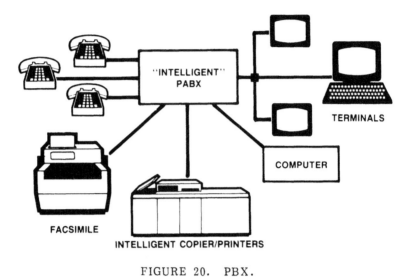

FIGURE 20.   PBX.

rectly received at the next storage point. Accordingly, NIUs need less
memory and can be simpler than packet switches. In a sense, LANs are
a new form of digital switching.

Clearly, circuit switches were designed for and are ideal for voice
communications but are inappropriate for the types of interactive computing
applications that require very short call setup times.

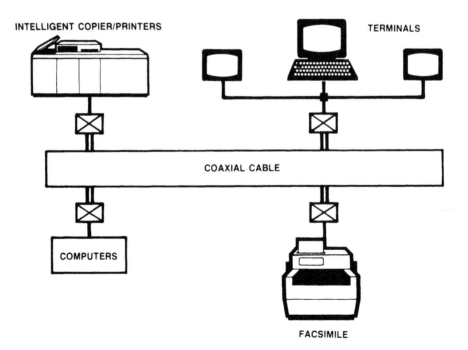

FIGURE 21.   LAN.

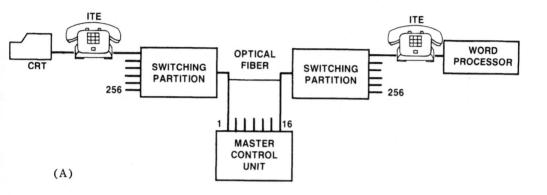

(A)

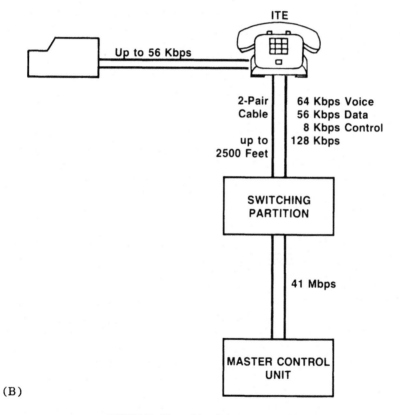

(B)

FIGURE 22.   (A, B) Intecom IBX.

Classical PBXs, i.e., circuit switches, are still appropriate for data connections or for file transfers where the destination need not be switched rapidly and there are no requirements for rapid alternate routing. As a matter of fact, many PBX vendors have added special high-speed connections for this purpose. For example, Intecom manufactures a PBX that they call the IBX (Integrated Business Exchange), which is illustrated in Figures 22A and B. Figure 22A shows that the central switch has switching partitions, each of which can handle 256 telephone and data terminals. Figure 22B shows that the lines are restricted to handle a single voice circuit at 64Kbit/sec and data at 56Kbit/sec, switched by the central circuit switch. However, for applications requiring connections to multiple hosts, flexible addressing, and other features, the LAN has more extensive capability.

Northern Telecom takes a somewhat different approach with their Meridian Series, as illustrated in Figure 23. Their PBX is called an SL-100 and has some similarities with the Intecom switch in that is also allocates 64Kbit/sec channels, but they can be used for either voice or data. However, as shown in Figure 23, it is also attached to a packet transport bus, which has a speed of 40Mbit/sec and to a LAN called LANLINK, which has a speed of 2.5Mbit/sec. Hence, the entire package, whatever it is called, is a combination of circuit switching and LANs. In this extended sense, of course, PBXs do indeed encompass LAN functions.

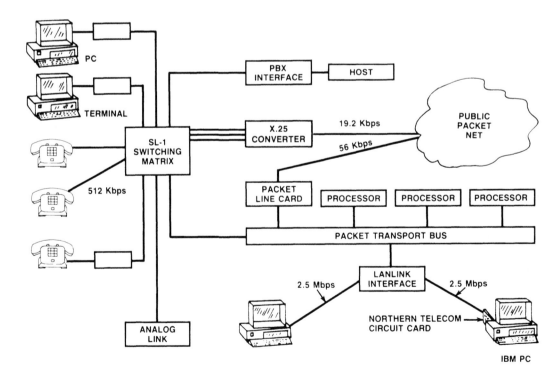

FIGURE 23.   Northern Telecom Meridian.

HIGH–LEVEL PROTOCOLS

The irony of LANs is that most of the standards and classifications deal with the lower level protocols, but most of the functionality and user interest service lies with the higher level protocols. Indeed, beyond connectivity, experts and market research ascertain that users look to LANs to provide "gateways;" i.e., connections to outside building systems. Next in importance is the ability to bring on new applications easily such as word processing, computer aided design, and electronic mail. Third in importance is the ability to add equipment from different vendors to the system. A consequence of this requirement is a need for a capability for protocol conversion. The requirement is specifically to convert the protocols of e.g., Digital Equipment Corporation, computers to the protocols of e.g., IBM equipment, for all the higher level protocols.

Protocols above the link level are usually referred to as high level protocols (HLPs). Unlike the link protocol, and despite the continual efforts by standards organizations, the HLPs differ drastically from one vendor to another. In the user community, the need for a number of elementary high-level protocols providing various types of services is apparent.

Three main groupings of such protocols may be defined: application oriented, executive oriented, and network induced, [2]. The motivation for this classification is the perspective of distributed systems as extensions of the single system environment. The goal of elementary protocols is to extend the array of system utilities, programs, and operating system services available on a single system to the total LAN. Hence, development of elementary LAN protocols is a basic step in evolving high-level operating systems for LANs. Application-oriented protocols will allow a process in one node to access files, retrieve and edit text, execute programs, execute modules, and debug programs at another node. These operations are analogous to the activities in a centralized operating system that supports conversion, file transfer, editing, computation, execution, and debugging.

Executive level protocols are defined to be interprocess communication lines and data formats that extend the operating system services, such as resource allocation, device or program service, and monitoring services of one node to an application process in another node. Examples of commonly used operating system services are commands like ASSIGN, TIME, and STATUS; examples of virtual terminal protocols are scrolling, screen, and page for alphanumeric and graphic terminals. Virtual terminals are generally supported by two elementary protocols: a virtual terminal display data transformation protocol and a control protocol. The data transformation protocol maps display commands from the sending process into the prescribed input data formats for the receiver process. The control protocol exchanges nondisplay information, such as change of state or status request for coordinating the interactions between the sending and receiving processes.

Network-induced protocols are defined to be interprocess communication rules and data formats that facilitate the operation of executive level and application level protocols in a LAN. Some of these protocols are as follows:

- *Network generation protocol:* Provides the mechanism for a LAN node to establish or disestablish addressable network ports in a directory, thereby allowing qualified processes in other nodes to become associated with processes assigned to this port. The protocol might serve normal and privileged processes in the application space, as well as network control functions within the operating system. This protocol provides a mechanism to identify "well-known" processes in a network directory.

- *Network directory service protocol:* Allows a process to request information about a node, another process, or an end user. It may also support custom menu services for each network user to promote the impression of a single integrated system.
- *Network access authorization protocol:* Allows a process to gain access to another process in the network. It includes log-on/ log-off support to end users and general process interconnection authorization, and interfaces with network security and privacy management information systems.
- *Transport control protocol:* Allows a process in one node to establish an association with a process in another node and to exchange messages in a virtual circuit or datagram mode.
- *Interprocess synchronization:* Provides a mechanism for two or more processes in two or more nodes to coordinate asynchronously executing functions.
- *Network system control protocol:* Provides the mechanism for establishing "built-in" maintenance and security subsystems in a LAN environment. It is envisioned that performance, maintenance, and security checks should permeate the LAN software, as well as hardware, subsystem. This protocol facilitates a unified specification of performance, maintenance, and security-related functions.

There has been less standardization of higher level protocols than of the lower layers. The most notable overall attempt has been for the field of manufacturing. The Engineering and Manufacturing Computer Coordination (EMCC) activity is responsible for corporate direction in the application of manufacturing process computers within General Motors. To facilitate information exchange pertaining to plant-floor computer data communications, the GM "Local Communication Networks Users Group" was sponsored by the EMCC in late 1979. On recommendation from this group, a task force was formed to investigate and identify a common communications standard for plant-floor systems. This task force was chartered in November 1980 as the "Manufacturing Automation Protocol" (MAP) Task Force [14].

The purpose of MAP is the preparation of a specification that will allow common communication among diverse intelligent devices in a cost-effective and consistent manner. To meet this purpose, the following set of objectives is followed:

1. Define a MAP message standard that supports application-to application communication.
2. Identify application functions to be supported by the message format standard.
3. Recommend protocol(s) that meet the functional requirements.

The function of MAP is not to create protocols but to adopt and enforce protocols as developed. Thus, e.g., the committee has adopted the IEEE standards for layers 1 and 2 and will enforce a layer-4 standard developed by the National Bureau of Standards.

At the network and transport layers, a number of different protocols have been developed, or adopted, for LANs. For example, the Xerox Corporation has introduced its Xerox Network System (XNS) for its Ethernet LAN. The XNS transport protocol is called the Sequenced Packet Protocol (SPP), and the Network Protocol is called the Internetwork Data Protocol (IDP). However, other layer-3 and -4 protocols have been developed for different purposes and added to LANs.

In the early 1970s, ARPA of the Department of Defense provided a testing ground for communications protocols over a packet-switched system. The ARPANET originally used the network control protocol (NCP) but later decided to transition to a new protocol called transmission control protocol (TCP). Under ARPA grants, experimental TCP implementations were also completed at both Stanford University in California and BBN Communications Corporation in Boston, Massachusetts. As a result of this research, the Department of Defense adopted TCP/IP as its standard communications protocol. TCP is the layer-4 protocol and the Internet Protocol (IP) is the layer-3 protocol [15, 16]. By then, the ARPANET consisted of several nodes across the country. These nodes were located at major universities and military installations. By 1972, 75% of the ARPANET machines used TCP/IP over a variety of physical media.

In the last 2 or 3 years, UNIX systems developers at Berkeley have produced version 4.2, which has TCP/IP integrated with the UNIX kernel. The LAN interface to the Ethernet was provided by the addition of a simple Address Resolution Protocol (ARP) that mapped TCP/IP addresses to Ethernet addresses. This event greatly expanded the TCP/IP arena. Many UNIX machines now being built have the same TCP/IP and network interfaces as 4.2 Berkeley UNIX.

The layer-5, -6 and -7 protocols session, application, and presentation are usually the concern of the user and vendor who attach computing equipment to the LAN. The LAN is often then transparent to these layers of protocol. However, the LAN can become a part of this process in three ways.

To the extent that attached computing equipment, both hardware and software, is part of a vendor architecture of protocols such as system network architecture (SNA) or Digital Equipment Corporation Network (DECNET), the first four layers of the LAN protocols may have to be the same as the four layers of the vendor architecture, or the LAN must be called upon to convert the vendor protocols.

The second involvement is an extension of the first. Often equipment from multiple vendors may be interfaced to a single LAN. It is often the case that layers 1 to 4 of the protocols differ for this equipment and almost always the case that the top three layers differ. In these cases, the LAN may be called upon to provide protocol conversion among the protocols of the different vendors. This conversion may be done in the NIUs, or it may be done on a dedicated processor attached to one port on the LAN.

Finally, the LAN is sometimes treated as a resource for providing some services at layers 5 to 7 of the protocols. For example, a file server is a service that allows users and computers to store files, transfer files reliably at high speeds, and share file accesses and updates. The file server may be provided as part of the LAN.

NETWORK CONTROL

As stated at the beginning of this article, distributed processing has been a driving force in the development of LANs. However, the same trend has led to the requirement for a powerful centralized network control center (NCC) for the LAN [17]. There are two reasons for this requirement. The first is that with hundreds, or even thousands, of pieces of attached equipment, there is a need for centralized management and troubleshooting. The second reason is that with the advent of LANs, communications managers for the first time have a vehicle to regain control of the proliferation of previously uncontrolled personal computers and other desktop equipment. Accordingly, NCCs have become an integral part of LANs.

There are three categories of requirements for NCCs:

1. Continuous status monitoring and display.
2. General network control requirements.
3. Specific integrated network control requirements.

Continuous status monitoring and display, although part of general network control, is broken out as a separate requirement category because of its relative importance.

Continuous Status Monitoring and Display

It is the responsibility of the NCC operator to identify and solve network problems quickly. The hope is that the problems can be corrected even before the LAN user detects them.

The consequence of the above is that a continuous status display is required, and exceptions to normal operation must be dealt with immediately. That is, exceptions must be displayed immediately and/or acted upon automatically by the NCC.

General NCC Requirements

In addition to the status display requirement, other general NCC requirements include the following:

1. *Downline loading the NIUs:* Downline loading means that new software can be entered into an NIU by sending a file on the LAN from an NCC, as opposed to carrying new memory boards to every NIU. If the NIUs can be downline loaded, the hardware units become more interchangeable. This means less spares and less time and money to swap out a malfunctioning unit. Furthermore, it is much easier to install the latest release of NIU software.
2. *Logging:* The NCC should receive and record all status changes and errors or abnormal conditions for all NIUs, NIU-connected devices, and the cable plant.
3. *Statistics:* The NCC should collect statistics on a regular basis for each NIU and each port. The port statistics should include measures that are meaningful for the particular protocol of the port. In addition to collecting and recording statistics, effective reports are needed. Also, the ability should be provided to allow the network manager to create his own reports easily from the statistics file(s).

4. *Device configuration control*: The NCC should provide a capability to obtain and redefine the device parameters of each NIU port. These parameters include speed, bits per character, local echo, and many more.

5. *Security:* The NCC and NIUs should maintain network log-on security data. In this way, log-on locks and keys can be centrally administered if necessary.

6. *Dianostics:* The NCC should assist the operator and the initial network cable plant installers with the diagnosis of cable plant problems and NIU problems.

Specific Integrated NCC Requirements

In addition to the continuous status display requirement and the six general NCC requirements listed above, there are requirements specific to an integrated NCC.

1. *Multiple subnetworks:* Clearly, an integrated NCC must monitor and control more than one subnetwork. These could be multiple distinct base-band subnetworks or multiple channels on a broad-band network, or both.

2. *Multiple vendors:* The NIUs to be monitored by an integrated NCC will include equipment from multiple original equipment vendors. For example, a CSMA/CD office network and a token bus network may coexist on the same broad-band system. Furthermore, a separate LAN may exist to serve personal computers as opposed to data terminals.

REPRESENTATIVE SYSTEMS

At present, there are hundreds of products being sold under the generic heading of LANs [18]. It is clearly impossible to describe them all. Hence, only a few will be introduced and classified very briefly; those few have been selected because they are representative of various categories already discussed or have particular historical significance, or both. The significance of each system is described, and the system characteristics are summarized in Table 3.

Each system is illustrated by a block diagram representative of the offering, derived from the vendor's own publicity material. For further information on these and other systems, the reader should contact the individual vendors directly. Their addresses are included in the bibliography at the end of the article.

Ethernet (Fig. 24) was one of first CSMA/CD systems introduced commercially, and it is trademarked by Xerox Corporation [19]. However, many people now think of Ethernet as the name for the CSMA/CD access method. Ethernet uses 50 Ω coaxial cable and, hence, is not compatible with broad-band systems using CATV equipment on 75 Ω coaxial cable.

Bridge Communications is another CSMA/CD system compatible with IEEE 802.2 and uses the Ethernet base-band protocols, as shown in Figure 25, on 50 Ω cable [20].

TABLE 3. Representative LANs

Vendor	System Name	Topology	Medium	Access Method	Base band/ Broad band	Number Channels	Channel Speed	Link Protocol
Xerox Corp.	Ethernet	Bus/tree	Single 50-Ω coaxial Cable	CSMA/CD	Base band	1	10Mbit/sec	IEEE 802.3
Bridge Communications Inc.	Ethernet System product line	Tree	Single 50-Ω coaxial Cable	CSMA/CD	Base band	1	10Mbit/sec	IEEE 802.3
Contel Business Networks	ContelNet	Tree	Single 75-Ω coaxial cable	CSMA/CD	Broad base	5	10Mbit/sec	IEEE 802.3
Sytek	System 20	Tree	Single 75-Ω coaxial cable	CSMA/CD and frequency agile modems	Broad base	120	128Kit/sec	Nonstandard
Wang Laboratories Inc.	Wangnet	Tree	Dual cable 75-Ω coaxial cable	Frequency Division multiplexing and CSMA/CD	Broad base	Multiple	Varying	Nonstandard

Company	Network	Topology	Medium	Access Method	Transmission		Speed	Standard
Network Systems Corp.	Hyperchannel	Bus	Single 50-Ω coaxial cable	CSMA/CD priority	Base band	1	50Mbit/sec	Nonstandard
Concord Data Systems, Inc.	Token/Net	Tree	Single or dual 75-Ω coaxial cable	Token	Broad base	5	5Mbit/sec	IEEE 802.4
Applitek, Inc.	UNILAN	Tree	Single 75-Ω coaxial cable	Token and CSMA/CD	Broad base	5	10Mbit/sec	Nonstandard
IBM	Token Ring	Ring	Optical fiber and wire pair	Token	Base band	1	4Mbit/sec	IEEE 802.2
AT&T	Information System Network (ISN)	Star	Four-pair Twisted Wire	Priority contention	Priority dynamically assigned	1	8.64Mbit/sec	Nonstandard

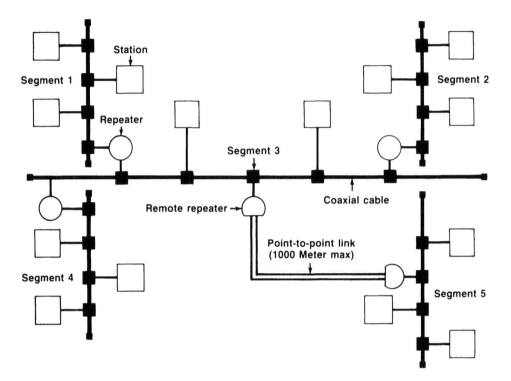

FIGURE 24.   Xerox, Ethernet.

Contel Corporation and Bridge Communications added a board to the Bridge BIU that enables the same signal to be sent in a 75 Ω broad-band system [29]. One resulting configuration is the ContelNet in Figure 26, which allows the user the same interface to base-band clusters or a broad-band backbone.

Sytek (Fig. 27) was one of the early vendors of broad-band systems and uses a 75 Ω coaxial cable [22]. Its System 20 is still unique in that it offers 120 128 Kbit/sec channels, with the NIU containing a "frequency agile modem" that can switch among the frequency bands. As a result of the low channel speeds, the system can extend to up to 50 kilometers without excessive signal degradation.

Wangnet is representative of systems that use dual cable, as shown in Figure 28 [23]. It is unusual in that it assigns frequency bands to different applications, as in Figure 29. Within each of the bands there are multiple channels of different speeds. For example, the Wang band for Wang hosts is a single 10 Mbit/sec CSMA/CD channel. However, the peripherals band for attachment of Wang peripherals, contains multiple 4.27 Mbit/sec channels.

Network Systems Corporation's Hyperchannel, shown in Figure 30, is a base-band system with a 50 Mbit/sec channel speed [24]. The system is tailored for high-speed file transfers among host processors. The BIUs

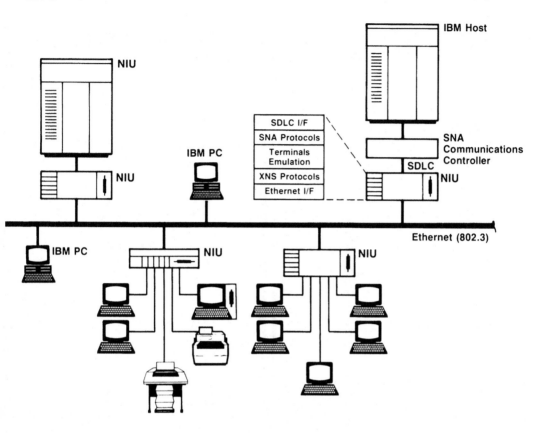

FIGURE 25. Bridge, Ethernet System Product Line.

perform the protocol conversion between different host protocols. The
access method is a modification of CSMA/CD that allows priorities so that
if a host is in the midst of a file transfer it is not interrupted.

Concord's Token/net is one of the first token systems and it meets the
IEEE 802.4 Standard [25].

Applitek's UNILAN, shown in Figure 31, is unique in that it allows both
token and CSMA/CD operation [26]. Time slots are allocated to a user or
group of users to be shared by token or CSMA/CD, depending upon user
requests and system congestion as measured by the system itself or as
assigned by a system manager.

IBM has introduced a number of different cabling schemes and LAN
products with different applications and properties [27]. IBM announced
its token ring in October 1985, as shown in Figure 32. The ring uses wire
pair or optical fiber in the backbone ring, with wire pair extending to individual terminals. The architecture uses existing wire closets as connection points to the ring. In this way, IBM tries to use existing telephone
wires in buildings.

The AT&T Information Systems Network (ISN) in Figure 33 uses a star
topology with a centrally located short bus at the hub [28]. The bus is
shared on a contention basis with priorities dynamically assigned to BIUs.

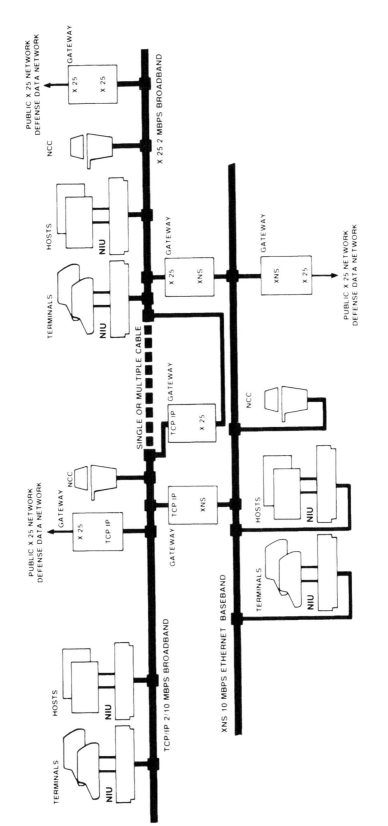

FIGURE 26. Contel, ContelNet.

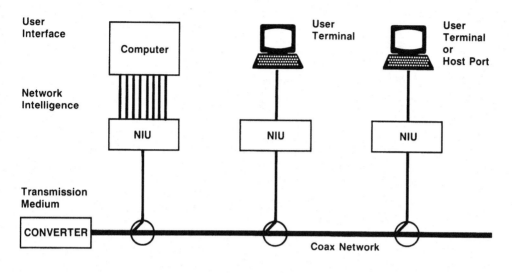

FIGURE 27.   Sytek, System 20.

The access medium is standard telephone four-pair twisted wire. Hence, AT&T combines some of the advantages of PBXs with LANs. The system capacity is 8.64Mbit/sec. AT&T has other offerings such as the 1Mbit/sec CSMA/CD STARLAN System to support 20 to 200 active workstations. Indeed, AT&T like IBM will have a variety of offerings for different users and needs.

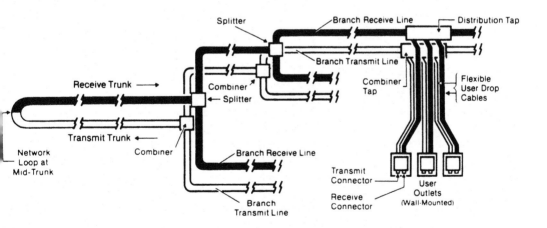

FIGURE 28.   Wang, Wangnet.

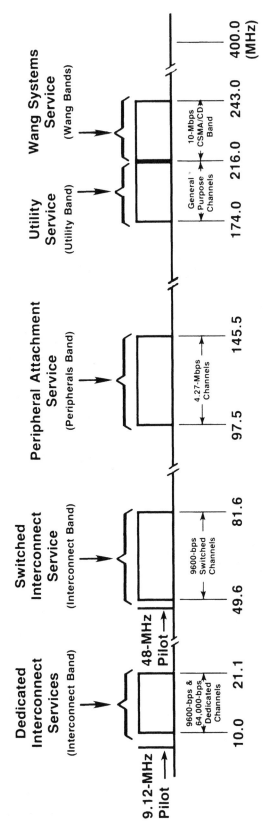

FIGURE 29. Wang, Wangnet.

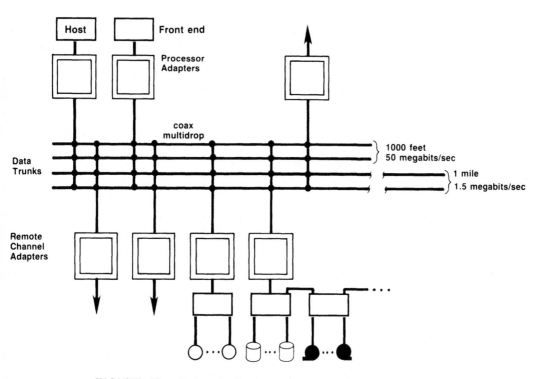

FIGURE 30.   Network Systems Corp., Hyperchannel.

Message Length	Performance Similar to	Applications
Variable	Token Passing & CSMA/CD	Mixed Environments
	Priority Token Passing	Synchronous Devices, Real Time Voice, Factory Control
	Priority CSMA/CD	Asynchronous Bursty Devices
Fixed	Dual Mode STDMA*	Highly Synchronous
	Reservation STDMA*	Applications or
	Contention STDMA*	Long Networks
*STDMA: Slotted Time Division Multiple Access		

FIGURE 31.   Applitek, UNILAN.

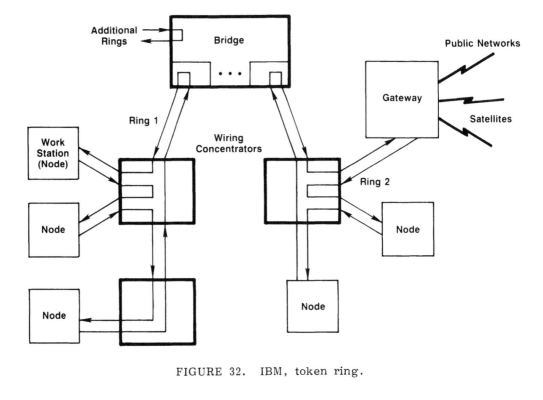

FIGURE 32. IBM, token ring.

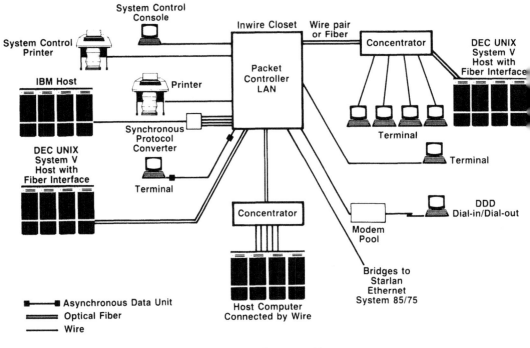

FIGURE 33. AT&T, ISN.

MARKETS

This article began with the premise that LANs were driven by the creation of distributed processing and built out of microprocessor-based NIUs near the user. Consequently, LANs are easily tailored to different applications, industries, and users.

One result of this flexibility is that specific products have emerged for different market segments. For example, for manufacturing facilities token systems have become popular for LANs involved in machine control. The reason for this is that for machine control there must be a guaranteed upper limit on response time. CSMA/CD cannot achieve this, but token systems can. For office environments, CSMA/CD is often used because of the sporadic inputs and large number of light systems users. Highly specialized systems have been developed for particular types of buildings such as hospitals. Some of the applications handled on a LAN in a hospital may include electronic patient-monitoring systems, call systems, emergency dispatch systems, master clock equipment, pharmacy order systems, and many others. In this environment, there are LANs that provide all the necessary interfaces to specialized medical equipment, as well as all the application packages to carry out the specialized functions.

The other result of this inherent flexibility is that LANs are adapted and new ones developed to meet new demands. For example, the number of personal computers in a business environment has grown tremendously. Users of these personal computers often want to network them. Furthermore, managers often encourage this networking so they can audit the systems, ensure uniform software and service, and impose security. When networking personal computers, the NIUs must be inexpensive because the personal computers are so low in price. Indeed, the NIUs are usually reduced to cards that are inserted into slots in the personal computers. Given this constraint, there is still a broad array of options to connecting the computers to an LAN.

Table 4 shows just some of the pros and cons of several options for LANs for personal computers. Specialized small low-capacity clusters for personal computers are considered. The other alternative shown is for a "full-scale network" which we can think of as a general-purpose broad-band LAN. For the sake of comparison, we have also included a stand-alone personal computer with multiple users. The best solution may depend upon the precise application intended for the personal computer. For example, the personal computer may

1. Act as a terminal to the mainframe.
2. Files may be transferred, a screen at a time between the personal computer and mainframe.
3. Entire files may be transferred between the personal computer and the mainframe with a single command.
4. The mainframe may act as a file server to the personal computer and the connection is transparent to the personal computer user.

Often, an effective economical solution under any of these circumstances is to allow low-cost specialized base-band clusters of personal computers to develop and then connect them to a broad-band backbone, as shown in Figure 34 [29].

The possibilities are limitless, and the field of LANs has become a mature technology with enormous scope for development and service.

TABLE 4. Alternatives to Full-Scale Networks

	Network Control	Resource Sharing	Expand- ability	Security	High Capacity
Multi-user Personal computer	N[a]	N	N	Y[b]	N
Personal computers	N	N	C[c]	C	C
Full-scale networks	Y	Y	Y	C	Y

[a]N, not available.
[b]Y, yes, easy.
[c]C, can be done.

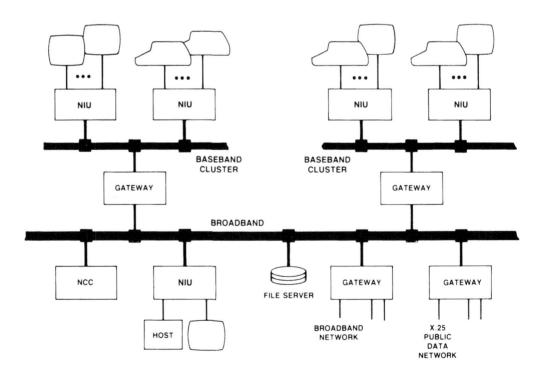

FIGURE 34. Broad-band backbone.

ACRONYMS

ACK	Acknowledgment
ARP	Address Resolution Protocol
ARPA	Advanced Research Projects Agency
ARPANET	ARPA Network
BIU	Bus interface unit
CAD/CAM	Computer aided design/computer-aided manufacturing
CATV	Cable television
CIU	Communications interface unit
CRT	Cathode ray tube
CSMA/CD	Carrier sense multiple access/collision detect
DECNET	Digital Equipment Corporation Network
DTE	Data terminal equipment
EMCC	Engineering and Manufacturing Computer Coordination
ETE	End-to-end
FDM	Frequency Division Multiplexing
Gbit/sec	Gigabits per second (billions of bits per second)
HDLC	High level data link control
HLP	Higher level protocols
IBX	Integrated Business Exchange
IDP	Internetwork Data Protocol
IEEE	Institute of Electrical and Electronics Engineers
IEEE 802	An IEEE Standards Committee
IP	Internet Protocol
ISN	Information System Network
ISO	International Standards Organization
Kbit/sec	Kilobits per second (thousands of bits per second)
Km	Kilometers
LAN	Local area network
MAP	Manufacturing Automation Protocol
MAU	Media access unit
Mbit/sec	Megabits per second (millions of bits per second)
MHz	Megahertz (million cycles per second)
Modem	Modulator/demodulator
μ sec	Microsecond (one millionth of a second)
msec	Millisecond (one thousandth of a second)
NACK	Negative Acknowledgment
NCC	Network control center
NCP	Network Control Protocol
NIU	Network interface unit
OSI	Open Systems Interconnect
PBX	Private branch exchange
PC	Personal computer
RAM	Random access memory
SDLC	Synchronous data link control
SNA	System network architecture
SPP	Sequenced Packet Protocol
TCP	Transmission Control Protocol
TCP/IP	Transmission Control Protocol/Internet Protocol
TIU	Terminal interface unit
TRU	Transceiver unit

UNIX   A computer operating system developed at Bell
                        Laboratories
XNS   Xerox Network System
X.25   An International standard to interface to a packet
                        switched network

REFERENCES

1. An American National Standard, "IEEE Standards for Local Area Net-
    works: Carrier Sense Multiple Access with Collision Detection (CSMA/
    cd) Access Method and Physical Layer Specifications," The Institute
    of Electrical and Electronics Engineers, Inc., Wiley-Interscience, John
    Wiley & Sons, Inc., New York, 1985.
2. T. Lissack, B. Maglaris, and I. T. Frisch, "Digital Switching in Local
    Area Networks," *IEEE Commun. Mag.*, 26–36 (1983).
3. I. T. Frisch, "The Evolution of Local Area Networks," *J. Telecommun.*,
    7–23 (Spring 1983).
4. T. C. Bartree, ed., *Data Communications, Networks, and Systems*,
    Howard W. Sams & Co., Inc., Indianapolis, IN, 1985.
5. A. S. Tanenbaum, *Computer Networks*, Prentice-Hall, Inc., Englewood
    Cliffs, NJ, 1981.
6. D. V. Glen, "Local Network Assesment," NTIA Report 85-174, U.S.
    Department of Commerce, Washington, D.C., April 1985.
7. H. Frank, "Broadband vs. Baseband Local Area Networks," *Telecom-
    munications*, 35–38 (March 1983).
8. W. R. Franta and I. Chlamtac, *Local Networks*, Lexington Books,
    D. C. Heath and Company, Lexington, MA, 1981.
9. J. F. Hayes, *Modelling and Analysis of Computer Communications
    Networks*, Plenum Press, New York, 1984.
10. C. Tropper, *Local Computer Network Technologies*, Academic Press,
    New York, 1981.
11. P. Hsi and T. Lissack, "Coaxial Cable Based Local Area Network
    Comparison Study," *Data Commun.*, McGraw-Hill, 56–66 (December
    1980).
12. An American National Standard, "IEEE Standards for Local Area Net-
    works: Logical Link Control," The Institute of Electrical and Electronics
    Engineers, Inc., Wiley-Interscience, John Wiley & Sons, Inc., New
    York, 1984.
13. An American National Standard, "IEEE Standards for Local Area Net-
    works: Token-Passing Bus Access Method and Physical Layer Specif-
    ications," The Institute of Electrical and Electronics Engineers, Inc.,
    Wiley-Interscience, John Wiley & Sons, Inc., New York, 1985.
14. "MAP, Manufacturing Automation Protocol," GMCC, GMME&D A/MD-13,
    GM Technical Center, Warren, MI 48090-9040.
15. "Transmission Control Protocol," Military Standard-1778, Department of
    Defense, Washington, D.C. 20301, August 12, 1983.
16. "Internet Protocol," Military Standard-1777, Department of Defense,
    Washington, D.C. 20301, August 12,1983.
17. J. S. Ambler, "Network Control Center Architecture for an Integrated
    LAN," in *Proceedings of the 1985 Symposium on New Developments in
    Local Area Networks*, Long Island Section of the IEEE, Uniondale,
    Long Island, New York, October 4, 1985.

18. *The LocalNetter Designers Handbook*, Architecture Technology Corporation, Minneapolis, MN 55424, 1985.
19. Xerox Corporation, 1341 W. Mockingbird Lane, Dallas, TX 75247.
20. Bridge Communications, Inc., 10440 Bubb Road, Cupertino, CA 95014.
21. Contel Business Networks, 4330 East-West Highway, Bethesda, MD 20814.
22. Sytek, 1225 Charleston Road, Mountain View, CA 94043.
23. Wang Laboratories, Inc., 1 Industrial Way, M/S 13A3B, Lowell, MA 01851.
24. Network Systems Corporation, 7600 Boone Avenue, Brooklyn Park, MN 55428.
25. Concord Data Systems, Inc., 303 Bear Hill Road, Waltham, MA 02154.
26. Applitek Inc., 107 Audobon Road, Wakefield, MA 01880.
27. IBM Data Products Division, 1113 Westchester Avenue, White Plains, NY 10604.
28. AT&T Information Systems, 1 Oak Way, Berkeley Heights, NJ 07922.
29. S. C. Foster, H. Frank, I. T. Frisch, W. J. Levitt and W. B. Roeca, "The Marriage of Broadband and Baseband LANs," *Telecommunications*, 85 ff (February 1985).

IVAN T. FRISCH

MACHINE TRANSLATION IN THE U.S.S.R.

INTRODUCTION

Machine (automatic) translation (MT) presents one of the most challenging problems of applied or computational linguistics. The concept of MT, once born, has greatly contributed to the development of methods of modern theoretical and applied linguistics, to the emergence of the idea of computational linguistics itself, and to the modeling of language and speech. Compiling dictionaries for MT has stimulated research in the fields of statistical lexicography, contextual analysis, methods of formalizing word meaning, etc. MT algorithms require the use of mathematical logics, algorithm theory, computational mathematics, mathematical linguistics, and programming languages. MT systems form a part of information systems and networks. MT has a direct bearing on the problem of artificial intelligence because the most difficult aspect of the MT problem can only be solved through the formalization of the semantic level. The status of MT stems from the essence of translation, which is based both on relatively simple operations, such as looking up words in a dictionary, and on complex operations, such as rendering certain syntactic structures or contents rich in original semantic connotations in a different language, etc. Rather often, the translator has to perform various creative operations on the text. MT problems are being solved in the following areas: the inclusion of state-of-the-art MT in current information services and the development of new and more effective reproductive linguistic models, which would produce higher quality results.

HISTORY OF MACHINE-AIDED TRANSLATION

The idea of MT was first put forward in 1949, soon after World War II, where electronic computational machines were used to decipher enemy codes, which gave some researchers the idea of applying these machines to the translation process [1]. Much earlier, in 1933, the Soviet inventor P. P. Smirnoff-Troyansky put in a claim for his invention, "A machine for automatic production of ready-made translations requiring only literary editing, from one language into several others simultaneously." He was issued author's certificate No. 40995 of the Soviet Union for "A machine for selecting and typing words while translating from one language into another" [2]. The inventor based his idea on the concept of the unique logical structure for all languages.

According to P. P. Smirnoff-Troyansky, logical analysis conducted by man consisted in the fact that grammatical information extracted from the text found explicit expression in special logical signs reflecting the syntactical structure of the sentence. He used the linguistic idea of the similarity of logical structures of different languages. P. P. Smirnoff-Troyansky's invention found no applications, but the idea of the unity of means of expression in language also inspired researchers of the next generation. New possibilities of electronic computers gave impetus to ideas of translation mechanization and automation. In 1952, the United States held the first conference on MT in which many specialists participated who had already started work on developing MT for various languages [3]. The Georgetown experiment conducted on the IBM 701 computer became a sensation in the scientific world; it may be considered as the beginning of the first period of MT development. The dictionary used in the experiment contained only 250 Russian words from the fields of politics, law, mathematics, chemistry, metallurgy, communication, and the military. L. Dostert and P. Garvin were in charge of the project. Every Russian word was supplied with a translation, or several translations, if the word was polysemantic. There were six syntactic rules. The selected Russian sentences consisted of words from the dictionary and were built according to the syntactic rules included in the analysis algorithm. The program contained 2,400 commands. Translating each of the sentences took 5 to 8 seconds [4].

The first MT experiment drew the attention of the scientific community. Before it, the problem had only narrowly interested some specialists at government institutions who had to deal with speedy translation of large bodies of texts. After the experiment, many European countries—the Soviet Union, Great Britain, France, Italy, West Germany, as well as the United States, Canada, Japan, and others—started their own research, mostly at universities and educational institutions, predominantly on the basis of government contracts.

In 1955, the first Soviet experiment in MT took place with the help of a computer, in which a small single text in mathematics was translated from English into Russian. I. K. Belskaya was in charge of the experiment [5]. The same year saw the start of MT experiments in the Soviet Union on a wide scale. The research was being conducted at U.S.S.R. academic institutes, at higher education institutes, and in research groups of information institutions, such as the Scientific Research Institute of Patent Information. In 1958, the Soviet Union conducted the first representative conference on MT. Immediately afterwards, a number of higher educational institutions opened departments for training specialists in MT.

The history of MT may be divided into four periods, approximately 10 years each. The first period began toward the end of the 1950s, with the emergence of the MT idea itself and the first works on MT. It lasted until 1966 and was characterized by a rather optimistic approach to MT and even, to a certain extent, by overevaluation of its possibilities. Thus, the idea of multiple MT for a large number of language pairs through an intermediary language was rather popular, though there was no clear-cut idea of the structure of such a language. But even then the researchers had substantial difficulties in formalizing and preparing algorithms for the analysis and synthesis of a wide range of language phenomena. It could be said that even during the first period, there were two approaches to the problem.

The first approach concentrated on linguistic contents. It was established that MT research was essentially in the mainstream of the approach of many linguistic schools that viewed language as a mechanism generating texts and divided it into language proper and speech, the plane of contents and the plane of expression—the approach considering formal, distributive, and statistical peculiarities of human language. Great attention was paid to the works of such linguists as F. de Saussure, L. Hjelmslev, L. Bloomfield, E. Sapir, N. S. Trubetzkoy, J. J. Baudouin de Courtenay, and L. V. Shcherba. The works of these scholars provided much of the material allowing the formulation of MT as a linguistic task which, in its turn, allowed scientific research of formal language properties and language properties capable of being formalized. The second approach concentrated on the mathematical properties of language and speech and introduced some notions of mathematical language modeling. But these notions themselves could not solve MT problems from the linguistic point of view.

No artificial "semantic" language can render the broad variety of meanings of language elements appearing in actual speech time and time again, depending both on the linguistic and extralinguistic context, on the non-linguistic situation of communication, etc. Therefore, the practical output of the intermediary language concept for MT did not amount to much, but the research conducted brought about new notions of language structure and language functioning, as well as new possibilities of formalization techniques with the purpose of translation. Along with theoretical research, the first period of MT history saw attempts to build and use some working MT systems. This not only allowed the researchers to test the basic principles of MT from the theoretical point of view but also from a practical aspect, and the tests were conducted on vast linguistic material. Among such systems one should mention the U.S. system of translating texts from Russian into English. The system was developed on the basis of the Georgetown University approach by M. M. Zarechnyak [6]. On the whole, the first period was rather important for the development of MT; it made it possible to realize the deficiencies in our knowledge of natural language principles. Unlike exact sciences, the humanities, and especially linguistics, which had no descriptions exact enough, turned out to be unprepared to use computational equipment. This led to long-term research in the field of creating language models. The report of the U.S. National Scientific Foundation Commission entitled "Language and Machines" is considered to be the end of the first period. The report summed up the results of MT research conducted in a number of U.S. organizations, evaluated their economic effectiveness, and made forecasts about the translation market and MT prospects. The report had a considerable impact on the further development of MT research in the United States and other countries, leading to their considerable curtailment [7].

The second period covered the 10 years from 1967 to 1977. During that time, working MT systems were put into operation in EUROATOM, in the United States, on the basis of the Georgetown system and some other approaches, in the Soviet Union (Central Research Institute of Patent Information and others), as well as in some other countries, such as Italy, Japan, and France. But the predominant feature of the second period was massive theoretical research directly or indirectly related to MT. The problem not only aroused considerable interest from universities but also from commercial organizations, because the demand for translations remained high and/or grew in accordance with the requirements of scientific and technical progress.

A number of theoretical principles were formulated, which contributed much to the development of both linguistics and contiguous branches of science. Thus, the principle of separating the language grammar from the algorithm of using the grammatical description, and the separation of analysis and synthesis was defined and found practical application; there was a great deal of research into the means of formalizing syntactic structure and semantics. Large natural language dictionaries were complied, with the aim of using them in MT systems and other systems of text information automatic processing. Contextual dictionaries appeared that could help to establish contextual nonsynonymity of lexical units [8]. One should especially note growing research in the field of language unit statistics and the application of information theory methods to solving linguistic problems. Great progress was achieved in the area where the "speech statistics" group was especially active, particularly in the Soviet Union [9]. MT influenced the development of research in automatic information search considerably. As a result of research during the second period, linguistics and contiguous branches of science concerning themselves with MT problems received an arsenal of new scientific and practical resources. Among such resources were algorithms for morphological analysis and synthesis for major and most widespread scientific and technical languages; algorithms and means of describing the lexical, syntactical, and semantic levels of language; software for corresponding linguistic tasks; and special dictionaries to be used in MT and information search systems. As the problem of coding and processing hieroglyphics and other types of written languages became especially pressing, much attention was paid to the machine analysis and translation from the Japanese language into European languages.

The third period may be considered to have started in 1975 to 1977 and it is not yet over. During the "Apollo–Soyuz" joint flight under the U.S.S.R.–U.S. space project, spacemen talked via MT (SYSTRAN system). MT systems ready for industrial use appeared on the commercial market. In 1974, the U.S.S.R. Centre for Translation of Scientific and Technical Literature and Documentation (VCP) was given the function of the central organization dealing with MT problems, which gave a powerful impetus to the further development of practical MT in the Soviet Union and determined the trends of theoretical research [10].

CONTEMPORARY STATE OF MT

Totally automated high-quality MT which, in one way or an other, was the goal of the first period research, is now considered to be an ideal unattainable in the immediate future. In present-day MT, the role of the editor is very important: There are pre-, inter-, and posteditors, preparing the text for translation or proofreading the machine output during or after the computer-translation process. Division of labor between man and computer is not a trivial thing; it demands sound research and special technology. The machine is ready to analyze all linguistic phenomena of the text, without noticing its own mistakes.

The linguistic status of MT, MT progress, and grounds for forecasts and prospects can be described in terms of two parameters: levels of linguistic representation and operable existing systems.

At the morphological level, analysis algorithms for the main European languages (English, German, French, Russian, and Spanish) have been produced and tested in an extended experiment; there has been research into Japanese, Arabic, Mali, the Indian languages, Portugese, Chinese, and a number of other languages. The morphological level analysis principle for MT, as well as for computational linguistics in general, differs from the traditional approach in linguistics. The traditional approach treats everything that characterizes the form of the word as a morphological level. In other words, traditional morphological analysis is determined by *what* it defines. For computational linguistics and MT it is important that through the analysis of word forms one can sometimes (depending on the language type and analysis algorithm) receive diverse information, not necessarily referring to form. Thus, while analyzing the Russian word form of "he was," one can see that within a sentence it performs the role of the predicative verb or the link verb of the compound predicate. This type of information cannot be considered morphological, but it is important for the subsequent analysis, and there is no point in omitting it while analyzing word forms. In other words, we have a different principle in this case: It is not important *what* is to be determined through word-form analysis, but *how*, i.e., the concept of morphological analysis for MT is an operational concept.

Morphological analysis for MT can be performed both with a word-stem dictionary and a word-form dictionary, the latter being necessary for obtaining grammatical information about the word form and for lemmatizing it. Morphological elements to be analyzed (endings, suffixes, affixes) are usually distributed in special tables. Word homonymy, if any, is dealt with by using special means of contextual analysis. On the whole, it can be said that automatic morphological analysis for the main languages of the world, in which most scientific and technical material is written, is the most developed and used component of MT linguistic analysis. It is also widely used in other tasks dealing with automatic processing of text information [11].

The problem of correcting orthographical errors needs particular mention. Automatic input of text information, which is a necessary stage in the work of contemporary automated systems of text processing, often results in spelling errors. Correcting these errors should also be done automatically, i.e., according to regularities operating at the morphological level and expressed statistically. Statistical distribution of letter combinations in various languages is widely used.

At the lexical level, special research has established that a MT is not understandable mainly through syntax or grammar but rather through the correct translation of words. It has also been found that to achieve the latter, it is possible and expedient to use contextually determined features of resolving lexical ambiguity.

In linguistics it is understood that the word as one of the main units of language description can contain a large volume of diverse information. Thus, a word may have paradigmatic, syntagmatic, and derivational (word-building) characteristics; syntactic information in dictionary entries of some syntactically marked words, e.g., conjunctions, may be rather complex. Nevertheless, algorithm variants and MT systems, in which dictionary information is complex and difficult to update, have been realized only in experimental systems, the reason for which is the fact that the lexical level of any language is a very mobile level subject to changes more than any other language level, due to constant additions and corrections caused by transfer to new sublanguages. If a dictionary entry is large and complex, it becomes difficult and expensive to compile new entries and to enter them into the system. On the other hand, automatic dictionaries with minimal information in entries, e.g., with only a translation, are not very convenient for MT, precisely because of information scarceness, for analysis sometimes requires other kinds of information besides translation equivalents. In general, there is obviously a problem in choosing the optimal volume of lexical entries in the input dictionary. The solution to the problem is important for MT [12].

The experience of compiling automatic dictionaries for MT translation and for rendering help to a human editor and translator, as well as the theoretical understanding of the problem, have given rise to a new linguistic science within the framework of computational linguistics: computational lexicography. It studies the problems of compiling and using automatic (machine) dictionaries in automatic text-processing systems [13].

To resolve lexical ambiguity in context, a special dictionary is used. It is a contextual dictionary, which helps to solve the polysemy problem through algorithms, As far as the author is aware, he was the first to describe such a dictionary, though the idea of using contexts had been discussed even during the first period of MT development, and some experimental dictionary entries of this kind had been published. The difficulty, however, is in the comprehensive approach to polysemy, where it is important to find out to what extent all words of a natural language (or their sufficient amount) are determined contextually, to what extent their lexical meanings are explicitly bound contextually, and to what degree it is possible to use these contextual features for making respective algorithms. In compiling an English—Russian dictionary, the author had to use the concordance of 700,000 uses of words, which took several years of hand work. A contexual dictionary systematizes contexts in which a polysemantic lexical unit displays their meanings relative to the target language. The theoretical basis for a contextual dictionary is the theory of determinants that has been developed and enriched with the aim of solving other problems, particularly those of lexical—grammatical homonymy [14].

The level of syntactic analysis is especially important for MT, because constructing a correct sentence at the exit and preserving the sense of the original is possible only after the syntactic structure of the sentence or some substituting information has been determined and rendered in the exit language. The fact that syntactic analysis has to be formal places great demands on the formalization and algorithmic nature of relevant procedures and descriptions. It is common knowledge that syntax is closely connected with semantics: Traditional parsing of the sentence is based on answers to such questions as "What is the subject? It is that which is spoken about in the sentence. What is the predicate? This is what the subject is doing," etc. Mo matter how complex an apparatus is used to describe semantics, syntax, and their relationship—practically at all levels of description, be it the functional sentence perspective or some other complex semantic—syntactic problems—the description is based on practically interminable a priori intuitive statements, and the fact that both semantic and syntactic types of analysis are so difficult to formalize is a consequence of the indeterminability of the initial fundamental ideas and concepts of the analysis, which are impossible to formalize. The machine cannot give a clear-cut answer to questions unanswerable by man. While defining syntactic roles of words within a sentence, it can rely only on formal, explicitly expressed features— morphological and lexical—and grammatical ones, i.e., information ascribed to clearly identifiable lexical units such as word forms. It cannot think. Therefore, the contemporary state of automatic syntactical analysis can be

characterized by the fact that there are no accepted suitable algorithms of
such analysis, that could be tested in new experiments or, at least, I am
not aware of their existence. What we have in mind is algorithms of complete syntactical analysis.

On the other hand, practical tasks of formal definition of syntactic
information within a sentence are satisfactorily solved by methods of approximate syntactic analysis. Most often, these methods are replicas of schemes
of analysis into parts of speech and sentence, which exists in most European languages in one modification or another. Automatic analysis makes it
necessary to modify the system, but its essence remains. The commonness
of the approach is due to the fact that the system is formalized best of all.
Practically every European language has a set of features that are formal or
easily formalized that provide the basis for describing members of the sentence and parts of speech capable of performing certain syntactic roles
within a sentence. Therefore, it is possible to maintain that contemporary
automatic syntactic analysis is realized through methods of consecutive
approximations underlied by systems based on determining the syntactic
functions of separate words and workd groups constituting the sentence [15].

At the semantic level it is important to consider the fact that contemporary MT systems are based on the principle of gradual acquisition of
knowledge necessary for translation; therefore, in most cases, semantic information does not present a separate block or a system component but is
spread through other algorithms, in particular those for lexical and syntactic analysis. Semantic means can be most diverse, ranging from using—in
syntactic analysis of semantic categories of words and word groups, such
as animateness—systems of differential semantic features to the semantics
of separate words and word groups in dictionaries compiled especially for
analysis and translation. A more detailed description of the semantic inventory would demand a special investigation and, more important, would go
beyond MT proper. The system of algorithms for analysis and synthesis,
i.e., the system of MT, together with dictionaries, is described by a rather
general theoretical model. Models underlying working systems of automatic
text processing are usually referred to in Soviet Linguistics as "reproductive linguistic models," as distinguished from purely theoretical, descriptive,
or explanatory models. Through a feedback apparatus, a reproductive model
helps to update algorithms and analysis systems where and when it is necessary. It is responsive to external changes and results [16].

The translation model, based on translation correspondence as described
in Soviet literature, can be represented by the block diagram shown in
Fig. 1. It should be noted that this model is the basis of all working MT
systems. The fact is that those who conduct research into practical MT
systems independently have arrived at rather similar distribution of their
material and stages of text processing.

The main contents of these stages in the scheme does not depend on
the choice of a concrete language pair, but each source and target language
and their correlation can certainly influence concrete conclusions. The
purpose of the block diagram of the described algorithm is a prompt retrieval of translation correspondence and translation of the text, with the most
difficult areas demanding thinking to be left for the editor. For each language pair the necessary syntactic and lexical sentence transformations are
performed through various mechanisms and means and located at different
stages of the analysis and synthesis. Thus, in Russian, there is no structural correspondence to English structures with phrases such as "there is,

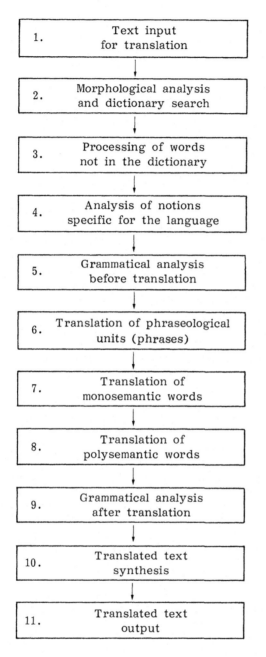

1. Text input
for translation

2. Morphological analysis
and dictionary search

3. Processing of words
not in the dictionary

4. Analysis of notions
specific for the language

5. Grammatical analysis
before translation

6. Translation of phraseological
units (phrases)

7. Translation of
monosemantic words

8. Translation of
polysemantic words

9. Grammatical analysis
after translation

10. Translated text
synthesis

11. Translated text
output

FIGURE 1   Block-diagram of MT algorithm.

there lies," etc. The necessary changes in the translating sentence word order may occur both with verbs and adverbs.

Text input for translation may be done through various carriers. An automatic reader is most effective. Morphological analysis is conducted with the help of a word-stem dictionary or a word-form dictionary and also has a number of algorithms. At the same time, correction of errors is taking place. An essential task is the processing of words not found in the dictionary. They are also analyzed and ascribed certain grammatical meanings necessary for further analysis. Thus, if a noun is not included in the dictionary and cannot be translated, it is ascribed the feature "noun," e.g., by reason of its having certain suffixes or inflections. Thus, the word fully participates in grammatical analysis. Such is the summary of the first three stages.

The fourth stage involves analysis of features specific for the given language, the preliminary examination of which may give substantial information useful for the subsequent stages of analysis. The purpose of grammatical analysis preceding translation is to determine syntactic functions of the words in the sentences. The analysis is conducted for every word form of the text according to certain algorithms oriented at lexical—grammatical word classes (corresponding, with certain modifications, to parts of speech). Besides determining the syntactic functions of words, this stage of analysis is able to solve other problems, e.g., to analyze frame structures in German, etc. The fifth stage may follow the identification and classification of phraseological units and set expressions, which makes grammatical analysis considerably easier.

Translation of monosemantic words is separated from translation of polysemantic words. The latter are defined as those having more than one translation equivalent. A variety of contextual dictionaries is used for translation. The translation of words is followed by grammatical analysis, which is necessary for putting the output sentence into grammatical shape in accordance with the grammatical norms of the target language, with account of corresponding grammatical elements at the input. Thus, in translation from a foreign language into Russian, certain categories necessary for synthesis can be determined only after the lexical units have been translated: English has no categories such as gender or case, and in the target text they are to be taken from the lexical meaning of the source units. Translation text synthesis is not only the synthesis of word forms but of the whole sentence. Sentence translation is actually a sum of translations of more or less large pieces of the sentence, in accordance with the data of syntactical analysis. The necessary transformations are provided for by the previous stages of translation. In all working MT systems, there are algorithms that effectively analyze ties outside sentences, such as anaphoric ties. The output can either be typed or displayed, with further editing by the editor or the translator working with the computer [14].

The more accurately they reveal translation correspondence for the language pair, the more effective models of translation are. Such correspondence, as a rule, forms a potentially open system. Adjusting MT algorithms for a new language subsystem will add considerably to the arsenal of translation correspondence.

At present the following systems of MT exist. In Europe, the United States, and Canada, SYSTRAN is the most popular system. It was developed in the United States on the basis of the Georgetown system and is based on principles of translation correspondence. The system has all elements of contemporary stages of analysis and synthesis; it has been designed for several language pairs and several scientific—technical sublanguages; it has been planned to be widely used for translation in the European Economic Community (EEC). A multilanguage MT system is being developed for the languages of the EEC. It is based on a new principle of using an intermediary language according to the principles worked out by the Grenoble group. The effort is known as EUROTRA. The Soviet Union has a system of English—Russian automatic translations of texts in computational technology, known as AMPAR. Its author is the All-Union Center of Translation. By now the system has translated nearly 10,000 pages of current scientific—technical documents, demanding different degrees of editing. Versions of the system are installed by different users to be operated by them independently. The All-Union Center of Translation has also worked out and put into experimental use the systems of French—Russian MT (FRAP) and of German—Russian MT (NERPA). The former is built on the principle of explicit processing of semantic information and has a complex component of syntactic and, separately, of semantic analysis. The German—Russian system is built on the principle of translation correspondence. These systems are being delivered to users.

There are also many systems in the world that occupy an intermediate position between MT and automatic dictionaries: They help human translators, editors, and specialists using foreign languages. Among them are such systems as ALPS, Siemens, TEAM, the Brigham Young University system, and a number of others. At the same time, MT proper is being perfected in the form of theory-oriented systems aimed at achieving higher quality at the expense of perfecting the theoretical model [17, 18].

PROSPECTS OF MT DEVELOPMENT

MT as a scientific problem largely depends on the appearance of new and more effective models of human translation activity, models of a reproductive type, which are not only called to explain but also to reproduce the activity with the help of automata. Such models are especially important at the level of translation correspondence, because it is at this level that practical problems of translation are solved for language pairs taken separately. This increases the importance of contrasting studies and of contrasting linguistics. Contextual dependencies, which alone can help solve translation problems proper, acquire new meaning in the light of MT tasks. The establishment of contextual dependence of language and text units relevant for translation is necessary for building certain algorithms. Different types of contexts should be described and various contextual dictionaries compiled. Modeling for MT purposes not only needs "translational lexis", i.e., lexis viewed through the prism of translation correspondence, but "translation grammar," a number of grammatical rules arranged so that it may be possible to gradually identify features necessary for finding translational correspondence. It can be said that such ideas are increasingly appreciated by the traditional translation theory that is turning to the translation process in its close relation to grammar [19, 20].

Language and speech frequency data are still of great importance for creating working MT systems. Dictionaries, lexical means of analysis and synthesis, and algorithms of morphological and other types of analysis are based on statistical data on speech in all of its varieties. It is important here to determine the strategy of moving phenomena from most frequent and statistically well described to more and more subtle ones that have no meaningful frequency but some of which appear frequently enough. Means of identifying formal characteristics of linguistic phenomena and the means of constructing algorithms of syntactic and semantic analysis are of great importance for making applied models of MT. Semantics of artificial intelligence in its present application to robots has little to do with text semantics necessary for MT. However, further developments of applied semantic analysis methods will undoubtfully play an important role in improving MT models.

Finally, MT has much to gain from the experience of automatic dictionaries being used in the man—computer context. Regularities for concrete language pairs will help to establish more general regularities common for the translation process in general. Thus, for MT it is not only important to follow the path of deduction, on which problems of semantic modeling are now being solved, but to use induction as well, which proceeds from experience and texts with the purpose of building working MT systems. The future of MT is in an optimal combination of theory and practice of information processing.

REFERENCES

1. W. Weaver, "Translation," in *Mechanical Translation of Languages*, (W. N. Locke and P. B. Booth, eds.), John Wiley & Sons, New York; Technology Press of M.I.T., 1955, pp. 15—23.

2. P. N. Denisov, *Printsipy Modelirovaniya Yazyka*, Moscow State University, Moscow, 1965, (in Russian).

3. V. H. Yngve, "The Machine and the Man," *Mechanical Translation*, *1*(2), 20—22 (August 1954).

4. L. Dostert, "The Georgetown—IBM Experiment," in *Mechanical Translation of Languages*, (W. N. Locke and P. D. Booth, eds.), John Wiley & Sons, New York; Technology Press of M.I.T., 1955, pp. 124—135.

5. I. K. Belskaya, *Yazyk Cheloveka i Mashina*, Moscow State Univeristy, Moscow, 1969, (in Russian).

6. M. Zarechnak and A. F. R. Brown, "Current Research in Georgetown University," in *Proceedings of the Natioanl Symposium on Machine Translation*, Prentice-Hall, Englewood Cliffs, NJ, 1961, pp. 63—87.

7. "Yazyk i mashini (Primenenije elektronnikh vichislitelnikh mashin v perevode i v issledovanii yazika. Otchiot Nabludatelnogo Komiteta po avtomaticheskoj obrabotke tekstov. U.S. National Academy of Sciences. Natsionalnyi nauchno-issle-dovatelskij sovet)," in *Nauchno-technicheskaya Informatsia*, U.S.S.R. Institute of Scientific Information, Academy of Sciences of the U.S.S.R., Informatsionnye protsessy i sistemy, seria 2, 1968, No. 8, pp. 25—37 (in Russian).

8. "Kontekstologicheskij slovar dlya mashinnogo perevoda mnogoznachnikh slov s anglijskogo yazyka na russkij," Compiled by Yu. N. Marchuk, Moscow, the U.S.S.R. Centre for Translation, 1976, Part 1—Part 2, pp. 264, 256 (in Russian).

9. R. G. Piotrovski, *Tekst, Mashina, Chelovek*, Nauka, Leningrad, 1975 (in Russian).

10. V. N. Gerasimov and Yu. N. Marchuk, "Sovremennoye sostoyanije mashinnogo perevoda," in *Mashinnyi Perevod i Avtomatizatsia Informat-*

sionnykh Protsessov. U.S.S.R. Centre for translation, Moscow, 1975, pp. 5–17 (in Russian).

11. A. L. Vasilevskij and Yu. N. Marchuk, *Vychislitelnaya Lingvistika,* Moscow Foreign Languages Institute, Moscow, 1970, Part I–Part IV (in Russian).

12. N. N. Leontyeva, I. M. Koudrashova, and E. G. Sokolova, *Semanticheskaya Slovarnaya Statya v Sistemje FRAP,* Institute of Russian Language, U.S.S.R. Academy of Sciences, Moscow, a preliminary edition, No. 121, 1979 (in Russian).

13. Yu. N. Marchuk, *Vychislitelnaya Leksikografia,* The U.S.S.R. Centre for Translation, Moscow, 1976 (in Russian).

14. Yu. N. Marchuk, *Problemy Mashinnogo Perevoda,* Nauka, Moscow, 1983 (in Russian).

15. Yu. V. Rozshdenstvenski, *Vvedenije v Obschuyu Filologiyu,* Vishaya Shkola, Moscow, 1979 (in Russian).

16. R. G. Piotrovski, *Inzshenernaya Lingvistika i Tooria Yazyka,* Nauka, Leningrad, 1979 (in Russian).

17. H. Bruderer, *Handbook of Machine Translation and Machine-aided Translation. Automatic Translation on Natural Languages and Multilingual Terminology Data Banks,* North-Holland Publishing Company, Amsterdam, Oxford, New York, 1978.

18. J. Slocum, *A Status Report on the LRC Machine Translation Systems,* Linguistic Research Center, University of Texas, Austin, Texas, 1982.

19. R. G. Kotov, Yu. N. Marcuk, and L. L. Neloubin, *Mashinnij Perevod v Nachalye 80 Godov.* Voprosi Yasykoznanija, Moscow, 1983, No. 1, pp. 31–38 (in Russian).

20. R. G. Piotrovsky, V. N. Bilan, M. N. Borkun, and A. K. Bobkov, *Metody Avtomaticheskogo Analiza i Sinteza Teksta,* Vysheishaya shkola, Moscow, 1985 (in Russian).

YU. N. MARCHUK

MICROCOMPUTER, SELECTION OF A

INTRODUCTION

Today, some 50 companies manufacture microcomputers in the United States, and over 2,000 software publishers supply programs that make these micro-computers useful and productive tools in government, education, and corporate organizations. Therefore, selecting microcomputers is an endeavor that may present considerable challenge to experienced computer and information systems professionals and much frustration to the new or inexperienced user of computer systems and software. Despite the dominance of IBM in the single-user personal microcomputer market, there are many IBM "clone" systems and other systems that possess specific strengths and weaknesses when considered for specific tasks. For example, the strongest challenger technology to IBM is Apple's Macintosh, designed for ease of use by noncomputer-oriented individuals. Whether this technology becomes very popular with large institutional organizations outside of higher education may become the biggest gamble Apple Computer will face.

In addition, there is a growing class of networked and multiuser micro-computers that afford differing capabilities. The local area network (LAN) microcomputer system using single-user personal computers attaches them by a cabling scheme to share large disks and other peripherals. These LANs are controlled through network server hardware and specific software to enable the system to function. True multiuser microcomputers, running multiuser operating systems such as Digital Equipment Corporation's RSX-11M on PDP-11 series, 16-bit word microcomputers or VAX/VMS on their MicroVAX 32-bit word microcomputer, AMOS on Alpha Microsystems, Inc., AM-1000 series microcomputers, and UNIX or PICK on systems such as the Altos Computers or General Automation Zebra afford even more powerful microcomputer alternatives where multiple simultaneous users require access to the same application program. These 32-bit systems are also very popular for running the UNIX operating system versions and applications for engineering design, scientific laboratories, computer-aided design/graphics, and similar applications where computational speed and power are required.

In this article we will give a primer for the non-data-processing professional who faces the selection of one or more microcomputers or systems using microcomputers as workstation devices or processors that might be used in building a distributed data processing system architecture.

In the United States and Europe, for single-user microsystems, major software houses are writing new software, mainly for the IBM Personal Computer in its respective models—the PC and PC/XT—and the relatively new Intel-80286-based PC/AT (Advanced Technology). Therefore, most software activity is concentrated on serving this IBM and clone system market and, secondly, on serving other microcomputers that use the Microsoft MS-DOS operating system as opposed to other operating systems. Some of these systems have very little or no compatibility with the IBM PC models.

The exception to this market-driven trend are developers who are readying programs for Apple's Macintosh computer which, although based on a Motorola MC68010 microprocessor, has its own proprietary operating system referred to simply as "System" rather than using XENIX, a UNIX derivative operating system most often found running on systems using this microprocessor family. Developers who have software products operating under CP/M-86 (Digital Research) or under their 8-bit CP/M version 2.2 or 3.0 may include some upgraded software but are not creating many new products for these systems because there are few new marketing opportunities in these operating systems. In essence, the IBM PC and its very powerful sibling PC/AT have become defacto industry standards.

In England and Europe, although similar trends toward IBM compatibility are evident, there is still a considerable installed base of microsystems noncompatible with IBM PCs, for which developers are continuing new software efforts. For example, the ACT Apricot is becoming a very popular machine with its IMb RAM (random access memory), and previously ACT's Sirius 1 (Victor 9000 in the United States) had and continues to maintain considerable installed user bases, as do other European-manufactured machines. Although IBM and clone machines are gathering European market share, noncompatible MS-DOS systems of non-U.S. manufacture continue their success more strongly in these markets due to the lack of traditional IBM dominance outside of North America. Also, there is still a major reliance on CP/M-86 and CP/M 2.2 and 3.0 in these markets in comparison to the North American scene, but this will continue to shrink.

Consequently, in North America, and increasingly in other parts of the world, the selection of a microcomputer that is a single-user system is colored by the dominance of IBM, the software that runs on these systems, and the add-on peripheral and accessory market offerings. Other companies designing microcomputers have concentrated on achieving as much compatibility as possible, but this does vary considerably. Due to the dominance of IBM and the resultant manufacture of clone systems by third-party firms, creativity has been stifled in a number of areas that contribute to the overall usefulness, capacity, and human factors associated with the microcomputer as a personal, professional workstation tool. The Apple Macintosh has met this human factor problem very well for the novice user and presents the most creative challenge yet to the dominance of IBM in the professional and business microcomputer-user community. Whether this challenge will be successful in the marketplace in business and industry remains to be determined in the 1985/1986 market year.

MICROCOMPUTER DESIGN FACTORS

The IBM PC models have established what amounts to a defacto business and professional microcomputer standard in both hardware and software aspects. What are some of these design factors that have become defacto standards?

First, the use of PC-DOS as the single-user operating system on the IBM PC has brought a new operating system standard to the foreground for the microcomputers largely built around the Intel 8088/8086 and successor models in this family of microprocessors. Version 2.2 of the popular control program/microcomputer (CP/M) had earlier established a standard operating system for 8-bit microprocessors, such as Zilog's Z80A and B and Intel's 8080. PC-DOS (currently in version 3.0 or 3.2 for running IBM's recently announced LAN) is the version of Microsoft's disk operating system (MS-DOS) used on the IBM PC, whereas MS-DOS versions (1.25 and 2.1) are used on the IBM clone compatibles and other non-IBM compatibles using 8/16- (Intel 8088) or 16-bit (Intel 8086) microprocessor architecture.

Therefore, Digital Research, Inc., the creator of CP/M, did not take the market by storm, although their CP/M-86 and Concurrent CP/M-86 operating systems for the Intel 8088/8086-based microcomputers, along with their multiuser MP/M-86, still have some following. However, little in the way of new software is being expressly written for CP/M-86 and its later versions, such as Concurrent CP/M-86. Some software developers for specific vertical market applications, such as the insurance brokerage application, continue to offer and support special application packages under these operating systems.

Although the Apple IIe and IIc, together with Macintosh, still dominate the secondary educational market, the IBM and compatibles are making some inroads in primary and secondary school systems. Some new 8-bit microcomputers are still appearing from time to time, but their sales are not capturing a significant sector of the personal computer market. In fact, some enterprising manufacturers have put together Intel 8088-based add-on microprocessor boards to enable these systems to run MS-DOS and its commercial compatible software. These boards retail for approximately $700 to $900 and enable the user to still maintain his/her software collection, processor, and peripherals under CP/M. This is the reverse of the so-called "bridge" microcomputers that were really Intel 8088 based but included a separate Z80 processor board to enable running software based on the CP/M 2.2 operating system. On these systems one normally ran CP/M-86 on the main processor and invoked the 8-bit system through a switching routine accessed from CP/M-86 command level.

There are many aspects to creating a true clone system to a given IBM PC model. First, a fully compatible clone must be able to run all of the software commercially available for the IBM PC and software written using IBM's BASICA programming language interpreter. A good test of this is to try programs such as Lotus Development Corporation's Lotus 1-2-3 and MicroLogic's Flight Simulator program. Because IBM uses a proprietary BIOS (basic input/output system) encoded in a ROM device, the clone manufacturers can only attempt to functionally duplicate this device. Herein lies one area of potential incompatibility. Second, a true clone will have to use the same physical 40-track floppy diskette recording standard so that IBM diskettes can be read on the clone and the clone's diskettes can be read on an IBM PC. Third, the clone must have a keyboard that is identically laid out to that of the IBM PC so that templates for the IBM keyboard will work and keyboard references in IBM version application software manuals will correspond. Fourth, the system must be able to accept expansion or accessory add-on cards in its expansion slots, which are made for the IBM PC models. Finally, the clone must use the same graphics screen resolution to enable correct screen displays to occur for both monochrome and color displays. Alternatively, the clone must automatically take care of any graphics resolution differences in its hardware and operating software including its firmware-encoded portions.

Until the introduction of the IBM PC/AT, the standard IBM PC diskette format enabled recording of 340 kilobyte on a double-sided 5.25-inch diskette under PC-DOS 1.x versions and 360 kilobyte under PC-DOS 2.x versions and later using 40 tracks per side. These diskettes are recorded at 48 tracks per inch (tpi). However, the IBM PC/AT uses a 5.25-inch diskette formatted 80 tracks per side and recording 1.2 megabytes on a dual-sided diskette using a constant speed rotation in the diskette drive. These diskettes are recorded at 96 tpi. Although this drive can read the 360 kilobyte floppies from an IBM PC and can write in this mode, these 40-track disks require formatting on a standard IBM PC or clone and not in the AT drives. However, the frequent user can configure the IBM PC/AT with a separate 40-track recording floppy disk drive to enable formatting and read/write of these disks on this separate disk drive. Although this 1.2 megabyte diskette will undoubtedly cause a new diskette standard to arrive, this diskette capacity in itself is not new nor is its capacity state of the art; the Sirius 1 (Victor 9000) had used, since its introduction, a variable speed rotation and 96-tpi recoding format to put 1.2 megabyte on a dual-sided floppy diskette. However, the IBM 1.2 megabyte format requires a special high-quality diskette that currently retails at twice the price of conventional 96-tpi dual-sided diskettes.

Newer storage media such as the Sony 3.5-inch cartridge floppy disk, used in the Hewlett-Packard HP-150, Apple Macintosh, and ACT Apricot, and popular lap-top portables such as the Data General One represent superior low-cost storage media. Depending on how this cartridge disk is formatted, this type of media will give 600 to 700 megabyte storage capacities with higher read reliability. The protective enclosure of this disk guards it against contamination and raises its reliability. Several briefcase portables also use this form of auxiliary storage; however, unless IBM adopts it, it is unlikely to become a widespread storage medium in North America. The dominance of IBM and its conservative design philosophies will impede the degree of acceptance of the Sony 3.5-inch medium or any of the other Japanese or American entrants to this cartridge diskette storage field.

Users who require larger storage capacity have obtained Winchester technology hard disks for their systems, either as built-in devices such as that found in the IBM PC/XT model with a 10 megabyte capacity disk or as a separately contained hard disk drive. The IBM PC/AT has one model incorporating a built-in 20 megabyte Winchester disk drive, and another can be added for a total of 40 megabyte of Winchester disk storage on this system. Third-party disk manufacturers offer even more storage for the PC/AT or for compatibles, such as the recently introduced Compaq Deskpro 286 clone PC/AT. This system is available with up to 70 megabyte of built-in Winchester disk and includes a built-in streaming tape backup system. Winchester drives afford larger storage and considerable improvement in operating speed. Even the portable version of this system, called the Portable 286, puts 20 megabyte of Winchester in the system cabinet.

If hard disk is needed, the user should consider just how he or she will perform disk backup as it may not be satisfactory to do only selective copying of files to floppy diskette, particularly with the size of files likely to occur with hard disk users who are using one of the popular data base management or application generator programs. Video recorders, in some cases, can be used to perform this backup, but today, the use of streaming cartridge magnetic tape to back up these relatively large hard disks is the norm. This is why a unit such as IOMEGA's Bernoulli Box, with a Winchester disk and a cartridge magnetic tape unit capable of serving as both a Winchester backup and as a serial, infinite storage device, is popular with users. The computer manufacturers have largely left this backup and external Winchester disk storage market to third-party vendors.

Another factor to mention if the user is interested in adding an external hard disk to an existing floppy disk system is the boot ROM, a read-only memory device that contains the program that initially reads in the system tracks from the floppy disk and performs some hardware diagnostics prior to loading the operating system. Some boot ROMs of the older variety, on some microcomputers originally configured as floppy-drive-equipped systems, will not allow the system to be booted from the external Winchester disk drive system volume. These boot ROMs can usually be replaced somewhat inexpensively but do require some chip and jumper installation work on the "motherboard," the internal location of the boot ROM.

Very soon, the storage situation may be revolutionized to some degree by the introduction of read/write optical disks, which will have storage capacities in the 500 megabyte range in a 5.25-inch format. Therefore, our desktop microcomputers of 1990 will very likely have substantial storage attached and today's 10 megabyte to 20 megabyte sizes of the Winchester disk will seem paltry. Watch for 3M Company to introduce their read/write optical storage media in this format in late 1986 or early 1987.

More realistically speaking, the 20 megabyte unit in a 3.5-inch size may become the new standard for built-in Winchester drives in desktop, transportable, and lap-top microcomputers in the next few years.

Another aspect of the microcomputer that is receiving considerable attention is the design of input devices. Although the IBM PC keyboard is a relatively poor one from a user's point of view, their PC/AT keyboard has largely cured these major faults. Clone machine and nonclone alike are putting emphasis on designing better keyboards. Systems with keyboards designed by Keytronics, Inc., usually have excellent keying and layout qualities. The other major input device to spring into fashion is the "mouse," which has been popularized by Apple's Macintosh. This device enables the user to move the cursor about the screen with a small hand motion applied to a device that usually has a contact ball in the base and one or two control buttons on its top. It is analogous to the "joystick" controls used on many video games and game-playing home computers.

Although currently not very popular, there could arise another cursor-controlling device known as a "trackball," which is really superior to the mouse. The trackball is in the keyboard housing itself and is a sphere with one hemisphere showing, which is rotated by the users's hand to control cursor positioning. Trackballs have been used largely in military and special-purpose systems but could spring into popularity to challenge the mouse and joystick. Trackballs have seen their greatest popularity in England. Because no external cord is required nor added desk space to attach and use this tool, the future prognosis is excellent that this device will ultimately come into its own.

Another input device receiving considerable attention is the optical reader, which is capable of scanning text via a handheld scanner. These are becoming more popular in text applications where other equipment, such as typewriters, are still producing documents that are not in machine-readable media that can easily be transferred to floppy disk. Also, digitizing tablets that enable input of graphic designs into a computer are becoming more popular peripherals due to the increase in computer-aided drafting, cartographic, manufacturing, and engineering applications. Optical readers may save considerable time in input if one has documents that routinely need to be input to a microsystem but originate from a source that cannot be used to download the data directly to the microcomputer. The digitizing tablets reduce image data to a series of coordinates and, with appropriate software, open a new horizon of applications to microcomputers.

RAM is also a changing design feature for the microcomputer workstation. At the birth of personal computers, the 8-bit word microprocessor prevailed and the user was served by a total of 64 kilobyte directly accessible memory. Later, some of these systems employed a technique known as "bank switching" to address more memory, but generally these systems were not popular with typical single-user 8-bit microprocessors. These 8-bit processors were adequate for many tasks that personal computer users require; however, with the advent of spreadsheet programs, such as Visicalc and integrated software packages such as Lotus 1-2-3 or Symphony or design packages such as AutoCAD from AutoDesk, much larger directly addressable memory microcomputers demonstrated their superiority. Working storage requirements for these kinds of programs are substantial, and the operating system and the application program space required are also substantially beyond that of the 8-bit microprocessor. Also, a faster processor speed is highly desirable to achieve more acceptable performance with such programs.

Thus, the microprocessor having a 16-bit memory address or word length has become the standard for current personal computers for professional use. Either an Intel 8088 microprocessor, which uses an 8-bit data transfer, or a true 16-bit microprocessor, such as the Intel 8086, became the basis, respectively, for the IBM PC and some clone systems. Now, most of these IBM look-alike systems use the newer members of this Intel chip family. IBM's new PC/AT uses the Intel 80286, which is a true 16-bit microprocessor. It operates at a clock rate of 6 to 11 MHz, whereas the IBM PC using the Intel 8088 operates at a clock rate of 4.77 MHz. These newer 16-bit microprocessors feature much larger potential memory address space, which is up to 4 megabyte on the IBM PC/AT.

However, IBM has chosen to implement only 640 kilobyte RAM as maximum on its PC-DOS-based microcomputers, even though the theoretic maximum for the Intel 8088 is 1024 kilobyte RAM. Some MS-DOS noncompatible or partially compatible microcomputers allow the user access of up to 896 kilobyte under this operating system. Although the IBM PC/AT can have 4 megabyte of RAM memory, under PC-DOS 3.0 it can only address 640 kilobyte. Undoubtedly, when the XENIX operating system becomes available to make the IBM PC/AT into a three-user system, it will have the ability to address the memory above the initial 640 kilobyte. It would have been appropriate though, for IBM to have increased this PC-DOS 3.0 memory maximum to at least 896 kilobyte for users who run large software applications and/or use RAM disk programs, as described below. Microcomputer purchasers should be aware that several third-party firms have produced hardware/software add-ons that transform a PC/AT system into a multiuser system capable of supporting memory beyond 640 kilobyte.

Newer systems using MC68000 family microprocessors, such as the Apple Macintosh, have 32-bit RAM address space or word length and use 16-bit data transfers. However, to keep costs down, Apple initially introduced Macintosh with 128 kilobyte RAM and only later introduced the "fat Mac" with 512 kilobyte as well as a RAM board, which is dealer installable to upgrade memory board for 128 kilobyte Macintosh owners. With the pictorial windowed or "icon"-driven human interface of the Macintosh family microcomputers, larger memory is needed to implement this feature. In summary, larger memory is becoming more of a necessity as the human interface to the system changes, as operating systems require more memory due to their improved capabilities, and as users perform more substantial applications on their systems or require speed improvements to their systems.

Programs such as Lotus Development's Symphony require 384 kilobyte RAM to load on an IBM PC. Therefore, a 640 kilobyte RAM system for a Symphony user is none too large. If the user wishes to improve the speed of certain programs, he or she may employ a special program called a RAM Disk or C Drive program. This program creates a virtual disk area in RAM into which a program and its overlay modules or specific parameter and driver routines can be loaded. This minimizes the need for the system to access the floppy drive or Winchester disk and can increase the speed of operating a floppy-disk-based microcomputer four to eight times with some programs. An example would be the use of a word processing program such as WordPerfect version 4.0, which includes a 100,000-word lexicon. This lexicon can be invoked at any time during text entry or editing to verify spelling. If this is done with the lexicon on the floppy disk system, one's speed is considerably slowed by waiting for the program to access the floppy disk. Less time would be wasted with a Winchester drive, but when this program works from a RAM disk area in RAM, the effect is instantaneous and utterly amazing to microprocessor users who have not experienced such a system configuration.

Finally, the microprocessor chips themselves are undergoing rapid development and will require less power due to CMOS (complementary metal oxide semiconductor) circuit technology. Such processors are now used in the lap-top and notebook-sized portable microcomputers. The Intel 80C86 microprocessor is one such chip that has been used in this class of microsystems.

Our future processors will implement additional memory, and basic systems will be packaged with memory sizes in excess of 256 kilobyte. Experienced microprocessor users who use RAM disk will appreciate at least a 512 kilobyte system if not a maximum 640 kilobyte system on IBM PC and clone class systems.

THE USER'S MICROCOMPUTER WORKSTATION

The predominant population of single-user microcomputers are used as personal workstation devices, equipped with a single-user operating system and application software. In larger organizations, the microcomputer LAN has emerged as one method to link these systems together to share the following:

- Large-capacity Winchester disk storage
- Application software
- Data files (where appropriate)
- Laser technology printers or other output devices

Another microsystem type is the multiuser microcomputer, which affords its users a system very similar to larger minicomputer host systems, except generally at lower cost per user and in-office operation. These systems use true multiuser operating systems with multitasking facilities. Application software in such a system is often the same as that operating on larger minicomputer systems requiring specially equipped computer room installation. Multiuser microcomputers are designed to permit multiple simultaneous users the ability to use these application programs. Smaller institutions without mainframe host computer facilities or larger minicomputer access have been the main installation bases for these systems. Popular applications for these systems have been office automation, engineering design, and manufacturing support.

The problems of compatibility of new systems with systems already in use and the phase over to a new system may be critical in larger organizations or where an older microcomputer is being replaced or augmented by a new system. Functional compatibility in application software and the transfer of data files from the old system to the new system usually present difficulties due to storage media incompatibilities in some cases and incompatible file formats or the inability to convert the existing file format to a universal data interchange file (DIF) format. Programs that can produce a DIF as output or a straight ASCII-type file will ease a later conversion and transfer to another system and to another application program. Data transfer between systems with incompatible diskette formats is best done through either a direct RS-232C serial-port-to-serial-port transfer or via modem-to-modem transfer using such programs as Woolf Software's Move-it or communications programs such as MicroStuf's Crosstalk XVI or Hayes Smart-Com II.

For multiuser microcomputer systems, there is no clear prevailing market share leader or really standard generic operating system. UNIX operating system versions have been popular in software development and scientific applications, whereas PICK operating system products have provided excellent business applications to their users. However, manufacturers' own proprietary operating systems still continue to be the norm for most multiuser microcomputer systems. Most of these are upward compatible to versions running on larger minicomputers. Examples are Digital Equipment Corporation's RSX-11M on the Micro PDP-11 or VAX/VMS on the MicroVAX.

Finally, institutional policy may also affect the user's microcomputer workstation situation. When remote "computer czars" establish policy on microcomputer purchase, it can present problems to the individual user, particularly if the desired application software does not run on the specific system chosen by the institution. Such policies usually stifle creative information system solutions and require users to either justify special situations or somehow compromise on their software selections.

Also, in a larger institution, the microcomputer user may have available attractive discount purchasing arrangements for both institution and personal purchases. This is typically the case in academe and in the for-profit sector where companies have established their own "computer stores" or "service centers." In some of these cases, up to a 40% discount from list prices prevail on certain systems and selected software. Prospective micro-computer buyers who have such arrangements at their disposal should take advantage of them. However, if the user has definite need for software that will not run on the systems being offered on this basis, it would be most advisable to purchase the needed software and the specific system best able to execute this software, seeing that it is the time of the pro-fessional or executive that is most valuable.

MICROCOMPUTER LANs

The major reason to install a LAN for microcomputers is to enable two or more single-user microworkstations to share peripheral devices, such as larger Winchester storage disk drives, or more elegant printers, such as the new laser technology units. Also, peripherals that often might not be needed by every user but that do come in very handy occasionally could be shared by several or more users. These could be color pen plotters, 35-millimeter color transparency makers, and other specialized devices. Depending on the nature of the software being used on such a network, some multiuser access to specific files can be built into the security scheme provided by the specific network software. However, few of the programs that run on these LANs are true multiuser programs. Uveon's Optimum is one rare example of a data base management system program that can offer multiuser support when implemented on a LAN.

Specific LANs permit the attachment of noncompatible microcomputers, each running different operating system software. For example, Corvus' OMNINET LAN product enables both IBM PC and compatibles to share a LAN with Apple II family microcomputers. Another competitor is Novell with their NetWare network, which also enables attachment of several brands of microcomputers into the network. On these networks attaching noncompat-ible microsystems, using different operating systems, the same software cannot run in these dissimilar microcomputers but each can share the Win-chester storage and other peripherals for both program and data storage. The recently announced Apple Macintosh Office is a LAN product designed to link Macintosh microcomputers into a shared network where Apple's new LaserWriter printer can be shared as well as larger Winchester storage. Read/write optical storage media will undoubtedly be a candidate storage device for these LAN facilities, as well as a replacement for the typical 10- to 20-megabyte Winchester disks built into present microcomputers.

The March 18, 1985, issue of *The Wall Street Journal* saturated its readership with advertisements of the Apple Office and third-party firms manufacturing peripherals and other Macintosh market products. Corvus featured OMNIDRIVE 126 megabyte hard disks and OMNITALK software so that users wishing to share data do not have to "turn their floppies into little frisbees." Corvus has had considerable success in LANs and intends to take the professional Macintosh market seriously. Cadmus announced its CADMAC Motorola 68000 UNIX supermicrocomputer workstation, which can serve as a network server for Apple Macintosh microcomputers and support up to a gigabyte of disk. Their workstations support 1024 × 800-pixel ele-ment screen resolution, which is almost twice that of the Macintosh. With the mouse, this product is designed as a software development workbench for those creating software for the Macintosh family microcomputers. Tecmar announced their MacDrive series of fixed and removable hard disk units for the Macintosh. Odesta Helix announced its Control Room system, an end user application development software product built around the Helix Database Management System Software. It enables text, numbers, and graphics images to be stored together. Helix will also drive the Apple LaserWriter printer and support the Corvus OMNIDRIVE. PFS software, a longtime favorite of many for the IBM PC and clones has implemented versions of its PFS File and PFS Report programs for the Macintosh.

Although microcomputer LANs offer some additional features, such as communications between attached microcomputers, larger electronic mail systems afford much greater communications services. The read/write optical storage media may obviate the need for installing LANs to share large-capacity peripheral storage. Price cuts for laser printers and other output devices may have the same effect. Therefore, users should carefully assess the cost benefits of microcomputer LANs before installing such a system because these networks do not substitute for true multiuser computer systems, general-purpose LANs using digital data and voice switches for a total digital communications network, or networks based on the Ethernet protocol, which afford considerably more benefits in the variety of devices able to be attached to the LAN.

CONCLUSIONS

Selecting microcomputers today requires that the potential purchaser and user have a thorough understanding of the uses to which the system will be put and the ability to discover and evaluate software capable of delivering these functions. The more microcomputer literacy the purchaser can acquire, the easier these choices will be and the less likely that the choice will be ill advised. Because the microcomputer hardware scene is changing daily and systems or models become technologically obsolete within a few years, it is best to purchase hardware with the view toward its expandability in RAM, peripherals, and accessories after one has initially determined the software of choice. Through this approach, your microcomputer can continue to function well with your initial software and grow in capability through the addition of new software and peripherals.

The innovative human interface presented by the Apple Macintosh is really the only fresh product on the market. To a lesser extent, ACT's Apricot also offers some fresh ideas and flexibility. Recently, a new product combining the Macintosh with an IBM PC compatible disk, microprocessor, keyboard extension, and software turns the Apple Macintosh into both an IBM PC compatible and the original Mac with the ability to transfer files back and forth between programs running under each environment. It is too early to tell, but this product might help win the IBM versus Apple institutional market war. Those users willing to sacrifice some speed in operation and wishing to have as much ease of use as possible might examine software and products for the Macintosh system and then examine the offerings for the IBM PC and other MS-DOS systems. The bibliography below gives some basic sources for detailed information on microcomputers, software evaluation, and selection.

Finally, your local area user group for the system you are interested in will be an invaluable source of help and information. You can find out about these user groups from local area computer newsletters and your local computer dealers. Also, large bookstore chains, such as B. Dalton and Walden Books, have large microcomputer book sections that have new titles added daily. Many of these are buyers'-guide-type publications geared to specific machines, such as Apple, IBM, Tandy, and so forth. Prepare yourself by gaining a good understanding of your application needs and the general types of available commercial software that might fill those needs and then begin actually contacting dealers. Remember, in most cases system selection is still best done from the software-first aspect and then the determination of suitable hardware that will run this software with the best price/performance, ease of use, and expandability. The more knowledgeable you are as a prospective purchaser, the more likely you are to be satisfied with your purchase in the longer term and the easier it will be in the future for you to continue to select software and additional or replacement systems.

BIBLIOGRAPHY

This bibliography is intended to assist those who are selecting microcomputer systems for business and professional applications. These references will help the reader gain general microcomputer background and familiarity and determine sources of further examination as he or she proceeds to search and select appropriate software and hardware.

Directories and Books Useful for Locating Software and Systems

Bowker's Complete Sourcebook of Personal Computing, 1985, R. R. Bowker, New York and London, 1985.

Chen, Ching-chih. *Microuse Directory,* Microuse Information, West Newton, MA, 1985.

Computing Information Directory, 1985, Compiled and edited by Darlene Myers Hildebrandt, Pedaro, Inc., Federal Way, WA, 1985.

DataPro Directory of Microcomputer Software, DataPro, Delran, NJ, 1985.

Directory of Library and Information Retrieval Software for Microcomputers, Compiled by Hilary Gates, Gower Publishing, Brookfield, VT, February 1985.

Nicita, Michael and Ronald Petrusha, *The Reader's Guide to Microcomputer Books,* Knowledge Industry Publications, White Plains, NY, 1984.

UNESCO Inventory of Software Packages, Edited by Carl Keren and Irina Sered, UNESCO, Paris, France, July 1983.

General Microcomputer Books for Those Selecting or Learning About Systems

Clapp, Doug, *Macintosh! Complete,* Softalk Books, North Hollywood, CA, 1984.

DeVoney, Chris, *IBM's Personal Computer,* 2nd ed, Que Corporation, Indianapolis, IN, 1983.

Foster, Dennis L., *The Addison-Wesley Book of IBM Software 1985: The Essential Consumer Guide to Buying Software for Your IBM PC, PC/XT, or PCjr.* Addison-Wesley, Reading, MA, 1985.

Foster, Dennis L., *The Practical Guide to the IBM PC/AT.* Addison-Wesley, Reading, MA, 1985.

Miller, Merl K. and Mary A. Myers, *Presenting the Macintosh.* Dilithium Press, Beaverton, OR, 1984.

Novogorodsky, Seth and Frederic E. Davis, *The Complete IBM Personal Computer: The Authoritative Guide to Hardware for Expanding the IBM PC, XT, AT, and Compatibles,* PC World Books (Simon & Schuster), NY, 1985.

General Microcomputer Journals

Byte, Byte, Inc., Peterborough, NH (monthly).

Dr. Dobbs Journal for the Experienced in Microcomputing, People's Computer Company, Palo Alto, CA (monthly).

InfoWorld, InfoWorld, Framingham, MA.

Microsystems, Ziff-Davis Publishing, New York.

Mini-Micro Systems, Cahners Publishing, Boston, MA (monthly).

PC World, PC World Communications, San Francisco, CA (monthly).

Personal Computing Plus, Hayden Publishing, Hasbrouck Heights, NJ (monthly).

Seybold Report on Professional Computing, Seybold Publications, Media, PA.

Small Systems World, Hunter Publishing, DesPlaines, IL (monthly).

Software News, Technical Publishing, Barrington, IL.

Selected Specific Microcomputer and Application Journals

Access Apple, Boston Publishing, Boston, MA (monthly).

Access IBM, Boston Publishing, Boston, MA (monthly).

Agricultural Computing, Doane Publishing, Columbus, MO (monthly).

Apple Education News, Apple Computer, Cupertino, CA (three per year).

Business Computing, Professional Computing and Penwell Publishing, Littleton, MA (monthly).

Buss: The Independent Newsletter of Heath Co. Computers (Heath and Heath/Zenith Computers), Sextant Publishing, Washington, D.C. (20 per year).

Collegiate Microcomputer, Allen Press, Lawrence, KS (quarterly).

Commander (Commodore Computers), Micro Systems Specialties, Tacoma, WA.

Data Based Advisor (dBASE II), Data Based Solutions, San Diego, CA (monthly).

Digital Review (Digital Equipment Corp. microcomputers), Ziff-Davis Publishing, NY (monthly).

Hot CoCo (Radio Shack/Tandy TRS-80 color computer), CW Communications, Peterborough, NH (monthly).

IEEE Computer Graphics and Applications, IEEE Computer Society, Los Alamitos, CA.

In Cider (Apple Computers), CW Communications, Peterborough, NH
(monthly).
Infosource (IBM PC), Query, Inc., Bogota, NJ (monthly).
Keywords: For Users of SPSS, Inc., Software Products, SPSS, Chicago,
IL (quarterly).
Lawyer's Microcomputer: A Newsletter for Lawyers (Radio Shack/Tandy
Computers), R. P. W. Publishing, Lexington, SC.
Medicine & Computer (medical micro applications), Medicine & Computer,
White Plains, NY (six per year).
National LOGO Exchange (teachers using LOGO computer language), Posy
Publications, Charlottesville, VA.
PC Tech Journal (advanced IBM PC users), P.C. Tech, NY (six per year).
Personal and Professional (Digital Equipment micros), Personal Press,
Springhouse, PA (six per year).
Pragma's Product Profiles (PICK operating system multiuser micros),
Semaphone, Aptos, CA (monthly).
Scientific Computing & Automation, Gordon Publications, Randolph, NJ
(six per year).
Unique (UNIX operating system), Infosystems, Denville, NJ (monthly).
UNIX Review. Unix Review Company, Denville, NJ (six per year).
80 Micro: The Magazine for TRS-80 Users. CW Communications, Peter-
borough, NH (monthly).

Abstracting and Indexing Sources on Microcomputers

Microcomputer Index, Database Services, Los Altos, CA (six per year).
PC Abstracts, Artrice Press, Jenks, OK (semiannual).
Periodical Guide for Computerists, Applegate Computer Enterprises, Grants
Pass, OR (annual).

AUDREY N. GROSCH

OCEANOGRAPHIC DATA SYSTEMS

The computer plays a vital role in the science of oceanography and is the primary tool for the acquisition, processing, analysis, display, interpretation, archiving, and dissemination of data and information. Modern marine sensors have caused a data explosion, which can only be managed by computer systems. Today, all types of computers can be found in the laboratory and aboard oceanographic research platforms.

A much needed, highly accurate three-dimensional worldwide satellite navigation system, Global Positioning System (GPS) has been developed for use by both the military and civilians. Microprocessors have made the development of the system possible, and they are embedded in both the transmission satellites and receiving equipment. This system will become the primary radio-navigation system by the year 2000.

INMARSAT, a worldwide satellite communications system, provides marine voice and data transmission services. These communication services provide a rapid exchange of information between the field site and the laboratory.

Satellites and other multidimensional sensor systems produce large quantities of data, which must be processed, interpreted, and archived. This is accomplished with the use of computer graphic image processors, which provide the ability to apply image-processing techniques to the data.

There are many oceanographic data bases in existence today that archive and disseminate raw and processed data and information. These data bases are rapidly expanding due to the data explosion created by modern sensor systems. A compatible data exchange format needs to be developed in order to share the data and information that has been and will be accumulated.

Today, we are very dependent upon the ocean for our basic needs, such as food, fuel, and minerals. Therefore, it is essential that we learn as much about the ocean as quickly as possible. Modern oceanographic sensor systems provide us with the data, but computer technology is needed to use the data to determine the microstructure of the ocean. Computer systems must be developed to manage and disseminate the large quantities of oceanographic data and information if we are to use the oceans' resources effectively.

INTRODUCTION

Computer science and technology have made a significant impact upon oceanography. Computers have revolutionized the way oceanography is performed, and with their help the microstructure of the oceans of the world is being determined. The technology has had a significant effect on the way oceanographic data are gathered, processed, analyzed, archived, and disseminated.

Both the civilian and military oceanographic scientific communities have made
substantial progress in applying computer science and technology to their
respective problems. Today, computers are used in oceanographic laboratories and platforms and are embedded in oceanographic sensors, marine
communication equipment, and navigational aids. The computer is used
universally in the science of oceanography.

The history of at-sea oceanographic data acquisition systems is provided for background purposes. Navigational systems were one of the first
uses of digital computers at sea and are currently required for modern-day
oceanography. The development of the digital data acquisition system used
at sea from the early 1960s to the systems of today are described along with
the major developments. Many examples of the computer systems used are
provided to inform the reader of the scope and limitations of computer technology at sea. Digital computer technology made possible satellite and aircraft oceanographic remote sensing platforms. The development of these
systems and future platforms are described. Satellites have become a data
transmission path for ship to shore, shore to ship, satellite to earth station,
and in situ oceanographic platforms. These developments are described as
they affected oceanographic digital data acquisition systems. The analysis,
display, and presentation of oceanographic data using modern digital graph-
ical and image-processing techniques are discussed because they are today's
analytical tools. Once acquired and processed, oceanographic data must be
archived and disseminated to the user community in a convenient format.
This is accomplished with the use of data base systems. The future developments in digital oceanographic data systems are delineated in the manuscript.
References and a selected bibliography are provided. A list of abbreviations and acronyms to aid the reader is available at the end of the chapter.

HISTORY OF OCEANOGRAPHIC DATA SYSTEMS

Perry and Smith [1] describe any scientific data acquisition system as having three parts: the sensor, the signal transmission and/or recording device,
and the data processing facility. This description fits the oceanographic
data system extremely well.

One of the first uses for computers at sea was in satellite navigation.
The satellite navigator reduced the problem of geographical location by
providing accurate navigational fixes so that the site of the experiment
could be firmly established. The quality of both on-station and underway
data improved significantly, and the microstructure and parameters of the
ocean could be measured with reasonable accuracy and experiments could be
repeated in the future.

Digital data acquisition and processing systems are used both at sea
and in the laboratory to acquire, process, analyze, display, archive, and
disseminate oceanographic data. Oceanographic digital data systems began
to appear in laboratories in the late 1950s and aboard oceanographic platforms in the early 1960s. At the time of their introduction to oceanography,
they had already been used extensively in other scientific, engineering, and
mathematical fields. The computer systems in the 1950s were large, relatively expensive, and very unreliable under the adverse conditions found
at sea. These adverse conditions were condensing water vapor, corrosion,
vibrating structures, unstable power, and lack of control over environmental conditions. Therefore, it is understandable why their use at sea
trailed their use in the laboratory.

Oceanographic data are collected in two operational modes: either on-station or underway. Although the type of data acquired varies depending upon the mode, the data acquisition methods do not generally change. Usually underway data collection has a higher data rate because parameters are a function of geographical coordinates and the data are being collected and often processed in real time. The on-station data are repeatable over short time periods and can often be post-processed by laboratory systems.

The types of measurements made at sea have not changed much in the past 50 years. However, the sensors and methods of collecting, processing, and disseminating the data have undergone significant changes. Generally, digital techniques combined with new collection systems have caused an explosion in the quantity and quality of oceanographic data, and processing, storing, and distributing the data are major problems. The types of on-station measurements include subsurface water temperature, salinity, sound velocity (which is directly related to temperature and salinity), ambient light, and depth. The underway oceanographic parameters include magnetic and gravity field intensities and anomalies, seismic measurements of sub-bottom structures, surface water temperature, stabilized narrow-band, wide-band, and multibeam bathymetry, and navigational parameters such as course, heading, speed, latitude, and longitude. Almost all of the parameters are functions of and referenced by time, latitude, and longitude. Oceanographic data collection platforms consist of ships, buoys, towers, piers, aircraft (fixed winged, helicopter, and blimp), and satellites. The type of data to be collected dictates the type of oceanographic platform used, and at times the platform used will dictate the type of measurements that can be made. An example of this trade-off is gravitational measurements, which can be done using a gravimeter aboard ship or aircraft. The ship would reduce the measurement problem to utilization of a commercially available gravimeter to survey the oceans of the world. Based upon the speed of a typical research vessel of 5 meters per second, it would take a long time to survey even a small area of the ocean, and surveying ice-covered areas by ship would be almost impossible. An aircraft would be a better oceanographic platform for gravity measurements because it travels at 150 meters per second and could survey the ice-covered areas easily. However, gravity measurements are usually made with sensitive accelerometers, which measure miniscule differences. Any vertical aircraft motion resembles a change in the gravitational field, which makes gravitational measurements from aircraft very difficult and complex.

Prior to the late 1950s at-sea oceanographic data acquisition was confined to manual methods of recording and strip chart and analog tape recorders. In the 1960s digital computer systems began to appear aboard research vessels. Mudie [2] describes the seagoing computer systems that began to appear on ships in the 1960s. A brief recorded history of non-military computer systems at sea starts with the use of an International Business Machines (IBM) 1710 computer system by Bowin at Woods Hole Oceanographic Institution (WHOI) aboard the R/V CHAIN in 1963. The computer system recorded bathymetry, navigational information, gravity, and magnetic field information. Other digital computer systems used in the mid-1960s were the Digital Equipment Corporation (DEC) PDP5 aboard the EVERGREEN to record magnetometer, gravity, and navigational data on punched paper tape during a 7-month patrol in 1965; a DEC PDP5 used aboard the R/V ATLANTIS II for off-line data processing; and an IBM 1800 computer system, installed and successfully operated aboard the Scripps Institution of Oceanography (SIO) R/V THOMAS WASHINGTON during a 6-month cruise. Since that time, other IBM 1800s were installed on SIO's research vessels and operated until 1984 when they were replaced by DEC VAX11/730 computers. In 1969, the Applied Physics Laboratory (APL) at the University of Washington used an IBM 1130 computer at sea. At approximately the same time, Lamont-Doherty Geological Observatory (LDGO), the University of Miami, Oregon State University (OSU), and the Marine Physical Laboratory of SIO used DEC PDP8 computers at sea. Also, Texas A & M used an SDS (Scientific Data Systems) computer, Dalhousie University used a LINC8 computer, Naval Oceanographic Office (NAVOCEANO) used an IBM 1130 aboard the USNS KANE, and the hydrographer of the Royal Navy installed computer systems aboard the HMS HECLA, HECATE, and HYDRA. The National Institute of Oceanography, England, installed an IBM 1800, and the Naval Underwater Weapons Center (NUWC), San Diego, used a UNIVAC 1218 computer. Numerous other computer systems were placed aboard oceanographic vessels during this time. The benefits of using computers at sea was firmly established during the late 1960s.

The first formal recognition of oceanographic data systems as part of computer science came about in 1969 at SIO when the first Oceanographic Data Systems (ODS) conference was sponsored by the Marine Technology Society. At the ODS conference, papers were presented on the utilization of computers at sea and the experiences of the scientists attempting to acquire and process oceanographic data. The conference was attended by over 100 scientists engaged in oceanography. The major topics, issues, and concerns at that time were the reliability of computers at sea and what applications the computers were best suited to solve while aboard ship.

Since the 1969 conference at SIO, four other ODS conferences have been held. In 1975, 1978, and 1983, WHOI hosted these conferences and SIO hosted the ODS conference in 1986. It is interesting to note that the number of attendees at the ODS conferences has remained relatively constant. The same laboratories and universities are, for the most part, still represented, but the issues have changes. As mentioned earlier, one of the major issues at the 1969 conference was whether or not the computer systems were well suited for seagoing operations aboard ship. At the 1975 conference, the major discussions centered around interfacing to the ocean and satellite communications (telecommunications). In 1978, major topics included interfacing to the ocean, telecommunications, remote satellite sensing and image processing, and the subject of standards. Also, in 1978 the concept of using an intelligent cathode ray tube (CRT) terminal for data collection and processing, (a forerunner of the personal computer [PC]) was introduced. In 1983, the major topics became automated data collection systems, interfacing to the ocean, graphics and imaging systems, and information exchange. The conference in 1986 centered on multibeam bathymetric systems, high-resolution navigation (specifically the Global Positioning System [GPS]), networking and communications, data acquisition systems (which included several papers on the use of PCs at sea), data base systems, and graphic and imaging systems.

The use of an aircraft as an oceanographic platform provides many benefits to the researcher, such as transiting to the experimental site quickly, conducting a fast survey of an area, and the ability to conduct the experiment over ice-covered regions. The first attempt at using general-purpose computers aboard fixed winged aircraft for oceanographic research is recorded by Steiger and Clamons in 1975 [3]. The hostile environment of the aircraft is far worse than any other oceanographic plat-form.   In 1975, a Hewlett—Packard HP1000 computer system with standard computer peripherals was placed aboard a Navy P3 anti-submarine warfare (ASW) aircraft to measure the acoustic signatures of large ships.   The computer system was proven reliable and resulted in on-board processing that had been performed only at the laboratory prior to that experiment. The computer system used during the experiment for data acquisition, pro-cessing, and display is shown in Figure 1.   The use of general-purpose computers in aircraft oceanographic experiments has increased significantly since 1975.

The state of the art in computer technology is rapidly changing, and the oceanographic community is making good use of the new technology. For example, compact microprocessors are being used in Artic research and in situ sensors where size and power requirements must be kept to a mini-mum.   High-performance computers are being used to solve nonlinear prob-lems and compute on large multidimensional data sets.   The use of array processors and general-purpose input/output (I/O) computers are permitting real-time computations on large quantities of data and the production of rapid graphic displays.   Imaging systems can now produce multidimensional images from satellites, which inform us better of the structure of the oceans and surrounding atmosphere.

FIGURE 1   Computer system used for data acquisition, processing, and display aboard Navy P3 ASW aircraft.

NAVIGATION

Celestial navigation was the primary method of navigation before and during World War II. LORAN-A was on naval vessels during the war, but the standard at-sea tools of navigation were the sextant, compass, chronograph, charts, tables, and almanacs. These devices were used to "fix" the position of the ship (establish the ship's latitude and longitude) at specific times, whereas dead reckoning was used between fixes.

LORAN-A was the first of the multiple transmitting radio-navigation systems that gave the navigator fixes using hyperbolic lines of position. There were 83 LORAN-A transmitting stations at one time, which operated at 2 megahertz and had an effective coverage of 1,200 kilometers at night and considerably less in the daytime [4]. These stations have been rapidly phased out and replaced by LORAN-C, which operates in the 100-kilohertz region and provides far more range and consistency between day and night operations. For land and coastal navigation, DECCA is available for distances less than 200 kilometers. DECCA operates in the 100-kilohertz range and uses a master and two slaves. The most recent of the systems is OMEGA, which began transmissions in 1966. OMEGA is an eight-station, very low frequency, continuous wave (CW) system operating in the 10- to 14-kilohertz range and provides a positional accuracy of approximately 3 to 6 kilometers [5]. Improvements in OMEGA's accuracy have been accomplished using the technique of differential OMEGA. The technique uses the phase changes at a monitor station and at the user's receiver to make corrections. A differential system developed by Teledyne Hastings–Raydist, called Micro-OMEGA, automatically corrects for propagational conditions and can improve positional accuracy by an order of magnitude over conventional OMEGA.

The radio-navigational systems were designed to provide offshore long-range navigation. For short-range and underwater navigation, acoustic transponder systems have been used for marking sites and precision surveys. These systems are not dependent upon shore stations, and they provide continuous navigational information without interruption and are not severely affected by the environment. The concept consists of placing acoustic transponders at known locations within the ocean. The transponders are interrogated and respond with a reply frequency. Figure 2 shows the concept of high-precision acoustic navigation. By using three transponders with measured baselines, triangulation can be performed and position precisely determined in three dimensions in real time. This computation is relatively complex and requires the use of a digital computer for real-time navigation. In fact, this was one of the early uses of commercially available computers at sea. A description of an underwater acoustic navigation system is given by Porta [6] and accurately represents the acoustic systems in use today.

In the early 1960s, satellite navigation became a reality and was first employed by the military. The first of these satellite navigation systems was known as TRANSIT. The first satellite was launched and became operational in 1960, with a total of six satellites by 1964 [7]. Since the early 1970s TRANSIT has been used commercially and by other governments. The most recent system based upon satellites is the NAVSTAR GPS. The system will consist of a total of 18 operational satellites and 6 spares when fully operational by the late 1980s and will be capable of providing very high-accuracy, three-dimensional navigational information of less than 10 meters for military use and 200 meters for commercial endeavors. The satellites

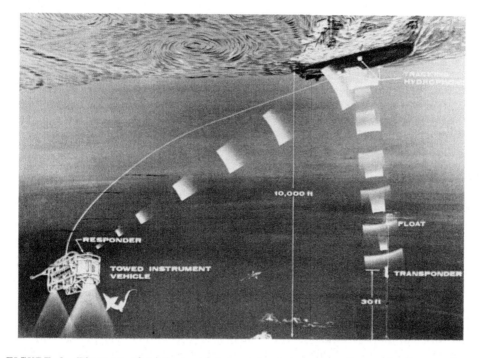

FIGURE 2   Diagram of high-precision underwater acoustic navigation system.

are positioned so that four satellites can be seen at any one time. However, only two satellites are required for a position fix. A ground control net-work uses the satellite signal to compute updated orbit and clock parameters and stores this information in the satellite's memory [8]. Each satellite transmits navigational signals to the users below in three dimensions. The GPS navigational satellites can be used in basically two ways: "P" code for high-precision military purposes and "S" code (formerly "C/A") for civilian use. The satellite transmits this information at 1575.42 and 1227.6 mega-hertz, respectively. Modulated on these frequencies is a bit stream defining the orbit and known clock error of the satellite. The S code is transmitted only at 1575.42 megahertz, repeating at a rate that is one tenth of the P code. Both of these transmissions are from the NAVSTAR satellites such that the time and position of each satellite is well known. The arrival times of transmission of four satellites with known positions are measured, and latitude, longitude, altitude, and GPS time can be calculated. The positional information is determined by measuring the time of arrival from each of four satellites at known positions referenced to precise time.

A technique of differential GPS has been developed with navigational accuracies having been measured in centimeters. Differential GPS is accom-plished by comparing signal arrivals from a satellite on two receivers at different locations. By differencing the frequency and phase measurements from each satellite, signal variations that secure the GPS P code need not be known to obtain high-resolution navigation [9]. The computer plays a major role in obtaining the navigational fixes from the satellite system.

GPS is expected to be fully operational by 1989 and, when combined with OMEGA, will provide the navigational accuracy requirements for both military and civilian use in the future. All other systems, although in widespread use throughout the world, will be gradually phased out by the year 2000.

Computers are an integral and necessary part of all modern navigational systems. The embedded computer is generally a microprocessor, whereas the general-purpose commercially available microcomputer or minicomputer is found at the system level. Computer technology has far surpassed navigational computational requirements, and almost every navigational system has a computer embedded. Several special-purpose navigational systems have been developed for geophysical research and harbor navigation where high accuracies are required. For geophysical studies, which include petroleum exploration, several navigational systems are usually employed and their results integrated by computer algorithms.

Radio-navigation systems, such as LORAN-A and now LORAN-C, provide repeatable navigational accuracies of 100 meters by the navigator using hyperbolic lines of transmission from multiple transmitting stations [10]. Computers were introduced into navigational systems with the advent of the Polaris submarines in the late 1950s. The TRANSIT system was deployed in 1964 to provide updates for the inertial navigation systems aboard the Polaris submarines [11]. The computer made the development of TRANSIT possible. "SATNAV" (TRANSIT) satellite navigation equipment was developed for military purposes by two vendors, International Telephone and Telegraph (ITT) and Magnovax [7]. The first of the full navigation sets from Magnovax was the ANWRN-4 receiver/computer followed by the MX-702CA unit. The MX-702CA used a commercially available general-purpose Hewlett—Packard HP2115 computer with a 16K word memory. In 1967, upon declassification of the TRANSIT system, the use of satellite navigation became available to the general public. At this time, the technology was transferred for worldwide use, and the navigational algorithms were made available to private industry. Today, TRANSIT is used by almost every country and many commercial enterprises. All TRANSIT systems have a computer as an integral part of the system. Two MX706 SATNAV receivers, a terminal to the shipboard computer, and a flatbed digital incremental plotter can be seen in Figure 3, which is the navigation room aboard the research vessel USNS HAYES.

There are both active and passive radio-navigation systems. Systems that use available information are called passive, and examples of these systems are LORAN-A, LORAN-C, TRANSIT, GPS, and OMEGA. Passive systems require a highly accurate reference timing system synchronized between the transmitter and mobile receiver. Active systems generate signals that provide navigational information. Examples of active systems are the underwater acoustic navigation system described earlier, GEOTRAC, GEONAV, and GEOSTAR.

GEOTRAC was developed in the 1970s by Texas Instruments (TI) for geophysical studies [12]. The GEOTRAC system makes extensive use of the computer by providing continuous navigational information. Also developed by TI is an active system called GEONAV, which was designed for marine geophysical studies. The system uses pulsed sonar Doppler, a gyrocompass, and a highly stable timing system to provide data to a minicomputer that computes the ship's relative position between satellite fixes.

The GEOSTAR Positioning System uses satellite technology to provide precise navigation in harbor areas under all weather conditions [13]. GEOSTAR uses three geosynchronous satellites orbiting the earth at 37,000

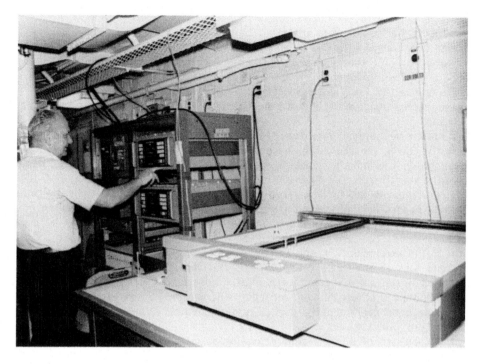

FIGURE 3   Navigation room aboard research vessel USNS HAYES.

kilometers to obtain positional information.   The user enters commands
through a transceiver which, in turn, relays the message through the satellites to a ground-station computer.   The ground-station computer requests
messages 100 times per second through the satellites.   The ground computer
uses the three satellites to calculate the position of the vessel, with an
accuracy of 7 meters.   GEOSTAR also operates in the differential mode to
eliminate known sources of errors.   Some of the applications projected for
GEOSTAR are harbor navigation, collision avoidance, and emergency transmissions.

OCEANOGRAPHIC DATA ACQUISITION SYSTEMS

Early marine data acquisition systems consisted of making measurements with
well-known land-sensing devices.   The data were originally recorded by
manual methods, then mechanical devices, and later electromechanical systems.
The initial sensors consisted of simple nets, coring tubes, thermometers,
Nansen bottles, and the bathythermograph, which is an example of an early
mechanical data acquisition system [14].   In the bathythermograph, the
recording is performed by a mechanically operated pen that scratches a plot
of temperature versus pressure on a thin film of gold deposited on a glass
plate.   Today, bathythermograph devices are expendable and can be deployed by aircraft as well as ships.   The measurements are transmitted by
radio from sensor to ship or aircraft.   The data are then recorded remotely.

Electronic tubes were invented in the early 1900s. In 1906, Lee de Forest added a grid to the Fleming diode that resulted in the triode. Shortly thereafter, electromechanical recording systems began to appear. However, significant progress in the development of automatic oceanographic data systems did not take place until World War II, when the science of oceanography became increasingly important for both military and civilian purposes.

Electromechanical data recording devices have been used extensively since the 1940s for recording oceanographic data, and these devices in their modern high-technology versions remain in use today. Analog computers played a significant role in real-time data processing in the 1930s and 1940s but were phased out for digital techniques in the 1950s. Multichannel analog data recorders, which are complex electromechanical devices, remain major data storage devices today due to their high-speed multichannel capabilities. Also, the analog recording of signals is relatively low cost compared with digital equipment, which is capable of achieving the same storage without data loss at the same rate. Often, the recorders are used as backup to digital systems, in the event of a digital failure and for data archival. It is anticipated that the analog recorder will remain in use for the forseeable future because high-density digital tape recording systems are still prohibitively expensive.

At-sea use of a commercially available, general-purpose digital computer system for data acquisition purposes was first recorded by Bowin in 1962 on an IBM 1710 digital computer [15]. To increase the processing speed and replace a labor-intensive digitizing process, Bowin used analog-to-digital (A/D) and digital-to-analog (D/A) conversion units. The IBM 1710 was later replaced in 1967 with a much smaller and less expensive Hewlett-Packard HP2116A computer. At that time, several innovative ideas were incorporated into the at-sea computers such as foreground/background software, which was a by-product of time-sharing, and the use of plotting equipment tied directly on-line to the real-time data acquisition and processing system. The advantage of using digital computers at sea, with their automatic mode of data acquisition and processing, far outweighed the difficulties of keeping the digital computer equipment operational under adverse environmental conditions.

In 1963, Marconi Space and Defence Systems Ltd. was established. The primary product was the development of an on-line shipboard data processing system for research and survey operations [16]. They installed a three-dimensional underwater tracking range using an Elliott MCS920A Computer in a military ship. In the next several years, they installed over 20 Elliott MCS900 series computer systems for various at-sea data acquisition and processing purposes.

In the mid-1960s, the use of digital data acquisition and processing systems at sea became widespread at oceanographic institutions and laboratories. The data conversion rates and number of sensors sampled at that time were relatively low by today's standards. Satellite navigation systems, such as TRANSIT, although operational in 1964, were not used in an automatic data acquisition and logging capacity until the 1970s. Other radio-navigational devices such as LORAN, DECCA, and LAMBDA were being interfaced into digital computers to form an integrated navigational system. Higher-level programming languages such as ALGOL and FORTRAN came into use for application programs, but the data acquisition programs were coded in assembly language.

Marine in situ data acquisition systems usually housed in buoys used analog technology to collect data. Data were recorded by electromechanical devices that made charts, analog tape recorders, and photographs. The chart and analog recordings were performed by well-known techniques that were used for many decades aboard research ships. The photographic recorder used a single or dual-ended camera to photograph instrument readings [17]. The camera was timed to take photographs at preset intervals. A dual-ended camera was capable of taking 4,000 data pictures of 12 different instruments. The use of in situ camera techniques gave way to digital techniques with the development of microprocessors. By comparison, typical in situ instruments today contain a microprocessor that acquires data from multiple sensors and records these measurements on high-density streaming magnetic tape devices in a highly compacted format. The information is then either transmitted from the in situ instrument via satellite to a shore station or saved until instrument recovery.

The typical seagoing computer system in 1969 consisted of computer core memories of 8K or 12K words ranging in size from 10 to 24 bits. Typical I/O devices consisted of a teletype, high-speed paper tape reader and punch, start/stop magnetic tape recorder, incremental magnetic tape drive, digital plotter, and a display device. A/D and D/A converters and equipment such as navigational systems, clocks, syncro-to-digital converters, and scanners were also interfaced to the computer. A typical shipboard system cost $150,000, and rarely did an experiment rely on only one system to remain operational throughout an extended cruise. The manufacturers of general-purpose computer equipment were most anxious to see their products being used in this new market. In several cases, manufacturers provided large computer systems to researchers along with spare parts and technician assistance to maintain the equipment during cruises. The computer systems proved to be seaworthy in most cases, and these loans resulted in purchases of their equipment. The most popular of these systems among researchers were IBM 1800s, DEC PDP8s, and the UNIVAC 1218 computers. Other computer systems were the IBM 1710, Hewlett—Packard HP2116A, Elliott MCS900, and Honeywell DDP24.

In the early and mid-1960s, scientist were primarily concerned with the feasibility, reliability, maintainability, and "cost effectiveness" of using "second-generation" computers (solid-state electronics) at sea. The major emphasis during this time was to prove how seaworthy the computer systems were and to justify their relatively high costs. By the late 1960s, the oceanographic community had generally accepted the computer as a viable and necessary tool to accomplish their work efficiently. Almost every major university and laboratory engaged in the ocean sciences was installing computers aboard ships. The major thrust at this time was using the computer to unburden the scientist and improve the quality of the measurements and reportable results. The type of computer-related tasks performed were automatic data logging, real-time processing, interfacing oceanographic sensors to the computer systems, compatibility between shipboard and laboratory systems, and maintainability of computer systems at sea.

Navigational problems for satellite, LORAN, and local acoustic navigation were worked on extensively during this period in order to improve the accuracy of fixes and make adjustments to the navigational data. Even today, navigational problems have a high priority in oceanography, military applications, and commercial enterprises because accurate geographical

position is required for geophysical measurements, operating and launching
military systems, and maintaining the most efficient course to minimize costs.

At WHOI and other laboratories, computer systems were employed for
logging magnetic, bathymetric, and gravity measurements. These measurements were displayed as smoothed ship's track showing bathymetry, the
gravity anamolies, and magnetic field strength [18].

By the late 1960s, almost all universities and laboratories engaged in
oceanography and underwater acoustics were developing seagoing computer
systems. At LDGO, seagoing computer systems were being used to predict
satellite fixes and for adjusting the ships track. The Bedford Institute of
Oceanography (BIO) used on-line and off-line techniques for entering data
by setting switches and pushing an "accept" button. When the button
(computer interrupt) was pushed, information from switches and other
sources was logged into the computer for retention and processing. The
computer was programmed to use these data to develop an automatic plot of
ship's track. Also, BIO developed a shipboard data logging system that
recorded navigational data and geophysical data (magnetics and gravity
measurements) on paper tape for future processing. Other developments at
BIO consisted of a remote recording of a digital thermometer used off-line
and an electronic bathythermograph used on-line by the computer.

The University of Washington used a digitizing tablet at sea to digitize
bathymetric data directly into the computer from acoustic profile records.
Once digitized manually by an operator with the aid of a digitizing tablet,
the data were merged with navigational information and plotted using computer programs as profiles along the track and contours. These methods
are still in use today. Another computer system developed by the University of Washington for seagoing operations was built around an IBM 1130
[19]. This system was designed for both real-time acoustic inputs using
A/D converters and manual inputs using a card reader and paper tape
reader and punch. The objectives of the computer system were to acquire
and process salinity, temperature, and depth (STD) acoustic data for
underwater sound velocity calculations and temperature microstructure data.
The system was placed inside a van for easy transport and higher reliability
at sea. Today, installing computer systems in vans is very popular because
the computer system can be set up and tested prior to shipping; the van
is highly portable, environmental conditions can be controlled easily; and
the van provides a high degree of protection for the equipment.

An IBM 1130 computer was used aboard the USNS KANE in December
1968 in a multilaboratory experiment [20]. The scientists were from NAV-
OCEANO, LDGO, and the APL of Johns Hopkins University. Utilization of
the computer was in an off-line mode and consisted of calculating satellite
fixes, drawing Mercator charts and profiles of the earth's magnetic field,
as well as processing data for sea-surface salinity and temperature, and
constructing topographical charts.

At SIO, automatic data logging and navigational systems were developed
in 1969 for a deep tow instrument system [21]. The instruments were
mounted on a cylindrical underwater-towed vehicle. The vehicle was towed
by a surface ship, and its position and depth were determined using acoustic navigation. The information from the towed body was transmitted
through a cable to the ship. The computer system aboard the ship automatically logged temperature and magnetic field data, using a frequency
counter and ship's course and speed parameters using shaft encoders.
Navigational information was entered into the computer manually through a

teletypewriter. This system was accomplished using a DEC PDP8 computer with 4,096 words of core memory. Also being developed and used at SIO were IBM 1800 computer systems, which were installed on the institution's research vessels. The IBM 1800 computer system has available a Time-Sharing Executive System, which provides real-time process control through the operating system. This capability, as well as the use of higher level languages such as FORTRAN, greatly reduced programming time and effort. Interfaces were developed for the connection of special-purpose peripheral hardware to the computer such as an A/D converter; MX-702CA Navigation Satellite Receiver; shaft position encoders; magnetometer; STD sensor; and digital switches. On-line programs logged and processed current meter data, bathymetric data, and marine geophysical data.

To study the temperature variations in the ocean, which affect underwater sound speed, the NUWC interfaced their thermistor chain to a UNIVAC 1218 computer for real-time data acquisition [22]. They employed an analog multiplexer followed by an A/D converter for digitization and entry into the computer. The data were supplemented with off-line entries and recorded on magnetic tape for future processing.

A UNIVAC 1230 computer was installed aboard the R/V SANDS by the Navy Underwater Sound Laboratory (NUSL) for acoustic data acquisition and processing [23]. Acoustic data from hydrophones suspended from the R/V FLIP were telemetered to the SANDS for processing up to 64 hydrophone channels through multiplexing and A/D converters in real time.

The hydrographer of the Royal Navy developed automatic logging systems for hydrographic research for their HECLA class ships [24]. They used an Elliott MCS900 series computer, which automatically logged navigational information from several sensors such as DECCA, LORAN, LAMBDA, and HIFIX. A precision depth recorder (PDR), magnetometer, gravity meter, gyrocompass, and several meterological instruments were interfaced. The computer system logged and processed this information automatically.

The Environmental Science Services Administration (ESSA, now known as the National Oceanic and Atmospheric Administration [NOAA]) survey ships OCEANOGRAPHER and DISCOVERER were outfitted with IBM 1800 computer systems for oceanographic data acquisition and processing [25]. The computer was used for automatic data logging of oceanographic data and to monitor events in the engine room. Oceanographic survey parameters such as gravity, magnetics, sea water temperature, and gyrocompass were logged automatically.

Smaller, more portable computer systems such as the Honeywell DDP24 were repackaged and used experimentally aboard U.S. submarines being built by General Dynamics Corporation as part of the Submersible Integrated Control Program [26]. A/D converters and syncro-to-digital converters were interfaced to the computer for automatic data logging of acoustic, oceanographic, and ship parameters such as speed, bearing, and inertial navigational outputs.

At the close of the 1960s, minicomputers were starting to have capabilities seen only before on larger computers such as real-time and time-shared software operating systems. General-purpose computers for at-sea data acquisition and processing in oceanographic research were firmly established. The computer no longer was left onshore because it was found to be seaworthy and the high cost was easily justified. Figure 4 shows a typical computer room aboard a research vessel.

FIGURE 4   Computer room aboard research vessel USNS HAYES.

In the early 1970s, the momentum in digital data acquisition systems took on new directions. For example, the computer has greatly improved the quality of the data and made high-resolution position fixing using satellite systems such as the SATNAV TRANSIT a reality. In 1975, there were 35 SATNAV Magnovox MX-706 receivers being used in the oceanographic community, as well as 101 MX-702CA receivers [27]. The MX-706 uses a special-purpose computer embedded into the unit to compute positional parameters. Both OSU and the Naval Research Laboratory (NRL) independently took on the task of interfacing the MX-706 to their shipboard computer systems. Both organizations were successful, using different techniques.

Telemetry systems or radio links to shore systems were developed for the transmission of data to processing facilities. These systems were the forerunners of the satellite data transmission systems used in oceanography. Remote sensing systems and in situ systems rely upon satellite communications for data collection. Telecommunications and teleprocessing were a new direction only mentioned briefly in the 1960s. Evans, Brown, and Van Leer [28], at the University of Miami, began using satellite transmission technology to telemeter their oceanographic data to shore stations for processing. Also, marine satellite communications (MARISAT) became operational at this time, and data were transmitted over voice communication type lines at 2,400 bits per second (bps) because voice grade commercial channels were used. In the mid-1970s NRL demonstrated that a computer system on a research vessel could be tied into an active local area network (LAN) on shore over the MARISAT communication system [29]. This technique, although technically feasible, is expensive and is only used for the transmission of essential software or data.

In 1974, NRL used a Hewlett—Packard HP2100 minicomputer system configured as a Fourier analyzer aboard a Navy P3 ASW aircraft (see Fig. 1) to collect and analyze ship-radiated acoustic noise data [3]. The air-craft sonobuoy (underwater acoustic transducer) receiver was interfaced to the computer system through the HP5451B analyzer. Five sonobuoys, spaced approximately 100 meters apart, were deployed from the aircraft in front of the oncoming vessel; the ship-radiated acoustic noise was acquired using the aircraft sonobuoy receivers, processed by the Fourier analyzer, and recorded on compatible digital magnetic tape. The locations of the sono-buoys were recorded by "marking on top" of the sonobuoys and automatical-ly recording geographical coordinates from the aircraft Litton Inertial Navi-gation System (LINS). The LINS was interfaced to the HP2100 computer through specially built digital hardware that buffered the data coming from the navigation system.

After the successful use of the commercial minicomputer aboard a research aircraft, an Airborne Geophysical Sensor Suite (AGSS) was develop-ed. The AGSS developed in 1975 acquired magnetic field strength using a Geometrics 801/3 Magnetometer and navigational information from the LINS. This geophysical data acquisition system was expanded in 1977 to include the measurement of gravity data using a LaCoste and Romberg S93 Air-Sea Gravity Meter mounted on an inertially stabilized platform [30]. Also, a HDUE GPS navigational P code prototype receiver manufactured by TI was installed, and a high-resolution radar altimeter for measuring aircraft verti-cal motion was designed and developed. The data acquisition equipment was interfaced to three HP2117F computer systems. Figure 5 shows the AGSS system on a Navy P3 ASW aircraft.

With the introduction of "third-generation" computers (integrated elec-tronic circuits), the physical size of the computer systems decreased dra-matically. Also, the development of microprocessors provided a whole new technology for in situ oceanographic systems. Timed film recorder systems were replaced with cartridge tape recorders. WHOI developed a 1-year unattended cartridge tape recorder to record in situ current parameters such as rotor, compass, vane follower, and time and temperature data at 15-minute intervals [31]. Eleven million bits of digital information were stored on the tape with no record gaps. The recorder was approximately 9.4 × 9.9 × 11.2 centimeters and weighed 1 kilogram. The microprocessors were used for general-purpose data collection and processing aboard research vessels. Their obvious advantages were size, low power consumption, and low cost; their disadvantages were processing speed, lack of vendor soft-ware support, and limited peripheral interfacing.

Environmental data buoys were deployed by the NOAA in 1972 [32]. The data buoys transmitted their information via satellite data links. The NIMBUS 6 meteorological satellite is capable of receiving and recording sig-nals from several oceanographic platforms. The Synchronous Meteorological Satellite/Geostationary Environmental Orbiting Satellite (SMS/GEOS) provides continuous meteorological observations from various platforms such as drift-ing ocean buoys, small weather platforms, and balloon-wind stations. NIM-BUS provides reports twice per day, whereas SMS/GEOS provides reports on demand.

As oceanographic researchers began to rely on computer systems for data acquisition and processing, they became aware of the many different approaches being taken by their peers even at the same laboratory. Also, researchers were interested in knowing what shipboard sensors were avail-

FIGURE 5   AGSS aboard Navy P3 ASW aircraft.

able before the experiment, as well as the type of interface required. An attempt was made by Mesecar and others [33] of OSU to introduce the concept of a sensor-to-computer interface standard. This data communication standard became known as the Serial ASCII Interface Loop (SAIL) and was accepted formally by the Institute of Electrical and Electronic Engineers (IEEE) Computer Society in 1985 (IEEE Standard 997—1985). It must be pointed out that this standard was only adopted by University–National Oceanographic Laboratory ships (UNOLS) because the interface is relatively slow for much of the work done in oceanography and many already existing ship interfaces were different from the standard.

    In the late 1970s microcomputers became "friendlier," with vendors providing operating systems for software development with both editor and assembler. With the advent of software development tools, several reseachers developed shipboard computer systems around microcomputers. One of these data acquisition systems was developed at the University of Rhode Island [34]. The microcomputer selected was a Motorola Exorciser with 16K

words of random access memory (RAM). The instrument package was interfaced to the oceanographic sensor using a peripheral interface adapter and
one asynchronous interface adapter. Interfaced to the microcomputer through
these devices were navigation equipment, A/D converters for expendable
bathythermographs (XBTs), wind direction and speed, magnetometer, sea
thermometer, and gyro. This data acquisition system basically logged the
data for future processing.

A microcomputer system was developed about the same time by Ocean
Electronic Applications for the acquisition of oceanographic data from a
moored buoy deployed by a fixed winged P3 ASW aircraft [35]. This system was deployed in the Artic from an aircraft so it had to withstand an
impact of 100G (acceleration of gravity, 9.8 meters per second) and operate
at −40°C. Each buoy contained two microcomputers sharing a 10Mbit memory.
Telemetry was used to transfer data from the moored buoy to the DEC PDP8E
computer processing system. Pragrammable read only memory (PROM) was
used with the microprocessors to store the program code. The software
was developed and tested on the DEC PDP8 prior to being burned into a
PROM for the microprocessor.

High-density digital recorders (HDDRs) came into use during the late
1970s [36]. The early recorders were capable of recording data on magnetic tape at over 2Mbits per second using 28 channels. These recorders
were used primarily by the acousticians to record multiple hydrophone channels at high sampling rates (greater than 1 kilohertz) for post-processing of
acoustic data. Also, the magnetic tape served as an efficient means of
archiving the data. Today, the HDDRs are still being used by the oceanographic community but will be replaced in a few years by high-density
optical recorders. The disadvantages of the HDDR recorders are their high
cost (units typically cost over $100,000), large size, and noncompatible
format from vendor to vendor.

High-speed array processors were taken out of the laboratory and used
at sea primarily for performing real-time multichannel spectrum analysis of
acoustic signals. At NRL, a real-time processing system was developed for
acoustic research that used a DEC PDP11/34 computer with two array processors [37]. The system could process up to 256 hydrophone channels of
analog data. The data were digitized by a high-speed A/D converter and
stored in two megawords of core bulk memory. The array processors
accessed the data from the buffer area and computed Fourier transforms
for each channel. Once the spectral content of the data was computed, the
data were further processed and displayed by the host computer.

Steiger at NRL introduced the concept of using intelligent computer
terminals (a computer terminal that contains a programmable microprocessor
embedded) for data acquisition and processing [38]. These terminals were
the forerunners of the PCs. A Hewlett−Packard HP2649 intelligent computer terminal was programmed to acquire and process XBT data and magnetics data aboard a Navy P3 ASW aircraft (see Fig. 6). The oceanographic
sensors were interfaced using 16-bit parallel transistor-transistor logic (TTL)
electronic level I/O interfaces. A magnetic tape cartridge built into the
computer terminal was used for storing the acquired data. The data processing, graphics display, and experimental monitoring were performed on
a graphics intelligent computer terminal. The data acquisition microprocessor
was programmed using a vendor-provided assembler for an Intel 8080 compatible microprocessor. The acquired data were stored on the built-in
cassette magnetic tape for processing by the graphics computer terminal.

FIGURE 6 Intelligent terminal data acquisition and processing system aboard
Navy P3 ASW aircraft.

The data were processed and a graph produced. This graph was copied by
using a graphics printer. The intelligent terminal was programmed in BASIC
and took advantage of prestored functions in read only memory (ROM) for
various I/O processing, such as reading compatible cartridge tapes and
producing hard copy output on preselected peripherals.

Today, PCs are used in much the same way as the intelligent terminals
were used in 1978, with about the same programming and interfacing difficulties. The PCs do not add to the cost of a computer system because when
they are not in a data acquisition mode they can be used as computer terminals or for other applications. The compact size, low weight, and small
power consumption of these systems makes them ideal processors aboard
aircraft and "ships of opportunity," and for research in ice-covered areas.

The SACLANT ASW Research Centre developed a high-speed signal
processing system for shipboard use in the late 1970s. The system used
array processors, beam formers, and microprogrammable minicomputers [39].
A unique characteristic of this system was the concept of user friendliness.

The system provided the user with high-level languages called Interactive Time–Series Analysis (ITSA) and Sound Propagation Digital Analysis (SPADA), which performed data acquisition, processing, and analysis. ITSA was capable of performing signal processing by the scientist specifying simple statements. ITSA was linked to BASIC to perform other functions. SPADA contained special hardware for recording up to 240K samples per second and performing analyses of the data.

In the early 1980s, the major contributions to oceanographic data systems were in the areas of graphics and imaging systems, the creation of data base systems for the storage and dissemination of large quantities of data, and an IEEE sensor-to-computer interface standard was established for use aboard the 27 UNOLS research vessels. Other noticeable changes were an expansion of remote oceanographic surveys and experimentation from fixed winged aircraft and satellites, more programmed intelligence in microprocessor-based measurement devices such as the conductivity, temperature, and depth (CTD) instrument, and the utilization of high-resolution navigation from GPS receivers.

Multibeam bathymetric survey systems, known as Sonor Array Sounding System (SASS), were formerly only available for military applications. Similar systems became available to civilian scientists in the early 1980s and are known as Sea Beam systems (see Fig. 7). Six of these Sea Beam sonar systems are now in operation and are located on the U.S. NOAA ship SURVEYOR, the Australian HMAS COOK, French CNEXO JEAN CHARCOT, the West German SONNE, SIO's R/V THOMAS WASHINGTON, and LDGO's R/V CONRAD. Their appearance was largely due to their ability to survey an area more rapidly by using multiple beams and their ability to generate higher quality hydrographic charts and maps. Major advances in high-speed signal processing using computer technology permitted the production of real-time contour charts of the area being surveyed. System hardware and

FIGURE 7 Diagram of multibeam bathymetric sonar system.

processing problems still exist for multibeam systems. One of the most significant of the processing problems is "image registration," which generally occurs when the navigational information is not accurate, making the matching of bathymetric data very difficult. Using GPS resolves the problem, but when not available, the data are registered using a combination of manual methods and image-processing computer algorithms developed for use on graphic image-processing computer systems. Efforts are under way by several laboratories processing multibeam bathymetric data to automate the processing procedures by developing complex computer algorithms. It is expected that this problem will be eliminated when GPS becomes fully operational.

In 1983, Bahamondes and others developed a single chip microcomputer system to control STD and CTD instruments [40]. Also, the microcomputer was used to acquire and store the data in local memory until it was time to transmit the data to a surface computer. The microcomputer was embedded within the underwater instrument to improve the quality of the data. Because the digitization process is located in close proximity to the sensor, there is no degradation in the measurement because of data transmission difficulties. The functions of the in situ instrument can be modified or adapted as conditions change, and very little power is required to operate the digital large-scale integrated (LSI) electronics. Ongoing continuous monitoring of the instrument can take place. Digital data transmission is accomplished by either a hard-wired or acoustic transmission link.

The SAIL standard developed for UNOLS vessels is the only standard instrument interface system used in the oceanographic community today. The standard is a network for connecting shipboard sensors and computers. The researchers need to know the shipboard sensing equipment available and how to interface to this equipment. Sensors can be added or deleted using the SAIL standard with no degradation in system performance. The standard is a 20-milliampere RS232 interface configured to support up to 20 sensors, but it does not support data rates above 9,600 baud. The SAIL system was originally proposed by Mesecar and others at OSU in 1978 and is well documented (see Refs. 41 and 42).

The Data Acquisition in Real-Time (DART) system was developed in 1983 to fill the needs of moored data acquisition systems [43]. The DART system has been designed for flexibility of operation. Several sensors can be moored with the same tether, and the data can be collected and sent to a central site for radio telemetry transmission via satellite to the shore station using a microprocessor. The system makes use of the SAIL communications link described earlier.

In 1983, Neil Brown Instrument Systems, Inc., developed a CTD instrument that contained a microprocessor embedded within it [44]. The CTD device is extremely compact (cylindrical in shape, 41 centimeters diameter and 63 centimeters high) and relatively lightweight with a 500-meter working depth. The microprocessor communicates digitally with the processing computer via an extended SAIL protocol and is capable of making measurements at five scans per second.

Another in situ microprocessor-bases system for underwater acoustic data acquisition and signal analysis is the Coherent Digital Data Acquisition System (CODDAS), developed by Daubin Systems Corporation in 1983 under a contract with the Naval Ocean Research and Development Activity (NORDA) [45]. The microprocessor system is capable of acquiring data from 16 channels at a sampling rate of 800 hertz, performing transient analysis on events of up to 12,000 samples, performing a fast Fourier transform (FFT) on up to 512 data samples, recording time—series data with a dynamic range of 76 decibels on blocks of 256 to 12,032 samples, performing demodulation of narrow-band signals, calibrating the acquisition system with four gain states possible, and providing a common time base for all signals. The data are stored on a 800-bits-per-inch (bpi) cassette tape. This system is packaged in a container less than 1/3 meter in diameter and 2 meters in length and has a weight of approximately 59 kilograms.

At WHOI, in 1983, an ambient noise measurement system was developed for underwater acoustic processing using two 16-bit microprocessors [46]. The system is capable of sampling ambient noise data at 0 to 200 hertz continuously, using a 14-bit A/D converter and performing a 2,048-point FFT in the arithmetic processor. The computed results are stored in bubble memory and transmitted to the external computer on a 30-day basis via the SAIL interface protocol. This represents the first recorded use of bubble memory for mass storage in an oceanographic data acquisition instrument.

The major new developmental efforts in the mid-1980s were the use of low cost, highly portable PCs for data acquisition and processing aboard oceanographic research platforms. The PCs are small in size and low in cost but have the processing power of much larger computer systems developed only a few years earlier. Several of these systems are currently in use today.

In 1982, an XBT data collection system was used aboard the M/V OLEANDER to collect meteorological data for the Shipboard Environmental Data Acquisition System (SEAS). A Hewlett—Packard HP-85 desktop computer was used to collect and process the data. The data were stored temporarily and transmitted through a GEOS satellite at the appropriate time in a standard format [47].

A test system for towed-array sonars was developed by Barkley and others of Planning Systems, Inc., for the Naval Underwater System Center (NUSC) [48]. The system used two AT&T 6300 personal computers for data acquisition, processing, and display. This system is part of their Sonar Evaluation Acoustic Operational Processing System (SEAOPS) group of computer systems. The system software was developed using a mix of FORTRAN programs and assembly language programs where high I/O rates were required. This system replaced a much larger mainframe computer. The size and cost of hardware have shrunk considerably, but there is a trade-off between computer size and flexibility and the time required to interface and program the PCs for real-time data acquisition and control. The cost savings of hardware could easily be absorbed by the increased software development costs because software is an ongoing expense. The SEAOPS computer system uses a two-channel spectrum analyzer to digitize the data and calculate the power in one-third octave bands. The data in real time are acquired from the spectrum analyzer and stored on magnetic tape. A second PC is required for the analysis and display of the data. Further expansion of this system is planned to accommodate up to 144 channels of analog underwater acoustic hydrophone data in lieu of the 2 channels today.

An ambient underwater acoustic noise spectral data acquisition system was developed by Prada at WHOI in 1985 [49]. The system uses NEC Advanced Personal Computer for data acquisition, processing, and display functions. The software development uses the CP/M-86 operating system, and C is the primary programming language. This system is employed during

underwater acoustic experiments to perform time–series analysis and display
spectra of frequencies up to 1 kilohertz with a 1-hertz resolution in real
time and serves to determine the best time to perform low ambient noise
measurement studies.

Super minicomputers with an array processor and general-purpose I/O
computer are being used at sea by NRL for underwater acoustic data acquisition and processing. The data acquisition system consists of a DEC VAX-
730 or VAX750 computer, HDDR, Floating-Point systems array processor,
APTEC general-purpose I/O computer, and RAMTEK or LEX90 graphics display system (see Fig. 8) [50]. The system is capable of processing data
from 50 hydrophone channels, computing FFT beam-former outputs, plotting
hydrophone power versus time, plotting signal power versus time, and storing other experimental information in real time. Due to the high cost of
this system, no backup system was provided. However, the system was
found to operate reliably throughout a 3-week experiment aboard a research
vessel. It would have been extremely difficult to have a system of this
nature a decade earlier, as the reliability of the equipment at that time was
much lower and backup systems were often required for successful data
collection at sea.

FIGURE 8   NRL high performance at-sea acoustic data acquisition, processing,
and display system.

COMMUNICATIONS

Satellite communication systems offer excellent opportunities for the transmission of oceanographic data between vessels, between scientific satellites
and ground stations, and for in situ data acquisition systems. In 1975,
Evans and others at the University of Miami proposed the development of
a satellite communications system for the transmission of messages and data
between ship and shore [28]. This development effort was supported by
the National Science Foundation (NSF) in cooperation with the National
Aeronautics and Space Administration (NASA), and satellite communications
using the ATS I and ATS III satellites were established for UNOLS vessels.
In an agreement with NASA in 1978, the oceanographic users receive three
1-hour periods per day for data transmission, which is subdivided among
the participating users. The system is capable of transmitting voice, facsimile, digital binary, and ASCII pulse code modulated (PCM) data streams.
The establishment of a data link between ship and shore provides options
that were not available to researchers previously. The mainframe computers
could remain on shore, as well as the personnel needed to program and
operate the computers. Small highly reliable microcomputer systems could
be used at sea with little or no expertise required to operate or maintain
them. The systems at sea had to be fast enough to acquire the data and
have enough storage capacity to save the data until their data transmission
window opened. With a relatively short transmission window and RS-232
transmission rates, the data exchange between ship and shore is very
limited. However, for low budgets and limited personnel, data satellite
transmission provides an effective way of processing oceanographic data.

Early Bird, the first commercial communications satellite, was successfully launched in 1965 [51]. In 1976, the first commercial maritime satellite
(MARISAT) was launched over the Atlantic Ocean in a geosynchronous orbit
above the equator. A second MARISAT satellite was launched to provide
communications over the Pacific Ocean and another over the Indian Ocean.
MARISAT provides both voice and teletype transmissions worldwide for
governments, the military, and commercial enterprises. MARISAT is being
used for direct computer-to-computer communications from ship to ship,
ship to shore, and shore to ship. In 1981, Eskinzes and Clamons demonstrated that the quality of the MARISAT data transmissions is sufficient to
permit a computer system on a vessel to be part of the LAN on shore [29].
MARISAT communications are also useful for providing shipping information
to custom officials, hazard avoidance, navigational information, air in rescue
operations, and general telephone communications.

The International Maritime Satellite Organization (INMARSAT), which
now operates MARISAT, was formed in 1979 and is now made up of over
40 member countries [52]. Each participating country has an investment
share in INMARSAT, with the United States, the Soviet Union, the United
Kingdom, and Norway holding major shares. INMARSAT uses some of the
existing MARISAT capabilities, as well as developing new ones. INMARSAT
has been designed to be compatible with MARISAT. At this time, three
satellites are being used for INMARSAT: one over the Atlantic Ocean, one
over the Pacific Ocean, and one over the Indian Ocean. The services currently available are voice, telex, facsimile, and 56Kbits per second data
communication ship to shore. The second-generation satellites are planned
for deployment in the 1988 through 1991 time frame [53]. A total of nine
satellites for INMARSAT will be available when the system is completed, with

three over the Atlantic Ocean, three over the Pacific Ocean, and three over the Indian Ocean [54]. These satellites will have greater capability, namely, wider bandwidths, increased power, voice actuation, and 200 voice channels. Higher data speeds of 1.544Mbits per second will be possible at that time.

Today, shipboard equipment, consisting of a minicomputer, acquires, stores, and transfers data to the earth station at 56Kbits per second through the MARISAT. The earth station has equipment to receive the data and retransmit it over private lines at the same rate of 56Kbits per second. GEONET services from Communications Satellite Corporation (COMSAT) World Systems makes use of the transmission rate of 56Kbits per second. GEONET operates a network of ground and transmission services for receiving and disseminating the data. The data can be transmitted over private communication lines or common carriers, spooled to magnetic tape for next day delivery, or transmitted by microwave communications links for rapid processing [55].

Using high-speed satellite data communications provides an almost real-time look at the data by the shore-based laboratory site, where high-performance computers can be used to provide current survey information to the operational vessel. This is a highly beneficial service because at-sea operations are expensive and often a great deal of time elapses before an area can be reinvestigated for missing information. The data link can provide the ship with navigational information, suspected malfunctions in equipment, identification of geological features by experts, and other operational information. Now, shore-based technical experts can process and analyze the data while the ship is on-station and direct the ship's further experimental plans. This shore-based guidance provides a more cost effective approach to gathering data while at sea. Also, data processing delays are minimized because the data are processed during the survey and not a month or two after the survey.

The seismic data collection and processing community has been helped greatly by the use of satellites for data transmission to shore sites. Seismic data shots typically produce over 4Mb of raw data and on a daily basis over 8 gigabytes (Gb) of raw data. Enough of this data can now be transmitted over INMARSAT at the current rate of 56Kbits per second to make processing of the data at the shore-based facility worthwhile. The data transmission rate of 56Kbits per second has provided for the processing of two-dimensional data on shore. INMARSAT will provide a transmission rate of 1.5Mbits per second in the near future, after which it will be possible to transmit three-dimensional data, which will be even more beneficial to the seismologist [56].

In situ moored and drifting buoys are very dependent upon satellites to transmit data to field stations. The data are transmitted to a shore station for processing and dissemination. The NOAA Data Buoy Office (NDBO) is actively deploying General Service Buoy Payload (GSBP) moored buoys in order to make in situ ocean surface measurements for meteorological and oceanographic measurements [57]. These measurements are used as an adjunct to satellite remote sensing for ground truth data and data enhancement purposes. The moored buoys measure meteorological and oceanographic parameters such as wind speed and direction, air temperature, pressure, surface temperature, and wave spectra. These buoys contain a programmable microcomputer that controls the acquisition, processing, and formatting of data for transmission via a satellite link. Many of these buoys have been deployed and are actively acquiring and transmitting oceonographic data to field-processing sites. The data from the buoys are transmitted via satellite to ground stations. The data are then transmitted via land lines to the National Earth Satellite Service (NESS) and NDBO stations for processing. NDBO maintains data base systems of current and archival data. Once a month the processed data are forwarded to the National Oceanographic Data Center (NODC) for analysis and archival, as well as for dissemination to the oceanographic community.

The ARGOS system has been designed to provide worldwide environmental information. The system was begun by an agreement in 1974 between NOAA and NASA of the United States and CNES of France [58]. ARGOS was first demonstrated in 1978 during a Global Atmospheric Research Program (GARP) experiment. During this experiment, ARGOS data collection systems were put aboard floating buoys for meteorological and oceanographic data acquisition. Two NOAA polar-orbiting satellites contained the ARGOS data collection and transmission package. Four positions per day were obtained in the equatorial region and as many as 28 in the polar region. Every time one of the satellites passed over any of the three telemetry-receiving stations (Wallops Island, Virginia; Gilmore Creek, Alaska; and Lannion, France), the recorded data were transmitted to the station. The data were relayed to the NESS-DIS/NOAA facility in Maryland and forwarded from there to the ARGOS Data Processing Center in Toulouse, France.

The ARGOS data acquisition package is instrumented for experiments in oceanography, glaciology, biology, hydrology, and geology. The oceanographic instrument package makes sea-surface and subsurface measurements, ocean swells and wave measurements, and acoustic studies. ARGOS also provides calibration "ground-truth" data for satellite imagery, as well as in situ field data. The drifting buoys are deployed from ships and aircraft. Their data are augmented by over 7,000 voluntary observing ships that transmit data messages on an irregular basis. It is projected that ARGOS will expand to 10,000 platforms in the late 1990s. The system will continue beyond the Television Infrared Observation Satellite (TIROS)-N series of satellites, and ARGOS will be part of the planned 10-year Tropical Ocean Global Atmospheric (TOGA) program.

NOAA has been tasked with marine weather forecasting. To provide current or near real-time forecasting, NOAA has developed a SEAS system that utilizes the GEOS satellite to receive and transmit meteorological and oceanographic data [59]. Information from vessels that carry a SEAS data acquisition unit is transmitted over the GEOS satellite. The information is received at a ground station at Wallops Island, Virginia, and then retransmitted to the NESS-DIS shore station in Suitland, Maryland, for reduction and evaluation.

Satellite data communications has revolutionized the way oceanographic data are processed at sea and transmitted to shore stations. The satellites bring the data from the field site to the shore-based laboratory and bring the resources of the laboratory to the field site. Powerful computer systems can now be employed in the reduction, processing, analysis, and display of the oceanographic data in near real time, which is very valuable, for example, in weather forecasting and seismology. The future of megabit-per-second data transmissions over satellite communications will aid researchers further in their endeavors to produce accurate data of the highest quality.

REMOTE SENSING SYSTEMS

The study of the earth from satellites and aircraft is referred to as remote sensing. Aircraft have been used as an oceanographic data acquisition platform since World War II, whereas satellite oceanography generally began in the early 1960s. The science of what is known today as satellite oceanography was recognized first at WHOI in 1964. Under the chairmanship of Ewing at WHOI, the first Oceanography from Space meeting was held [60].

The properties of the ocean that are currently sensed from aircraft and satellites are water-surface temperature, water depth (shallow water bathymetry), salinity, currents, geoid anomalies, tides, sea state, surface winds, ice floes, icebergs, ice coverage, oceanic fronts, concentration of suspended particles, and petrochemicals. The advantage of using aircraft and satellites for oceanographic measurement purposes instead of other oceanographic platforms is the rapid and extensive coverage that can be obtained, as well as the ability to make measurements over ice-covered regions.

Satellites are divided into two types, operational and experimental, and further subdivided into geostationary or polar orbiting [61]. NESS, under NOAA, has the responsibility for all operational satellites, whereas NASA has the responsibility for developing experimental satellites and sensors and placing them into space.

The satellites that have provided oceanographic data were the TIROS for weather observations in the 1960s; the NIMBUS program from 1964 to 1978; the GEMINI manned series in the 1970s; the manned SKYLAB experiments in 1973 and 1974; the GEOS series in 1975, 1977, and 1978; and SEASAT in 1978 [62].

NIMBUS and GEMINI satellites provided images that were used to study sea-surface temperature, currents, sea state, marine biology, and sea ice [63]. The SEASAT satellite, which was dedicated to oceanography, was only in operation for approximately 100 days, but it provided the oceanographic community with a great deal of data over that short period [62]. The satellite had five sensors that measured sea state and winds at the ocean surface with a microwave radiometer; sea-surface topography and wave height with a precision radar altimeter; surface winds from Doppler return using a scatterometer; wave lengths, sea state, and ice boundaries with a synthetic aperature radar; and cloud and surface temperatures with a visible infrared radiometer.

SEASAT demonstrated that remote sensing from satellites was extremely valuable to the oceanographic community. The data the sensors provided have been analyzed and published in research reports for several years, and analysis is still not completed. The sensors are being employed in future satellites.

Experimental satellites to be launched in the near future are Geodetic Satellite (GEOSAT) for the Defense Mapping Agency, which will use a high-resolution altimeter; Defense Meteorological Satellite Program (DMSP) meteorological satellites for the U.S. Air Force, which will employ a Special Sensor Microwave Imager (SSMI) for the study of sea ice, snow cover, surface winds, and atmospheric water; MOS, to be launched in 1986, is a series of Japanese sun-synchronous orbital satellites, which will be used to collect oceanographic data; European Space Agency (ESA) Remote Sensing Satellite (ERS-1) is a satellite to be launched in 1988 in a sun-synchronous orbit to study the oceans; Navy Remote Ocean Sensing Satellite (NROSS) to be launched in 1989 is a U.S. Navy satellite with NOAA and NASA participation, which will be designed to meet the needs of the operational Navy and will be in a sun-synchronous orbit; Ocean Topography Experiment (TOPEX), to be launched in 1989, will complement NROSS and have a dedicated altimeter to study the general circulation of the oceans; a Japanese Earth Resources Satellite (ERS-1) satellite, to be launched in 1990, will be used to study terrestrial mapping for nonrenewable resources; POSEIDON, to be launched in 1990, is a French satellite that uses altimetry for ice and ocean studies; Geopotential Research Mission (GRM), to be launched in 1991, is a two-satellite system for the study of the earth's magenetic and gravitational fields; RADARSET, a Canadian satellite to be launched in 1991, will monitor and predict sea ice; and several other satellites, not mentioned here, are in the planning stages. To validate the satellite data, many in situ experiments will have to be conducted using vessels and data buoys containing various instruments.

Instruments proposed for use on future satellites for oceanographic research include an altimeter for the measurement of sea-surface topography and wave height; a color scanner using a radiometer to obtain ocean color; an infrared radiometer to measure sea-surface temperature; a microwave radiometer to measure wind speed, water vapor, rain rate, sea-surface temperature, and ice coverage; and a scatterometer (microwave radar) to measure the sea-surface roughness, which yields the amplitude of short surface waves. A synthetic aperture microwave radar will provide information on swells, internal waves, currents, amplitude of short surface waves, sea ice floes, and their location.

The various stages of satellite data processing for oceanographic research are identified as data handling, image processing, and pattern recognition [64]. Oceanographic satellites provide an extremely large quantity of data that must be reduced, processed, and analyzed. The data are usually recorded by the sponsoring agency on digital magnetic tape and transmitted in that format to the oceanographic processing agencies. The raw data may consist of as much as 50Mb in a data file, as well as calibration data and sector registration data. The data are processed to produce sectorized two-dimensional files and must be corrected for the geometric distortion of the earth. The large quantities of data, as well as the data central processing unit (CPU) intensive processing requirements, usually dictates that the processing be performed on at least a high-performance minicomputer system. Each data element must be referenced to geophysical coordinates in order to be meaningful. This is accomplished by using the latitude, longitude, altitude, roll, pitch, and yaw when available. Otherwise, the data must be fitted to known landmarks. The data are recorded in sectors, usually in two-dimensional arrays, of 512×512 data points, as most image-processing systems have resolutions of at least this size. Each pixel (smallest addressable electronic element on a CRT display) must be localized with geophysical position (latitude and longitude), and calibration values must be taken into account.

The environmental satellite data are archived at NOAA's Satellite Data Services Division (SDSD) in Suitland, Maryland [62]. This facility is located with NESS, who became the managers of the operational environmental satellite program in 1980 [65].

Image processing takes place after the data reduction. It encompasses the restoration, enhancement, and registration of the image. The arrays of data are processed and displayed on graphic image-processing systems.

There are many such systems that utilize minicomputers, as well as large mainframe computers. The image displays, manipulation of data, and the addition of color usually result in highly intensive CPU and I/O processing activities.

Pattern recognition requires a knowledgeable scientist to interpret the enhanced images that are produced. The scientist will analyze the image displayed and make a determination as to what has occurred. Actual readings from the data can be made, such as wind velocities, temperatures, and wave heights. To speed the processing and analysis of the data, complex computer algorithms are being developed.

COMPUTER GRAPHICS IN OCEANOGRAPHY

Computer graphics has been defined by Mufti [66] as "the use of the computer to define, store, manipulate, interrogate, and present pictorial output." Oceanographic researchers have used graphics to convey their findings for a long time. This began with geographic maps and charts of the oceans and shore lines, simple bathymetric charts from early surveys of harbor areas, temperature charts, and meteorological charts. In the 1950s, CRT displays were interfaced to computers at the Massachusetts Institute of Technology (MIT), and computer graphics became a reality.

Hard copy computer grahipcs devices, such as incremental pen plotters, emerged at about the same time as the CRT, and many of these initial technological developments remain in use today. The CRT graphics displays are the key ingredient of interactive computer graphics-technology today. The computer graphics industry has progressed rapidly in the past 30 years, having developed highly sophisticated hardware and software algorithms. The science has progressed to multidimensional graphics using pseudo or false color. Several successful attempts have been made to standardize the software so that the computer graphics developments will be transportable among different computers. The graphics revolution has touched all science, business, and artistic endeavors. Computer graphics technology provides fast solutions to previously tedious, time-consuming, and repetitive tasks and the display of large quantities of data in a easily managed form.

Digital computer graphics devices were first used to produce the standard charts that were done manually. The first seagoing computers in the mid-1960s used digital incremental plotters and CRTs as part of their complement of digital computer equipment. These digital plotters were operated either on-line by the computer or through an off-line digital magnetic tape controller. The plotting was generally confined to those standard laboratory two-dimensional plots such as acoustic ray tracing and propagation; navigational charts and cruise tracks (vessel geographical position); bathymetric profiles and contours; magnetic and gravity geophysical measurements; and STD graphs. Real-time graphics were usually confined to plotting vessel position from the output cf a navigational device. As mentioned earlier, one of the first uses of computers at sea was to perform local acoustic navigation during underwater searches. The computer was used to calculate the vessel's position based on the arrival times of interrogated underwater acoustic transponders and plot the process of the search vessel in real time on a digital incremental plotter. In this way, the search vessel could be navigated precisely so that all geographic areas could be searched.

These navigational techniques were used in the underwater searches for the lost submarines USS THRESHER and USS SCORPION.

In the early 1970s, interactive graphics became available to the oceanographic researcher. The digitizing tablet revolutionized the way the researcher reduced analog data from charts. Researchers no longer had to employ manual methods of reading analog charts, converting the values to a number, and entering the numeric value into a computer file. This process could be done quickly by developing computer programs to read the values directly from a digitizing tablet and storing these values in either raw or processed digital form. For large data sets, such as those obtained on geophysical surveys, this method has speeded the process of developing bathymetric charts by an order of magnitude and significantly improved the quality of the data. The use of a digitizing tablet to perform this task is still in use today.

The next major technological change in computer technology that affected the oceanographic community was satellite images. Satellites with oceanographic sensors are being used to record the physical properties of the oceans of the world. These images must be enhanced, reduced, analyzed, interpreted, and archived. Several graphic image processors have been developed and used by the oceanographic community for this purpose. As a natural extension of this work, multidimensional analysis, which includes color as a dimension, has been applied to the oceanographic data.

The development of digital image processing systems is a relatively new science. The image processor functions can be divided into three main elements: image acquisition, processing, and display [67]. Sensors have been developed to take a "snapshot" of a scene and digitize the acquired information. The processing of this information consists of enhancing the image; applying color, brightness, and gray tones to data values; edge detection; spectral analysis; and multidimensional as well as multiple image displays. Typically, this process generates large quantities of data that require large random access storage devices. The emerging technology of optical disk storage devices offers an excellent media for the storage and retrieval of this information. Several gigabytes of data may be stored relatively inexpensively and made available on-line to users.

Scientists at the Jet Propulsion Laboratory, an installation of NASA, have developed a Pilot Ocean Data System (PODS) that uses interactive graphics. The SEASAT data base was selected for the development and testing of this system [68]. As discussed earlier, the SEASAT satellite used an altimeter, scatterometer, and microwave radiometer to remotely sense ocean temperature, wind speed and direction, wave height, and other atmospheric parameters. The data, which exceeded 50Gb, was selectively compressed to 700 Mb and stored on a hard disk for on-line access. Scientists now have direct access to the data base for scanning purposes.

PODS provides graphics capability for producing linear plots of one parameter versus time or position, histograms, scatter plots, and contouring capabilities. These graphics are used to browse through the data in order to select areas for analysis. The graphics system provides several interactive features such as color and two- and three-dimensional transformations. The U.S. Central Intelligence Agency's World Data Bank I provides detailed world coastline data and is available on this system. The data can be projected onto four specified grids: Polar Stereographic, Mercator, Linear, and Eckert VI. By using PODS, the researcher can scan and test data quickly for selection purposes. Once selected, the data can be transmitted through communication lines or by other media, such as magnetic tape, depending upon the quantity.

To enhance the informational content of multidimensional data gathered from multibeam bathymetric, towed array, or satellite systems, gray tones and real and false color can be added using an image-processing system. The addition of either gray scale or color aids in the analysis, interpretation, and presentation of the data.

A color-imaging sonar has been developed by Mesotech Systems Limited [69]. The sonar solves the problem of obstacle avoidance and navigation by using high-resolution imaging techniques. Both navigation and obstacle avoidance are by visual observation on the CRT display. The system is capable of operating at a depth of from 5 to 100 meters in five different modes. It is used primarily to survey offshore sites, recover lost equipment, and inspect underwater installations. The system consists of three parts: the sonar, the sonar processor, and the CRT. The sonar processor consists of a microprocessor, line-scan converter, and main memory. The CRT is a red, green, and blue (RGB) 512 × 512-pixel display with 8-bit color resolution of which 7 bits are used to display as many as 128 colors. The four operating stages consist of data acquisition, data processing, data display, and data output. The data are read continuously with five display modes available: side scan (scrolls right to left), polar, sector, linear (horizontal is angle, vertical is range), and perspective. Permanent recordings are on video cassette recorder (VCR), screen photographs, and chart plots.

The development and use of nonmilitary multibeam bathymetric systems aboard research vessels conducting geophysical studies has generated new interest in image-processing systems. These systems are capable of producing real-time contour charts of the topography of the ocean that is being surveyed. NOAA, U.S. Geological Survey (USGS), SIO, LDGO, and many others are engaged in acquiring and processing high-resolution bathymetric data using multibeam sonar syatems. Although most of the multibeam bathymetric systems are hull mounted, there is also a towed sonar system called SAR.

The multibeam systems provide bottom depth as a function of along-the-track and across-track directions. This information provides a two-dimensional description of the topographic features of the ocean floor. A computer-generated three-dimensional perspective of an underwater seamount is shown in Figure 9. The data used to produce this graph were acquired by a multibeam sonar system and processed and plotted on a Hewlett—Packard HP1000 computer system by Czarnecki and Bergin at NRL [70]. They also used these data to statistically characterize ocean bottom roughness as a function of topography.

The processing problems on all multibeam sonar systems are relatively complex because they must compensate for ship or vehicle motion; have exact navigational coordinates; and correct for flat, slanting, and uneven sea floors [71]. If the sonar is mounted on a towed vehicle, the mathematics are further complicated by the position, rotation, and crabwise drift of the towed vehicle. Several software systems are currently under development on microcomputers and minicomputers to solve these problems. The input to the system is vessel parameters, navigational information, and sonar bathymetric recordings from multiple beams. The output of the processor is image and contour plots of the area being surveyed. From the processed raw data, a latitude and longitude is assigned to each depth value. Each

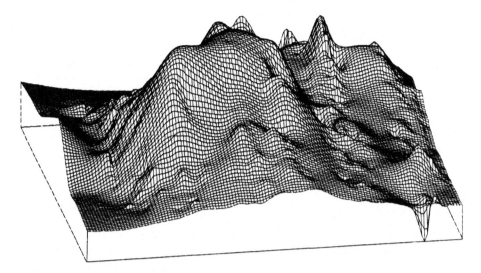

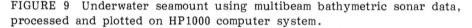

FIGURE 9 Underwater seamount using multibeam bathymetric sonar data, processed and plotted on HP 1000 computer system.

of the soundings is used to generate an image. Where values do not exist in the pixel matrix, linear interpolation is often used. Once the pixel matrix is in place, an image of the geographic area can be produced. False color can be added to the images in order to get a good representation of the topographic features, with either two-dimensional contours or three-dimensional geographical representations of the area. Problems exist in the processing that are still unresolved, such as matching different swaths [72] and image registration. Swaths of multibeam bathymetric data often overlap, and there is always the uncertainty of where, geographically, the vessel was when the measurement was taken. Image-processing systems are now being employed to deal with this problem of data registration. These systems are also capable of enhancing the data set, as well as correcting for anomalies.

The Sea Mapping and Remote Characterization (SeaMARC) System is a towed side-scan sonar system that also carries a magnetometer and compass and depth, speed, and fish attitude sensors [73]. The system is capable of recording and displaying images 50 meters to 20 kilometers wide of the ocean bottom, depending upon tow depth, at towing speeds of 0.25 to 5 meters per second. SeaMARC communicates with an on-board data acquisition system over a duplex digital communications system and an analog system for acoustic sonar signals. The digital uplink is used for transmitting the digital data for real-time processing. The digital processor has 2,000 pixels in the across-track direction for display and signal-processing purposes. Backscatter images from acoustic returns, as well as bathymetric contour maps generated from acoustic arrival times, are produced by the digital processing system.

Digital image processing has been applied to the study of temperature variance in the ocean [74]. Ocean temperature data are obtained by towing a vertical thermistor array through the area of interest and by using a CTD profiler. Extremely large quantities of temperature data, as well as other supporting oceanographic information are obtained in order to study the

microstructure of the ocean and the physical reasons for its composition.
False color is applied to a two-dimensional image of the computed temperature variance data. The areas of high energy become very discernible to
the human eye, whereas the microstructure of the ocean remains well hidden
without the introduction of color imaging in the analysis. These color-
imaging techniques are being applied to other areas of oceanography where
the microstructure of the ocean and atmosphere are being investigated.

Digital image-processing techniques have been applied to the study of
oceanographic parameters effecting the James River in Virginia [75]. The
effect of changes in river geometry, salinity, and bottom fill are analyzed
with the aid of modern image-processing equipment and techniques. As
with all imaging systems, the data normally consist of a two-dimensional
equally spaced data set. The graphics processor used is an International
Imaging Systems image processor interfaced to a Prime minicomputer. The
use of the image-processing system in this analysis provides the scientist
with the ability to observe the river's temporal changes, the tidal propagation, and the effects of man-made changes. Other parameters undergoing
investigation using imaging techniques are temporal variations of the three-
dimensional current fields and their effects on organisms to salinity gradients.

An interactive data processing station for oceanographic digital image
processing has been developed by Global Imaging, Inc. [76]. The computer
used is a 32-bit Hewlett–Packard HP9000 microcomputer. The software
includes geometric satellite corrections, earth location, remotely sensed data
registration, and sensor-specific programs. The standard utilities have been
designed to handle data sets from XBTs, Synthetic Bathymetry Processing
System (SYNBAPS) charts, imagery from advanced very high resolution
radiometer (AVHRR), Costal Zone Color Scanner (CZCS), and other sensors.
This system has been designed for the image processing of oceanographic
remote sensing data received from satellites.

The use of graphics by the oceanographic community has become increasingly more popular and important in the analysis, interpretation, and
presentation of oceanographic data. The modern color image-processing
system is the basic tool required to perform the analyses required from
multidimensional data. Most of the future work in oceanography will use the
data acquired by satellites, aircraft, and multibeam bathymetric ssytems.
All of these data collection platforms will require the development of sophisticated and complex computer-processing methods and algorithms, and it will
become necessary to use these tools to process large data sets. Techniques
using graphics image-processing systems must be developed quickly along
with standard processing and analytical methods. Also, there must be a
standard data format developed for the exchange and dissemination of the
data; otherwise, the entire oceanographic community will not be able to
benefit from the information.

OCEANOGRAPHIC DATA BASE SYSTEMS

On-station data acquisition systems, remote sensing systems, and in situ
digital oceanographic data systems have provided an overwhelming quantity
of oceanographic data. Once digitized and processed, these data must be
stored in a digital format for future recall so that they may be used by the
oceanographic community. This is accomplished by storing the data in data
base systems. The data base systems are digital computer systems of data

storage, maintenance, and recall. Data bases got their start in the 1960s, and their development is a recent technology.

The NODC recognized the need for a central clearinghouse of oceanographic data, and they established a data base in the mid-1970s. The quality depends upon the post-analysis of the data by the researcher. There are many different data base systems developed for each special application, with very few being software compatible. The oceanographic data bases are always expanding, with new data being added to an already large reservoir of past and historic data. These previous data are valuable for reference and comparison purposes and are rarely removed from the data base.

Most of the data bases developed prior to the 1980s use hierarchical or network structures. In the hierarchical data base, the data reside in one primary file, and a specific field within a record delineates the data type. Therefore, expending or altering a hierarchical data base is difficult and time consuming due to its lack of flexibility. Network data bases have more complicated structures that allow arbitrary relationships between nodes. To retrieve information from either the hierarchical or network data base, the language is usually procedural and the user must navigate through the data base to obtain the desired information. Relational data bases use simple two-dimensional tables and provide automatic navigation through the data base. The relational data base was first developed by IBM researcher Codd in 1972 [77]. He developed a new method of viewing data in the form of relations or tables. Its advantages, as originally viewed by Codd, were its simplicity and power and the fact that mathematical theory could be applied.

Relational data bases began to appear commercially in the late 1970s. Data bases built before that time were generally of the hierarchical type; the later ones were of the relational type. Relational data bases consist of separate files that are related to each other through the use of a unique data item called a key. The use of relational data bases in the storage and retrieval of oceanographic information provides flexibility in defining the data structure. The data structure can be easily modified or expanded as required to meet the needs of the scientist. Relational data base systems seem to be the designer's choice today, mainly due to their flexibility. Many data bases have been designed and developed for the oceanographic community; however, almost no two are alike or data compatible except for those that have selected ASCII code as their data storage format.

The oceanographic data acquisition systems that are responsible for the data explosion today are the multibeam bathymetry systems, which provide a two dimensional swath of data recorded every few seconds as the vessel transits through the ocean; acoustic systems, which are sampled at relatively high rates (approximately 1,000 samples per second or greater) for sometimes several hundred hydrophones; remote sensing platforms such as aircraft and satellites, which provide vast amounts of multidimensional data; towed array systems that measure the microstructure of the ocean and in situ systems, which continuously measure and telemeter back marine environmental and meteorological conditions.

The researcher, in general, has more data than can be processed and analyzed. The raw data are usually archived on magnetic tape for long-term storage, whereas the processed data are placed in one or more data bases where the data may be accessed. The consumers of the information must have access to the data and convenient methods of recalling and viewing the data in order to select the data of interest. Once the selection of data is made, the consumer can process the data locally or remove a portion of the data from the data base for processing elsewhere. Standard digital data transmission media such as networks, digital magnetic tape, and other commonly used file transfer methods are used to transfer the data among data bases by scientists.

Environmental, meteorological, and geophysical data products are provided to both military and commercial consumers by the Environmental Data and Information Service (EDIS) of NOAA. The data that produced these products were obtained by NOAA or contributed by others engaged in oceanographic measurements for their own special purposes. EDIS consists of three major data centers where the oceanographic data are stored in data bases and disseminated to users: the NODC, the National Geophysical and Solar—Terrestrial Data Center (NGSDC), and the National Climate Center (NCC). NODC provides consumers with bathythermograph (temperature versus depth) data; oceanographic station data, which includes temperature, salinity, oxygen, nutrient chemistry, and organic compounds; surface and subsurface current information; and biological data [78]. NGSDC provides consumers with bathymetric data, seismic profiles, gravimetric measurements, geomagnetic total field measurements, and other geological data. NCC provides consumers with marine meteorological and environmental data. Its satellite data services provide cloud photos, infrared imagery, and data on ocean currents, sea ice, and tropical cyclones. The products disseminated by NOAA are in the form of reports, weather maps and charts, and computer-generated magnetic tape. EDIS also operates the Environmental Science Information Center (ESIC), which provides comprehensive computer-based literature searches on more than 100 data bases.

The Coastal Upwelling Ecosystem Analysis (CUEA) Project has developed an Interactive Real-Time Information System (IRIS) to accept standard data files to bring compatibility to the many oceanographic data sets throughout the CUEA oceanographic community [79]. The format for the standard data files was defined at that time, and all data are coded in this format. The IRIS General Automated Data System (IGADS) was developed based upon the standard data files in 1975. Under IGADS, the standard files are processed by a variety of application programs. The programs included are hydrography/STD/CTD, data reduction routines, statistical routines, and interactive editing routines. Plotting programs are available for x—y plots, contouring, and multidimensional displays. The standard data sets are used nationwide by scientists engaged in this project. Based upon the standard, the scientists can begin data entry into the data base and use the analysis routines that have been developed under IGADS.

The Navy Oceanographic Data Distribution System (NODDS) is an on-line data base system operated for the U.S. Navy Fleet Numerical Oceanographic Center (FNOC), which provides real-time meteorological and oceanographic observations to users [80]. The system operates using data sent in real time to the FNOC for analysis and makes forecasts for up to 72 hours. The users access the data base from a DEC PDP11 data communications link. The forecast data include wind speed and direction, surface pressure and temperature, and wave spectra (energy as a function of frequency and direction). The products are available in either tabular or graphic form, and the users are required to have a computer or Tektronix display to receive the graphic output.

In Canada, the Marine Environmental Data Service was established as the focal point for processing, archiving, and disseminating oceanographic data [*81*]. The Canadian Marine Data Inventory (CAMDI) system has been designed to perform this task and has been implemented around a commercial data base management system known as SYSTEM 2000. Its primary purpose is to archive and maintain oceanographic data along the Canadian coasts. The CAMDI data base and data management system uses seven forms for input, and the entry is defined as having a collection of these forms. One of the forms identifies the originator and general program information, whereas another form contains general comments. The other forms contain cruise data, current meter data, wave measurements, tide and water levels, and special research data sets. The data entry format is a sequential (fixed length coded) file containing CAMDI records. The software developed for the system consists of an on-line interactive program to input the data, a program to load the entry into the data base, and a data retrieval program. The data base is kept on-line so that users in Canada can have immediate access to the data and perform their own searches. The CAMDI data base system attempts to pull together all data sets on the physics, chemistry, biology, and geology of the oceans. A search of the CAMDI data base begins with a selected geographic ocean area. The search can be further narrowed to time and other parameters and qualifiers. The system has expanded rapidly because of current events, which include concerns about pollution and the environment, as well as the research, commercial, and military user needs.

The Ocean Assessment Division (OAD) of the National Ocean Service (NOS) of NOAA is producing data atlases related to marine pollution [*82*]. The atlases contain maps of sea-surface temperature, sedimentation, currents, living organisms, and other parameters related to study of marine life and pollution. Data from the collection program is stored in a large expanding data base from which information is used to produce interpretive reports, a specimen archive, and a newsletter. The OAD uses this data base to provide information to a user community that consists of academia, commercial enterprises, and governmental agencies engaged in policy-making decisions.

The MARMAP Ecosystem DataBase Information system (MEDBIN) is used for the processing, analysis, and retention of data collected by the National Marine Fisheries Services [*83*]. The system is based upon a scientific data base developed by the Environmental Protection Agency called DATMAN. The system is capable of accepting new data types and new paths for entry of data, which is critical to the success of the data management system. A relational data base structure provides this flexibility. A successful scientific data management system requires file protection so that the users can read the data but only authorized scientists are permitted to alter the data. The user must have the capability of computing on the data and performing common algebraic and trigonometric manipulations. Also, the user must be able to select subsets of the data by using logical operators and output data in a standard format such as ASCII for data transfer and portability among systems. The MEDBIN system has three levels of data: (*a*) raw data, which is processed and organized into tables to form (*b*) the second data level, and (*c*) the third data level, which is the fully processed data. These data are organized into broad categories and are considered the permanent library data, available to all users.

The Equatorial Pacific Information Collection (EPIC) is an oceanographic data archival and retrieval system designed by the NOAA Pacific Marine

Environmental Laboratory (PMEL) to manage large quantities of data collected from climate study programs such as Equatorial Pacific Ocean Climate Studies (EPOCS) and TOGA [84]. The system, designed to operate on a DEC VAX 11/785 under the VMS software operating system, is written in FORTRAN 77. The system contains over 2,000 CTD, XBT, and current profiling data sets collected on EPOCS cruises. Data sets are interactively selected by specifying latitude, longitude, time, and depth. Programs have been developed that will generate contour plots, data plots, and listings. The system requires no programming knowledge and is being expanded to include time—series measurements.

The USGS has developed a Seismic Data Analysis (SDA) software data base system to analyze and archive their seismic marine data. The SDA system provides a whole range of data processing and analysis programs that include software for digitizing seismic profiles, seismic velocity versus depth information (velocity semblance curves), calculation of depth to seismic reflectors, smoothing of velocities, merging of navigational data, and graphic displays of seismic data as profiles and maps [85]. The programs are used to generate a seismic reflector data base and are executed in either an interactive or batch mode. The system has been implemented on a Hewlett—Packard HP1000 computer system under the RTE-IVB operating system. FORTRAN IV was the main programming language, and graphics are performed using the USGS MAGPEN computer programs. Sequential ASCII files are utilized with the SDA programs and are easily edited by the operating system software. The file format includes geographic coordinates, two-way travel time, RMS and interval velocity, and depth. The identification header is 80 characters and is the first record of the file. This record includes identifying information such as cruise and ship information, seismic line number, data collection time, and shot number. SDA programs are classified into eight categories: data entry, graphics display, data merging, navigation merging, depth calculation, editing, smoothing, and entry of processed data. The programs are also being developed using the C programming language for transportability to other systems.

The Harbor Branch Foundation in Fort Pierce, Florida, has been engaged in the development of relational oceanographic data bases to meet their needs. They have used a commercial data base management system, INFO, which was originally used for business applications and adapted for their scientific purposes [86]. INFO has both a programmable query language and applications software. The relational architecture of INFO permitted a rapid development of the scientific data base system with an open-ended structure for modifying or expanding the data base. Harbor Branch has developed this system on their Prime 750 computer, which has over 80 terminals attached and is connected in an Ethernet LAN arrangement at their laboratory. By using INFO with its relational data base, scientific applications are developed more rapidly than what had been achieved over the previous hierarchial data bases. Also, additional applications software for analysis, graphics, word processing, and spreadsheets have been integrated to simplify the process of data reduction and publication.

The storage and dissemination of data can best be accomplished with the utilization of digital data base systems. Although each organization has its own data base systems designed to meet its own needs, a standard data exchange format must be developed so that data can be shared easily. An early data exchange format was specified by NOAA, called MGD77. This data exchange format was quickly outdated with the changes in sensor technology that provided multidimensional Sea Beam data. Currently under way by NOAA and others is the development of a new data exchange format that will handle multidimensional data. In the future, most data bases will be of the relational type due to their inherent ability to expand easily. The conversion from existing hierarchical data bases to relational data bases is a monumental task due to the present investment in software and the existing data stored in the data bases. Technology is rapidly changing oceanography, and the data base system must change in order to meet the needs of the consumers. Otherwise, much valuable information about the oceans will be lost.

FUTURE OCEANOGRAPHIC DATA SYSTEMS

Oceanographic data systems will play an increasingly important role in our future scientific endeavors as well as in our daily lives. Current oceanographic sensor systems are providing more data today than can possibly be processed, analyzed, and archived by current digital computer systems. These data will be selectively processed and analyzed based upon a priori knowledge of what the data contain and the geographic area of interest. Raw oceanographic data will be accumulating at faster rates due to the new remote sensor systems (satellites and aircraft) and multidimensional and in situ data acquisition systems. The consumers of the data will continue to be commercial enterprises, government regulatory agencies, scientific researchers, and the military. These data will be collected to augment and enhance the scientific knowledge of physical, chemical, and biological oceanography; atmospheric science; underwater acoustics; hydrodynamics; optics; sea floor geology and geophysics; and other scientific areas [87].

Several data-sensing and gathering systems already in use and planned for the late 1980s will provide much of the oceanographic data in the future. For example, the proliferation of multibeam bathymetric systems for new and existing research vessels will generate large quantities of two-dimensional swath data as these ships survey the oceans of the world. With high-resolution GPS navigation becoming more available, areas of the world that have already been surveyed will be resurveyed for data comparison and data correction. The oceanographic community believes that the oceans have been largely "undersampled" and much guesswork has gone into registering the measurements. Two new oceanographic satellites, TOPEX and NROSS, are currently planned for launch in the late 1980s. These satellites will have SEASAT-type sensors such as microwave radiometer, precision radar altimeter, scatterometer, infrared radiometer, and synthetic aperature radar. Large quantities of continuous data will be transmitted by the satellites during their long operational lives. Also, other systems such as SeaMARC and AGSS will create large quantities of data to be processed.

High-resolution navigational systems such as GPS will have a profound effect upon future oceanography. With navigational accuracies in the sub-meter range, the oceans of the world can now be surveyed with repeatable results expected. These surveys will become reference points for future work in the ocean. GPS is the offshore navigation system of the future. When completed, the system will have 18 active satellites and spares deployed, which will provide continuous worldwide coverage by the early 1990s and will be the only high precision system in operation by the year 2000. The system will serve the military with P code transmissions and civilians with S code transmissions. Current plans call for S code to be transmitted at one-tenth the rate of P code, but the debate continues as to how far S code should be degraded. One suggestion that has been made by researchers is to provide GPS information in a delayed mode so that research data can be corrected as to geographical coordinates. In this manner, real-time navigation would be denied to potential enemies. OMEGA, with a navigational accuracy of 4 to 8 kilometers, is the backup system to GPS. OMEGA is currently operational worldwide at this time.

Digital technology is currently providing the tools required for oceanography in the future. Almost all computers today are available in small portable packages. For example, the processing power of a DEC VAX 11/780, which has been a reference point for the scientific computer industry for quite some time, is now available as a Micro-VAX which is approximately the size of a PC. Furthermore, computers that exceed the processing power and I/O capabilities of the VAX line of computers are already available and are being used in oceanography.

New oceanographic research platforms in the form of ships, satellites, aircraft, and in situ systems are planned for the immediate and distant future. The UNOLS fleet of ships are relatively old and do not meet the present or future research needs. Plans are already underway to upgrade and replace many of the 27 research vessels. The UNOLS Fleet Replacement Committee has identified six ship types required in the future in order to match capabilities with scientific endeavors. These six ship types are large high endurance; general-purpose medium endurance; general-purpose high performance (swath); general-purpose, special geology, and geophysics; intermediate general purpose; and costal general purpose [88]. The plan is to either modernize or provide new ships for the fleet over a 30-year period. The NROSS satellite has been designed to provide ocean-sensing capabilities as demonstrated by SEASAT. The TOPEX satellite will complement NROSS and will have a dedicated altimeter to study the currents of the ocean. Communication satellites currently capable of transmitting data at 56Kbits per second will be upgraded to 1.5Mbits per second, making data communications between ship and shore economically feasible.

Oceanographic sensors are becoming more sophisticated with better resolution and higher sampling rates. The information is being digitized at the transducer to avoid data degradation during transmission to the processing computer. The use of fiber optics has been introduced into the design of oceanographic sensors and digital transmission links. One example is a new in situ chemical sensor demonstrated aboard the deep submersible vehicle ALVIN. Microprocessors have become small and economical enough to be embedded with the many hydrophones on an underwater acoustic array and used in acoustic underwater ASW research. The data are sampled and digitized immediately to avoid any degradation in the signal that is transmitted from the hydrophone array to the analysis platform.

The computer hardware that will be used to process the vast quantities of data expected in the future will have the same attributes as the computer hardware has today. The equipment must first be rugged enough to go to sea and survive the adverse operating conditions found there, such as moisture; unstable power; motion, shock, and vibration; insufficient cooling; and dirty physical surroundings. Also, the hardware must remain highly portable, consume relatively small amounts of power, and be easily interfaced to sensors aboard the research platform. For systems acquiring and processing high-speed data, such as that obtained from acoustic hydrophone arrays, an array processor is required. Array processors are relatively well packaged and have already been used at sea. For acoustic and satellite transmitted data, due to the high data rates, general-purpose I/O computers with high bandwidths are required. These computers maintain very high transfer rates with a programmable microprocessor controlling the I/O. The data, once acquired, must be stored for processing in a high-capacity, high-speed random access device such as a magnetic disk and must be eventually archived in both raw and processed form. Optical disks hold much promise for solving the high-capacity storage problem. Today, optical disks are capable of storing several gigabytes of random access data on a single platter in a "write once, read many times" mode. However, the access and transfer rates for data stored on the optical disks are much slower than a magnetic disk today, making this technology of limited use to the oceanographic community at the present time. It is expected that future optical storage systems, both write once, read many times and the erasable optical disk, will be used by the researcher when the technology is ready. For multidimensional data systems, such as multibeam bathymetry and satellite imagery, color graphic image analysis systems on research platforms will be used. Recent developments have rapidly applied the graphics and imaging sciences to the problems of oceanography. These graphic systems are becoming available today from commercial vendors and their deployment at sea is anticipated.

Many future oceanographic data systems will use PCs for their at-sea data acquisition and processing. For low data rates and single application systems, the PC is an ideal choice. The PC is inexpensive and has all of the salient features required for sea duty. Due to their low cost, multiple systems can be used and they can be networked together. PCs have recently been used for underwater acoustic ASW research purposes at NUSC and WHOI. Generally, high-performance computer systems are required for underwater acoustic ASW applications. The NUSC system, SEAOPS uses a spectrum analyzer to perform the spectral calculations, which is a computationally bound task, and the PC is used as a controller to the spectrum analyzer. Also, a second PC system is used to perform data calibration and to store computed results. The WHOI PC system does the spectral calculation in real time, calibrates the data, and stores the result. This system, however, results in data loss, which is not a problem, because the system is only being used for monitoring purposes.

The software systems today are far friendlier than they were when digital computers first went to sea. At that time, computer programmers, electronic engineers, and the forerunner of computer scientists were all required personnel. Today, with more reliable hardware and friendlier software, personnel aboard ship can often be reduced, depending upon the complexity of the experiment. In the future, with natural languages being developed and packaged commercial software available, marine computer systems will be easier to develop and use.

In situ systems and oceanographic satellites will transmit vast quantities of data through communication satellites to ground stations. Once received at the ground station, the data are transmitted over standard commercial connections to the laboratory processing site. Standard high-performance processors are employed to process and analyze these large quantities of data directly in research laboratories. Therefore, sensors of this type will not require added at-sea hardware or software.

Standardization of computer interfaces has been accomplished on the UNOLS ships. However, in practice, the standard causes difficulties as well as solutions. The SAIL standard interface was designed for relatively slow RS232 data rates, which are inadequate for a large class of oceanographic experiments. Also, this interface does not conform to all sensor outputs, which results in an intermediate interface having to be designed to match the shipboard SAIL. Attempts at standardization will continue, especially in the networking area. However, because research objectives are continuously changing, there may not be any standard or group of standards that will satisfy all requirements.

Artificial intelligence (AI), a computer technology that is in its infancy, can be thought of as consisting of three primary areas: decision making, robotics, and computer speech. Knowledge-based expert systems being developed today assist in analyzing problems and making decisions [89]. Since 1980, the technology has been developed in research laboratories, and many useful products have emerged, such as systems to schedule tasks, perform medical diagnosis, troubleshoot mechanical systems, and synthesize speech. AI systems in oceanography will be used in the future to process and analyze the vast quantities of data expected. Also, AI will be employed to replace, where possible, the analyst in the data reduction and interpretation process. Although oceanography will not be the driving force behind AI technology development, oceanography will make good use of the technological advances in the field. Work has already begun in looking at ways to use the technology. Image enhancement and analysis, underwater detection, and the ability to search and retrieve information are all promising applications for AI research. The U.S. Navy has designated NRL as their lead AI laboratory. NRL researchers are busy working on the development of military applications, with major benefits anticipated for the civilian community as well. Currently almost all universities are engaged in AI research, but there are no known projects that are specifically targeted for oceanography. AI in its present development uses "brute force" techniques to perform tasks that are almost trivial for a human. This will change as AI technology develops, and oceanography will be among the beneficiaries.

Fiber optics have already begun to play a major technological role in land-based communication networks. As a digital data transmission media, fiber optic cables have been found to be a highly reliable and secure means of communications. Also, fiber optics provide high data transmission bandwidths, economical transmission paths, immunity from magnetic field interference, and electronic countermeasures [90]. Fiber optics would serve shipboard purposes extremely well as they can be used to carry analog and digital data transmissions on the ship without interference or signal degradation. These transmissions are currently being contaminated and degraded due to cross talk, signal loss, and external shipboard influences.

The physical properties of fiber optics makes them well suited as oceanographic sensors for both military and civilian purposes. At NRL in 1979, under the Fiber Optic Sensing System (FOSS) research program, it was demonstrated that fiber optic hydrophone sensors could be fabricated with characteristics that match or exceed the best conventional hydrophones today [91]. Because of the Navy's desire to expand its underwater sensing capabilities, a need has been developed for these optical sensors and for data processing equipment to manage the large, high-speed data requirements. High-speed processing may also be accomplished by using optical devices, because the properties of optics are relatively well understood and optical signal processors have very high computation speeds along with their relative simplicity and reliability.

The oceans have become increasingly more important to our civilization in the last three decades. The study of the ocean has risen exponentially during this time due to its importance in military and commercial endeavors. Today, much of our civilization depends heavily on the ocean as its source of food, fuel, and raw materials. Many of the future natural resources required for maintaining life will be provided by the ocean. Many of the secrets of the ocean or "inner space" must be unlocked, as well as the mysteries of the ice-covered regions of our world. The sensors are being put in place now and new ones are planned for the future. But the key to understanding the microstructure of the ocean, and solving the ice-covered regions mysteries is digital computer technology and the scientists who will turn the key.

Unfortunately, the disaster of the space shuttle Challenger will have a significant effect on the oceanographic time table. Future satellites for GPS navigation, maritime communications, and oceanographic research (NROSS and TOPEX) will be delayed until an alternative means of launching these satellites is found. It is important that the technical decisions be made quickly, so that the newly awaited technologies can be fully utilized by the oceanographic scientific community.

ABBREVIATIONS AND ACRONYMS

AGSS—Airborne Geophysical Sensor Suite
AI—Artificial intelligence
APL—Applied Physics Laboratory
ARGOS—Worldwide environmental information system
ASW—Anti-submarine warfare
ATS—NASA communication satellite
AVHRR—Advanced very high resolution radiometer
baud—A signaling speed, interchangable with bits per second.
BIO—Bedford Institution of Oceanography
bpi—bits per inch
bps—bits per second
byte—Eight consecutive binary digits operated upon as a unit
C/A—Course/acquisition
CAMDI—Canadian Marine Data Inventory
CODDAS—Coherent Digital Data Acquisition System
COMSAT—Communications Satellite Corporation
CPU—Central processing unit
CRT—Cathode ray tube
CTD—Conductivity, temperature, and depth
CUEA—Coastal Upwelling Ecosystem Analysis (Project)
CW—Continuous wave
CZCS—Coastal Zone Color Scanner
DART—Data Acquisition in Real-Time (System)
DEC—Digital Equipment Corporation
DECCA—A radio navigational aid
DMSP—Defense Meteorological Satellite Program
Early Bird—First commercial communications satellite

EDIS--Environmental Data and Information Service
EPIC—Equatorial Pacific Information Collection
EPOCS—Equatorial Pacific Ocean Climate Studies
ERS—ESA's Remote Sensing Satellite
ERS—Japan's Earth Resources Satellite
ESA—European Space Agency
ESIC—Environmental Science Information Center
ESSA—Environmental Science Services Administration
Ethernet—A local area network defined by DEC, Intel, and Xerox
FFT—Fast Fourier transform
FLIP—SIO research vessel that can be flipped vertically
FNOC—Fleet Numerical Oceanographic Center
FOSS—Fiber Optic Sensing System
g—The acceleration due to gravity, 9.8 meters per second
GARP—Global Atmosphere Research Program
GEMINI—Manned space flight
GEONAV—A passive navigation system designed for geophysical studies
GEONET—A satellite ground and transmission network
GEOS—Geostationary Operational Environmental Satellite
GEOSAT—Geodetic Satellite
GEOSTAR—A geosynchronous satellite for message transmissions
GEOTRAC—A radio navigation system developed by Texas Instruments
Gigabyte (Gb)—One billion bytes
GPS--Global Positioning System
GRM—Geopotential Research Mission
GSBP—General Service Buoy Payload
HDDR—High-density digital recorder
HDUE—Prototype GPS P code receiver (Texas Instruments)
IBM—Internatioanl Business Machines
IEEE—Institute of Electrical and Electronic Engineers
IGADS—IRIS General Automated Data System
INMARSAT--International Maritime Satellite Organization
IRIS--Interactive Real-Time Information System
ITSA—Interactive Time—Series Analysis
ITT—International Telephone and Telegraph
K—Denotes 1,000 or 1,024 when describing computer memory
Kilo—A unit of measure equal to 1,000
Kilobits (Kbit)—A unit of measure equal to 1,000 bits
Kilobyte (Kb)--A unit of measure equal to 1,000 bytes
Kilohertz—A measure of frequency equal to 1,000 cycles per second
Kilometer—A unit of measure equal to 1,000 meters
LDGO—Lamont—Doherty Geological Observatory
LAMDA—A radio navigational aid
LAN—Local area network
LINS—Litton Inertial Navigation System
LORAN—A radio-navigation aid
LSI—Large-scale integrated
MARISAT—Maritime satellite
MEDBIN—MARMAP Ecosystem Data Base Information (system)
Mega—A unit of measure equal to 1,000,000
Megabit (Mbit)—A unit of measure equal to 1,000,000 bits
Megabyte (Mb)—A unit of measure equal to 1,000,000 bytes
Megahertz—A measure of frequency equal to 1,000,000 cycles per second

Milliampere—A unit of current denoting one-thousandth of an ampere
Millimeter—A unit of measure denoting one-thousandth of a meter
MIT—Massachusetts Institute of Technology
MOS—A Japanese sun-synchronous orbital satellite
NASA—National Aeronautics and Space Administration
NAVOCEANO—Naval Oceanographic Office
NCC—National Climate Center
NCSC—Naval Coastal Systems Center
NDBO—NOAA Data Buoy Office
NESS—National Earth Satellite Service
NGSDC—National Geophysical and Solar—Terrestrial Data Center
NIMBUS—A meteorological satellite
NOAA—National Oceanic and Atmospheric Association
NODC—National Oceanographic Data Center
NODDS—Navy Oceanographic Data Distribution System
NORDA—Naval Oceanographic Research and Development Activity
NOS—National Ocean Service
NRL—Naval Research Laboratory
NROSS—Navy Remote Ocean Sensing System
NSF—National Science Foundation
NUSC—Naval Underwater Systems Center
NUSL—Naval Underwater Sound Laboratory
NUWC—Naval Underwater Weapons Center
OAD—Ocean Assessment Division
ODS—Oceanographic Data System
OSU—Oregon State University
PC—Personal computer
PCM—pulse code modulated
P code—Military GPS transmitted information
PDR—Precision depth recorder
pixel—Smallest addressable picture element in electronic display
PMEL—Pacific Marine Environmental Laboratory
PODS—Pilot Ocean Data System
POSEIDON—French satellite that uses altimetry
PROM—Programmable read only memory
RADARSET—Canadian satellite to monitor sea ice
RAM—Random access memory
RGB—Red, green, and blue
ROM—Read only memory
RS232—Computer communications standard
R/V—Research vessel
SAIL—Serial ASCII Interface Loop
SAR—INFERMER towed acoustic sonar system
SASS—Sonar Array Sounding System
S code—Civilian (C/A) GPS transmitted information
SDA—Seismic Data Analysis
SDSD—Satellite Data Services Division
Sea Beam—Multi-beam sonar system
SeaMARC—Sea Mapping and Remote Characterization (System)
SEAOPS—Sonar Evaluation Acoustic Operational Processing System
SEAS—Shipboard Environmental Data Acquisition System
SEASAT—First satellite dedicated to oceanography
SDS—Scientific Data Systems

SIO—Scripps Institution of Oceanography
SKYLAB—First U.S. manned space station (1973—1974)
SMS—Synchronous Meteorological Satellite
SPADA—Sound Propagation Digital Analysis
SSMI—Special Sensor Microwave Imager
STD—Salinity, temperature, and depth
SYNBAPS—Synthetic Bathymetry Processing System
TI—Texas Instruments
TIROS—Television Infrared Observation Satellite
TOGA—Tropical Ocean Global Atmosphere
TOPEX—Topography experiment
TTL—Transistor—transistor logic
UNIX—Software operating system copyrighted by Bell Laboratory
UNOLS—University—National Oceanographic Laboratory ships
USGS—U.S. Geological Survey
VCR—Video cassette recorder
WHOI—Woods Hole Oceanographic Institution
XBT—Expendable bathythermograph

REFERENCE

1. K. E. Perry and P. F. Smith, "The Importance of Digital Techniques for Oceanographic Instrumentation," *Ocean Sci. Eng.*, *1*, 398—404 (1965).

2. J. D. Mudie, "Applications of Sea-Going Computers," in *Under Sea Technology Handbook Directory*, 1969, pp. A/3—A/7.

3. D. Steiger and J. D. Clamons, "NRL's Oceanographic Computer Systems: Present Capabilities and Future Enhancements," Working Conference on Oceanographic Data Systems, WHOI, Woods Hole, MA, 1975, pp. 57-70.

4. Sea Technology Staff, "Basic Radiopositioning Systems Spawn Versatile Offshoots," *Sea Technol.*, 26—31 (March 1978).

5. J. L. Hoerber, "An update on Worldwide Navigation Ssytems—The Present and the Year 2000," *Sea Technol.*, 10—13 (March 1981).

6. D. W. Porta, "An Acoustic Navigation System for Offshore Positioning Applications," *Sea Technol.*, 18—20 (May 1977).

7. L. L. Booda, "Satellite Navigation: Technology Transfer from Military to Civil Use," *Sea Technol.*, 19-22 (June 1981).

8. T. A. Stansell, "Meeting the GPS Challenge," *Sea Technol.*, 48,51,53, 55,70,71 (April 1983).

9. P. F. MacDoran, "Codeless GPS Positioning Offers Sub-Meter Accuracy," *Sea Technol.*, 10—12 (October 1984).

10. N. Zinn, "Is There Life After GPS," *Sea Technol.*, 85 (March 1984).

11. J. C. Fuechsel, "Global Positioning: A New Policy Form with an Enthusiastic Following," *Sea Technol.*, 26—28 (November 1981).

12. P. Chappell, "Computerized Navigation System-Key to Future Petroleum Exploration," *Sea Technol.*, 10—16 (March 1976).

13. W. L. Whalen, "Geostar Positioning System Using Satellite Technology," *Sea Technol.*, 31—34 (March 1984).

14. G. L. Lawrence, "Electronics in Oceanography," Howard W. Sams, 1967, pp. 7—20.

15. C. Bowin and J. Allen, "Geophysical Data Base and Processing System," in *Fourth Working Symposium on Oceanographic Data Systems*, IEEE, SIO, La Jolla, CA, 1986, pp. 178-183.
16. E. E. Clark and B. Matthews, "Experience With Shipborne Computer Systems for Research and Survey Applications," in *Electronic Engineering in Ocean Technology*, 1970, pp. 211–278.
17. J. W. Harford and E. D. Van Reenan, "Data Recording Device for Underwater Instrumentation," *Instrum. Soc. Am. 1,* 88–90 (1961).
18. E. H. Coughran, "Scope of Current Usage of Shipboard Computers," in *Transactions of the Applications of Sea Going Computers*, 1969, pp. 5–9.
19. T. E. Ewart, "Design Philosophy and Operational Experiences of a Seagoing Computer and Data Acquisition System," in *Transactions of the Applications of Sea Going Computers*, 1969, pp. 159–174.
20. T. L. Holcombe, "An Experiment in Computer Processing of Oceanographic Data Aboard the USNS KANE," in *Transactions of the Applications of Sea Going Computers*, 1969, 45–61.
21. C. D. Lowenstein, "Navigation and Data Logging for the MPL Deep Tow," in *Transactions of the Applications of Sea Going Computers*, 1969, pp. 91–98.
22. P. G. Hansen, "A Sea Going UNIVAC 1218 Interfaced with NUWC's Thermistor Chain," in *Transactions of Sea Going Computers*, 1969, pp. 105–114.
23. R. W. Hasse and R. L. Martin, "Real-Time Processing of Acoustic Oceanographic Data at Sea," in *Transactions of Sea Going Computers*, 1969, pp. 115–130.
24. D. J. Mabey, "An Automatic Data Logging and Computing System for the Hydrographer of the Royal Navy," in *Transactions of Sea Going Computers*, 1969, pp. 175–186.
25. E. E. Jones, "Computer Data Acquisition Systems Aboard ESSA Survey Ships," in *Transactions of Sea Going Computers*, 1969, pp. 201–207.
26. K. J. Fein and D. G. Williams, "Development and Use of Portable Digital Computer Systems for Submarine Experiments," in *Transactions of Sea Going Computers*, 1969, pp. 209–222.
27. T. A. Stansell, "Extended Applications of the TRANSIT Satellite Navigation System," in *Magnavox Research Laboratories Technical Report*, MX-TR-2018-71, 1971.
28. R. Evans, O. Brown, and J. Van Leer, "Computers at Sea: Is Satellite Communication a Viable Alternative?," in *Working Conference on Oceanographic Data Systems*, WHOI, Woods Hole, MA, 1975, pp. 81-94.
29. J. Eskinzes and J. D. Clamons, "Accessing Shipboard Computers Through Satellite Links," NRL Memorandum, 1981.
30. J. D. Clamons, J. M. Brozena, and L. J. Rosenblum, "Marine Gravity Measurement System for Fixed Winged Aircraft," in *Third Working Symposium on Oceanographic Data Systems*, 1983, pp. 15–21.
31. J. R. McCullough, "A digital Data Logging Technique for Remote Recording Instruments," in *Working Conference on Oceanographic Data Systems*, WHOI, Woods Hole, MA, 1975, pp. 72-77.
32. E. Kerut, L. Livingston, G. Haas, and J. Sharp, "Advantages and Limitations Associated with Satellite-Oceanographic Data Transmission Systems," in *Working Conference on Oceanographic Data Systems*, 1975, WHOI, Woods Hole, MA, pp. 109-139.

33. R. Mesecar and F. Evans, "A Partitioned Data Communications System," in *Second Working Conference on Oceanographic Data Systems,* WHOI, Woods Hole, MA, 1978, pp. 372-383.

34. M. McClure, "A Micro-Processor Based Data Acquisition System," in *Second Working Conference on Oceanographic Data Systems,* 1978, pp. 49–61.

35. E. J. Sottley, "The Microcomputers for ADOM," in *Second Working Conference on Oceanographic Data Systems,* 1978, pp. 62–69.

36. R. A. Robinson, J. W. Peterson, and E. L. Brickner, "Adaptable Data Acquisition and Processing System," in *Second Working Conference on Oceanographic Data Systems,* 1978, pp. 112–118.

37. D. T. Deihl, "A Flexible Digital, Multi-Channel, Real-Time Acoustic Processing System for Field and Shipboard Use," in *Second Working Conference on Oceanographic Data Systems,* 1975, pp. 119–130.

38. J. D. Clamons and D. Steiger, "Can Intelligent Terminals and Modern Calculators Replace Oceanographic Computer Systems?" in *Second Working Conference on Oceanographic Data Systems,* 1978, pp. 152–164.

39. R. Seynaeve, "Real-Time and Shipborne Processing at SACLANT Centre," in *Second Working Conference on Oceanographic Data Systems,* 1978, pp. 292–304.

40. M. A. Bahamondes, J. A. Vignolo, and H. F. Milovic, "Applications of Microcomputer Technology to Oceanographic Instruments," in *Third Working Symposium on Oceanographic Data Systems,* 1983, pp. 30–33.

41. E. Mellinger and M. Jones, "A Baseline SAIL System Controller," in *Third Working Symposium on Oceanographic Data Systems,* 1983, pp. 39–43.

42. A. M. Bradley and W. E. Terry, "A Coherent Approach to Instrument Inter-Communication and Testing Using SAIL," in *Third Symposium on Oceanographic Data Systems,* 1983, pp. 51–54.

43. R. N. Lobecker, P. D. Higly, and R. J. Robbins, "The DART System for Real-Time Acquisition of Oceanographic Data," in *Third Working Symposium on Oceanographic Data Systems,* 1983, pp. 64–68.

44. N. L. Brown, R. J. Robbins, and A. J. Fougere, "A Microprocessor Based Conductivity, Temperature and Depth Profiler," in *Third Working Symposium on Oceanographic Data Systems,* 1983, pp. 119–124.

45. S. C. Daubin, "Microcomputer Implementation of Current Data Reduction, Processing, and Display," in *Third Working Symposium on Oceanographic Data Systems,* 1983, pp. 125–128.

46. K. Prada, K. von der Heydt Koelsch, E. Mellinger, S. Liberatore, and F. Schuler, "A Deep Ambient Noise Spectra Recording Instrument," in *Third Working Symposium on Oceanographic Data Systems,* 1983, pp. 129–134.

47. S. K. Cook and V. Zegowitz, "An At-Sea Automated Data Acquisition and Satellite Transmission System," *Sea Technol.,* 48–49 (October 1983).

48. G. K. Barkley, W. P. Kruger, C. A. Halpeny, P. Lane, and J. R. England, "Design Evolution for a Sea-Going Automated Test System," in *Fourth Working Symposium on Oceanographic Data Systems,* IEEE, SIO, La Jolla, CA, pp. 106-109.

49. K. E. Prada, "Real-Time Ambient Noise Spectra Acquisition and Display," in *Fourth Working Symposium on Oceanographic Data Systems,* 1986, IEEE, SIO, La Jolla, CA, 1986, pp. 199-207.

50. B. A. Decina and J. S. Padgett, "A VAX-11/750 Based Ocean Acoustic Data Acquisition and Processing System for Shipboard and Laboratory Use," in *Fourth Working Symposium on Oceanographic Data Systems*, IEEE, SIO, La Jolla, CA, 1986, pp. 137-144.

51. C. Dorian, "The Mariner's Satellite," *Sea Technol.*, 14–15 (May 1975).

52. L. B. Heitman, "Geophysical Data Move Faster by Satellite," *Sea Technol.*, 10–13 (May 1982).

53. D. W. Lipke, "Planning for New Generation of Maritime Satellites," *Sea Technol.*, 19–20 (May 1983).

54. L. B. Heitman, "Marine Satellite Communications Update," *Sea Technol.*, 11–15 (May 1983).

55. R. D. McCormick, "The 'INMARSAT Interconnect'—High Speed Data Rides the Waves," *Sea Technol.*, 22–26 (August 1984).

56. J. R. Fricke, "Geophysical Applications of Satellite Data Communications," *Sea Technol.*, 10–14 (August 1983).

57. E. G. Kerut and G. Haas, "Geostationary and Orbiting Satellites Applied to Remote Ocean Buoy Data Acquisition," NOAA Technical Report 00E3, 1979.

58. A. E. Shaw, "Collecting and Disseminating Environmental Satellite Data," *Sea Technol.*, 60–64 (April 1985).

59. M. W. Szabados and C. M. Roman, "Upgrading Global Weather Forecasts with SEAS," *Sea Technol.*, 10,11,14 (August 1985).

60. G. A. Maul, "Introduction to Satellite Oceanography," Martinus Nijhoff, 1985, pp. 3–67.

61. B. H. Needham, "Satellite Data Handling," *14*(6), 41–46 (1981).

62. B. H. Needham, "U.S. Environmental Satellite Data," *Sea Technol.*, 38–39 (October 1981).

63. L. L. Booda, "Oceanography from Space: An Update," *Sea Technol.*, 10–15 (September 1984).

64. M. H. Byrne, "Satellite Data Processing for Oceanographic Research," *Marine Technol. Soc. J.*, *14*(6), 32–40 (1981).

65. L. L. Booda, "Satellites Come into Their Own in Earth Sensing," *Sea Technol.*, 10–11 (October 1981).

66. A. A. Mufti, *Elementary Computer Graphics*, Reston Publishing Company, 1982, p. 3.

67. A. Bridges, "Merging of Technology Accomplishes Realistic Scene Simulation," *Comput. Technol. Rev.*, 145–153 (Summer 1985).

68. *Sea Technology* Staff, "Interactive Graphics Eases Managing Ocean Data from Space," *Sea Technol.*, 41–45 (February 1984).

69. D. Friedman, "Versatile Imaging Sonar Enhances Underwater Operations," *Sea Technol.*, 38,41,43,44 (April 1984).

70. M. Czarnecki and J. Bergin, "Statistical Characterization of Small-Scale Bottom Topography as Derived from Multibeam Sonar Data," in *Fourth Working Symposium on Oceanographic Data Systems*, IEEE, SIO, La Jolla, CA, 1986, pp. 15-24.

71. J. M. Augustin, "Side Scan Acoustic Images Processing Software," in *Fourth Working Symposium on Oceanographic Data Systems*, IEEE, SIO, La Jolla, CA, 1986, pp. 221-228.

72. W. A. Kruse and R. W. Schmieder, "High-Resolution Graphic Images of EEZ Data: Cordell Bank California," in *Fourth Working Symposium on Oceanographic Data Systems*, IEEE, SIO, La Jolla, CA, 1986, pp. 4-13.

73. J. G. Kosalos, "Sonar Developments Catalyze Mapping Technology Progress," *Sea Technol.*, 28-31 (November 1983).

74. L. J. Rosenblum, "Digital Imaging of Ocean Temperature Fine-Structure Patches," in *Fourth Working Symposium on Oceanographic Data Systems*, IEEE, SIO, La Jolla, CA, 1986, pp. 208-210.

75. E. P. Ruzecki, P. V. Hyer, K. Kiley, and M. S. Jablonsky, "Imaging System Techniques Applied to Analysis of Hydraulic and Finite Element Model Experiment Results," in *Fourth Working Symposium on Oceanographic Data Systems*, IEEE, SIO, La Jolla, CA, 1986, pp. 211-220.

76. S. Gordon, S. Borders, and M. Guberek, "An Interactive Data Processing Workstation for the Ocean Sciences," in *Fourth Working Symposium on Oceanographic Data Systems*, IEEE, SIO, La Jolla, Ca, 1986, pp. 52-53.

77. J. Baker, "SQL: A New Standard," *Computerworld Focus*, 55-58 (February 19, 1986).

78. P. Hughes, "NOAA's EDIS Ocean Data Used Worldwide," *Sea Technol.*, 10-14,30 (February 1981).

79. J. Rix and J. C. Kelly, "Standard Data Files—A Standardized Data Base System," in *Second Working Conference on Oceanographic Data Systems*, WHOI, Woods Hole, MA, 1978, pp. 410-436.

80. S. Lazanoff, "The Naval Oceanographic Data Distribution System," *Sea Technol.*, 38-39 (September 1983).

81. P. A. Bolduc and H. A. C. Jones, "Marine Data Inventory," in *Third Working Symposium on Oceanographic Data Systems*, 1983, pp. 173-177.

82. S. E. Dixon, "NOAA's Data Atlases, Data Bases," *Sea Technol.*, 16-17 (August 1985).

83. R. L. Sand, J. R. Goulet, and S. H. Koelb, "The Design and Management of a Large Ecosystem Database Using a Scientific Database Management System," in *Fourth Working Symposium on Oceanographic Data Systems*, IEEE, SIO, La Jolla, CA, 1986, pp. 169-173.

84. A. E. Shaw, "Collecting and Disseminating Environmental Satellite Data," *Sea Technol.*, 60-64 (April 1985).

85. E. L. Wright and J. P. Hosom, "Seismic-Reflector Database Software," in *Fourth Working Symposium on Oceanographic Data Systems*, IEEE, SIO, La Jolla, CA, 1986, pp. 184-190.

86. T. Cerwonka, "Advantages of Scientific Relational Databases," in *Fourth Working Symposium on Oceanographic Data Systems*, IEEE, SIO, La Jolla, CA, 1986, pp. 191-195.

87. Adm. J. B. Mooney, "Advancing the State of Ocean Science," *Sea Technol.*, 30-35 (January 1986).

88. W. D. Barbee, "U.S. Academic Research Fleet: Status and Plans for Orderly Replacement," *Sea Technol.*, 27-30 (January 1986).

89. P. Harmon and D. King, *Expert Systems: Artificial Intelligence in Business*, John Wiley, New York, 1985, pp. 1-12.

90. J. J. Pan, "Fiber Optics for Undersea Applications," *Sea Technol.*, 18-24 (November 1983).

91. C. M. Davis and R. E. Einzig, "ASW: What Role Will Fiber Optics Play?" *Sea Technol.*, 20-23 (November 1979).

SELECTED BIBLIOGRAPHY

Abbott, J. L. G. S. Morris, and J. D. Mudie, "Scripps' Seagoing Computer Centers," in *Transactions of the Applications of Sea Going Computers,* 1969, pp. 187–200.

Abbott, J. L., S. M. Smith, J. S. Charters, P. G. Downes, T. Hylas, R. L. Moe, J. M. Moore, and D. V. Stuber, "Scripps Seagoing Computer Centers: Real-Time Data Acquisition and Processing," in *Fourth Working Symposium on Oceanographic Data Systems,* 1986, pp. 123–129.

"Acquiring Data in Deepwater Operations," *Ocean Ind.,* 57 (August 1982).

Anderson, G. M., "Mobile Satellite System Will Serve Remote Areas," *Sea Technol,* 19–22 (May 1984).

Anderson, V. C., W. S. Hodgkiss, J. C. Nickles, and G. L. Edmonds, "A High Speed Recording System," in *Fourth Working Symposium on Oceanographic Data Systems,* 1986, pp. 98–105.

Apel, J. R., "Some Recent Scientific Results From the Seasat Altimeter," *Sea Technol.,* 21,23–25,27 (October 1982).

Appell, G., "A Real-Time Current Monitoring System," *Sea Technol.,* 10–12, 15 (February 1984).

Austin, T., "Remote Sensing and Fisheries," *Sea Technol.,* 21–22 (January 1981).

Austin, T. S., "Changes and Challenges in Ocean Data and Information Services," *Sea Technol.,* 12–14,33 (February 1978).

Balboni, M. J. and W. E. Walsh, "The Expendable Sound Velocimeter (XSV)," *Sea Technol.,* 38–40,42 (November 1978).

Barbagelata, A., "The Present SACLANTCEN Equipment for the Digital Recording of Multichannel Broadband Acoustic Signals, Their Edition and Their Transfer to a Digital Computer," in *Digital Analysis Working Group at SACLANTCEN,* May 1971, pp. 7–16.

Barbagelata, A. and B. Diess, "A Conversational Processing System of Acoustic Data for Use on Land and at Sea: SPADA," in *Digital Analysis Working Group at SACLANTCEN,* May 1971, pp. 50–69.

Bender, E., "Drifting Buoys Collect Meteorological Data," *Sea Technol.,* 25–27 (August 1978).

Bender, E., "New Techniques Advance Marine Geophysical Survey," *Sea Technol.,* 10-13 (September 1978).

Bender, E., "NAVSTAR Passes Sea Trials," *Sea Technol.,* 29–30 (March 1979).

Bender, E., "Satellite, Radio Teletype Communications Grow," *Sea Technol.,* 10–13 (May 1979).

Bender E., "Director System Has Marine Surveys," *Sea Technol.,* 39–46 (September 1979).

Bender, E., "INMARSAT Plan 1982 Deployment," *Sea Technol.,* 16–17 (May 1980).

Bennett, A. S., "Computer Data Display," in *Transactions of the Applications of the Sea Going Computers,* 1969, pp. 99–103.

Bennett, A. S., C. S. Mason, and E. A. Bendell, "The Bedford Institute Shipboard Data Logging System," in *Transactions of the Applications of Sea Going Computers,* 1969, pp. 63–69.

Booda, L. L., "Marisat Takes First Operational Step," *Sea Technol.,* 10–12 (May 1976).

Booda, L. L., "NAVSTAR: Three Dimensional Satellite Positioning with Ten Meter Accuracy," *Sea Technol.,* 19–21 (March 1977).

Booda, L. L., "Oceanographers Check Nutrients with AutoAnalyzers," *Sea Technol.*, 34–35 (November 1978).

Booda, L. L., "Omega Becomes Worldwide System," *Sea Technol.*, 20-21 (May 1980).

Booda, L. L., "Satellites Aid Surveys, Data Transmission: Geophysical Exploration Grows More Sophisticated," *Sea Technol.*, 10–13 (October 1980).

Booda, L. L., "SURTASS, RDSS Augment Ocean Surveillance," *Sea Technol.*, 19–20 (November 1981).

Booda, L. L., "Integration of U.S. Radio-Navigation Systems," *Sea Technol.*, 22–25 (March 1982).

Booda, L. L., "Seasat Research Could Make Ocean 'Transparent' for ASW," *Sea Technol.*, 10–14 (November 1983).

Booda, L. L., "Civil Use of Navstar GPS—A Matter of Debate," *Sea Technol.*, 17–18 (March 1984).

Booda, L. L., "Navigation Accuracy Depends on Naval Observatory Time," *Sea Technol.*, 55–58 (March 1985).

Booda, L. L., W. S. Wilson, and W. C. Patzert, "Oceanography from Space: An Update," *Sea Technol.*, 10–13 (September 1984).

Boutacoff, D. A., "Navstar Forecast: Cloudy Now, Clear Later," *Def. Electron.*, 90,92,94,96,99–100 (May 1986).

Bowin, C. O., "Experience with a Sea-Going Computer Systes: Lessons, Recommendations, and Predictions," in *Transactions of the Applications of Sea Going Computers*, 1969, pp. 141–157.

Bowra, J. W., "The Honeywell Array Processor Family: Faster and Smaller, on Less Power," *Sea Technol.*, 65–68 (April 1982).

Bradley, A. M. and D. L. Dorson, "A Microprocessor-Based Acoustic Correlator," in *Second Working Conference on Oceanographic Data Systems*, 1978, pp. 70–80.

Branham, D. W., "Shipboard Oceanographic Survey System," *Mar. Technol., Soc.*, *1*, 341–362 (1965).

Brozena, J. M., A Preliminary Analysis of the NRL Airborne Gravimetry System," *Geophys. Soc.*, *49*(7), 1060–1069 (1984).

Christensen, J. L., "Theory and Performance of a Doppler Current Profiler," in *Third Working Symposium on Oceanographic Data Systems*, 1983, pp. 88–92.

Christensen, J. L., "A New Acoustic Doppler Current Profiler," *Sea Technol.*, 10–13 (February 1983).

Ciesluk, A. and F. C. W. Olson, "NCSC Environmental Measuring System," *Sea Technol.*, 20,23,25 (April 1979).

Clamons, J. D. and J. G. Eskinzes, "A Computer Interface to a Magnavox 706 Satellite Navigator," in *Working Conference on Oceanographic Data Systems*, 1975, pp. 26–37.

Clamons, J. D., J. M. Brozena, and L. J. Rosenblum, "A Marine Gravity Measurement System for Fixed Winged Aircraft," in *Third Working Symposium on Oceanographic Data Systems*, 1983, pp. 15–21.

Clark, J. W., R. B. Lawrence, and G. Flimlin, "Satellite Observed Oceanographic Analyses and Sea Surface Thermal Analyses," *NOAA NESS/NWS*, May 6, 1983.

Clay, A. F., "Shipboard Data Highway," in *Third Working Symposium on Oceanographic Data Systems*, 1983, pp. 69–73.

Clifford, P., "Real Time Seafloor Mapping," *Sea Technol.*, 22–26 (May 1979).

"Computer System Monitors Vessel Systems Efficiently," *Sea Technol.*, 60–61 (March 1983).

Covey, C. W., "Hydrographic Surveys at Sea in Real-Time," *Sea Technol.*, 18–19 (February 1974).

Covey, C. W., "Analog Computer Determines Ship Cargo Distribution," *Sea Technol.*, 20–21 (October 1974).

"Cubic's ARGO DM-54 System Makes Pinpoint Positioning a Reality," *Sea Technol.*, 21–22 (August 1978).

Dauphinee, T. M. and H. P. Klein, "A New Automated Laboratory Salino-meter," *Sea Technol.*, 23–25 (March 1975).

DeCarlo, G., "Computer Techniques for Offshore Corrosion Protection," *Sea Technol.*, 25–30,37 (September 1981).

"The Defense Meteorological Satellite Program," *Sea Technol.*, 37,39 (August 1983).

Digre, T., "Effective Utilization of Microprocessors for Shipboard Data Systems," in *Working Conference on Oceanographic Data Systems*, 1975, pp. 154–170.

Dingee, A. L. M., Jr. and A. F. Feyling, "Timing Control Methods Available for Self-Contained Recording Systems," Marine Sciences Publication, Publication of *Instrum. Soc. Am.*, 1, 77–79 (1961).

Dixon, T. H., M. Naraghi, M. K. McNutt, and S. M. Smith, "Bathymetric Prediction From SEASAT Altimeter Data," *J. Geophys. Res.*, 88(C3), 1563–1571 (1983).

Doutt, J. A., "Digital Acoustical Processing at Woods Hole," in *Digital Analysis Working Group at SACLANTCEN*, 1971, pp. 95–96.

Drummond, S. E., "SWATH Ship—Calming Seas for Operating Efficiency," *Sea Technol.*, 33–34 (August 1983).

Edy, C., "Automatic Mapping with Multibeam Echosounder Data," in *Fourth Working Symposium on Oceanographic Data Systems*, 1986, pp. 229–238.

Erskine, F. T., G. Bernstein, and E. R. Franchi, "Imaging Techniques for Analysis of Long-Range Acoustic Backscatter Data from Ocean Basin Regions," in *Third Working Symposium on Oceanographic Data Systems*, 1983, pp. 160–164.

Eschelbach, R. E., "Automatic Oceanographic Systems for Multipurpose Research Vessels," in *Second Working Conference on Oceanographic Data Systems*, 1978, pp. 211–241.

Evans, F. and R. Mesecar, "Common Computer Interface Advantages," in *Working Conference on Oceanographic Data Systems*, 1975, pp. 257–270.

Evans, R. H. and O. B. Brown, "Design and Implementation of a Software Analysis System for Support of Oceanographic Data and Satellite Image Processing," in *Second Working Conference on Oceanographic Data Systems*, 1978, pp. 305–317.

Evenden, G. I., "The MAPGEN Cartographic System," in *Fourth Working Symposium on Oceanographic Data Systems*, 1986, pp. 239–245.

Fitzpatrick, J. C., "Oceanographic Data Collection Systems," in *ISA Marine Sciences Division Symposium*, 1966.

Flittner, G. A., "Computers Are Better on the Shore," in *Transactions of the Applications of Sea Going Computers*, 1969, pp. 11–16.

Foley, J. D. and A. Van Dam, "Fundamentals of Interactive Computer Graphics," in *The Systems Programming Series*, Addison-Wesley Publishing Company, Reading, MA, 1982, pp. 1–28.

Fuechsel, J. C., "Satellite Issues Continue to Dominate NOIA TPC Programs," *Sea Technol.*, 49–52 (January 1986).

Galloway, J. L., "Applications of SAIL Systems at I. O. S.," in *Third Working Symposium on Oceanographic Data Systems*, 1983, pp. 74–77.

Garofalo, D., "Air and Spacecraft Remote Sensing Applied to Coastal Geomorphology," *Oceanogr. Mar. Biol. Ann. Rev.*, 17, 43–100 (1979).

Gautier, C. and M. Fieux, eds., *Large-Scale Oceanographic Experiments and Satellites, Series C: Mathematical and Physical Sciences*, D. Resdel Publishing Company, *128* (1983).

Gay, J. P., "The Role of Navigation for the Offshore Petroleum Industry," *Sea Technol.*, 24–29 (March 1983).

Georgi, D. T., R. C. Millard, and R. W. Schmitt, "Conductivity Microstructure Measurements with a CTD," in *Third Working Symposium on Oceanographic Data Systems*, 1983, pp. 5–14.

Giloi, W. K., "Interactive Computer Graphics," in *Data Structures, Algorithms, Languages*, Prentice-Hall, Englewood Cliffs, NJ, 1978, pp. 3–22.

Goody, R., "Satellites for Oceanography—The Promises and the Realities," *Oceanus*, 24(3), 3–5 (1981).

Gottholm, B., T. Bethem, and P. Eichelberger, "The Development of a Real-Time Acquisition System for the Collection and Display of Conductivity-Salinity-Temperature-Depth (CSTD) Data," in *Third Working Symposium on Oceanographic Data Systems*, 1983, pp. 34–38.

Graham, D. M., "Fifteen Years of Precise Positioning," *Sea Technol.*, 37–41 (March 1984).

Graham, D. M., "NOAA's Seattle Center Emphasizes 'Service'," *Sea Technol.*, 43–46 (March 1984).

Graham, D. M., "Instrumenting the NOAA Research Fleet," *Sea Technol.*, 22,23 (February 1985).

Grandvaux, G., "A Direct Digital/Acquisition System," in *Digital Analysis Working Group at SACLANTCEN*, 1971, pp. 25–27.

Hadsell, P., "Standards for Data Exchange," in *Working Conference on Oceanographic Data Systems*, 1975, pp. 272–275.

Hanson, W., "INMARSAT's 56-Kilobit Service for Seismic Surveys," *Sea Technol.*, 17 (August 1983).

Harmel, N. A. and R. S. Doar, "A Passive Ranging System for Marine Navigation," in *The Western Electric Engineer*, October 1972.

Hearn, D. and M. P. Baker, *Microcomputer Graphics Techniques and Applications*, Prentice-Hall, Englewood Cliffs, NJ, 1983.

Heitman, L. B., "A Multi-Function Data System for the Offshore Seismic Industry," *Sea Technol.*, 22,23,25,27,31 (September 1979).

Heitman, L. B., "Satellite Data Sommunications—The Technology Revolution Continues," *Sea Technol.*, 10–12,16 (May 1985).

Henderson, G. C., "Computer Methods for Analyzing Marine Gravity and Magnetic Data," *Mar. Technol. Soc.*, 1, 432–439 (1965).

Hodgkiss, W. S., V. C. Anderson, G. L. Edmonds, J. C. Nickles, and R. L. Culver, "A Freely Drifting Infrasonic Sensor System," in *Fourth Working Symposium on Oceanographic Data Systems*, 1986, pp. 79–84.

Hoff, B. J. and F. B. Chmelik, "Shallow Water Operations-Better Shallow Water Seismic Data," *Ocean Ind.*, 19–23 (June 1982).

Holland, C. R., R. T. Miles, and L. B. Stogner, "Adaptive Multiprocessor Data Acquisition System," in *Third Working Symposium on Oceanographic Data System*, pp. 55–59.

Hollinger, A. B. and J. F. R. Gower, "Programmable Imaging from the Air," *Sea Technol.*, 34–35 (August 1985).

Jaeger, J. E., "Evolution of Salinity/Temperature/Depth Instrumentation," *Sea Technol.*, 18–19 (June 1975).

Johnson, G. L., D. A. Horn, O. M. Johannessen, S. Martin, and R. D. Muench, "MIZEX," *Sea Technol.*, 18–22 (May 1985).

Johnson, J. D. and L. L. Booda, "Spacecraft Oceanography: Ocean Scientists Finally Have a Satellite to Call Their Own," *Sea Technol.*, 10–15 (October ±978).

Kalafus, R. M., "Differential GPS Standards, Satellite Navigation System Is a Promising New Tool of High Accuracy," *Sea Technol.*, 52–54 (March 1985).

Kao, C. N., "Future of Optical Fiber Systems for Undersea Applications," *Sea Technol.*, 13–15 (May 1980).

Kelley, J. C., "Portable Real-Time Minicomputer System Acquires and Displays Dynamic Ocean Data," *Sea Technol.*, 20–21, 23, 27 (February 1979).

Kelley, J. C. and C. S. Smyth, "Reduction and Presentation of Acoustic Reflection Data with the Aid of a Shipboard Computer," in *Transactions of the Applications of Sea Going Computers*, 35–44 (1969).

Kerut, E. G., O. Anderson, and D. P. Kozak, "Global Weather Experiment Shows Usefulness of Drifting Buoys," *Sea Technol.*, 23, 34–35 (June 1980).

Keyes, D., "Submarine Speed Measurement with Doppler Sonar," *Sea Technol.*, 26–30 (February 1984).

Kontopidis, G. D., "Design and Implementation of Streaming Tape Data Loggers," in *Fourth Working Symposium on Oceanographic Data Systems*, 1986, pp. 156–165.

LaBrecque, J. L. and E. Draganovic, "A General Purpose Computer System for Oceanographic Research Vessels," in *Second Working Conference on Oceanographic Data Systems*, 1978, pp. 242–253.

LaHain, P., "Telesystems Introduces New Low Cost Maritime Terminal," *Ocean Eng.*, 10(1), 77 (1983).

Lahore, H., "PRIME: The Seagoing Supermini Computer for You?," in *Second Working Conference on Oceanographic Data Systems*, 1978, pp. 164–169.

Lancaster, R. W., "Current Profiling in Near Real Time," *Sea Technol.*, 24–28 (February 1985).

Lancaster, R. W. and G. Baron, "Measuring ASW Oceanographic Parameters with XCTD Profiling Systems," *Sea Technol.*, 18, 19, 21, 23 (November 1984).

Latham, D. C., "The Federal Radionavigation Plan from a Department of Defense Perspective," *Sea Technol.*, 10–13 (March 1983).

Laufer, C. A., "Telemetry System Offers Deep Ocean High Data Rate," *Sea Technol.*, 29–33 (October 1984).

LeDrew, E. F. and S. E. Franklin, "Microcomputer Based Satellite Image Analysis," *DEC Professional*, 17–20, 22, 26–27, 29, 32–33 (December 1985).

Little, W. S., "Data Processing and Analysis in Oceanographic Research,"
    Sea Technol., 10–17 (February 1980).
LoVecchio, J. A., "Planning Marine Radionavigation Systems, National
    Decision on Future Systems Mix Is Expected in 1987," *Sea Technol.*,
    61–63 (March 1985).
Lydecker, R., "Remote Sensing of Waves Successful," *Sea Technol.*, 29–30
    (February 1981).
Malkin, B., "NRL Scientists Develop Improved Maser Clock," *NRL Labstracts*,
    November 29, 1985, p. 1.
Marchal, A. W., "SPOT Radiopositioning System, Eliminating Skywaves as
    a Range-Limiting Factor," *Sea Technol.*, 16–18 (March 1985).
Martin, R. L., "Real-Time Processing of Acoustic and Oceanographic Data
    at Sea," in *Digital Analysis Working Group at SACLANTCEN*, 1971,
    pp. 48–49.
McCann, M. J. and R. J. Panter, "The ARL Shipborne Computer System,"
    in *Digital Analysis Working Group at SACLANTCEN*, 1971, pp. 17–18.
McFarlane, C. F. and J. T. Byrne, "Improving the Success Rate In Obtain-
    ing Oceanographic Data," *Sea Technol.*, 19–21,44 (November 1977).
Mesecar, R. and W. Dillion, "Proposal for the Exchange and Recording
    Media of Research Vessel Parameter Data (SAIL)," in *Third Working
    Symposium on Oceanographic Data Systems*, 1983, pp. 179–182.
Mesecar, R., J. Wagner, and L. Powers, "A Digital Instrumentation Sys-
    tem for Vertical Profiling of Ocean Parameters," in *Third Working
    Symposium on Oceanographic Data Systems*, 1983, pp. 97–102.
Mesecar, R., J. Wagner, W. Dillon, and O. Page, "A Digital Measurement
    and Control System Coupled with an Undulating Profiler," in *Fourth
    Working Symposium on Oceanographic Data Systems*, 1986, pp. 85–89.
Miller, H. C., "A Coastal Data System for Long-Term Comprehensive
    Measurements of Nearshore Processes," in *Fourth Working Symposium
    on Oceanographic Data Systems*, 1986, pp. 62–69.
"Minicomputers Aid Oceanographic Research," *Sea Technol.*, 26–29
    (September 1978).
Montgomery, B. O., "NAVSTAR GPS-A Giant Step for Navigation and
    Positioning," *Sea Technol.*, 22–23 (March 1984).
Morgan, J. G., "Uses of Navigation Satellites by Oil Explorers," *Sea
    Technol.*, 10–13 (March 1982).
Morris, C. C., "Getting the Data Back: Update on Inmarsat," *Sea Technol.*,
    10–12 (May 1984).
Morris, W. P., J. P. Dugan, B. S. Okawa, C. W. Martz, and W. P. Rudd,
    "Towed Thermistor System for Marine Research," in *Third Working
    Symposium on Oceanographic Data Systems*, 1983, pp. 147–153.
Mortensen, E., "Data Bases Move In," *Computer Focus*, February 19, 1986,
    pp. 49–54.
Morton, R. W. and R. D. Jones, "Accuracy: Key to Sampling Success,"
    Sea Technol., 23–26 (August 1985).
Moyer, J. R. and N. Raimondo, "The New Integrated Navigation Systems,"
    Sea Technol., 18–19 (September 1975).
Mulcahy, M., "U.S. LORAN C Coverage: An Update," *Sea Technol.*, 15,17,
    42–43 (March 1977).
Mulcahy, M., "The U.S. Research Vessel Fleet," *Sea Technol.*, 24–28 (June
    1977).

Mulcahy, M., "A Solid State Water Current Meter for Wave Direction Sensing," *Sea Technol.*, 14–16 (July 1978).

Mulcahy, M., "University of Miami's Rosenstiel: Oceanography Flourishing in South Florida," *Sea Technol.*, 17–20 (February 1979).

Mulcahy, M., "Transition From MARISAT to INMARSAT Is Expected to Be Smooth in 1982," *Sea Technol.*, 17–20 (May 1981).

Mulcahy, M., "Sixteen Years of Ocean Instrumentation," *Sea Technol.*, 20–21 (February 1982).

Mulcahy, M., "Positioning a Critical Factor in Summit Geophysical Surveys," *Sea Technol.*, 14–18 (March 1982).

Mulcahy, M., "Scripps Marine Physical Laboratory 30 Years of Excellence in Ocean Research," *Sea Technol.*, 24–28 (June 1983).

"Multibeam Bathymetric Swath Survey Systems," *Sea Technol.*, 28–31 (June 1982).

Munro, D. F., "A New Ocean/Meteorological Data Buoy," *Sea Technol.*, 35–39 (April 1983).

Nagy, A., "Navigation and Positioning Systems Come of Age," *Sea Technol.*, 11-13 (March 1977).

"NOAA's Environmental Research Laboratories," *Sea Technol.*, 26–27 (October 1981).

"Oceanographic Data, Tactical Lifeblood of the U.S. Fleet," *Sea Technol.*, 10–15 (February 1982).

O'Hagan, R. M., and P. F. Smith, "The Use of a Small Computer with Real-Time Techniques for Oceanographic Data Acquisition, Immediate Analysis, and Presentation," *Mar. Technol. Soc.*, 1, 458–471 (1965).

Orrick-Johnson, M., "Electronic Chart Applications, VIEWNAV Systems Find Their Way into the Maritime Community," *Sea Technol.*, 38–42 (April 1985).

Ostenso, N. A., "An Ocean Renaissance," *Sea Technol.*, 81 (September 1965).

Ott, G. E., and P. Chappell, "Conquering Marine Positioning Problems," *Sea Technol.*, 22,24,26 (March 1985).

Padgett, J. S., and D. M. Dundore, "A VAX-Based Data Acquisition and Processing System for Multichannel Acoustic Data," in *Fourth Working Symposium on Oceanographic Data Systems*, 1986, pp. 130–136.

Pasque, G., and D. Goodfellow, "Automated Position Fixing," *Sea Technol.*, 40–41 (March 1981).

Pearson, C. A., G. A. Krancus, and R. L. Charnell, "R2D2: An Interactive Graphics Program for Rapid Retrieval and Display of Oceanographic Data," in *Second Working Conference on Oceanographic Data Systems*, 1978, pp. 318–329.

Pierson, C. B., Jr., "A High-Precision Radio-Positioning Offshore Navigation Buoy," *Sea Technol.*, 35–39 (March 1982).

Quartley, C., "Navigation/Positioning System for Mediterranean Pipeline Survey," *Sea Technol.*, 25–27 (March 1981).

"Raydist-76 Offers Third Shore Station," *Sea Technol.*, 17–18 (March 1976).

Reynolds, M., "A Simple Meteorological Buoy with Satellite Telemetry," *Ocean Eng.*, 10(1), 65–76 (1983).

Richards, C. Z., "Tracking ROV's Acoustically," *Sea Technol.*, 10–14 (March 1985).

Riordan, A., and Sethu Raman, "Keeping an Eye on Winter Storms," *Sea Technol.*, 18–21 (August 1985).

Robb, D., "From Sextant to Satellite: Institute Follows Navigation Growth," *Sea Technol.*, 14–15 (March 1981).

Robb, D., "Data Acquisition Company Celebrates Tenth Anniversary," *Sea Technol.*, 38–39 (October 1982).

Robb, D., "Precision Instrument Manufacturer Finds Worldwide Ocean Market," *Sea Technol.*, 28–30 (August 1982).

Rougeau, A., "Echoscan Fills in the Gaps," *Sea Technol.*, 36–38 (August 1985).

Ryan, J. W., and Ma Chopo, "A Small Data Base Handler for Scientific Applications," in *Second Working Conference on Oceanographic Data Systems*, 1978, pp. 330–342.

"Satellite Communications," *Sea Technol.*, 13,15–16 (May 1977).

Scrivens, R. F., "Wave Detection by Buoy," *Sea Technol.*, 25–28 (February 1981).

"SEASAT—An Ocean-Dedicated Satellite," *Sea Technol.*, 33–36 (May 1978).

Sentz, J. D., and J. D. Wiley, "Radar's Growing Problem in Ice, Pollution Surveillance," *Sea Technol.*, 27–29 (August 1985).

Seynaeve, R., "The SACLANTCEN Interactive Time Series Analysis System," in *Digital Analysis Working Group at SACLANTCEN*, 1971, pp. 85–94.

Sikorski, R. W., "Positioning Accuracy: An Economical Approach," *Sea Technol.*, 28–32,68 (March 1985).

Smith, J. G., "A New High Precision Range/Azimuth Position Fixing System," *Sea Technol.*, 33–36 (March 1983).

Smutz, M., "Applications of Optical Fibers at Sea," *MTS Ocean Sci. Eng.*, 9(4), 457–465 (1984–1985).

Smutz, M., "Fiber Optics At Sea," *MTS Ocean Sci. Eng.*, 9(4), 447–456 (1984–1985).

Spencer, D. W., "Ocean Science and Ships," *Oceanus*, 25(1), 3–14 (1982).

Stanley, H. R., "The Geos 3 Project," *J. Geophys. Res.*, 24, 3779–3783 (1979).

Stansell, T. A., "The Global Positioning System," *Sea Technol.*, 35–38 (January 1984).

Steiger, D., "Real-Time Oceanographic Data Acquisition Systems Aboard Aircraft," in *Third Working Symposium on Oceanographic Data Systems*, 1983, pp. 27–29.

Stephenson, A. G., "New Methods in Hydrographic Survey," *Sea Technol.*, 21-23,38–39 (March 1978).

Stewart, R. H., "Satellite Oceanography: The Instruments," *Oceanus*, 24 (3), 66–75 (1981).

Sullivan, D. H., "Seismic Data Processing: Yesterday, Today, and Tomorrow," *Sea Technol.*, 16–19 (February 1982).

Talwani, M., J. Dorman, and R. Kittredge, "Experiences with Computers Aboard Research Vessels VEMA and ROBERT D. CONRAD," in *Transactions of the Applications of Sea Going Computers*, 1969, pp. 17–25.

"Telemetering Wave and Current Data in Real Time," *Sea Technol.*, 32–34 (September 1983).

Thompson, D., "An Acoustic Processor for ASW Use," *Sea Technol.*, 16–17 (November 1977).

Tollios, G., "The Future Role of Computers in Supporting Oceanographic Research at Sea," in *Second Working Conference on Oceanographic Data Systems*, 1978, pp. 170–183.

Torsen, H. O., J. M. Hovem, and T. Knucsen, "Instrumentation Of An Underwater Vehicle for High Precision Topographic Surveys," North-Holland Publishing Company, ±976.

Tripe, R. L. K., "Automated Data Acquisition and Processing within the Canadian Hydrographic Service," in *Second Working Conference on Oceanographic Data Systems*, 1978, pp. 406–409.

"Undersea Cable Communication Offers Improvements Over Satellites," *Sea Technol.*, 19–20 (December 1974).

Vigliotti, V., J. E. Coolahan, D. L. James, and R. E. Ball, "A Small Oceanographic Data Acquisition (SODA) System," in *Fourth Working Symposium on Oceanographic Data Systems*, 1986, pp. 114–122.

Vito, J., and R. Mesecar, "Input/Output Communicator for the Magnavox (706) Satellite Navigation Systems," in *Working Conference on Oceanographic Data Systems*, 1975, pp. 15–25.

Voss, A. J. R., J. Sherwood, C. S. Jackson, and F. P. Bilimoria, "A Standards Based Distributed Oceanographic Computing System," in *Fourth Working Symposium on Oceanographic Data Systems*, 1986, pp. 145–154.

Voyles, Q., and D. Clayton, "A Submersible-Based Data Display and Data Logging Systems," in *Fourth Working Symposium on Oceanographic Data Systems*, 1986, pp. 70–78.

Wagner, J., and R. Msescar, "DECODE: A simple Algorithm for Digital Data System and Database Applications," in *Fourth Working Symposium on Oceanographic Data Systems*, 1986, pp. 58–61.

Washington, R., "The Advanced Signal Processor (ASP) for ASW," *Sea Technol.*, 20–25 (February 1980).

"Watching At-Sea Weather Automatically," *Sea Technol.*, 25,27–31 (August 1983).

White, H. H., "The Potential Role of Remote Sensing in Marine Pollution Monitoring," *Sea Technol.*, 15–19 (October 1981).

Wilson, W. S., "Oceanography from Satellites?," *Oceanus*, 24(3), 10–16 (1981).

Wood, V., "Collecting Data in the Ice Age," *Sea Technol.*, 36–37 (February 1985).

Wunsch, C., "The Promise of Satellite Altimetry," *Oceanus*, 24(3), 17–26 (1981).

DANIEL STEIGER

OPTICAL CHARACTER RECOGNITION

INTRODUCTION

Optical character recognition (OCR) refers to the ability of a machine to automatically read printed characters that reside on some machine-scannable medium such as paper. Although document and page reading are the most common applications for OCR, the function is also employed in many special-purpose media applications such as reading characters from microfilm, stamped numbers on parts in a manufacturing line, price and stock numbers on merchandise labels for sales and inventory controls, and characters keyed on a display for the quality testing of computer keyboards.

With the growth of computer technology, the need for OCR machines became quickly apparent. With the high speeds of data processing, a major concern of the user has been how to enter data into the computer efficiently. Because the primary method of data entry is manual keying, the data entry personnel become a major portion of the total data processing costs. This cost continues to increase as labor rates escalate. Therefore, it was savings in data entry costs that provided the necessary justification to develop commercial OCR machines that would automatically convert data from human-readable form to computer-usable input.

Although research has been going on in the OCR field for more than 100 years, it was not until 1951 that David Shephard designed the first commercial OCR reader [1]. His company, Intelligent Machines Research Corporation (which later became part of Farrington and now Lundy-Farrington), built OCR machines for the banking, publishing, and oil industries. Another much heralded pioneer in OCR is Jacob Rabinow, who, after forming his company, Rabinow Engineering (which later became part of Control Data Corporation), designed OCR equipment for the U.S. Postal Service.

Some of the earliest OCR approaches employed optical mask matching [2]. In these techniques, the masks consisted of stencils or photographic negatives of the characters to be recognized. Each mask would be aligned mechanically with the printed character positions, and the light reflected from a character position through the mask would be measured. Because character strokes are black and hence absorb light, the mask that permitted the least amount of light to be transmitted (below some minimum threshold) was considered a match and selected as the correct recognition.

It was not until the evolution of more advanced electronic technologies in the 1960s that OCR began to flourish. During this period, the major OCR manufacturers were Control Data Corporation, IBM, Lundy-Farrington, Recognition Equipment Incorporated (REI), and Scan Data [3]. Of course, many other U.S. and European companies also participated in this field, and the list continued to change and grow throughout the 1970s. From the late 1970s to the present, Japanese manufacturers have become increasingly active in the OCR marketplace.

One characteristic of these early OCR machines is that they are very large in size. For example, the IBM 1287 reader is 3 × 5 × 15.5 feet and weighs up to 3,900 pounds. Their highly mechanized document feeders and transports were the fulfillment of many a mechanical engineer's dreams and frustrations. Depending on their size and content, documents could be generally processed at rates from 100 to 1,000 documents per minute. The REI OCR/S2000 machine was capable of processing Swedish Giro (Postal bank) documents at rates up to 2,400 documents per minute. Based on their document-handling capability, speed, and overall recognition function, these OCR machines ranged in price from $50,000 to over $600,000. As a result of these high costs, OCR machines could be justified only for applications requiring very large volumes of documents to be processed. Such applications included processing of utility billings, credit card sales vouchers, order sheets, warranty claims, payroll records, insurance remittances, vehicle licensing, etc.

Commercial OCR machines have employed many different types of recognition algorithms. Two of the more classic approaches for recognizing characters are mask (or template) matching for machine print and curve following for handprint. Illustrations of these techniques are shown in Figures 1 and 2. The mask-matching algorithm consists of having a set of Boolean logical masks that define the shape of each character class and then logically comparing each mask to a scanned character pattern. A recognition is obtained if one and only one mask is matched (i.e., logically satisfied). The contour-following algorithm uses various techniques to trace the edges of the character pattern and relates the directions and distances traveled to predetermined references that define the tracing sequences for each character class. A recognition is obtained if a match is found with a reference while following the character outline.

As noted above, the early and expensive OCR machines have very high recognition speeds. Their recognition algorithms are implemented directly into hardware logic circuits, and recognitions are made at speeds permitted by the hardware technologies. For example, in Figure 1, a binary scanned pattern is shifted through a hardware register with the combinatorial logic

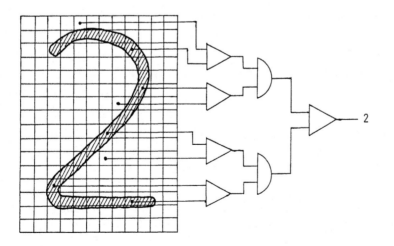

FIGURE 1 Mask matching by Boolean logic.

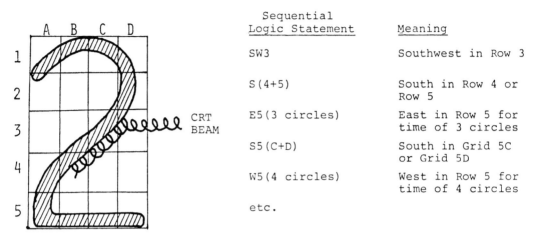

	Sequential Logic Statement	Meaning
	SW3	Southwest in Row 3
	S(4+5)	South in Row 4 or Row 5
	E5(3 circles)	East in Row 5 for time of 3 circles
	S5(C+D)	South in Grid 5C or Grid 5D
	W5(4 circles)	West in Row 5 for time of 4 circles
	etc.	

FIGURE 2   Curve following.

masks wired directly to the register. All logic masks are active, and a recognition can be obtained as fast as the character black/white bit pattern can be shifted through the register. Figure 2 illustrates the analog technique to curve follow a hand-printed character that is used in the IBM 1287/1288 OCR machines [4]. A cathode ray tube (CRT) beam is used to follow the outline of the character by first tracing the character to determine its size for superimposing it on a normalized grid and then tracing the character a second time to determine the contour characteristics relative to the superimposed grid. Again, this recognition approach is very fast and reliable for recognizing handprinted characters.

OCR PERFORMANCE

The most critical and controversial characteristic of an OCR machine is its recognition performance—controversial because many factors have to be considered in describing and understanding the machine's real performance. In discussing OCR performance, it is necessary to understand some basic definitions. The percentage of characters recognized correctly is called the *recognition rate*. The percentage of characters not recognized correctly is called the *error rate*. The error rate consists of two types of errors, called substitutions and rejects. *Substitutions* are those character patterns that are read incorrectly, and *rejects* are those patterns for which no recognition can be determined and are labeled as unrecognizable by the machine. The sum of the recognition, substitution, and reject rates equals 100%.

Reject and Substitution Trade-off

Of the two components of error rate, the substitution error is the more serious. This is because it is undetected in the recognition process and, hence, becomes more costly than rejects for the user to correct at a later time. As a result, the substitution error rate must be kept as low as possible, at least to the point where the cost to correct additional rejects is less than fixing a substitution error. Figure 3 shows the nonlinear

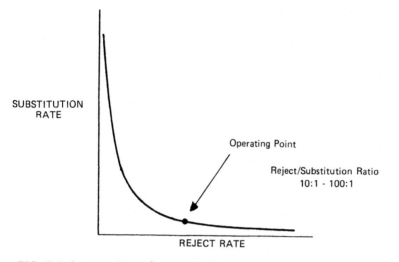

FIGURE 3 Relation of substitution and reject performance.

inverse relationship between substitution and reject rates. As the substitution rate becomes smaller, increasingly more rejects occur. The ideal
operating point is slightly to the right of the knee of the curve. Commercial OCR machines strive to have operating points with a reject/substitution
ratio in the range of 10:1 to 100:1 [5]. Table 1 provides typical performance values obtained for various OCR tasks. As can be seen, the OCR
performance varies with the type of input being recognized. It should be
noted that the performance of the general public alphanumeric handprint is
well below the desired range of reject/substitution ratios, which is an
indication of its difficulty and lack of commercial success.

Machine Print Versus Handprint

Due to character shape and size inconsistencies, it is expected that handprint recognition is more difficult and less reliable than machine-print recognition. Not so obvious, however, are the performance variances within
different machine-print fonts themselves. These differences result from the
style of the font, as well as its associated print quality in a typical application. For example, serif fonts are usually more difficult for OCR than sans
serif fonts because, in many cases, the serifs interfere with the pattern of
the adjacent character. Also, some fonts provide little or no distinguish-
ability between some of their symbols. For example, the zero (0) and
letter "O" and the 1 and lowercase "l" are the same symbols in many fonts
and can only be distinguished in the context of their use. Print quality
factors that affect a font's performance are stroke thicknesses, character
slurring, character tilt, character breaks or voids, and random character
noises due to dirt, smudges, paper impurities, and stroke fuzz. These
print quality factors are, for the most part, attributable to the characteristics of the printing device. For handprint, breaks due to pen skips,
extraneous pen ticks, linking characters, and just poor penmanship are
particularly troublesome print quality conditions.

TABLE 1   OCR Performance Values

Type of OCR	Recognition Rate	Reject Rate	Substitution Rate
Standardized OCR Ronts	0.9999	0.00009	0.00001
Omni Typewriter Text	0.999	0.0009	0.0001
Standardized Numeric Handprint	0.99	0.009	0.001
Gen. Public Numeric Handprint	0.95	0.045	0.005
Gen. Public Alphanumeric Handprint	0.90	0.08	0.02

OCR Font Standardization

To help alleviate the foregoing problems, standardized OCR fonts have been defined. Two fonts that are defined by American and International standards are called OCR-A and OCR-B [6—9]. These fonts are for machine-print use and basically are an attempt to maximize the shape differences between the individual characters for best recognition performance. OCR-A has a distinctive style that typifies it as a font designed more for machine than for human reading. Conversely, OCR-B has a style similar to normal printing and would not be associated with OCR by the casual reader. The character sets of both fonts have a full repertoire of symbols and are specified in three different character sizes for various application uses. To illustrate the style difference between OCR-A and OCR-B, the numeric and uppercase symbols of each font are shown in Figure 4. These fonts minimize the alphanumeric shape conflicts that occur in other fonts, as in the case of the letter "O" versus zero (0).

Cost/Performance Trade-Offs

Another factor in the OCR performance trade-off is cost. As shown in Figure 5, the performance or recognition rate of an OCR algorithm is a function of the cost of implementation. The optimum cost/performance would be slightly to the right of the knee of the curve because beyond this point little performance can be gained with additional costs. The slope of this curve will change, depending on the font being recognized. As expected, the best cost/performance trade-off curves can be achieved with the OCR-A and OCR-B standard fonts, whereas general public handprint will have a much worse cost/performance trade-off. For this reason, there are users who retype handprint (or written) data to an OCR font in order to obtain the higher recognition reliability. These cases are usually referred to as OCR retype applications and are justified on the basis that one OCR machine with multiple typewriters is a more cost-effective solution for data entry than a large and complex on-line system of specialized data-entry equipment.

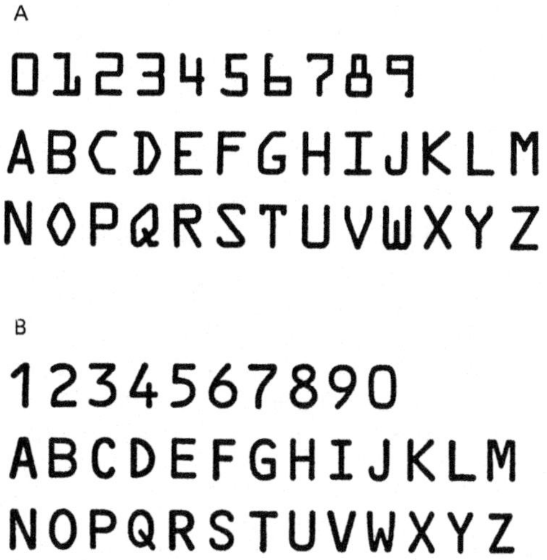

A
0123456789
ABCDEFGHIJKLM
NOPQRSTUVWXYZ
B
1234567890
ABCDEFGHIJKLM
NOPQRSTUVWXYZ

FIGURE 4 OCR font styles. (A) OCR-A subset. (B) OCR-B subset.

RECOGNITION
RATE
Optimum
Cost/Performance
RECOGNITION COST

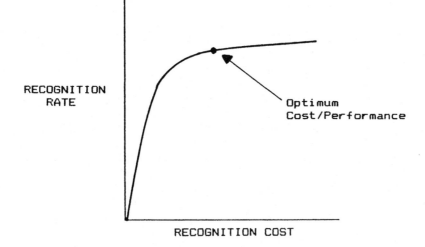

FIGURE 5 Relation of recognition cost and performance.

Depending on the OCR method and implementation, the costs in Figure 5 can be measured either in hardware circuits or microcode storage.

Postprocessing

For many OCR applications, additional performance can be obtained by further processing the OCR results with special application-dependent or context-oriented functions. These functions may range from simplistic error-correction codes for numeric data to complex spell-checking algorithms for text data. Also, most applications already have self-checking, balancing, and reconciliation procedures that can be utilized effectively in the postprocessing function. Postprocessing is designed primarily to detect substitution errors because, as noted earlier, these are the most costly to fix at a later time.

Design Considerations

An important but often unheralded factor of OCR performance is the methodology and care used in the design of the recognition logics. Early OCR development utilized manual design techniques that relied on the designer's knowledge and intuition to cover the expected shape variations in the design. Today, computer design techniques employ statistical algorithms to generate the recognition logics automatically.

In preparing a character design base for statistical methods, it is important that character classes are well-balanced in size and cover the wide range of print quality and shape variations found in real-world applications. For example, machine-print design samples should come from as many different printer types as possible in order to increase the design's performance on real-world data. Because design data are difficult and expensive to obtain, scanned characters can be produced artificially and used to complement real data to stress the recognition design. Synthesis of artificial characters can be accomplished by either modifying real characters or by constructing them directly from their centerline definitions. However, if such artificial data are to be used beneficially, their generation must be carefully controlled for realistic shape and quality representation. Even then, for best design results, only a portion of the total design data (preferably no more than one-third) should consist of artificial data.

Care must be taken to ensure that all characters in the design base have proper identification labels (IDs). This is required so automatic design programs can effectively analyze the characters for proper class separation and efficient design convergence. Incorrect pattern IDs can cause wasteful and unreliable logic paths.

During the development of an OCR design, the designer should plan periodic checkpoints and tests. It is essential that the data used in the testing be independent from the design data in order to ensure that performance results are unbiased and are representative of the true expected performance.

Limitations

Although the cost/performance of OCR has continued to improve over the years, there are still some areas where performance shortcomings are observed. In general, the automatic handling and recognition of data on general forms is still not readily achievable with today's technology. If the forms are redesigned under stringent guidelines, conventional OCR techniques are usable. Significant progress has been made in processing free-formatted text recognition where there is no interference from preprinted form backgrounds. Handprint algorithms still require certain constraints, like printing the characters in predefined boxes or areas. Also, the reliability of recognizing alphanumeric handprint is generally less than desired for most applications. Therefore, the advantage of OCR is still primarily derived from applications requiring processing of controlled handprinted numeric data and, in areas of text, OCR-A or OCR-B font reading.

FUNCTIONAL DESCRIPTION OF AN OCR SYSTEM

An OCR system consists of three major functions: data capture, video preprocessing (VPP), and recognition. Although many variations of these functions exist, a general description of each follows.

Data Capture

The data capture function in the OCR process is the ability of a machine to collect and convert human-readable information into a machine-readable form. Although often overlooked, the first step in this function is document formatting. In preparation for this step, users are usually required to take on the painstaking task of redesigning their forms for reliable OCR processing. They then perform the formatting step to provide the machine with a definition of how the documents are to be processed. This definition is usually in the form of tables that contain information on each document such as field locations, font types, character pitches, etc. The format tables are stored in the machine and are used in the overall control of the OCR process.

Good document formatting and control capability allow the OCR machine to process complex documents efficiently. Under format control, only the areas of interest are captured and processed by the machine. This enables higher productivity for the OCR system. Many OCR machines have automatic format control whereby a preprinted format number on the document is first read by the machine, which automatically identifies the format table to be used for processing the remainder of the document [10]. In this mode, the user can intermix document types, and the machine can automatically change format tables and process the documents without interruption. For documents that do not have preprinted format numbers, other means of entering the format ID can be used, such as inserting a separate header sheet in front of the document (or batch of documents) or manually entering the format number through machine switches or keyboard, etc.

The above table method of format control is required when processing complex documents that contain a combination of handprint and different machine-print fonts and to avoid non-OCR areas such as handwriting, diagrams, etc. In today's market, there is another type of document formatting referred to as "free formatting," which allows the machine to process documents dynamically without the use of format tables. These machines are restricted for text recognition use and usually recognize a number of typewriter print styles. The types of documents that can be processed in free-format mode are text documents, such as letters, manuscripts, reports, etc. The free-formatting algorithm automatically determines and retains the format of the document to enable its reproduction at a later time.

After the formats have been loaded, the next step in the data capture function are to scan and threshold the document. A typical scanning system consists of an incandescent light source, a lens, and a light-sensing mechanism. The light source shines light onto the document; the light, in turn, is reflected through a lens and focused on the sensor device. Light paths typically range from 18 to 24 inches in length in order to obtain the appropriate magnification ratios (i.e., document width to sensor width). To enable compact packaging of the optical system, one or two mirrors can be used strategically to fold the light path as necessary.

There are two methodologies used in establishing a scanning system. In one, the transport moves a document under (or by) a fixed scan station; in the other, the document is held stationary and the scanning mechanism is moved. The first method is generally preferred because it is easier and less costly to move paper than to move the scan station. Also, scanning mechanisms are adjusted very precisely, and it is best to avoid moving such mechanisms if possible.

There are many different types of scanning devices. Early machines used CRTs to move a beam of light across the document, and the reflected light was sensed by a photomultiplier tube. Most of today's OCR machines use a lamp to flood the document scan area with light and use a linear charged coupled device (CCD) array to sense the reflected light. The linear CCD array is a solid-state device that consists of a series of photo-cell-like elements (as many as 2,048) that span some scan area or window. As a document is moved past the scan window, the CCD charges according to the amount of reflected light from the scan area, where each element sees only its corresponding small area on the document. A thresholding algorithm is then employed to convert the analog charges of the CCD elements to digital black or white bits referred to as picture elements (pels or pixels). Each pel represents only a very small area on the document. The sequence of pels from one CCD charge cycle is called a scan line, and the resolution of the scanner is defined by the number of pels captured in a scan line relative to the document distance represented by the scan line. Common OCR resolutions are 200 and 240 pels per inch in both the horizontal and vertical directions. These black and white pels contain the information on the scanned document and are used in the subsequent steps of the recognition process.

The quality of the resulting digital video is extremely important in obtaining an overall reliable and optimum recognition system. For this reason, it is essential to select a thresholding algorithm that provides the best possible representation of the actual character patterns. If strict control of the document design, i.e., format, paper, and ink specifications, can always be maintained, OCR machines will perform very well with a fixed thresholding scheme. In this situation, video signals above a fixed value are called white pels, and those below are called black pels. The fixed threshold value can be determined by a calibration function that is executed once when the machine is turned on or, in more sophisticated machines, executed repeatedly at the beginning of each document to be read. The latter approach will compensate for background differences that occur from document to document.

Where input documents are less controllable, better thresholding algorithms are needed. Most machines today employ some form of dynamic thresholding algorithm. Dynamic thresholding algorithms are aimed at maintaining consistent character stroke widths, sharp character edge transitions, and uniform character openings over a wide range of dark to light printing and document backgrounds. This is accomplished by the algorithms maintaining ongoing histories of the white and black profiles that are used to continuously update the thresholding levels as a document is being processed [11].

Video Preprocessing

After a digitized video representation of the document has been captured, the next function required to locate and prepare the character patterns for recognition is referred to as VPP. Although the steps utilized in this function can vary, the ones defined below are generally considered to be traditional and have been used in various OCR machines. Again, the quality of these algorithms play an important role in the final recognition performance.

Field-Cut Algorithm

The field-cut algorithm uses the document-formatting information to locate and cut out the designated areas required for recognition. For general OCR processing, the algorithm must be able to handle multiple horizontal or vertical adjacent fields. If the machine has a full-page buffer, the fields can be cut out individually and processed independently. However, with only partial document buffering, a more powerful algorithm is required to process multiple adjacent fields. In this case, the field-cut algorithm must additionally act as the VPP control logic so that multiple fields can be cut out and processed concurrently as they are encountered on the document [12].

When processing text-only documents with free formatting, the entire document is treated as a single field. This is considered the trivial case for the field-cut algorithm because, in the general sense, it needs to be supported from a control standpoint but no specific field cutting is required.

Line-Find Algorithm

Once a field has been located, the next step in the VPP function is to find and track the lines of characters in the field. The line-find algorithm uses various minimum character requirements and line profile information to help identify line-starting conditions. Depending on the capability of the OCR machine, the line-find algorithm may be required to process only single-line fields, multiline fields, free-format text fields, or any combination thereof. As expected, the complexity of the algorithm becomes greater as its capability increases. For free-format text, the line-find algorithms must also compensate for the printer or typewriter line skew, as well as any document transport skew.

For users who require processing of complex OCR documents in formatted mode, the multiline-find algorithm can simplify the document-formatting step. With this capability, consecutive lines of the same font can be defined collectively as a single multiline field and, hence the amount of format information required is significantly reduced.

Segmentation

After the starting location of a line of characters has been found, the seg-mentation algorithm is used to locate and isolate the individual characters sequentially encountered in the line. One of the more traditional and simplest segmentation schemes is called "blank scan segmentation." In this technique, the segmentation point is determined by looking for the first blank scan (white column) that separates adjacent characters. The technique works well for good-quality printing where few characters touch and a font is used that has no character space overlap.

Many segmentation algorithms utilize character pitch information when processing known character fonts with fixed pitches. Depending on the algorithm, either the pitch is provided as part of the document-formatting information or the segmentation algorithm has to calculate the pitch before it can begin processing. Even when the pitch is used, reliable segmentation, especially for handprint, depends on the ability of the algorithm to locate a proper starting point and to adjust segmentation points as necessary to compensate for printing irregularities, optical nonlinearities, and other system distortions [13].

More complex algorithms are required to segment printing with propor-tional spacing and fonts that create difficult overlap situations. In these cases, the character patterns and their associated boundaries have to be examined more closely to arrive at more sophisticated character blocking and serpentine segmentation approaches. Techniques employing histograms of the character profiles within the line can also be used successfully to determine optimum segmentation points in touching character situations.

Ancillary Segmentation Processing

There are a number of other VPP operations that can enhance the quality of the recognition system and are usually implemented in conjunction with the segmentation function. These are noise filtering, blank detection, data presence testing, and special VPP measurements. A brief description of each follows.

During the line-find and segmentation algorithms, extraneous noise due to dirt, ink smudges, paper impurities, and extraneous markings is usually removed using various noise-filtering techniques. Generally, the filtering procedures are based on geometric and size characteristics of groups of pels that fail to meet certain minimum character or cluster requirements. Another type of filtering is the removal of single pels near or along the edges of the character strokes. This is sometimes called fuzz or feather noise, and its filtering provides a smoothing function on the character strokes. Fuzz removal has the drawback that it requires special hardware logic to imple-ment efficiently. For this reason, most microprocessor-based recognition units will bypass this filtering.

Blank detection is another function of the segmentation process. Be-cause the segmentation algorithm analyzes each character position very methodically as it moves down a line, it is a rather straightforward process to detect the occurrence of one or more blanks. In conventional OCR pro-cessing, only an indication that a blank space has occurred is sufficient, and the exact number of blanks is not required. For text processing, a precise means of recording all blanks is required to permit a good represen-tation of the document after recognition has been completed.

Data presence detection is a function that checks for the presence or absence of data in a predefined area on the document. Usually this is required for processing forms that contain one or more boxes to be checked (or not checked) when the form is completed. It can also be used to detect the presence or absence of signatures and other data in predefined areas on the document. To implement this function, some straightforward tests can be incorporated at appropriate points in the segmentation logic.

During the VPP function, information about the character patterns that is not available in the later steps of the recognition process is encountered. Therefore, it is necessary to make appropriate measurements to extract and save this information in a compact form for later use. An example of these VPP measurements is the height and width of the segmented characters. This information is useful in distinguishing uppercase and lowercase characters. Without the VPP measurements, this information would be lost whenever characters are normalized prior to recognition. Other VPP measurements could be segmentation touching or overlap conditions, character-density characteristics, ascender/descender information, and any other preprocessing data that a designer may consider useful for the recognition process.

Normalization

For OCR algorithms that recognize multiple fonts or handprint, the use of a normalizing function is generally required. After a character has been segmented, it undergoes the normalization function. The purpose of normalization is to equalize the size of all character patterns in order to present more uniform pattern shapes to the recognition algorithms. This provides better alignment of character patterns of the same class which, in turn, reduces the complexity required for the recognition logics.

There are many different algorithms for normalizing character patterns. Most only normalize downward because there is less distortion in a reduced pattern than in an expanded pattern. Also, the resolution of most scanners provides sufficient height and redundancy in the original (unnormalized) patterns to allow the reduction to a normalized size without critical information loss. In this case, delimiter characters, such as periods and commas, which are smaller than the normalized size, are left in their original form.

Most normalization algorithms modify the pattern physically whereas some may only scale the pattern logically. An example of the latter is the IBM 1287 Contour-Follower method shown in Figure 2. As noted earlier, the CRT beam will initially trace the outline of the pattern to determine its size and then overlay a uniform grid that is scaled to the pattern's size. This effectively normalizes the pattern to the uniform grid. Algorithms that physically modify the patterns can range from very simple to complex transformations. Simplistic approaches usually employ some form of uniform deletion or combination of pels in the original pattern, whereas complex algorithms will examine a neighborhood of pels in the original pattern to determine the value of a single pel in the normalized pattern. Generally, uniform pel detection with minimal logic adjustments is sufficient for the desired quality and implementation effectiveness. After normalization, all characters are registered (aligned) in a consistent manner for the recognition function. Typical registration schemes are centering and lower left or lower right justification.

Recognition

The final function in the OCR System is recognition. The objective of this function is to identify the individual character patterns that were prepared by the VPP function. The recognition process consists of two steps: first, a measurement step called feature extraction, and second, the identification step called decision. A further description of these steps is given below.

Feature Extraction

After the completion of the VPP function, the information that is available for recognition is the normalized character and the VPP measurements. For recognizing most single machine print fonts, this information is adequate. A technique such as the Boolean mask-matching technique (described in Fig. 1) could be used. However, this information alone would not be sufficient for optimally handling the more difficult handprint and omnifont recognition problems. To handle these problems, additional measurements are required to compensate for the localized shape variations that occur in characters belonging to the same class. There are many approaches to developing invariant measurements; some are geometrically intuitive, whereas others are mathematically abstract. In either case, these measurements are considered to be identifying features of the characters; therefore, the term feature extraction.

An example of one method of feature extraction is shown in Figure 6. Generally, measurement results or features are represented by a single binary bit which, when set, indicated whether the feature is present or absent in the pattern. As shown in Figure 6, the value of each feature is stored in a feature vector, which is saved for later use by the recognition algorithm. The features in Figure 6 are only conceptual; in reality, they become much more complex but remain geometrically intuitive. Some other types of information that have been used in feature definitions are contours, sequences, run lengths, stroke intersections, transition properties, statistical properties, and transformations. Regardless of the type of information, it is extremely important that the algorithm encompasses a quality set of features to obtain the extendibility that is desired in the final recognition performance.

Decision

All of the information about the character has been assembled and prepared for the final classification algorithm to decide the identity of the character. Decision (or classification) is the step that is most widely discussed in OCR theory, because these algorithms generally have a strong mathematical basis. There are many books and papers that provide a good service to this aspect of the science [2, 14, 15], but due to the wide scope of this paper, these theoretical details cannot be described here.

From a technological standpoint, there are many different types of classification algorithms. Some of these, like contour following and mask (template) matching, were discussed in the Introduction. Other major methods include Bayesian probabilistic techniques, such as Boolean logic discriminants and linear hyperplane discriminants; information theory techniques, such as sequential tree structures; and artificial intelligence (AI) techniques, such as syntactical grammars and parsers. An illustration of the Boolean logic discriminant technique is shown in Figure 6.

FEATURE EXTRACTION

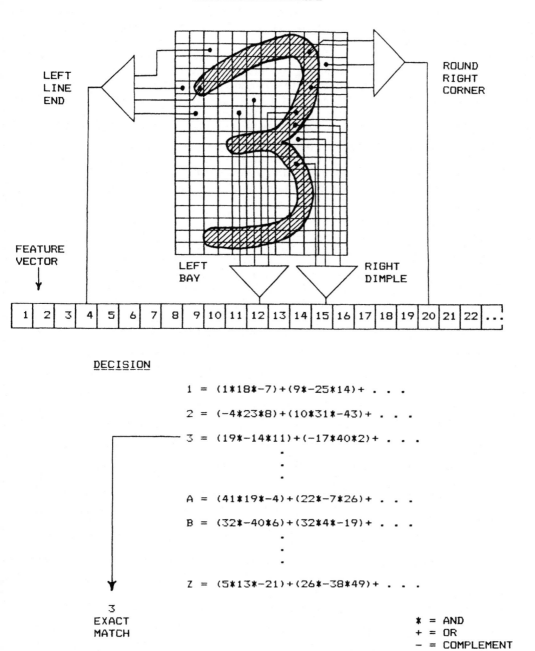

FEATURE VECTOR

LEFT LINE END

ROUND RIGHT CORNER

LEFT BAY

RIGHT DIMPLE

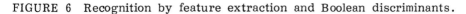

DECISION

$$1 = (1*18*-7)+(9*-25*14)+ \ldots$$

$$2 = (-4*23*8)+(10*31*-43)+ \ldots$$

$$3 = (19*-14*11)+(-17*40*2)+ \ldots$$

$$A = (41*19*-4)+(22*-7*26)+ \ldots$$

$$B = (32*-40*6)+(32*4*-19)+ \ldots$$

$$Z = (5*13*-21)+(26*-38*49)+ \ldots$$

3
EXACT
MATCH

* = AND
+ = OR
- = COMPLEMENT

FIGURE 6   Recognition by feature extraction and Boolean discriminants.

Generally, the classification algorithm will have access to the character pattern and its associated measurements and features for analysis in its decision process. As in Figure 6, some classification algorithms use only the feature results. The algorithm will evaluate all of the available information using its predesigned logics to determine the identity of the character. For those cases where the algorithm cannot recognize the character with some predetermined confidence factor, the algorithm will assign a reject code to the character. Some algorithms permit the user to adjust the reject confidence level in order to better tailor the algorithm's reject/substitution rate to the customer's application requirements. Also, after a reject situation, some algorithms will provide a retry by changing the registration position of the character pattern and re-executing the classification. Usually on retry situations, higher confidence levels or some means of voting are required.

EFFECT OF MICROPROCESSORS ON OCR TECHNOLOGY

The advancement of microprocessor technology has enabled OCR technology to migrate from strictly hard-wired implementations in the 1960s, to special-purpose microprocessors with hardware assist in the 1970s, to general-purpose low-cost microprocessors in the 1980s. This evolution to the general microprocessor has also caused (required) new directions in OCR algorithms, machine characteristics, and system strategies.

Algorithm Direction

New ideas and innovation had to go into the complete renovation of OCR algorithms for use with the general-purpose microprocessor. The old algorithms were created for high speed, parallel operation, and hardware implementations and were too costly and slow for emulation in a microprocessor environment. The basic functions of an OCR system (described earlier) are still the same today, but the algorithms and techniques to achieve these functions had to become more efficient for microprocessor implementation.

The major technical advantage that microprocessors have provided for OCR algorithm development is flexibility. With microprocessors, diverse algorithms can be combined readily because all functions become microcode. This enables the designer to be creative in selecting and mixing the strengths of many algorithms, along with new heuristics to provide enhanced function and performance. This diversity cannot be obtained in hardware implementations.

In video preprocessing, microprocessor-oriented algorithms have provided inroads for the free-formatting capability of text-recognition systems. Continued progress in this area will be seen. Because microprocessors are not efficient bit manipulators, the new algorithms in VPP and feature extraction are becoming more byte oriented for better productivity. For the decision function, the sequential tree structure and AI syntactical grammars are probably the most utilized classification schemes with microprocessors. For throughput considerations, these approaches fit well with the sequential operation of a microprocessor. Also, this has inspired engineers to invent more efficient ways to partition and organize these sequential algorithms into more complex structures, as shown by the tree-verifier structures [16] in Figures 7 and 8.

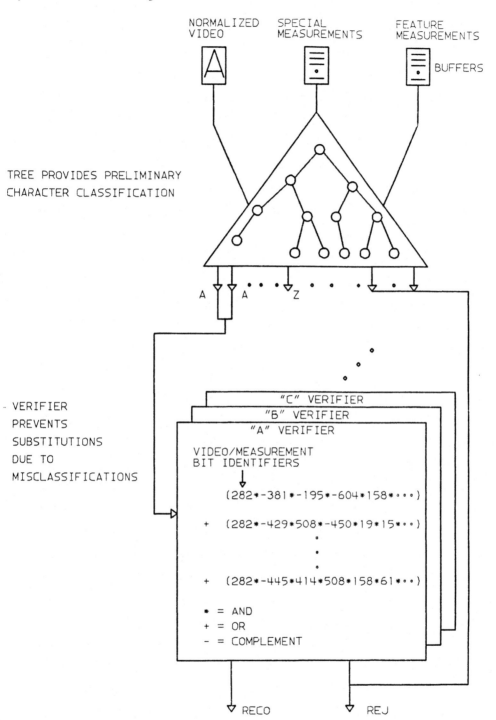

FIGURE 7 Tree-verifier recognition algorithm.

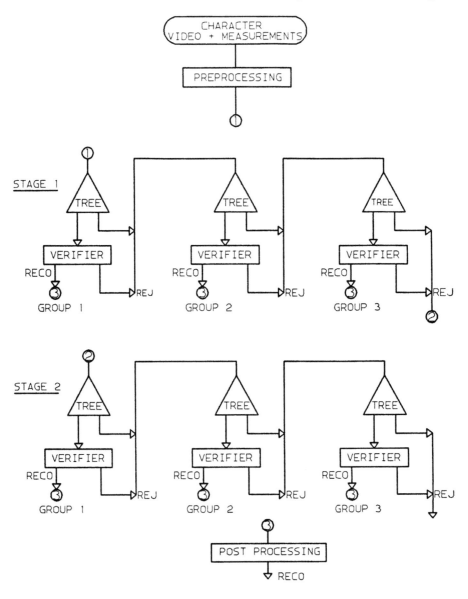

{Total Char. set} = {Group 1} U {Group 2} U {Group 3}

Character Frequencies of: Group 1 > Group 2 > Group 3

FIGURE 8   Frequency-oriented multiple tree recognition structure.

Machine Characteristics

Today's OCR machines are lower in price, richer in function and, in general, have improved recognition performance rates over earlier machines. However, the one area where today's machines fall short is in document throughput. Technology limitations here are the scan speed of CCD sensors and micro-processors speeds for implementing OCR algorithms. As sensor technologies continue to improve and multiprocessor architectures become more attractive, OCR speeds will also improve.

Most new OCR machines today are of the workstation variety. Full-page readers currently range in price from approximately $2,500 to $40,000. A good multiple-font tabletop reader costs about $10,000. These machines range in speed from one to twelve pages per minute. OCR wands and docu-ment slot readers are less then $2,000 and are manually operated. They are used primarily in retail stores, banks, and other cashiering applications. OCR is available today for applications that could not afford the earlier high throughput machines.

System Strategy

In the past, OCR readers have been built and sold as special-purpose hard-ware boxes. In most cases, the boxes are quality machines that were superbly engineered with the latest hardware technologies. Unfortunately, these great machines were very expensive, difficult to install, and came with little software support. As with many other devices, manufacturers have been providing a box solution but no system solution. For OCR, the diffi-culty has been even greater because the systems problem was compounded by the high price and installation problems. This has limited the accept-ability of OCR to only large centralized operations that could justify over-coming the above problems on their own.

With the evolution to microprocessor implementations, the cost/perfor-mance of OCR has improved significantly. This, combined with growth in systems networking concepts, opens new opportunities for OCR as decentra-lized system devices. This strategy would permit the use of lower speed machines because documents could be processed at distributed stations. In most applications, this would be more cost effective than transporting batches of documents to a centralized facility. Also, this OCR approach would provide improved device redundancy for larger processing stations where several devices could be utilized economically. For this strategy, it is even more critical that a sound system solution be provided that includes the necessary software support to simplify the OCR installation and inter-facing to customer applications.

IMAGE PROVIDES NEW LOOK TO OCR

Another means of capturing data with a scanner, which is becoming increas-ingly important, is image capture. The image of a document is basically an electronic copy of the document, represented by black and white pels. In 1971, an image capture option was introduced on the IBM 1287 OCR document reader, and in 1975, this option was extended to the IBM 1288 page reader. These options enabled images to be captured either on a character basis for reject correction or on a field basis for verification of critical data, signature capture, image statement printing, etc. In 1979, image was incorporated on the REI TRACE (Transaction Control and Encoding) OCR system for use by banks in check truncation, and was called the TRIM (TRACE Image) system [1].

An image of an 8.5 × 11-inch page scanned at 200 pels/inch is 3.74Mb in size. This large size has limited the use of image because of inadequate channel bandwidths, insufficient system software, and excessive storage costs. With continued improvements in communications and software and storage technologies (such as optical disks) and the use of better compression algorithms to reduce the size of an image (by a factor of 10 to 15), the capability to work effectively with image data is becoming more viable. As a result, the image opportunity will continue to grow as more applications are developed and better systems are provided.

Image can be used with OCR to overcome some of the difficulties of the conventional OCR process. The tedious task of defining document formats can be simplified greatly with the use of image. In the past, document formats were defined directly by measuring the document for the required field information. With image, a document could be scanned and displayed, enabling the user to define the document format interactively. This could be a very natural process where the user could use a keyboard with a light pen or mouse to locate and define the OCR fields. The program would compile the format table automatically for use in the OCR process.

Image-Assisted Data Entry

All data-entry processes contain errors. As a result, it is necessary to provide suitable data verification and error correction. For key-entry applications, verification of critical data is usually accomplished by comparing results of a second keying operation. Errors are detected and corrected where mismatches occured.

Conventional OCR has always caused user problems in dealing with errors. Although rejects are detected, to correct them the operator must go back to the original documents to locate and key the reject corrections, which is a laborious and time-consuming process. Substitution errors are not detected and, therefore, are even more costly to locate and correct. The type of data that are suitable for OCR are also limited. For example, script handwriting, graphics, and other types of data cannot be processed reliably with today's OCR technology.

Image desensitizes the above data-entry and OCR performance limitations. An image/OCR system would have the combined advantages of automatic data entry for OCR data, key from image of non-OCR data, and verification from image for all data. This process provides an easy and cost-effective way to correct rejects and substitutions. The operator no longer has to be encumbered with large quantities of documents and can take advantage of programmed productivity aids to enter, verify, and correct data from image efficiently.

OCR Cost-Performance Trade-Offs with Image

The introduction of image into an OCR system has an inherent effect on the OCR cost-performance trade-offs and requirements. It is plausible that the ease of image reject correction allows for some desensitization, i.e., relaxation, of the reject rate. This would enable OCR algorithms to recognize traditional fonts at lower costs and would encourage new algorithm development for more difficult recognition tasks. As shown in Figure 3, relaxing the reject rate can also reduce substitution errors, which is greatly desired in most applications.

Having image with an OCR machine also permits handling the data verification/correction step as an asynchronous process. This step can be completely independent of time or order in which the documents were scanned. This enables the user to better control and balance workloads which, in many applications, reduces the need for the ultra high-speed document-handling capability required by OCR-only machines. This, in turn, reduces the cost of OCR machines for more affordable marketing.

Optimum Document Capture

There have been many document scanners built to handle either image-only or OCR-only, but few (e.g., IBM 1287/1288 and REI TRIM) that can do both. However, it is the integrated image/OCR system that provides the optimum document capture solution. In this system, the OCR would be used to convert character data to coded information, and image would be used to convert all other data to noncoded information. OCR-coded information reduces a document's storage requirements significantly. For example, the storage requirements for two typical typewritten letters are shown in Table 2. The advantage of coded data is quite dramatic. Also, coded data can be used intelligently by a computer and can be revised easily by the user. Therefore, a combined image/OCR capture system provides optimal storage, intelligence, and utility for most applications.

PRESENT/FUTURE DIRECTIONS IN OCR

Intelligent Workstation Systems

The proliferation of the personal computer has paved the way for the success of the intelligent workstation in business. New network communications approaches such as local area networks (LANs) have been developed to support the interconnection of intelligent workstations in a total system fashion. Likewise, this distributed intelligence capability has provided a new dimension for the utility and function of OCR.

TABLE 2 Coded versus Image Storage for Typewritten Correspondence[a]

Document[b]	Raw Image (Bytes)	Compressed Image (Bytes)	OCR Coded (Bytes)	Image/OCR Ratio
Letter 1 at 3 l.p.i	456,192	26,213	1,350	19:1
Letter 2 at 6 l.p.i.	457,920	37,485	1,843	20:1

[a]Courtest of IBM, Charlotte, NC, 28257.
[b]l.p.i., lines per inch.

Producing a low-cost personal computer terminal has forced other traditional computer attachments such as hard disks and printers to follow suit. The impact of these devices has also caused OCR machines to address the low-cost intelligent workstation attachment. These OCR machines are referred to as desktop scanners because most are small enough to fit nicely in a PC workstation configuration. The lower cost machines are single-sheet hand-fed machines, but compact batch-fed machines are also available. Most desktop machines are designed for text recognition and can read from 10 to 12 different type styles.

Office Automation

In recent years, great strides have been made in migrating office functions to computer-based systems. This includes electronic mail, text creation/ editing, automatic spell-checking, calendar maintenance, filing, and many other functions. Even with the increase in computer-generated information, there is still a large amount of paper handling in today's office, which is assumed to be externally generated paper, for the most part. This forces the office to maintain dual document administration systems; one for auto-mated files and the other for paper files. Therefore, the use of image/OCR machines in the future can play a major role in facilitation the migration of the paper files to a consolidated electronic office system.

An image/OCR scanner will have to have good ergonomic characteristics for it to be an effective tool in the future office. The machine must be as natural and easy to use as a copier yet provide the advantage of utilizing OCR for character data and image for all other data. The types of docu-ment formatting and processing required in an office environment are shown in Figure 9. The OCR-coded data output is compatible with present text/ office systems that include effective tools for editing and automatic proofing. The inclusion of image manipulation with these functions will enable users to handle all types of document processing at their personal workstations. This capability, combined with good networking communications and system software, will most likely become the office automation solution of the future.

Central Host Systems

The use of current OCR machines in centralized document processing is still required, but demand for this requirement is declining. Manufacturers are investing less in the development of expensive, high-speed, central process-ing OCR equipment. Instead, most of today's development is being directed toward low-cost decentralized OCR terminals.

There are many central and back-office applications that continue to rely on OCR. Utility remittance and financial credit-card processing are two applications that still use OCR to process large volumes of documents in central locations. A newer OCR application called "lock box" is a service offered by many of today's larger banks to handle a company's remittance processing. In this case, customer-returned payments are addressed to a post office box and are picked up, processed, and deposited directly to the company's account by the bank. This provides the company with the benefit of earning interest on its payments earlier while the bank benefits from its service fee.

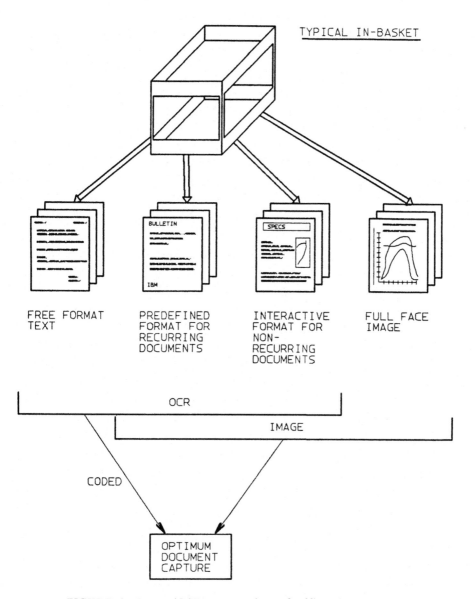

FIGURE 9   Image/OCR processing of office documents.

Some government applications for image/OCR systems in the future might be the processing of federal and state income tax returns, state licensing registrations, U.S. patent submissions, federal, state and municipal court documents, U.S. mail, and U.S. Customs documents. Also the transportation and distribution industries are areas where future image/OCR systems can thrive. Most of these applications will require a combined central and decentralized system.

Impact of Other Data-Entry Technologies

The reason for the projected decline in centralized high-speed OCR machines is the advances in distributed system processing. In some cases, this is handled by decentralized, lower-cost image/OCR units, but, to a large extent, many of the traditional central applications will be replaced by other non-OCR data-entry techniques. For example, the major credit-card companies are looking to electronic funds transfer systems (EFTS) to replace the central processing of paper sales vouchers. EFTS will provide an on-line computing network that will allow a store to debit a customer's bank or credit-card account automatically for his purchase.

As proven with banking self-service machines, migrating the data entry to the user does reduce paper and the need for OCR or key entry by the bank employees. Another future data entry approach and growth area is in home personal computer networks. Video text systems will provide home computer attachments through the telephone networks to allow one to conduct banking, shopping, bill-paying, social planning, etc., directly from his home terminal. For this service to be generally accepted, lower usage costs and network data security will be required.

Advances in OCR Algorithms

As microprocessor speeds and technologies continue to improve, advances in OCR will also continue. Improvements in the following areas are expected:

Thresholding

More sophisticated digital thresholding techniques will use gray-level pels to better represent the document contrast variations. If gray-level images for the documents can be retained, it would be a straightforward process to adjust the thresholding of the rejected OCR characters and retry them in recognition. This would improve the reject rate which, in turn, could be traded for better substitution performance. Gray-level images would also allow different thresholding for different parts of a document in order to maintain the highest quality image for each part. For example, a halftone thresholding algorithm could be used for non-OCR areas such as pictures, whereas a dynamic gradient thresholding could be used for the OCR areas [17].

General Text Recognition

To improve the utility of text recognition, further development is necessary in the area of free formatting. Algorithms that automatically separate readable text from image areas within a document need to be perfected. An arthitecture that supports complete intermixing of coded and noncoded data with minimum overhead is required for true system flexibility [18]. The system should default to image for any data that cannot be recognized. OCR systems with improved VPP algorithms will enable the recognition algorithm to handle a wider variety of print styles and sizes. Basically, any legible print should be readable by the OCR machine.

Automatic Learning

Automatic learning is the capability of an OCR algorithm to train itself to read new characters, as well as to improve its recognition performance on current characters. The concept is not new, but there is renewed interest in this capability, with current emphasis on low-cost workstation OCR scanners, which would allow the user to personalize OCR for his own needs. New training algorithms have been developed to provide better human interaction and performance reliability [19].

The major disadvantage of automatic learning algorithms has been their inadequacy to recognize the variety of font styles that a typical user encounters without the constant need for complete retraining. The noticeable loss of recognition performance on some symbols after training new symbols has been another user frustration and deficiency of learning methods. A learning algorithm that would retain the essential information with continually less training to eventually recognize omnifont would reduce this sensitivity.

Katakana and Kanji Recognition

In recent years, the Japanese have been major contributors to the advancement of OCR algorithms with their work in Katakana and Kanji recognition. Katakana is their phonetic alphabet consisting of 73 symbols, and Kanji is their written language consisting of over 10,000 complex symbols called ideographs. Kanji is a subset of the original Chinese language consisting of over 30,000 symbols. The Japanese have developed algorithms to recognize handwritten and machine-printed versions of these languages.

There are certain Katakana symbols that can occur with or without special diacritical marks. Although the Japanese Industry Standard (JIS) for Katakana Handprint OCR requires that these diacritical marks be written in a separate character box following the base character, the natural way the Japanese write these diacritical marks are together in a single box with the base character. The IBM 4751 (a Japan-only machine) is capable of reading the diacritical marks either way.

The Kanji font poses the double difficulties of having an extremely large number of symbols, as well as having complex symbol shapes. As a result, the Japanese have invested much time and research in hierarchical structures where the first level of logic will partition the total set of characters into smaller subsets which, in turn, are further separated by subsequent logic levels. Because key entry of Kanji symbols is itself a slow and tedious process, most Kanji key entry today is done by operators keying multiple Katakana symbols for each Kanji symbol, and the terminal or system automatically converts the Katakana to Kanji. With these data-entry difficulties, reliable OCR for Kanji would be extremely valuable.

CONCLUSION

OCR has made great advancements in cost/performance going from large expensive machines in the 1960s to low-cost desktop units in the 1980s.

Today's scanner/recognition units are generally applicable to conventional OCR, text recognition, and image capture. Integrated image/OCR provides an optimum document capture solution, where OCR-coded data provide significant document storage savings and are compatible with persent text/office systems.

With the continued advancement in microcomputer technology, further improvements in OCR can be expected. OCR machines using dedicated microprocessors will be able to achieve greater speeds and, therefore, be more effective in satisfying traditional OCR applications. An admirable goal would be to have three to five low-cost machines handle the workloads of the early high-speed OCR machines. This would provide a user with advantages in machine availability, distributed workload, and system flexibility. With the additional benefit of image, such a system could be extremely effective for the user.

As the cost of OCR continues to decrease, it will become a more desirable function in machines such as transaction printers, self-service terminals, cashiering terminals, etc. However, the more noticeable increase in OCR will be in conjunction with intelligent workstations for office systems. As microcomputers advance in speed and memory costs continue to decline, the OCR function will run as a program in the workstation as opposed to a function in the scanner. This will permit lower cost image scanners to be placed at the workstation and OCR will become like any other image function such as cut, paste, magnify, rotate, etc. In this way, the user will have an opportunity to create more varied applications of OCR in the future.

REFERENCES

1. H. F. Schantz, *The History Of OCR*, Recognition Technologies Users Association, Manchester Center, VT, 1982.

2. J. R. Ullman, *Pattern Recognition Techniques*, Crane, Russak, & Company, Inc., New York, 1973.

3. *Auerbach Guide to OCR and Mark Sense Readers*, Auerbach Publishers, Inc., Philadelphia, PA, 1974.

4. W. S. Rohland, P. J. Traglia, and P. J. Hurley, "The design of an OCR System for Reading Handwritten Numerals," in *Proceedings of Fall Joint Computer Conference*, 1968, pp. 1151–1162.

5. G. Nagy, "Optical Character Recognition—Theory and Practice" (P. R. Krishnaiah and L. N. Kanal, eds.), *Handbook of Statistics*, North-Holland Publishing, 1982, Vol. 2, pp. 621–649.

6. "Character Set and Print Quality for Optical Character Recognition (OCR-A)," *American National Standard*, ANSI X3.17-1974, American National Standards Institute, New York, 1974.

7. "Alphanumeric Character Sets for Optical Recognition—Part I: Character set OCR-A—Shapes and Dimensions of the Printed Image," *International Standard*, ISO 1073/I-1976 (E), International Organization for Standardization, Switzerland, 1976.

8. "Character Set for Optical Character Recognition (OCR-B)," *American National Standard*, ANSI X3.49-1975, American National Standards Institute, New York, 1975.

9. "Alphanumeric Character Sets for Optical Recognition—Part II: Character set OCR-B—Shapes and Dimensions of the Printed Image," *International Standard*, ISO 1073/II-1976 (E), International Organization for Standardization, Switzerland, 1976.

10. S. G. Aden, G. M. Bedner, S. P. Hartman, and R. G. Pierlott III, "Document Format Selection and Control Process," *IBM Tech. Disclosure Bull.*, *26*(9), 4718--4719 (February 1984).

11. M. R. Bartz, "The IBM 1975 Optical Page Reader—Part II: Video Thresholding System," *IBM J. Res. Dev.*, *12*(5), 354–363, (September 1968).

12. G. B. Fryer and D. A. Stepneski (IBM), "Video Image Field-cut Processing," U.S. Patent 4,493,108, January 8, 1985.

13. G. M. Bednar and G. B. Fryer, "Method and Apparatus for Segmenting Character Images," U.S. Patent 4,562,594, December 31, 1985.

14. R. O. Duda and P. E. Hart, *Pattern Classification And Scene Analysis*, John Wiley & Sons, Inc., New York, 1973.

15. C. K. Chow and C. N. Liu, "Approximating Discrete Probability Distributions with Dependence Trees," *IEEE Trans. Inf. Theory*, *IT-14*(3), 462--467 (May 1968).

16. A. J. Atribun, G. M. Bednar, G. B. Fryer, and J. C. Harmon, "Two-Level Character Recognition," *IBM Tech. Disclosure Bull.*, *23*(8), 3663–3664 (January 1981).

17. Y. Chin, F. C. Mintzer, and K. S. Pennington, "A Binary Representation of Mixed Documents That Compresses," in *Proceedings of IEEE-IECEJ-ASJ International Conference on Acoustics, Speech, and Signal Processing*, April 1986.

18. K. Y. Wong, R. G. Casey, and F. M. Wahl, "Document Analysis System," *IBM J. Res. Dev.*, *26*(6), 647--656 (November 1982).

19. R. G. Casey, S. K. Chai, and K. Y. Wong, "Unsupervised Construction of Decision Networks for Pattern Classification," *Proceedings of the Seventh International Conference on Pattern Recognition*, August 1984, pp. 1256--1259.

GREGORY M. BEDNAR

SYMBOL MANIPULATION PACKAGES

1 COMPUTER ALGEBRA

A newcomer to the study of computer algebra (CA) will be struck by the
large number of synonyms for it. Calmet [1] has remarked that almost any
combination of the words *algebraic*, *symbolic*, *computation*, *manipulation*,
and·*applied mathematics* has been used to describe CA. Indeed, Calmet
could have added the words *analytical*, *computing*. *formula*, and *symbol*,
among others, to his list.

Some synonyms for CA are formula manipulation [2], symbolic mathematical computation [3], symbolic and algebraic computation [4], symbolic algebraic computing [5], and symbolic computation [6]. In deference to what
seems to be increasingly common usage, the name CA is used henceforth in
this article.

The following definition of CA is based on those given by Ng [4], Yun
and Stoutemyer [7], and Loos [8].

Definition 1.1

CA is that part of computer science in which the design, analysis, computer
implementation, and application of algorithms for performing symbolic mathematical operations are studied such as those that occur in algebra and analysis.

It is clear from the preceding definition that the study of CA requires
considerable knowledge of both mathematics and computer science. What is
not clear, however, from the definition of CA is the almost inestimable value,
to the user, of the software produced by computer algebraists.

In this article, the term symbol manipulation package (SMP) is used generally to represent a software system that implements one or more CA algorithms. The importance of CA to scientists and engineers lies in the SMPs
created by computer algebraists: SMPs make possible the transfer of large
amounts of mathematical ability to the user; they are also able to compute
large amounts of tedious algebra very rapidly without the errors that are
usually produced by humans.

CA seems to have its origin in the work of Kahrimanian [9] and Nolan
[10] on symbolic differentiation. Effective CA software began to appear in
the early 1960s. In 1966, Sammet [11] produced an annotated CA bibliography containing about 300 items. In 1968, Sammet [12] produced a revised
bibliography containing about 380 items. In 1968, 1969, and 1970, Wyman
[13–15] produced supplements to Sammet's 1968 bibliography, bringing the
total number of items to about 550. At the present time, the number of
articles on CA in existence is vast and rapidly increasing, and the number
of SMPs in existence probably exceeds 60. The most significant developments in CA up to 1966 have been described by Sammet [2,11,16], and those
up to 1971 have been described by Sammet [17,18] and by Moses [19].
Some significant developments in CA up to 1973 have been surveyed by

Moses [20]. Unfortunately, there appears to be no historical survey of CA for the period 1973 to 1985.

During the last two decades, several authors [2,3,5,7,17,21−24] have written survey articles in which applications of CA and SMPs are described. Several conference proceedings [4,25−32] also contain articles in which applications of CA and SMPs are given. A large bibliography containing references to many applications of MACSYMA has been published [33], and is regularly updated. The interested reader is referred to this work and to others cited in subsequent sections of this article for records of interactions between SMPs and users, which occur when specific problems are being solved.

Some of the fields in which SMPs have been used successfully are as follows.

Algebra

Polynomial factorization.
Expansion of polynomial factors.
Determination of polynomial greatest common divisors.
Polynomial addition, subtraction, multiplication, and division.
Partial fraction decomposition of rational functions.
Simplification of algebraic expressions.
Indefinite and definite summation.
Vector, matrix, and tensor manipulation.
The analytical solution of polynomial equations.
The analytical solution of systems of linear algebraic equations.
Analytical matrix inversion.
Analytical determinant evaluation.
The analytical solution of systems of nonlinear algebraic equations.
The manipulation of expressions involving exponential, logarithmic, and
    trigonometric functions.
The manipulation of truncated power series.
Group theory.

Calculus

Differentiation.
Indefinite integration.
Definite integration.
The analytical solution of ordinary differential equations.
The manipulation of Laplace transforms.
The determination of Taylor, Poisson, and Laurent series.
The determination of asymptotic expansions.
The determination of limits.

Numerical Analysis

Unconstrained and constrained optimization.
The numerical solution of systems of nonlinear algebraic equations.
The numerical solution of boundary-value problems.
The generation of families of difference approximations for use in the
    numerical solution of partial differential equations.
The approximation of functions.

Physics

General relativity.
Celestial mechanics.
Quantum electrodynamics.
Particle dynamics.
Electron optics.
Plasma physics.

Engineering

Fluid mechanics.
Aeronautical engineering.
Electrical engineering.
Industrial mechanics.

Introductions to CA and SMPs for the computer-literate newcomer to the subject are to be found in Refs. *34–38*.

Very few books and easily obtainable monographs on CA and SMPs exist at present. The only actual introductory text for users of SMPs is the book by Howard [6], which is a self-contained account of the use of the SMPs REDUCE and MACSYMA to problems in aeronautics, particle dynamics, fluid mechanics, and cosmology. Rall [39] has written a very readable monograph on symbolic differentiation and some of its applications, and Davenport [40] has done the same for symbolic integration, although Davenport's book will be found to be mathematically demanding by most users who are not mathematicians.

To understand CA algorithms as opposed to merely using them, it is necessary to acquire a knowledge of abstract algebra and algebraic algorithms. The most readable texts for the algorithmic aspects of CA still seem to be Knuth [41] and Aho et al. [42], and an excellent introduction to the abstract algebraic aspect of CA for computer scientists in particular is Lipson [43], which contains several useful references.

2 SOME SYMBOL MANIPULATION PACKAGES

Yun and Stoutemyer [7] have given an excellent introduction to the uses and capabilities of the SMPs ALTRAN, CAMAL, FORMAC, MACSYMA, mu-MATH-79, REDUCE, SAC-1, SCRATCHPAD, SYMBAL, and TRIGMAN. Also, van Hulzen and Calmet [44] have surveyed SMPs with reference to ALTRAN, SAC-2, MATHLAB-68, SYMBAL, FORMAC, TRIGMAN, CAMAL, REDUCE, MACSYMA, SCRATCHPAD, muMATH-79, CAYLEY, and CAMAC-79, among others. Information on more recent developments in the design, uses, and capabilities of SMPs is to be found in the major international CA conference proceedings (see, in particular, Refs. *30* and *31*), in the 1982 through 1986 issues of the *SIGSAM Bulletin*, and in the *Communications of the ACM* and *Journal of the ACM*.

In this section, some recent developments in the field of SMP implementation for microcomputers are mentioned.

Until the beginning of this decade, SMPs were large pieces of software that ran on mainframe computers. The approximate sizes of some of the more well-known SMPs of this sort are as follows:

SMP	Size (Kb)
ALTRAN	280
CAMAL	200
FORMAC	140
MACSYMA	1125
REDUCE	300
SCRATCHPAD	1200
SYMBAL	200
TRIGMAN	113

In 1979, Rich and Stoutemyer [45] described muMATH-79, an SMP that needs a maximum of 64Kb of primary memory and appears to be the first significant SMP for microcomputers. At present, muMATH is available for Intel 8080, Intel 8085, and Z80-based computers, under the CP/M, IMSAI, IMDOS, and CDOS operating systems.

Originally, muMATH was intended to be used for educational purposes. Experience with muMATH, in which several interactions with the user are exhibited, has been described by Shochat [46], and recent experience with the use of muMATH in Austrian high schools has been described by Aspetsberger and Funk [47]. A brief survey of the capabilities of muMATH and an illustrative example are given by Yun and Stoutemyer [7].

The SMP muMATH is diveded into modules, which are loaded as needed. Details are given in Refs. 7 and 46.

The SMP PICOMATH-80 [48] is even smaller than muMATH and is intended for small microcomputers with 16Kb of random access memory using BASIC; currently supported machines include Apple, Atari, and Pet.

The SMP NLARGE [49] is an algebraic system that has been written in LISP for Z80 microcomputers with 24Kb of RAM. Some of the capabilities of NLARGE are expansion of expressions such as $(1+x)^{10}$; simplification of expressions such as $(x + 2)(x + y)^{10}/(x + y)^9$, yielding $x^2 + 2x + 2y + xy$; the calculation of rational forms such as $(x + y)^m/(x + z)^n$, where m and n are integers; and the symbolic inversion of matrices (e.g., the 2×2 Hilbert matrix). An example of the interaction between NLARGE and a user is given in Ref. 49.

Encouraged by their experiences with NLARGE, Marti and Fitch have implemented a large portion of REDUCE-2 on some 64Kb Z80 CP/M microcomputer systems [50]. Marti and Fitch conclude that CP/M REDUCE is a considerable improvement on NLARGE and that a small symbolic calculator is possible with conventional technology.

Fitch [51] has described the implementation of the SMP REDUCE on a Motorola 6800-based computer and concludes that "a new style of personal algebraic computer is now possible, which is both fast and reasonably priced and as such provides a cheaper base system for algebraic research than mainframes or LISP hardware."

A fairly recent and very promising addition to the list of SMPs that are implementable on microcomputers is Maple [52,53]. When work on it began in 1980, the primary purpose of Maple was to provide accessibility to symbolic computation for large numbers of students on a mainframe computer in a time-sharing environment, or on microcomputer-based workstations. The designers of Maple have been motivated by the need for portability between several kinds of computer systems and by the need to provide an efficient system for both student and general-purpose scientific usage.

Several features in the design of Maple are discussed in Ref. 52, and several interactions between Maple (version 3.0) and a user are exhibited in Ref. 53.

The mathematical facilities provided by Maple 3.0 include

Integer, modular integer, and rational arithmetic.
Long real arithmetic.
Multivariate polynomial arithmetic, expansion, and greatest common divisor.
Differentiation.
Univariate Taylor, Laurent, and asymptotic expansions.
Definite and indefinite summation.
Simple indefinite and definite integration.
Simple limits of real-valued scalar functions.
Solution of systems of linear equations and simple polynomial and transcendental equations.

Programming facilities that are currently available include

A user-level interpreted ALGOL-like programming language.
Two-dimensional output of expressions.
Built-in data structures: numbers, names, finite sequences, series, lists, sets, arrays, and tables.

Facilities that the designers of Maple hoped to add were multivariate polynomial factorization and the Risch integration algorithm [54,55]. More detail is provided in Ref. 53.

3 A SIMPLE SYMBOL MANIPULATION PACKAGE

In this section, a few of the problems that must be solved when designing even a simple SMP are illustrated with reference to the SMP ALGLIB [56].

The SMP ALGLIB was intended originally to be a software tool for use with programs implementing new algorithms for numerical optimization and for the numerical solution of systems of nonlinear algebraic equations, with and without the use of interval arithmetic (described in Refs. 57–60) and has subsequently been used in work that is described in Refs. 61–65.

The principal capabilities originally required of ALGLIB are as follows:

1. ALGLIB should interface with programs written in S-ALGOL [66], and in Triplex S-ALGOL [67–69].
2. ALGLIB should be easily implementable in high-level programming languages such as Pascal, Ada, FORTRAN 8X when it finally becomes available, ALGOL-68 and C.
3. ALGLIB should be usable in interactive or batch mode.
4. ALGLIB should be able to construct and manipulate the data structures corresponding to computable factorable functions (see Definition 3.2 below) efficiently without recreating structures that already exist.

5. ALGLIB should be capable of evaluating multivariate expressions efficiently in floating-point real arithmetic or in rounded interval arithmetic [70,71].

6. ALGLIB should be able to combine and compose multivariate expressions.

7. ALGLIB should be able to determine mixed partial derivatives of all orders of multivariate expressions originally read as strings or generated during execution of the program interfaced with ALGLIB.

8. ALGLIB should be able to write expressions in a reasonably readable one-dimensional form.

9. It should be possible to use the full capabilities of ALGLIB by invoking a carefully selected set of ALGLIB procedures that are made visible to the user.

10. It should be possible to introduce new capabilities such as those that are offered by Maple into ALGLIB without major reorganization of the package.

Capabilities 1 through 9 have been realized in ALGLIB-0, the initial version of ALGLIB, which is written in S-ALGOL and in Triplex S-ALGOL. Work is under way on ALGLIB-1, in which it is hoped to realize capability 10.

Currently, ALGLIB is implemented on a DEC VAX-11/785 computer under VMS, and it is hoped soon to implement it on a microcomputer.

Before describing some of the problems that must be solved in order to realize capabilities 1 through 9, it is necessary to define the set of objects that ALGLIB is designed to manipulate.

Most of the real-valued functions of several real variables that need to be manipulated in applications of mathematics to science and engineering are what McCormick [72] calls factorable functions.

Definition 3.1

The function $f: R^n \to R^1$ is a *factorable function* if and only if the expression $f(x)$, where $x = (x_j)_{n \times 1}$, is the last in a finite sequence of expressions $f_j(x)$ in which

$$
f_j(x) =
\begin{cases}
x_j & (j=1,\ldots,n) \\[2mm]
f_k(x) + f_l(x) & (k,l<j; \ n<j) \\[1mm]
\text{or} & \\[1mm]
f_k(x) f_l(x) & (k,l<j; \ n<j) \\[1mm]
\text{or} & \\[1mm]
g(f_k(x)) & (k<j; \ n<j)
\end{cases}
$$

where $g: R \to R$ is a given function.

Example 3.1

Let the function $f: R^3 \to R^1$ be defined by

$$f(x)=\cos(x_1 + x_2 x_3),$$

and let $f: R^3 \to R^1$ $(j=1,\ldots,6)$ be defined by

$$f_1(x)=x_1$$

$$f_2(x)=x_2$$

$$f_3(x)=x_3$$

$$f_4(x)=f_2(x)f_3(x)$$

$$f_5(x)=f_1(x) + f_4(x)$$

$$f_6(x)=\cos(f_5(x))$$

Then $f(x)=f_6(x)$ and f is a factorable function.

The SMP ALGLIB is required to manipulate interval-valued functions of several interval variables [71], as well as real-valued functions of several real variables [70]. Furthermore, it is necessary in practice to restrict the set of functions g in Definition 3.1 to a subset of the set of computable functions that is most frequently encountered in scientific and in engineering problems. Therefore, ALGLIB has not been designed to manipulate the set of factorable functions, but the set of computable factorable functions.

Definition 3.2

Let X be the set R of real numbers or the set I(R) of real bounded closed intervals. The function $f: X^n \to X^1$ is a computable factorable function (CFF) if and only if the expression $f(x)$, where $x=(x_i)\in X^n$ is the last in a finite sequence of expressions $f_j(x)$ in which

$$f_j(x)= \begin{cases} x_j & (j=1,\ldots,n) \\ f_k(x) * f_l(x) & (*\in[+,-,.,/])(k,l<j;\ n<j) \\ \text{or} & \\ g(f_k(x)) & (k<j;\ n<j) \end{cases}$$

where $g(.)\in F$, the set of unary operators defined by

$$F=[\ -(.),\ \text{sqrt}(.),\ \exp(.),\ \ln(.),\ \sin(.),\cos(.),\ \text{atan}(.),\ \text{abs}(.),\ (.)^m$$
$$(m\in Z)]$$

In Definition 3.2, $*\in[+,-,.,/]$ means that the binary operator $*$ can be addition, subtraction, multiplication, or division. The set F of unary operators in Definition 3.2 may be extended to include any other computable function from X to X.

It would seem that there is currently considerable demand among would-be users for a simple SMP that manipulates CFFs and is readily interfaced with a high-level language of the user's choice; ALGLIB has these capabilities, although it is still in an experimental form.

In the remainder of this section, some of the problems that must be solved in order to realize capabilities 1 through 9 in ALGLIB are discussed.

Capabilities 1, 2, and 3 have been realized by expressing ALGLIB in a pseudocode form that is easily implementable in such high-level languages as Pascal, ALGOL-68, Ada, S-ALGOL, Triplex S-ALGOL, etc. This makes it possible for a user with only a good working knowledge of his chosen programming language to acquire a CA capability which, although not comparable with that provided by the best available SMPs, is an effective aid for teaching and even for research, especially in numerical mathematics.

Having defined the primary purpose of an SMP and its capabilities, it is necessary to design the data structures corresponding to the objects that must be manipulated. In common with many SMPs, the important data structures in ALGLIB are vectors, linked lists, and binary trees [73].

The objects that are manipulated by ALGLIB are to a large extent dictated by Definition 3.2. Corresponding to each CFF $f: X^n \rightarrow X^1$ is a finite sequence of terms $f_j(x)$. Each term $f_j(x)$ belongs to one of four classes, which are exemplified as follows:

1. c *(constant)*
2. x_j *(variable)*
3. $f_k(x) * f_l(x)$ $(k,l<j)(* \in [+,-,.,/])$ *(binary term)*
4. $g(f_k(x))$ $(k<j)(g \in F)$ *(unary term)*

In order to store a *constant*, it is necessary to store its name and its value. Thus, a data structure of the form

<constant name> <constant value>

where <constant name> is a string and <constant value> is a real number in floating-point form, rational form, etc., could be used to store a *constant*.

To store a *variable* (or indeterminate), it is necessary to store only its name. Thus, a data structure of the form

<variable name>

where <variable name> is a string, could be used to store a *variable*.

To store a *unary term*, it is necessary to store a unary operator, and its argument, which is itself a *constant*, a *variable*, a *unary term*, or a *binary term*. Thus, a data structure of the form

<operator name> <pointer to argument>

where <operator name> is a string and <pointer to argument> is a pointer to the argument of the unary operator, could be used to store a *unary term*.

To store a *binary term*, it is necessary to store a binary operator and its left and right arguments, which are themselves *constants*, *variables*, *unary terms*, or *binary terms*. Thus, a data structure of the form

<left> <operator name> <right>

where <left> is a pointer to the left argument, <operator name> is a string, and <right> is a pointer to the right argument, could be used to store a *binary term*.

Using the data structures that have been described so far, a CFF f could be represented by binary tree as follows. If $f_1(x),\ldots,f_m(x)(=f(x))$ is a finite sequence of terms corresponding to f, then the head of the tree corresponds to $f_m(x)$, each node corresponds to a term in the sequence $f_1(x),\ldots,f_m(x)$, and the nodes that terminate each branch of the tree correspond either to *variables* or to *constants*. An example is given in Ref. 56.

The data structures that have been described so far are not adequate for the realization of capabilities 4 and 5. A partial derivative of a CFF is a CFF itself, and so may be stored as a binary tree. To store the n first-order partial derivatives of the CFF $f:X^n \rightarrow X^1$, a new field is introduced into the *unary terms* and the *binary terms*. This field is a vector of n pointers, the ith element of which points to the head of the tree that represents $\partial f/\partial x_i$. It is not necessary to introduce the new field into the *constants* and the *variables* because the partial derivatives of *constants* and *variables* are easily determined.

If two trees containing the same term are created, unless measures are taken to avoid it, this term will be duplicated, one copy being used in one tree and the other copy being used in the other tree. To avoid storing several copies of the same object, the data structure corresponding to a new term must be compared with those that have already been created. If a duplicate is found, the new data structure must be replaced with the duplicate.

To facilitate searching for duplicate data structures, the data structures corresponding to *constants*, *unary terms*, and *binary terms* are put into separate ordered linked lists. When a new *constant* is encountered, it is compared with those in the linked list of *constants*. If a duplicate is found, the pointer to the new *constant* is replaced with a pointer to the duplicate. Otherwise, the new *constant* is inserted into the ordered linked list of *constants*. A similar procedure is used for *unary terms* and *binary terms*.

Because certain constant terms occur very frequently, pointers to the data structures of class *constant* that correspond to these terms are stored in a vector rather than in a linked list to increase access speed. A new *constant* is compared with the frequently used *constants* before being compared with those in the ordered linked list of *constants*.

To maintain the ordered linked lists of *constants*, *unary terms*, and *binary terms*, it is necessary to introduce the additional fields <index> (an integer) and <next> (a pointer) into the data structures of classes *constant*, *unary term*, and *binary term*. These are the additions to the original data structures that are needed to realize capability 4.

To store the numerical values corresponding to *variables*, *unary terms*, and *binary terms* and to avoid unnecessary reevaluation, it is necessary to introduce the additional field <value> (an element of X) into the data structures corresponding to *variables*, *unary terms*, and *binary terms* and to introduce the additional field <known> (a Boolean variable) into the data structures corresponding to *unary terms* and *binary terms*. When a CFF is to be evaluated, the appropriate values are inserted into the <value> fields of the *variables*. If the value of a term in the CFF corresponding to these variable values is known, its <known> field will contain the value *true*, and the value in its <value> field can be used in the evaluation of the CFF. Otherwise, the term must be reevaluated. The addition of the <value> fields to the appropriate data structures is needed to realize capability 5.

Finally, another field <root> (a pointer) is introduced into the data structures of classes *constant*, *variable*, *unary term*, and *binary term*. The pointer <root> points to a data structure of class *root*, which contains pointers to the *variables*, frequently used *constants*, the ordered linked lists of *constants*, and the ordered linked lists of *unary terms* and *binary terms* corresponding to the *variables*. This greatly facilitates many of the operations that must be performed within ALGLIB.

The complete data structures that are used in ALGLIB-0 are as follows.

constant

<name> <index> <value> <root> <next>

variable

<name> <index> <value> <root>

binary term

<left> <right> <op> <grad> <index> <known> <value> <root> <next>

unary term

<arg> <op> <grad> <index> <known> <value> <root> <next>

root

<cons> <uns> <bins> <common> <vars>

The meanings and the data types of the field names are as follows:

<name>	:	The name of a *constant* or of a *variable*; a string.
<value>	:	The current value of a term; an element of X.
<index>	:	The index value of a term; an integer.
<left>	:	A pointer to the left argument of a *binary term*.
<right>	:	A pointer to the right argument of a *binary term*.
<arg>	:	A pointer to the argument of a *unary term*.
<op>	:	A unary operator name or a binary operator name; a string.
<known>	:	The current status of the <value> field; a Boolean.
<grad>	:	A vector of pointers to partial derivatives.
<root>	:	A pointer to the *root*.
<next>	:	A pointer to the next data structure in the ordered linked list of *constants*, *unary terms*, or *binary terms*.
<cons>	:	A pointer to the ordered linked list of *constants*.
<bins>	:	A pointer to the ordered linked list of *binary terms*.
<uns>	:	A pointer to the ordered linked list of *unary terms*.
<common>	:	A vector of pointers to the frequently used *constants*.
<vars>	:	A vector of pointers to the *variables*.

Mathematical expressions are usually passed to SMPs in the form of strings of characters that are read either from a data file or from a terminal and that look as much like the expressions that they represent as possible. For example, the expression

$$x^2 + y^2 + 1$$

may be presented to ALGLIB as the string

$$"x^2+y^2+1".$$

An SMP must determine whether a string that it has read (or is reading) represents a member of the class of expressions that it is designed to manipulate. Having read a string that represents a valid expression, an SMP must create a representation of the expression in terms of the data structures that have been designed for the purpose.

A first step in the solution of the problem of how to analyze a string to determine whether it is or is not valid consists of constructing a rigorous definition of validity. The approach that is adopted in the design of ALGLIB consists of constructing a grammar, the rules of which must be satisfied by any string that is a valid expression. A string is a valid ALGLIB expression if and only if it satisfies the rules of the ALGLIB grammar. The ALGLIB grammar and its implementation are based on the principle of recursive descent [74], which has been used extensively in compiler writing. The sentences of the ALGLIB grammar are valid expressions that represent CFFs.

The ALGLIB grammar is expressible in BNF (Bachus Nauer form, or Backus normal form) in which the syntax of expressions is written as a set of *productions* of the form A::=B, where A and B are strings. Examples from ALGLIB syntax will be used to illustrate the BNF notation.

The production

$$\text{<letter>::= "a" ... "b" ... "z" "A" ... "Z"}$$

means that the *nonterminal* symbol <letter> may be any one of the *terminal* symbols a,b,...,z,A,B,...,Z only. A terminal symbol cannot appear on the left-hand side of a production because a terminal symbol is fundamental and therefore, cannot be defined in terms of any other symbol.

The production

$$\text{<digit>::= "0" "1" ... "9"}$$

means that the nonterminal symbol <digit> may be any one of the terminal symbols 0,1,...,9 only.

The production

$$\text{<literal>::={<digit>}["." [{<digit>}]]}$$

means that the nonterminal symbol <literal> is one or more <digit>s optionally followed by a stop (.), optionally followed by one or more <digit>s. Thus, permissible <literal>s are 1, 1.2, 12.3, 0.2, etc. The production

$$\text{<standard constant>::= "pi" "epsilon"}$$

means that the nonterminal symbol <standard constant> is exactly one of the alternative strings "pi" and "epsilon."

The complete grammar for the real form of ALGLIB-0 is as follows:

<term>::=<expression1>

<expression1>::=<expression2>[{(" + " " – ")<expression2>}]

<expression2>::=[" + " " – "]<expression3>

<expression3>::=<expression4>[{(" * " " / ")<expression4>}]

<expression4>::=<expression5>[{ " ^ " [(" + " " – ")]<integer>}]

<expression5>::=<unary expression> <variable> <constant> " (" <expres-
   ression1> ")"

<unary expression>::=<standard function> " (" <expression1> ")"

<standard function>::= " – " "inverse" "sqrt" "exp" "ln" "sin" "cos"
   "atan" "abs"

<variable>::=<identifier>

<constant>::=<standard constant> <literal>

<standard constant>::= "pi" "epsilon"

<Identifier>::=<letter>[{<letter> <digit> " . "}]

<literal>::=<integer>[" . " [<integer>]]

<integer>::={<digit>}

<digit>::= " 0 " ... " 9 "

<letter>::= " a " ... " z " " A " ... " Z "

The sets of objects that define <standard function>s and <standard constant>s may, if necessary, be enlarged to accomodate the expressions that it is required to manipulate.

To illustrate the application of the ALGLIB-0 grammar, consider the string "cos(x1+x2*x3)". Clearly x1, x2, and x3 are <variable>s, which may also be regarded as <expression2>s, and x2*x3 is an <expression3>, which may also be regarded as an <expression2> because the sign is optional in the production for <expression2>s. So the string "x1+x2*x3" is an <expression1>. Therefore, from the production for <unary expression>s, the string "cos(x1+x2*x3)" is a <unary expression> and is therefore a valid ALGLIB expression.

The construction of the tree representing a valid ALGLIB expression consists of two parts, namely *lexical analysis* and *syntactic analysis*. Lexical analysis consists of breaking up the input string corresponding to the expression into the *basic symbols* that are recognized by ALGLIB. For example, the valid ALGLIB expression "exp(x+y)" contains the basic symbols "exp", "(", "x", "+", "y", and ")". Syntactic analysis consists of generating—from the set of basic symbols that make up the input string and that have been determined from the lexical analysis—the tree that represents the CFF corresponding to the input string. The implementation of lexical and syntactic analysis for the S-ALGOL compiler is described in detail in Ref. 74; the implementation of lexical and syntactic analysis for ALGLIB-0 is similar, except that the S-ALGOL compiler produces S code, whereas the ALGLIB-0 analyzer produces data structures that represent CFFs.

An important problem that must be addressed when designing an SMP is that of simplification. The problem of deciding which expressions are to be simplified, what is to be done to simplify them, and how the simplification is to be achieved is difficult and is surrounded by controversy in all but the simplest cases.

Very readable introductions to the difficulties that are inherent in simplification have been written by Moses [19], Fitch [75], and Yun and Stoutemyer [7], and an advanced survey of the subject, which contains 142 references, has been written by Buchberger and Loos [76].

It is necessary, even in simple SMPs such as ALGLIB, to include some form of simplification in order to realize capabilities 6 and 7, without excessive intermediate expression swell. It is also necessary to provide the user of an SMP with a certain amount of control over the simplification that occurs, especially during symbolic integration and the analytical solution of ordinary differential equations, for example.

The simplification capabilities that exist in the current real form of ALGLIB-0 include the recognition of such identities as

$$0 \times u = 0$$

$$u - u = 0$$

$$0 + u = u$$

$$u - 0 = u$$

$$1 \times u = u$$

$$u/1 = u$$

$$u^1 = u$$

$$1^m = 1 \quad (m \in Z)$$

$$u^0 = 1 \quad (u \neq 0)$$

$$0^m = 0 \quad (m > 0)$$

$$(-u)^m (-v)^n = \begin{cases} u^m v^n & (m+n \text{ even}) \\ -u^m v^n & (m+n \text{ odd}) \end{cases}$$

$$(au) * (bu) = \begin{cases} (a*b)u & (* \in \{+,-,.\}) \\ a * b & (* = / \text{ and } u \neq 0) \end{cases}$$

$$u^i v^j u^k v^l = u^{i+k} v^{j+l} \quad (i,j,k,l \in Z)$$

$$(u^m)^n = u^{mn} \quad (m,n \in Z)$$

$$(uv)^m = u^m v^m \quad (m, n \in Z)$$

$$\mathrm{inverse}(u^{-1}) = u \quad (u \neq 0)$$

$$\exp(u)\exp(v) = \exp(u+v)$$

$$\exp(u)/\exp(v) = \exp(u-v)$$

$$(\exp(u))^m = \exp(mu) \quad (m \in Z)$$

$$\ln(u) + \ln(v) = \ln(uv)$$

$$\ln(u) - \ln(v) = \ln(u/v)$$

$$\ln(u^m) = m\{\ln(u)\} \quad (m \in Z)$$

$$\exp(\ln(u)) = u \quad (u>0)$$

$$\ln(\exp(u)) = u$$

$$\sin(-u) = -\sin(u)$$

$$\cos(-u) = \cos(u)$$

$$\mathrm{atan}(-u) = -\mathrm{atan}(u)$$

$$\exp(0) = 1$$

$$\ln(1) = 0$$

$$\sin(0) = 0$$

$$\cos(0) = 1$$

$$\mathrm{atan}(0) = 0$$

The simplification capabilities in the current version of ALGLIB are rudimentary but will be extended in subsequent versions.

Let $f: X^n \to X^1$ and $g: X^n \to X^1$, where $X=R$ or $X=I(R)$ be given CFFs. ALGLIB can *combine* f and g to give the CFF $h: X^n \to X^1$ defined by

$$h(x) = f(x) * g(x)$$

where $* \in \{+, -, ., /\}$. Furthermore ALGLIB can combine $c \in X$ with $f: X^n \to X^1$ to give the CFFs $p: X^n \to X^1$ and $q: X^n \to X^1$ defined by

$$p(x) = c * f(x) \quad \text{and} \quad q(x) = f(x) * c$$

where $* \in \{+, -, ., /\}$.

Example 3.2

Let $f: R^2 \to R^1$ and $g: R^2 \to R^1$ be defined by

$$f(x) = x_1 \exp(x_2) \quad \text{and} \quad g(x) = x_1^2 + x_2^2$$

and let $c \in R$ be given by $c=3$. Then, ALGLIB can construct and store representations of CFFs such as h, p, and q, where

$$h(x)=f(x)g(x)=(x_1^2 + x_2^2)x_1\exp(x_2), \quad p(x)=c - f(x) = 3 - x_1\exp(x_2),$$

and $q(x)=g(x) - c = x_1^2 + x_2^2 - 3$

Let $f:X^n \to X^1$ and $g_i:X^n \to X^1$ $(i=1,\ldots,n)$ be given CFFs and let $g:X^n \to X^n$ be defined by

$$g(x)=(g_1(x),\ldots,g_n(x))$$

ALGLIB can *compose* f with g to give the CFF $h:X^n \to X^1$ defined by

$$h(x)=f(g(x))=f(g_1(x),\ldots,g_n(x))$$

Example 3.3

Let $f:R^2 \to R^1$, and $g:R^2 \to R^2$ be defined by

$$f(x)=x_1\ln(x_2) \text{ and } g(x)=(g_1(x), g_2(x))$$

where

$$g_1(x)=\sin(x_1)\cos(x_2) \text{ and } g_2(x)=x_1^2 + x_2^2 + 1$$

Then ALGLIB can construct and store representatives of CFFs such as $h:R^2 \to R^1$, where

$$h(x)=f(g(x))=g_1(x)\ln(g_2(x))=\sin(x_1)\cos(x_2)\ln(x_1^2 + x_2^2 + 1)$$

Let $f:X^n \to X^1$, where $X=R$ or $X=I(R)$, be a CFF. Then ALGLIB can determine mixed partial derivatives of f of any order and can also determine the gradient $g:X^n \to X^n$ and the Hessian $G:X^n \to M(X^n)$ of f, defined by

$$g(x)=(\partial_i f(x))_{n \times 1} \text{ and } G(x)=(\partial_j\partial_i f(x))_{n \times n}$$

where $M(X^n)$ is the set of square matrices of order n with elements in X, and for $i,j=1,\ldots,n$,

$$\partial_i f(x)=\partial f(x_1,\ldots,x_n)/\partial x_i \text{ and } \partial_i\partial_j f(x)=\partial^2 f(x_1,\ldots,x_n)/\partial x_i\partial x_j$$

Example 3.4

Let $f:R^2 \to R^1$ be defined by

$$f(x)=\exp(x_1^2)\sin(x_2)$$

Then ALGLIB can construct and store representations of partial derivatives of f such as $\partial_1^2\partial_2 f:R^2 \to R^1$, where

$$\partial_1^2\partial_2 f(x) = 2(1 + 2x_1^2)\exp(x_1^2)\cos(x_2)$$

and the gradient $g: R^2 \to R^2$ and Hessian $G: R^2 \to M(R^2)$ of f, where

$$g(x) = \begin{bmatrix} 2x_1\exp(x_1^2)\sin(x_2) \\ \exp(x_1^2)\cos(x_2) \end{bmatrix}$$

and

$$G(x) = \begin{bmatrix} 2(1 + 2x_1^2)\exp(x_1^2)\sin(x_2), & 2x_1\exp(x_1^2)\cos(x_2) \\ 2x_1\exp(x_1^2)\cos(x_2), & -\exp(x_1^2)\sin(x_2) \end{bmatrix}$$

When $g(x)$ or $G(x)$ is evaluated, ALGLIB can recognize that expressions such as $\exp(x_1^2)$, $\sin(x_2)$, $\cos(x_2)$, and x_1^2 need to be evaluated once only, even though they occur several times in the expressions for $f(x)$ and $G(x)$.

The following examples are intended to illustrate how ALGLIB could be used. It is assumed that an S-ALGOL implementation of ALGLIB is available and that the program in which ALGLIB is used is also written in S-ALGOL.

Initially, the names of the variables that are to be used in the expressions that ALGLIB is to manipulate must be known. Suppose that the variables x_1 and x_2 are to be used. A vector of strings containing the variable names is created by the statement

    let names = @ 1 of string ["x1" , "x2"]

in which names(1) points to the string "x1" and names(2) points to "x2". The data structures of classes *variable* and *root* corresponding to the vector names are created by invoking the ALGLIB procedure define.variables using the statement

    let variables = define.variables(names)

The entity variables is a vector of pointers to the *variables* corresponding to x_1 and x_2.

If the CFFs f and g are as defined in Example 3.2, the strings f.string and g.string representing the expressions $f(x)$ and $g(x)$, respectively, may be constructed by using the S-ALGOL statements

    let f.string = "x1*exp(x2)"

    let g.string = "x1^2+x2^2"

and the corresponding ALGLIB data structures are created by invoking the ALGLIB procedure string.to.function, as follows:

let f := string.to.function(variables,f.string)

let g := string.to.function(variables,g.string)

The entities f and g are pointers to the data structures corresponding to the CFFs f and g, respectively. The assignment operator := declares f and g to be of type variable pointer, so that both f and g may be assigned to subsequently. The assignment operator = declares f.string and g.string to be of type constant string, so that neither f.string nor g.string may be assigned to subsequently.

If it is desired to add the data structures pointed to by f and g to the appropriate linked lists after first simplifying them, the ALGLIB procedure add.to.list may be invoked, as follows:

f := add.to.list(f)

g := add.to.list(g)

If the CFFs h, p, and q are as defined in Example 3.2, the corresponding ALGLIB data structures and pointers h, p, and q are obtained by invoking the ALGLIB procedures function.op.function, real.op.function, and function.op.real, as follows:

let h = function.op.function(f,"*",g)

let p = real.op.function(3,"−",f)

let q = function.op.real(g,"−",3)

The procedures function.op.function, real.op.function, and function.op.real all simplify the data structures that they create before adding them to the appropriate linked list.

let $u:R^2 \to R^1$ be defined by

$$u(x)=\sin(f(x))=\sin(x_1\exp(x_2))$$

Then the ALGLIB data structure corresponding to the expression u(x) and a pointer u to the data structure are created by invoking the ALGLIB procedure op.function, as follows:

let u = op.function("sin",f)

let $r:R^2 \to R^2$ be defined by

$$r(x)=(p(x),q(x))=(3 - f(x),g(x) - 3)$$

and let $v:R^2 \to R^1$ be defined by

$$v(x)=f(r(x))=p(x)\exp(q(x))$$

Then a pointer r to the vector of pointers (p,q) is created by using the S-ALGOL statement let r = @ 1 of pntr [p,q]

and the ALGLIB data structure corresponding to the expression v(x) and a
pointer v to the data structure are created by invoking the ALGLIB procedure compose, as follows.

    let v = compose(r,r)

    The procedures op.function and compose simplify the data structures
that they create before adding them to the appropriate linked lists. The
ALGLIB procedures function.op.function, real.op.function, function.op.real,
op.function, and compose realize capability 6.
    The ALGLIB data structures corresponding to the partial derivatives of
CFFs may be created by invoking the ALGLIB procedure partial. For ex-
ample, the data structure corresponding to $\partial_1 f(x)$ and $\partial_2\partial_1 f(x)$, and the
pointers d1f and d2d1f to them are created by

    let d1f = partial(f,variables(1))

    let d2dif = partial(d1f,variables(2))

whereas the data structures corresponding to the gradient and the Hessian
of f and pointers grad.f and hess.f to them are created by invoking the
ALGLIB procedures gradient and hessian as follows:

    let grad.f = gradient(f)

    let hess.f = hessian(f)

Here, grad.f points to a vector of two pointers grad.f(1) and grad.f(2),
which point to the data structures corresponding to $\partial_1 f(x)$ and $\partial_2 f(x)$, respectively, and hess.f points to the matrix of four pointers hess.f(i,j),
(i,j=1,2), where hess.f(i,j) points to the data structure corresponding to
$\partial_j\partial_i f(x)$.
    The ALGLIB data structure corresponding to the Jacobian $J:R^2 \to M(R^2)$
of $r:R^2 \to R^2$, where

$$J(x)=(\partial_j r_i(x))_{2\times 2}$$

is created by invoking the ALGLIB procedure jacobian, as follows.

    let jacob.r = jacobian(r)

Here, jacob.r points to the matrix of four pointers jacob.r(i,j) (i,j=1,2),
where jacob.r(i,j) points to the data structure representing $\partial_j r_i(x)$.
    The procedures partial, gradient, jacobian, and hessian all simplify the
data structures that they create before adding them to the appropriate linked
list and realize capability 7.
    The expression corresponding to a given ALGLIB data structure may be
written by invoking the ALGLIB procedure function.format, which creates a
string corresponding to the given data structure: The string can then be
written by using the S-ALGOL write clause. The following code causes expressions corresponding to the CFFs f,g,h,p,q,u, and v to be written.

```
write "'nf(x)= ",function.format(f),

        "'ng(x)= ",function.format(g),

        "'nh(x)= ",function.format(h),

        "'np(x)= ",function.format(p),

        "'nq(x)= ",function.format(q),

        "'nu(x)= ",function.format(u),

        "'nv(x)= ",function.format(v),
```

Here, the characters 'n cause a new line to be taken on the output device. The output is as follows:

```
f(x)=1*exp(x2)

g(x)=1^2.+x2^2.

h(x)=1*exp(x2)*(x1^2.+x2^2)

p(x)=3.-x1*exp(x2)

q(x)=x1^2.+x^2.-3.

u(x)=sin(x1*exp(x2))

v(x)=(exp(x1^2.+x2^2.-3.))*(3.-x1*exp(x2))
```

Clearly, there is considerable room for improvement in the procedure function.format. This is a detail that will receive attention in subsequent versions of ALGLIB.

The vector of expressions corresponding to the data structures pointed to by a given vector of pointers may be written by invoking the ALGLIB procedure write.expression.vector. For example, the expressions corresponding to the CFFs $r:R^2 \rightarrow R^2$ and the gradient of $f:R^2 \rightarrow R^2$ may be written by using the statements

```
write.expression.vector(r,"r(x)")

write.expression.vector(grad.f,"The gradient of f.")
```

The output is as follows:

```
r(x)
───────────────
expression(1):

3.-x1*exp(x2)

expression(2):

x1^2.+x2^2.-3
───────────────
```

The gradient of f

---

expression(1):

exp(x2)

expression(2)

x1*exp(x2)

The matrix of expressions corresponding to the data structures pointed to by a given matrix of pointers may be written by invoking the ALGLIB procedure write.expression.matrix. For example, the 2×2 matrices of expressions corresponding to jacob.r and hess.f may be written by using the statements

write.expression.matrix(jacob.r, "The Jacobian of r.")

write.expression.matrix(hess.f, "The Hessian of f.")

The output is as follows:

The Jacobian of r.

---

expression(1,1):

−(exp(x2))

expression(1,2):

−(x1*exp(x2))

expression(2,1):

2.*x1

expression(2,2):

2.*x2

The Hessian of f.

---

expression(1,1):

0.

expression(1,2):

exp(x2)

expression(2,1):

exp(x2)

expression(2,2):

x1*exp(x2)

The ALGLIB procedures function.format, write.expression.vector, and write.expression.matrix realize capability 8.

Expressions corresponding to CFFs may be evaluated by invoking the ALGLIB procedure evaluate. The following code causes the CFF $f: R^2 \rightarrow R^1$ to be evaluated in real floating-point arithmetic with $x_1=2$ and $x_2=1$.

```
let x = @1 of real [2,1]

let f.value := evaluate(f,x)
```

Here, f.value is a variable of type real, which has the value $f(2,1)=2\exp(1)$. The S-ALGOL statement

```
write "f(x)= ",gformat(f.value)
```

produces the output

```
f(x)= 5.43656
```

let $s: R^2 \rightarrow R^1$ be defined by

$$s(x)=\sin(x_1)\exp(x_2)$$

and suppose that it is desired to evaluate $s(x)$ with the same values of x_1 and x_2 as were used to evaluate $f(x)$, namely $x_1=2$ and $x_2=1$. Although the ALGLIB procedure evaluate may be used, it is more efficient to invoke the ALGLIB procedure re.evaluate, as follows.

```
Let s := string.to.function(variables, "sin(x1)*exp(x2)")

    s := add.to.list(s)

   let s.value := re.evaluate(s)
```

The S-ALGOL statement

```
write "g(x)= ",gformat(g.value)
```

produces the output

```
g(x)= 2.47173
```

Here, the CFF s is evaluated with the values of x_1 and x_2 unchanged. Both the data structure corresponding to $\exp(x_2)$ (which was created when the data structure corresponding to $f(x)$ was created) and the value of $\exp(x_2)$ (which was computed when the value of $f(x)$ was computed) are reused.

Vectors and matrices of expressions corresponding to CFFs may be evaluated at a given point by invoking the ALGLIB procedures vecevaluate and matevaluate, respectively. For example, the values of r and of the gradient of f with $x_1=2$ and $x_2=1$ may be computed by using the statements

```
let r.x = vecevaluate(r,x)

let grad.f.x = vecevaluate(grad.f,x)
```

and the values of the Jacobian of r and of the Hessian of f with $x_1=2$ and $x_2=1$ may be computed by using the statements

    let jacob.r.x = matevaluate(jacob.r,x)

    let hess.f.x = matevaluate(hess.f,x)

Here, r.x and grad.f.x are pointers to the real 2×1 vectors containing the values of $r_1(x)$ (i=1,2) and $\partial_i f(x)$ (i=1,2), respectively. Also jacob.r.x and hess.f.x are pointers to the 2×2 real matrices containing the values of $\partial_j r_i(x)$ (i,j=1,2) and of $\partial_j \partial_i f(x)$ (i,j=1,2), respectively.

    The ALGLIB procedures evaluate, re.evaluate, vecevaluate, and matevaluate realize capability 5.

    Vectors and matrices of real numbers may be written by invoking the ALGLIB procedures write.real.vector and write.real.matrix, respectively. For example, the vectors of real numbers pointed to by r.x and grad.f.x may be written by using the statements

    write.real.vector (r.x, "r(x)",true,0,6)

    write.real.vector (grad.f.x, "The gradient of f at x is",false,0,0)

The resulting output is as follows:

    r(x)

    $-0.243656e+01$

    $0.200000e+01$

    The gradient of f at x is

    2.71828

    5.43656

    The matrices of real numbers pointed to by jacob.r.x and hess.f.x may be written by using the statements

    write.real.matrix(jacob.r.x, "The Jacobian of r at x",true,0,16)

    write.real.matrix(hess.f.x, "The Hessian of f at x",false,0,0)

The resulting output is as follows:

    The Jacobian of r at x

    This is a 2×2 matrix written by rows.

    $-0.2718281828459045e+01$ $-0.5436563656918091e+01$

    $0.4000000000000000e+01$ $0.2000000000000000e+01$

    The Hessian of f at x

This is a 2×2 matrix written by rows.

0.	2.71828
2.71828	5.43656

The parameter lists for the procedures write.real.vector and write.real. matrix each contain five parameters. The first is a pointer to the memory locations containing the real numbers to be written, the second is a string containing the heading, the third is a Boolean, the value of which determines whether a format similar either to FORTRAN E format or FORTRAN G format is to be used, and the fourth and fifth parameters are integers, the values of which specify the number of decimal digits before and after the decimal point, respectively.

Using ALGLIB procedures such as those described in this section, it is possible to implement a wide variety of mathematical algorithms in which algebraic manipulation is necessary or desirable. In particular, many algorithms for the numerical solution of systems of nonlinear algebraic equations and for the numerical solution of unconstrained and constrained optimization require analytical expressions for partial derivatives of the problem functions. These partial derivatives are easily determined and efficiently evaluated using an SMP such as ALGLIB.

4 THE FUTURE

Scientific computing may be said to have experienced its first revolution with the advent in 1954 and the appearance in 1957 of FORTRAN [77]. For the first time, scientists and engineers were able to write programs that resembled, albeit rather poorly, the mathematical algorithms being implemented.

Unfortunately, the use of finite-precision floating-point machine arithmetic gave rise to phenomena that were understood by few users other than numerical analysts. Consequently, it became necessary for libraries of widely used algorithms to be implemented by numerical analysts who specialized in writing numerical software.

The second revolution in scientific computing has begun. It is now possible for mathematicians, scientists, and engineers to use CA embodied in SMPs such as REDUCE and MACSYMA as a research tool, thereby obtaining results that would otherwise be unobtainable. The use of CA will have a major impact on science and technology. Soon, pupils in secondary education will have access to SMPs on microcomputers. This will have a more drastic effect on the curriculum than the pocket calculator. The SMP muMATH runs under CP/M, and muMATH is already available for microcomputers such as the HP 110 and could be made available in a hand-held computer if there were sufficient demand for computer manufacturers to do so. It is therefore likely that within a few years SMPs in hand-held and pocket computers will be available and inexpensive.

It is probable that as the available RAM on small computers increases, all mathematical topics that are encountered in secondary and undergraduate teaching will be represented in SMPs that run on such machines. The interested reader is referred to *SIGSAM Bulletin*, Volume 18, no. 4, November 1984, and Volume 19, no. 1, February 1985, which contain several articles about the impact of SMPs on teaching curricula. The views of several eminent computer algebraists on the future development of CA are contained in *SIGSAM Bulletin*, Volume 18, no. 2, 1984.

Specialized SMPs for solving problems in science and in engineering, which allow the user to pose a problem in terms of that user's discipline rather than in mathematical terms will almost certainly appear.

The new SMPs will combine algebraic manipulation, numerical computation, and graphics and will present intelligent interfaces to the user, who will be able to communicate with them by using speech, and writing, for example.

It is very probable that in the near future, CA and SMPs will transform the teaching and learning process in disparate fields of knowledge and will make possible very great increases in both the variety and size of computational problems in science and engineering that can be successfully addressed. Indeed, those who are familiar with current applications of SMPs know that these things have already begun to happen.

REFERENCES

1. J. Calmet, "Introduction," in *Proceedings of EUROCAM '82, European Computer Algebra Conference*, Marseilles, France (J. Calmet, ed.), *Lecture Notes in Computer Science 144*, Springer-Verlag, Berlin, Heidelberg, New York, 1982.

2. J. E. Sammet, "Survey of Formula Manipulation," *Commun. ACM*, 9, 555–569 (1966).

3. R. G. Toby, "Symbolic Mathematical Computation—Introduction and Overview," in *Proceedings of the Second ACM Symposium on Symbolic and Algebraic Manipulation* (S. R. Petrick, ed.), 1971.

4. E. Ng, ed., "EUROSAM 1979," in *Proceedings of the International Colloquium on the Methods of Symbolic and Algebraic Computation*, Marseilles, France, 1979.

5. W. S. Brown and A. C. Hearn, "Applications of Symbolic Algebraic Computation," *Comput. Phys. Commun.*, 17, 207–215 (1979).

6. J. C. Howard, *Practical Applications of Symbolic Computation*, IPC Science and Technology Press, Guildford, England, 1980.

7. D. Y. Y. Yun and D. R. Stoutemyer, "Symbolic Mathematical Computation," in *Encyclopedia of Computer Science and Technology*, Volume 15 Supplement, Marcel Dekker, New York and Basel, 1980.

8. R. Loos, "Introduction," in *Comput. Suppl.*, 4, 1–10 (1982).

9. H. G. Kahrimanian, "Analytical Differentiation by a Digital Computer," M.A. Thesis, Temple University, Philadelphia, PA, 1953.

10. J. Nolan, "Analytical Differentiation on a Digital Computer," M.A. Thesis, MIT, Cambridge, MA, 1953.

11. J. E. Sammet, "An Annotated Descriptor Based Bibliography on the Use of Computers for Non-Numerical Mathematics," *Comput. Rev. 7*, B1–B32 (1966).

12. J. E. Sammet, "Revised Annotated Descriptor Based Bibliography on the Use of Computers for Non-numerical Mathematics," in *Proceedings of the IFIP Working Conference on Symbol Manipulation Languages* (D. G. Bobrow, ed.), North-Holland Publishing Company, Amsterdam, 1968.

13. J. Wyman, Addition No. 3 to Ref. *12*, *SIGSAM Bull.*, (10) (October 1968).

14. J. Wyman, Addition No. 4 to Ref. *12*, *SIGSAM Bull.*, (12) (July 1969).

15. J. Wyman, Addition No. 5 to Ref. *12*, *SIGSAM Bull.*, (15) (July 1970).

16. J. E. Sammet, "Survey of the Use of Computers for Doing Non-numerical Mathematics," IBM, Systems Development Division, Poughkeepsie, New York, Technical Report no. TR 00.1428, March 1966.

17. J. E. Sammet, "Formula Manipulation by Computer," in *Advance in Computers* (F. Alt and M. Rubinoff, eds.), Academic Press, New York, 1967, Vol. 8, pp. 47–102.

18. J. E. Sammet, "Software for Nonnumerical Mathematics," in *Mathematical Software* (J. R. Rice, ed.), Academic Press, New York and London, 1971.

19. J. Moses, "Symbolic Integration: The Stormy Decade"; "Algebraic Simplification: A Guide for the Perplexed"; *Commun. ACM 14*, 548–560; 527–537 (1971).

20. J. Moses, "The Evolution of Algebraic Manipulation Algorithms," in *Proceedings of the IFIP Congress 1974*, North-Holland Publishing, Amsterdam, 1974.

21. D. Barton and J. P. Fitch, "A Review of Algebraic Manipulative Programs and Their Application," *Comput. J., 15*, 362–381 (1972).

22. J. Calmet and J. A. van Hulzen, "Computer Algebra Applications," *Comput. Suppl., 4*, 245–258 (1982).

23. R. J. Fateman, "Symbolic Manipulative Languages and Numerical Computation: Trends," in *The Relationship between Numerical Computation and Programming Languages* (J. K. Reid, ed.), North-Holland Publishing, Amsterdam, 1982.

24. R. Pavelle and P. S. Wang, "MACSYMA from F to G," *J. Symbolic Comput. 1*, 69–100 (1985).

25. D. G. Bobrow, ed., "Symbol Manipulation Languages and Techniques," in *Proceedings of the IFIP Working Conference on Symbol Manipulation Languages*, North-Holland Publishing, Amsterdam, 1968.

26. S. M. Petrick, ed., *Proceedings of the Second ACM Symposium on Symbolic and Algebraic Manipulation*, 1971.

27. R. Fateman, ed., *Proceedings of the 1977 MACSYMA Users' Conference*, Berkeley, MIT, Cambridge, MA, 1977.

28. V. E. Lewis, ed., *Proceedings of the 1979 MACSYMA Users' Conference*, Washington D.C., MIT, Cambridge, MA, 1979.

29. P. S. Wang, ed., "SYMSAC'81," *Proceedings of the 1981 ACM Symposium on Symbolic and Algebraic Computation*, 1981.

30. J. Calmet, ed., "EUROCAM '82," *Proceedings of the European Computer Algebra Conference*, Marseille, France, 1982.

31. J. A. van Hulzen, ed., "Computer Algebra," in *Proceedings of EUROCAL'83, European Computer Algebra Conference*, London, England, *Lecture Notes in Computer Science 162*, Springer-Verlag, Berlin, Heidelberg, New York, Tokyo, 1983.

32. J. Fitch, ed., "EUROSAM 84", *Proceedings of the International Symposium on Symbolic and Algebraic Computation*, Cambridge, England, *Lecture Notes in Computer Science 174*, Springer-Verlag, Berlin, Heidelberg, New York, Tokyo, 1984.

33. Bibliography of Papers Referencing MACSYMA, Document no. SM 10500130.003.4, Symbolics Inc., September 1985.

34. "Algebra Made Mechanical," *Nature, 290* (March 1981).

35. L. A. Steen, "Computer Calculus," *Sci. News, 119* (April 1981).

36. R. Pavelle, M. Rothstein, and J. Fitch, "Computer Algebra," *Sci. Am., 245*, 102–113 (1981).

37. H. S. Wilf, "The Disk with the College Education," *Am. Math. Monthly, 89*, 4–8 (1982).

38. S. Wolfram, "Computer Software in Science and Mathematics," in *Computer Software* (a collection of articles that first appeared in *Scientific American* in 1984), W. H. Freeman, New York, 1984.

39. L. B. Rall, *Automatic Differentiation: Techniques and Applications*, *Lecture Notes in Computer Science 120*, Springer-Verlag, Berlin, Heidelberg, New York, 1981.

40. J. H. Davenport, *On the Integration of Algebraic Functions*, *Lecture Notes in Computer Science 102*, Springer-Verlag, Berlin, Heidelberg, New York, 1981.

41. D. E. Knuth, *The Art of Computer Programming, Vol. 2, Seminumerical Algorithms*, Addison-Wesley, Reading, MA, 1969.

42. A. V. Aho, J. E. Hopcroft, and J. D. Ullman, *The Design and Analysis of Computer Algorithms*, Addison-Wesley, Reading, MA, 1974.

43. J. D. Lipson, *Elements of Algebra and Algebraic Computing*, Addison-Wesley, Reading, MA, 1981.

44. J. A. van Hulzen and J. Calmet, "Computer Algebra Systems," in *Comput. Suppl.*, 4 221–243 (1982).

45. A. D. Rich and D. R. Stoutemyer, "Capabilities of the muMATH-79 Computer Algebra System for the INTEL-8080 Microprocessor," in *Proceedings of EUROSAM'79, the International Symposium on Symbolic and Algebraic Manipulation*, Marseille, France, 1979.

46. D. D. Shochat, "Experience with the muSIMP/muMATH-80 Symbolic Mathematics System," *SIGSAM Bull.*, 16, (3), 16–23 (August 1982).

47. K. Aspetsberger and G. Funk, "Experiments with muMATH in Austrian High Schools," *SIGSAM Bull.*, 19, (1), 4–7 (February 1985).

48. D. R. Stoutemyer, "PICOMATH-89: An Even Smaller Computer Algebra Package," *SIGSAM Bull.*, 14, (3), 5–7 (August 1980).

49. J. Fitch and J. Marti, "NLARGEing a Z80 Microprocessor," in *Proceedings of EUROCAM'82, the European Computer Algebra Conference*, Marseille, France, 1982, Lecture Notes in Computer Science, 144, Springer-Verlag, Berlin, 1982.

50. J. Marti and J. Fitch, "REDUCE-2 for CP/M," *SIGSAM Bull.*, 17, (1), 26–27 (February 1983).

51. J. P. Fitch, "Implementing REDUCE on a Microprocessor," in *Proceedings of EUROCAL '83, the European Computer Algebra Conference*, London, England, 1983.

52. B. Char, K. O. Geddes, W. M. Gentleman, and G. H. Gonnet, "The Design of Maple: A Compact, Portable, and Powerful Computer Algebra System," in *Proceedings of EUROCAL '83, the European Computer Algebra Conference* (J. van Hulzen, ed.), London, England, March 1983.

53. B. Char, K. O. Geddes, and G. H. Gonnet, "The Maple Symbolic Computation System," *SIGSAM Bulletin*, 17, (3/4), 31–42 (August/November 1983).

54. R. H. Risch, "The Problem of Integration in Finite Terms, *Trans. Am. Math. Soc.*, 139, 167–189 (1969).

55. R. H. Risch, "The Solution of the Problem of Integration in Finite Terms," *Bull. Am. Math. Soc.*, 76, 605–608 (1970).

56. J. M. Shearer and M. A. Wolfe, "ALGLIB: A Simple Symbol Manipulation Package," *Commun. ACM*, 28, 820–825 (1985).

57. J. M. Shearer, "Interval Methods for Nonlinear Systems," Ph.D. Thesis, University of St. Andrews, Scotland, 1985.

58. J. M. Shearer and M. A. Wolfe, "Some Algorithms for the Solution of a Class of Nonlinear Algebraic Equations," *Computing 35*, 63–72 (1985).

59. J. M. Shearer and M. A. Wolfe, "Some Computable Existence, Uniqueness, and Convergence Tests for Nonlinear Systems," *SIAM J. Numer. Anal.*, 22, 1200–1207 (1985).

60. J. M. Shearer and M. A. Wolfe, "An Improved Form of the Krawczyk-Moore Algorithm," *Appl. Math. Comput.*, *17*, 229–239 (1985).
61. J. M. Shearer and M. A. Wolfe, "A Note on the Algorithm of Alefeld and Platzoder," *SIAM J. Sci. Stat. Comput.*, 7, 362-369 (1986).
62. J. M. Shearer and M. A. Wolfe, "An Interval Form of Brown's Method," 1986, unpublished manuscript.
63. I. Mohd and M. A. Wolfe, "An Algorithm for Global Optimization in which Interval Arithmetic is Used," Read at the International Conference on Numerical Optimization and Applications, Xi'an Jiaotong University, Xi'an, Shaanxi, China, June 1986.
64. M. Monsi and M. A. Wolfe, "Some Modifications of Sisser's Algorithm," 1986, unpublished manuscript.
65. M. Monsi and M. A. Wolfe, "An Algorithm for the Simultaneous Inclusion of Real Polynomial Zeros", in press, *Applied Mathematics and Computation*, 1988.
66. A. J. Cole and R. Morrison, *An Introduction to Programming with S-ALGOL*, Cambridge University Press, Cambridge, England, 1982.
67. A. J. Cole and R. Morrison, "Triplex: A System for Interval Arithmetic," *Software-Pract. Exper.* 12, 341–350 (1982).
68. P. J. Bailey, A. J. Cole, and R. Morrison, *Triples User Manual*, *CS/82/5*, University of St. Andrews Department of Computational Science, Scotland, 1982.
69. R. Morrison, A. J. Cole, P. J. Bailey, M. A. Wolfe, and J. M. Shearer, "Experience in Using a High Level Language that Supports Interval Arithmetic," in *Proceedings of ARITH6, the sixth Symposium on Computer Arithmetic*, sponsored by the IEEE Computer Society Technical Committee on Computer Architecture and Aarhus University, Aarhus, Denmark, 1983.
70. R. E. Moore, *Methods and Applications of Interval Analysis*, SIAM Publications, Philadelphia, PA, 1979.
71. G. Alefeld and J. Herzberger, *Introduction to Interval Computations*, Academic Press, New York, 1983.
72. G. P. McCormick, *Nonlinear Programming, Theory, Algorithms, and Applications*, John Wiley, New York, 1983.
73. N. Wirth, *Algorithms + Data Structures = Programs*, Prentice-Hall, Englewood Cliffs, NJ, 1976.
74. A. J. T. Davie and R. Morrison, *Recursive Descent Compiling*, Ellis Horwood, R. Fateman, ed., Chichester, England, 1982.
75. J. P. Fitch, "On Algebraic Simplification," *Comput. J.*, *16*, 23–27 (1973).
76. B. Buchberger and R. Loos, "Algebraic Simplification," *Comput. Suppl.*, *4*, 11-43 (1982).
77. *History of Computing in the Twentieth Century*, (N. Metropolis, J. Howlett, and G. Rota, eds.), Academic Press, New York, 1980.

J. M. SHEARER

M. A. WOLFE